Cruising
the Central
American Route

Revised 6.5 Edition

Capt. Patricia Miller Rains

Another of the authorative
Rains Guides,

a companion guidebook to

Mexico Boating Guide

Point Loma Publishing
San Diego, California, USA

This book and its text, chartlets, illustrations and photos are to be used for planning and reference purposes only. They are specifically not to be used for navigation. Some of this book's chartlets are referenced from the latest DMA, NIMA, SM, NOAA and British Admiralty Charts, and some of the previously charted shorelines and soundings have been updated and or corrected to agree with high-resolution satellite imagery. For the sake of clarity, the publisher has deleted some ship-relevant soundings and added new shoreline data such as breakwaters, marinas, fuel docks, shoals and rocks. Other chartlets and text pages in this book were created from the author's and her husband's sketch charts, created from onsite GPS triangulations, depth soundings collected aboard a variety of vessels, and referencing government issued topo maps and private aerial photos.

The text has been carefully prepared, based on the author's and her husband's personal inspections, on official publications and other data deemed reliable, with the objective of making the recreational boater's voyage more enjoyable. Every reasonable effort has been made to achieve up-to-date accuracy, but the infinite complexities of personal observation and a constantly changing world render total accuracy impossible.

Thus all sailing, navigation, anchoring and docking information in this book must be checked against the skipper's own eyes, ears and experience of the immediate conditions, on the skipper's navigation equipment and latest government-issued charts and publications. Every skipper alone is responsible for the safety of his or her crew and vessel, and he or she must plot the safe course.

The author and publisher therefore both specifically disclaim any and all personal liability for loss or risk of loss to persons or property or both, which might occur either directly or indirectly from any person's use or interpretation of any information contained in this book. No publication can substitute for good sea sense.

Library of Congress Control Number: 2006934587
ISBN 0-9638470-2-3
EAN 9780963847027

14 15 16 17 18 19 20   15 14 13 12

Cruising Ports: the Central American Route - 6.5 Edition
Capt. Patricia Miller Rains
6.5 edition in the "Cruising Ports" series, another of the trusted Rains Guides

© Point Loma Publishing
Post Office Box 60190
San Diego, California 92106
USA
www.CentralAmericanBoating.com

Cruising Ports:
the Central American Route

Who needs this nautical guidebook?

Cruising Ports is tailored for the owners of recreational power and sailing yachts who are interested in the popular cruising route from either Texas or Florida along the Gulf Coast, Yucatan Channel and Western Caribbean to the Panama Canal - AND for West Coast boaters who are departing from southern Mexico (hopefully after using our companion book, Mexico Boating Guide) and cruising along the Pacific Central American coast to Panama. Both routes culminate with the Panama Canal transit.

How to use this book?

Cruising Ports works generally southward toward Panama, first down the Pacific Coast, then from the East Coast (from both TX and FL) down through the Western Caribbean. We ordered the Central American route this way in response to overwhelming feedback from cruising boaters we've met at seminars, boat shows and down here underway.

Use this book as planning and dream book at home - and again on the chart table aboard your boat underway or at anchor. If you're still in the dreaming stages, *Cruising Ports* will ignite your imagination as it fills in the blanks on your itinerary with facts and a justified sense of realism. Each destination starts with Why-would-we-go-there? information. With it, you'll plan to spend more time exploring some cruising grounds, less in others. You'll pick ports where guests can easily fly down to join you for awhile, then fly out somewhere down the coast. Overall planning chartlets throughout the book can help you organize your itinerary.

As you're preparing your boat and crew, turn to the Preparation chapters to see what's unique about this route, for practical advice and check lists. Turn to the Paperwork chapter for blank Crew List forms and instructions. The *Resource Directory* at the back provides valuable contacts for marinas, yacht clubs, fuel docks, haul-out yards and ship's agents, so you can reach them in advance by telephone, website or email.

Already underway? *Cruising Ports* provides chartlets for the approaches, anchorages and ports. Text tells where to anchor, find a marina slip or land your dinghy, how to check in with local port officials, where to get fuel, water, provisions, repairs, land transport, worthy side trips plus a dab of local history & culture.

Who wrote *Cruising Ports* and why?

Capt. John E. Rains began delivering yachts from Florida to California via Panama way back in 1980, but so little was published about this route that many insurance brokers asked him to write a detailed itinerary before they would insure the vessel outside U.S. waters. In 1982, John turned all those itineraries into the 1st editon of *Cruising Ports: Florida to California via Panama*. In 1984, Capt. Patricia Miller Rains (former sailboat cruiser) joined her husband's yacht delivery team, and since then *Cruising Ports* has been expanded, updated and greatly improved with new material and technologies during more than 50 yacht deliveries over the Central American route. Since 2007, both Captains Rains retired from delivering yachts, freeing time to cruise this route for pleasure with their friends on a variety of nice boats. Capt. Pat Rains has a B.S. in Communications, U.S. Coast Guard 100-ton Masters license and Ham call sign KB6HBI. She writes several newspaper and magazine columns and continues to update these nautical publications.

Acknowledgements

Thank you! Gracias!

The author wishes to thank all those who helped create and improve this 6th edition of the comprehensive Cruising Ports nautical guidebooks - but listing them all is impossible a single page. Of course, infinite *abrazos y besos* go to my husband, the captain of my heart, Capt. John E. Rains - for sharing all these adventures with me on myriad yachts, and who kept me from getting True and Magnetic mixed up. His retirement from yacht delivery opened the door for us to go cruising again - which is where we both started.

Thank You, our generous advertisers. Most of them are friends John and I made underway and ashore along the Central American Route, whose services we found most valuable ourselves. Thank you to each of them for believing in this nautical guidebook - and for their patience despite its many delays.

Thanks go to our yatista friends who invite us to go cruising with them, who wait patiently while we sound murky bottoms, measure dinghy docks and chat with pangueros and port officials - yet who still invite us back! We protect their privacy, but they know who they are. Abrazos, amigos.

Several fellow yatistas sent me sections of their log books, some of their high-resolution photos and their worthy recommendations for improving the previous edition (***Cruising Ports: Florida to California via Panama***), for which I am very grateful. Please keep them coming, because the 7th edition is not far over the horizon. In particular I wish to thank Michelle & Karl Mech of S/V Arclyd, Monty Navarre and family, Hal Wayman at Barefoot Cay for their photos and facts. One of our most excellent crew members, Scott Atkins, shared many of his photos from our yacht deliveries and from his own voyages along the Central American Route. Scott's father, Martin Atkins, crewed for my husband, John, on John's first yacht delivery quite a few years ago. Scott is presently circumnavigating the globe on his Tayana 37, Avventura.

I'm grateful to Point Loma Publishing for upgrading this edition to color, and for providing spectacular images from some talented professional photographers who live and work along the Central American Route, such as Dave Shuler, Larry Benvenuti, Beverly Factor and Gustavo Gotera. Thanks to the Belize Tourism Bureau for photos by Tony Roth, Dave Humphries and Alex Nunez. Thanks to Yucatan Secretary of Tourism Lic. Maria Isabel Buenfil Pasos for her photos. Also, Point Loma Publishing furnished extreme high-resolution satellite imagery from SatPrints.Inc., charting what I think is a wonderful new course toward cartographic accuracy for recreational mariners.

Big thanks to Juan Wright, Heriberto Pineda and the folks at Barillas Marina Club for loaning me their plane and pilot for exploring all of El Salvador and the Gulf of Fonseca, not just their corner. Thanks to about 100 dock masters and Port Captains for sharing their time and local knowledge with me. Thanks to Duncan McIntosh and his crew at *SEA Magazine* and *The Log Newspapers* for their support and patience when I was late with my columns because I was off researching this book. Same thanks go to the editors at *Cruising World, Power Cruising,* etc. My own talented editorial and production team includes Rebecca Go, Hamilton Avocet, Darla Dunham, Shannan Palmer, Adam Rains, Patrick Ennis, Ada Garcia and Ann Kinner. Without all these folks and their cameraderie, talent and long hours of enthusiasm, ***Cruising Ports: the Central American Route*** wouldn't be as worthy as I'm sure you'll find it, and it might never have seen the light of day.

And I extend my humble thanks to the 60,000 *yatistas* who buy and use our nautical guides. May your spirit of adventure lead you onward and inward, and may you always find smooth seas!

Sincerely,
Pat Rains

Fundación
Adelante
Unity, Discipline, Hard Work and Courage

Thanks to you ... for helping support a very worthy cause - the Adelante Foundation.

A small percentage of the price you paid for this nautical guidebook is being contributed to the Adelante Foundation of Honduras. For each new edition of our nautical guidebooks, Point Loma Publishing pledges financial support to at least one non-profit group that significantly benefits the people and-or the environment through which we travel.

Adelante Foundation was selected as our sole recipient for this 6th edition of the Cruising Ports guides, which for the first time visits the mainland coast of Honduras, an area still struggling to recover from hurricane devastation. Using the same amazingly successful Grameen Bank micro-credit principles that won the Nobel Peace Prize, Adelante Foundation is working 4,800 minor miracles every day in rural Honduras - just out of sight from the marinas, behind the beach berm, up the next estuary channel. Want to see it in action?

You are hereby invited by Mike Wiesner, new director at the Adelante office in La Ceiba, Honduras, to come ashore for a "cultural tourism day." He'll take small groups of yatistas to meet some of Adelante's micro-credit recipients and to visit their workshops and markets, perhaps share lunch at their Pulperia or buy a bag of homemade breads, jams, honey, eggs, cheese, fruits or veggies produced by these women. To make arrangements or a donation, contact Mike Wiesner by email, Mike@AdelanteFoundation.org or call in country (504) 443-1198. Mail: Adalante Foundation, P.O. Box 4473, Denver, Colorado, 80155. US phone (303)662-5209.

Recipient of Adelante Foundation micro-credit business loan in Honduras.

Here's a word from former director Ashley Hooker:

Adelante's mission is to improve the standard of living of extremely poor women living in Honduras. Since 1999 Adelante has provided small loans to very poor women so they can start and grow their own small businesses. Over time, the women use their profits to buy better food for their families, to improve their homes, to buy medicine when necessary, to send their children to school, and to plan and save for the future.

Adelante also provides business, health and human rights education. The business education helps our borrowers learn the skills necessary to make their businesses successful. The health education provides vital but difficult to find basic health information for the whole family.

Adelante provides opportunity rather than charity to 4,800 women in Honduras – a hand up rather than a hand out. Adelante relies on the financial contributions of our supporters to provide hope and opportunity to thousands of women in Honduras. Help us help those who help themselves.

Recipient of Adelante Foundation micro-credit business loan in Honduras.

Gracias!

Table of Chartlets

Table of Contents

Cruising Ports: the Central American Route

Boat Preparations for the Central American Route

Let's assume you're not a novice at coastal cruising and have made a few offshore passages in the boat you're taking on the Central American route. Without reinventing the wheel, let's look at what's unique about preparing your boat for this route, as opposed to general cruising stateside.

Then I have an Outfitting & Spares Check List and a Provisioning Check List, both very concise and focused on this route.

Veteran cruisers on the Central American Route (power & sail) who I speak with at boat shows, seminars and down here doing it are happy to share what they've learned. They frequently urge newcomers to focus their boat preparations on (a.) living safely and comfortably at anchor; (b.) managing power and water needs; (c.) coping with heat and humidity; (d.) staying self reliant and secure.

Anchor Often

Even if your cruising kitty is unlimited, marinas are still fairly rare along this coast. Plan to anchor overnight about 90% of the time. If you're safe and comfy on the hook, you'll enjoy this route.

Above: Dual anchoring set-up on yacht trawler.
Right: Dinghy way of life in the tropics.

Dual anchoring set-up on cruising sailboat.

Ground tackle is the best place to go overboard, the cheapest insurance you can buy. You're already good at anchoring your boat in changeable conditions, through radical wind shifts and the turn of several tides, right? Have 2 complete bow anchoring suites, one stern anchor and rode, plus one monster anchor and swivel for storms. Never anchor too close to coral reefs, because your chain will destroy delicate living formations that are centuries old.

Your dinghy and outboard are your only way ashore. An inflatable with a hard bottom and floorboards is most practical, with a transom-mounted

Hoist dinghy out of the water in theft-prone areas.

in a bag tied into the corner. Build a 3-point towing bridle, because the eye often fails off shore.

Some outboard brands are not common down here, so finding parts is a problem. Be prepared to adjust your outboard for higher sulfur gasoline. Buy the best gas tank and jerry jugs you can afford, along with extra stoppers and threaded parts. Keep them neatly covered to prevent sun damage.

Power & Water

At small ports in the tropics, water and dirt sometimes contaminate diesel storage tanks. Yachts need a well designed fuel filtration system. We recommend dual Racor filters with vacuum gauges and an electric prime pump. Use a biocide treatment when ported very long. Carry as many fuel filters as you have room for. You can't have too many.

Sailboaters who may frequently haul diesel in jerry jugs from remote villages (often stored in 60-gallon steel drums) should consider using what's called a "Baja fuel filter," a large box-shaped stainless-steel funnel with 3 screened compartments that filter out water and dirt while transferring fuel, a slow but sure process.

outboard. Cheap dinghies don't survive constant use in the tropics. About a third of the way through this route, many cruisers start searching for a larger dinghy and motor. Canvas covers protect the pontoons and your fanny. If cruising with children, consider a second dink. Consider dinghy wheels that are not too difficult to remove and stow occasionally.

Your dinghy gear may include an extra fuel tank, pulling oars with dependable oar locks, spare oar lock, bailer, dinghy anchor with rode, extra PFD or floatation, flashlight and water jug. Stow loose stuff

Perform an amperage-draw survey to see if you generate sufficient power for comfortable cruising in the tropics. Can you run the water maker and one air conditioning unit at the same time? How long do you need to run the water maker to fill your tanks? What else can't you run while you're making water? Can you run a power drill if bread is baking in the oven? If you don't have enough 110-volt power, consider installing a larger or second generator or buying more solar panels and low-amp appliances – or doing without some high-draw comforts.

All power boats and most sailboats cruising Mexico and Central America have an RO water maker, because it's safer, frees you from the marina circuit and makes the difference between long-range cruising or merely camping at sea. But do carry filters and spare parts, because they're hard to find until you reach the Panama Canal region.

Panama's tap water has been

Dinghy wheels up, canvas covers.

excellent. But if you must take on suspect water, you can treat it with household chlorine bleach as you fill. I use 1/8 to 1/4 cup of regular Clorox per 100 gallons of fresh water. Add chorine only a few teaspoons at a time while filling, not all at once. Too high a concentration can corrode pipe connections and destroy the water-heater sensor. Leave the fill tube open to vent chlorine gas for at least 4 hours. To improve the flavor of water in a chlorine-treated tank, add a bottle of white wine.

Heat & Humidity

Think 5% drenching rain, 95% blistering sun and 100% humidity. Fans, awnings, dorades and wind scoops are essential for sailboats. Windshield covers, window blinds and port covers help a lot, especially the honey-combed or thermal-refracting kinds.

Robust ventilation below decks is more critical the farther south you go. I could sell a dozen 10" oscillating fans every time I pass through Panama. Mount and hard-wire a wall fan in each cabin. To promote ventilation, refit solid cupboard and cabin doors with louvered panels.

Air conditioning (a/c) is not a luxury. Have a professional test the whole a/c system, clean the lines, upgrade if necessary and top off the refrigerant. Turning an a/c unit on, holding your hand up to the vent and saying "that feels fine" is self-delusion. Under heavy load in tropical humidity, most marine a/c systems barely suffice.

Prevent mildew by hanging dehumidifying products using non-toxic anhydrous calcium sulfate. They absorb half their weight in moisture from the air but turn to liquid so must be replaced regularly.

Non-toxic Crocodile! insect repellent from www. DancingRoots.com is effective, safe for kids & pets.

Grains not refrigerated get buggy, so don't buy in bulk. A freezer mounted in a lazarette is more likely to die of heat stroke than one mounted on deck under a canvas cover is likely to corrode to death.

Plan to lightly scrub your bottom paint a bit more frequently in these warmer waters. Even if you don't scuba dive for sport, using a tank and hookah rig helps you do a better job more often. Zincs may need to be replaced more frequently in the Panama Canal region and near big ports or Navy bases.

Self Reliance & Security

Radar, GPS, a reliable depth sounder, HF radio, WX-fax, water maker and proper charts are required safety gear for this route. Charts and chart plotters for the countries on this route are not always GPS accurate, so in close proximity to land and offshore hazards, rely on your eyes, depth sounder and radar ranges more than GPS.

Production running lights usually are insufficient for this route. Don't hesitate to install heftier wiring for brighter bulbs; install beefier light housings; seal

Cruising Ports: the Central American Route

Low, wimpy running lights are not adequate for the Central American Route.

the housings better than the package recommends; carry spare bulbs. Running lights can fail without your knowledge due to shorts, heavy rain, pounding in a head sea, nearby lightning and old age.

HF email, Skype, Ham radio, SSB, cell phones and satellite phones let you communicate with the world from remote anchorages. Check out the latest com gear reviews at www. CruisingWorld.com But a satellite phone and WX routing service do not replace onboard WX fax or SSB.

Lightning strikes often in Costa Rica, Panama and Honduras, so be prepared to suddenly lose anything electrical – radios, autopilot, radar, GPS, engine controls, plotters, lights, pumps, etc.

Petty theft in areas of extreme poverty can be an issue, so pay attention to the "coconut telegraph" (VHF, SSB and Ham radio networks) for problems in specific anchorages or ports. Don't show theft prone items on deck. When anchored overnight in remote coves or problem areas, bring the dink on board, remove fenders and close the life lines. When cruising Mexico alone, I rigged a motion-sensor frog that croaked loudly if anything moved on deck. See "guard frog" below.

Dinghy theft is the most common security problem. But broadcasting a huge reward usually inspires a rash of dinghy thefts. Read above about dinghy security. To keep packs of beach children from bouncing on your inflatable or playing fort inside, hire one kid to keep it safe from the others. Carry a fully charged hand-held VHF whenever you go off in the dinghy.

Medical Issues: Don't embark on this adventurous route if you're not healthy, agile or can't tolerate exercise in high heat and humidity. Take along copies of your prescriptions with generic equivalents, because you'll be asked for copies during drug boardings. Big-port *farmacias* stock most common medicines, but few exotics. I've had good experiences with doctors in Cuba, Mexico, Guatemala, Costa Rica and Panama.

You can buy an extensive offshore medical kit customized for your needs, along with a supporting doctor's advice at www.medicalofficer.net This site has medical seminars for offshore cruisers, free articles and good advice ranging from safety drills to the ditch kit.

If you put together your own medical kit, "*Advanced First Aid Afloat*," 5th edition, has a

Running errands in the dinghy.

*Provisioning for produce is good
in Bocas del Toro, Panama.*

good outline. *"Where There Is No Doctor"* is also excellent to read on this route.

Provisioning Check Lists

If you absolutely must have tangerine chutney or Norwegian goose pate, stock up before heading south, because you won't find them at the *Mercado Municipal* and waterfront *fruterias* where you'll do most of your shopping. (Don't bring cardboard cartons on board, as they're cockroach nurseries.)

But along this route you'll find large air-conditioned grocery stores (CostCo, Sam's Club, Soriana's, El Rey, WalMart) with deli shops, custom butchers and US brands in the following cities: San Salvador, San Jose, Balboa, Panama City, Veracruz, Progreso, Merida and Playa del Carmen.

Some popular food items that are difficult to find in Mexico's Gulf Coast, Central America and the western Caribbean are:

1. albacore packed in water
2. canned chicken
3. cranberries
4. whole turkey
5. brown rice, wild rice
6. ground decaf coffee
7. low fat coffee creamer
8. whole wheat flour (refrigerated)
9. bread machine mixes (refrigerated)
10. soy flour, soy milk, tofu
11. low sugar ketchup & peanut butter
12. canned whole tomatoes
13. sun-dried tomato puree
14. herbal & balsamic vinegars
15. plain yogurt
16. dry yogurt culture
17. instant soup cups
18. seedless jams

Top-quality paper products (paper plates, towels, TP, tampons, tissues) are improving in Latin America, and US brands are sometimes available but more expensive. Some other non-food items to stock up on before heading south are:

1. TP for the holding tank
2. zip-locking plastic bags
3. microwaveable storage containers
4. air-tight storage containers
5. hypo-allergenic laundry detergent
6. hypo-allergenic bath soap
7. cleaners: teak, stainless, fiberglass
8. non-toxic insect repellents

*Super Mercados are found in major ports
along the Central American Route.*

Outfitting & Spares Check List

Spare parts for common engines like Detroit Diesel and Caterpillar are found in most major Central American capitals. However parts unique to yachts must be ordered, shipped down and cleared through Customs. So outfit your boat with as extensive a spare-parts inventory as you can. These items are difficult to find down here:

1. autopilot spares (check with your manufacturer).
2. watermakers: filters, membranes.
3. light bulbs for running lights and navigation lights.
4. charts, plotter programs, nav tools.
5. WX fax paper, parts.
6. diaphragms, seals & 0-rings for all hydraulics, steering system & stabilizers.
7. fuses for all electrical and electronic devices, check each manual for spares recommendations.
8. bilge pump and float switch.
9. fresh-water pump, or repair kit & back-up motor for burn out.
10. 3 very large fenders (ball or teardrop type, not tubular).
11. 4 Panama Canal lines (with eyes, 125' each) or 600' spool of 3-strand.
12. courtesy flags for Mexico, Cuba, Grand Cayman, Honduras, Guatemala, Colombia, Panama, Costa Rica, El Salvador, Nicaragua.
13 Q-flag (yellow quarantine flag).

Crew Preparations for the Central American Route

While you're preparing your boat to cruise the Central American route, here are a few personal preparations you might make.

Since you're not a novice cruiser, you already can anchor safely overnight, night after night, right? And by now, you're comfortable being underway at night whenever a safe anchorage is not available. You know how to gather the critical weather forecasts, maintain and fix most of your mechanical stuff and treat minor medical events, right? You and your crew operate as a team, you've developed shipboard hobbies to prevent boredom, worked out marital kinks and are physically healthy.

What's different?

Since you've accomplished everything above, what else is different about cruising this route as opposed to stateside cruising?

1.) Spanish Language: West Coasters arriving in Central America from southern Mexico had to have picked up some Spanish. But East Coasters jumping from Key West to Isla Mujeres to Roatan might meet only marina staffers who speak English. Even if you somehow hop from one gringo resort marina to another, you'll eventually need some Spanish. Without the language, you're isolated in a gringo bubble and unable to participate in your new environment. It's not enough to order "*mas cerveza, por favor*" in a beach palapa.

Can you understand a storm report broadcast by the Port Captain? Can you explain to a mechanic that your transmission seals were replaced after the noise started, not before? Can you find out whether or not the bus you're boarding comes back the same day? For quick reference, see the Appendices for our Spanish lexicon of nautical terms.

Get together with other cruising boaters ("*yatistas*") heading south and hire a Spanish teacher, tailor the curriculum to your needs. Get fluid (not necessarily fluent) in (a.) the present tense and (b.)

Simple Spanish is key to participating in life afloat and ashore.

the easy future using "ir" plus an infinitive. Learn when addressing a stranger in the familiar is OK and when it's rude. The rest will be forgiven.

2.) Money: Most countries covered in this guidebook have cash machines at banks and larger stores, but there's a daily limit and it's in local currency only. Before you depart, ask your home-port bank how you can access your accounts from abroad. Be sure your credit-card accounts are paid monthly in your absence (See below.), or after one late payment your card may be declined. Major credit cards like Visa and MasterCard are often (not always) accepted for paying marina and fuel dock bills under $500; some others are not. Some fuel docks want cash.

Start off with some US dollars. Unfortunately, $100 bills can be very difficult to break if they're not in perfect condition (no bent or missing corners) and because no one ever has change. Take plenty of $20s in good condition. When arriving in a new country, make a bank visit to convert some cash to the local currency. Otherwise, if you spend dollars on the street, you'll lose in the conversion. Travelers checks are often accepted in larger stores and exchange houses

Sharing water with locals, we learn where the best fishing and diving are found.

– but seldom in smaller shops. Clerks want to write your passport number on each traveler's check.

3.) Tropical Clothing: Once embarked on the tropical voyage this book covers, most yatistas live in shorts and T-shirts. Pure 100% cotton and mostly-cotton-blend fabrics are most successful. Flip flops and sport shoes suffice for shore. In really hot weather you might spend all day in a swim suit.

For women, a pareo wrap or shorts and a T-shirt, halter or bikini top are typical attire for casual visits or cocktails in your neighbor's cockpit. Some men dress up for these non-occasions by switching to a non-holey T-shirt. This is fine within the narrow yatista community.

But for a trip to the Port Captain's office or other local authorities – or going downtown in the bigger cities or to big airports, dressing too casually is taken by the locals as a sign of social disrespect to them. For such occasions, we recommend that men wear their most presentable shorts or long pants. For women, either longer shorts, long skirts or slacks are much better than short-shorts and bikini tops.

For tropical downpours, your rain gear jacket should be as light-weight and well ventilated as possible. Because of the humidity, most folks don't

Many marinas have activities for children, like this handicrafts class.

bother with the bottoms. You can wear a safety harness over or under the jacket for traveling in squally weather. A fleece windbreaker and a few cotton sweaters serve for rare cool evenings on the hook.

4.) Communication: Skype is one of the most practical new ways to keep in touch with your home base while you're cruising Latin America. For this you need to be comfortable using a keyboard, preferably on a laptop that you can take ashore. Internet cafes are everywhere.

SSB email is usually SailMail, and Ham email is WinLink, but others are cropping up for HF radio at sea and WiFi at marinas.

Cell phone coverage outside big ports is spotty, and

except in El Salvador and Belize, it's not seamless even within the same country. But a cell phone is almost indispensable when you spend a big chunk of time in one port.

Satellite phones are still coming down in price, still improving in reliability, but they have lots of room for improvement in offshore coverage areas – such as the western Caribbean.

Pre-paid phone cards are handy if you go ashore to make calls. Fewer phones still accept coins, but phone cards are sold in corner stores throughout Latin America. However, before you buy a packet of cards, find out what geographic area that brand of card is good for within that country.

On some phones, you can access your home-port long-distance carrier by using your home-port long-distance provider's credit card, then conveniently charge the call to your home phone account. But to do this, you must ask your phone service for their access number for each country you plan to visit.

Beware of phone booths that advertise that they'll bill your credit card for calls to the US, because the extra charges and local taxes are exorbitant. In

Above: Scuba & snorkeling are major yatista activities and great exercise.

Right: SSB radio, lap top with email program, modem (right) are portable, inexpensive & easy to use - chat with the whole world, receive WX reports.

Cruising Ports: the Central American Route

Emergency drills are more awkward when wearing a PFD - so try it.

Mexico and most of Central America, a collect call to the US is much less expensive than paying the local rate. Ask the operator in advance to calculate the total charges per minute. These calls don't appear on your bill for several months. After a couple 5-minute calls that cost $100 each, we avoid such scams.

5.) Keep the Home Fires Burning: The more smoothly your financial and familial affairs back home continue to operate, the more free you'll be. Designate one responsible person to act with your "power of attorney" to open your mail and email, field calls, forward important stuff to you, make deposits and pay bills. Keep this person informed of your whereabouts and changing itinerary.

He or she might also be your "social liaison," to coordinate when friends and family fly down to join you – off in the wild blue yonder in places they can't pronounce, places the travel agents don't believe exist. And if you should ever "go missing," it will certainly hasten your rescue – or prevent a needless Search & Rescue mission.

6.) Security: Passports are required for port clearance. Make a copy of the first 2 pages, and carry the copy as ID when you travel off your boat – even if you also carry the passport tucked away. Passport theft has increased since 9-11.

Guns are prohibited. Mexico strictly enforces its prohibition on guns onboard while transiting their waters, and Mexico lies astride the water route between Florida and California. Each country has its own laws about foreigners carrying guns, and when you're boarded in their waters, one of the first question they ask is "Are there any firearms on board?" Then they search. Having a gun could land you in jail, your boat confiscated.

The nautical radio networks (VHF, SSB, HAM) alert listeners as soon as a security problem occurs, but don't be passive about security. Using radar and binoculars, pay attention to any vessel approaching you underway or at anchor in remote spots. Stow theft-prone items below decks, especially when entering a new port. Pull in your boarding ladder and fenders, close lifelines, ship the dinghy at night. For personal protection, consider a flare pistol, spear gun, pepper spray or mace (requires training). My personal favorite is a sling shot and pocket of marbles.

Watch your life raft inflate during a demonstration at a cruisers fair. Many don't inflate properly, lack water or other critical components. An "offshore" type life raft is best for this route.

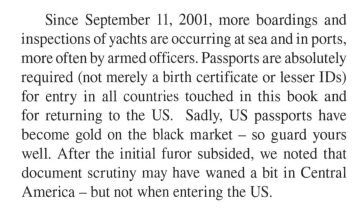

Paperwork Cha Cha for the Central American Route

About Port Clearance

Entering and leaving foreign countries in a private yacht is much more exciting and interesting than taking commercial flights in and out of international airports that all look and function pretty much alike.

First-time *yatistas* (yacht visitors) are always astounded at the huge number of documents, paper copies, rubber stamps and rounds of office visits they must wade through in order to enter a country by sea or to move their boat from one Port Captain's jurisdiction to another. We copyrighted the phrase Paperwork Cha Cha for the normal Latin American port-clearance process, because it's like the Cha Cha dance – you take 2 steps forward, 2 steps back, 2 steps left, 2 steps right, always going back to square one.

Every Port of Entry along this Cruising Ports route is utterly unique. Why? These balmy shores have experienced Aztec, Mayan and Caribe cultural wars, Spanish voyages of exploitation, sea battles between European square-riggers and Men of War, 100s of pirate attacks and shipwrecks, Cold War politics, hurricane devastation and population explosions right up through 2007.

International trade treaties, tourism developers and marina associations have streamlined some of the most cumbersome paperwork requirements that strangle nautical tourism, and each year we see improvements. Mexico and El Salvador get gold stars.

History and culture have shaped the ports and officialdom in Mexico, Guatemala, El Salvador, Honduras, Nicaragua, Costa Rica, Panama, Belize, Cuba and the Western Caribbean islands. So, please don't expect consistency from one country to the next – not even from one port to the next. As long as you allow plenty of time and stay cool, port clearance can be a rewarding cultural experience. Don't get your knickers in a twist, OK?

Since September 11, 2001, more boardings and inspections of yachts are occurring at sea and in ports, more often by armed officers. Passports are absolutely required (not merely a birth certificate or lesser IDs) for entry in all countries touched in this book and for returning to the US. Sadly, US passports have become gold on the black market – so guard yours well. After the initial furor subsided, we noted that document scrutiny may have waned a bit in Central America – but not when entering the US.

Documents Before You Leave Home

1.) Passports. Apply for passports for each person well in advance, because they can take 90 days. (http://travel.state.gov/passport/passport_1738. html) If your old passport might expire before you are done cruising, renew it before departing the US. For yourself and each crew member, make several color copies of the 2 inside front pages and keep these copies in a safe place on board, separate from the original passports.

2.) Visas. Some countries touched in this book may require non-US citizens to apply for and receive a visa before arriving in country. Check out this State Department website for the latest entrance requirements for each country you plan to visit by boat, plane or land. http://travel. state.gov/travel/travel_1744.html This has not applied to US citizens recently, but things can change.

3.) Vessel document or registration. One for each boat, dinghy, motorized toy, trailer or vehicle taken outside the US. The original must be on board with the correct annual renewal sticker. Make at least 24 copies of your primary boat document before leaving home, because several

Cruising Ports: the Central American Route

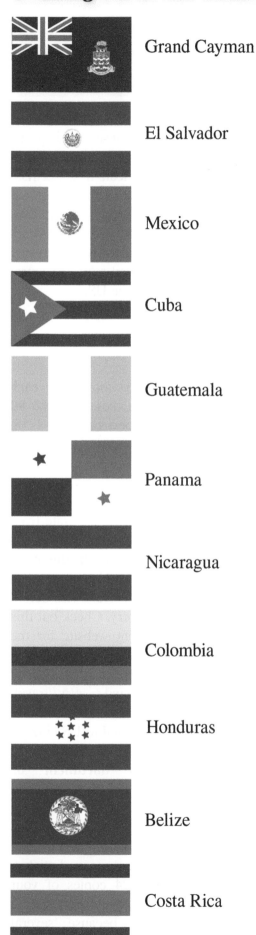

Grand Cayman

El Salvador

Mexico

Cuba

Guatemala

Panama

Nicaragua

Colombia

Honduras

Belize

Costa Rica

Here are the courtesy flags for all the countries on this route.

copies will be surrendered for each port clearance.

4.) Crew List. (See our Crew Lists for Mexico and Spanish-Speaking Countries" at the end of this chapter.) Make lots of copies of our blank forms for your personal use. When you arrive in your first non-US port, have at least 6 copies filled out with the name of the boat, the fact that it's a yacht, departure port and date, destination, document number, home port, gross and net tonnage, list each crew member, their nationalities, positions on board, ages, passport numbers. The Crew List must be signed by the vessel captain, and if everyone is a US citizen, no visits to consulates or payments for Cruising Permits are necessary before departure. Each country requires a fresh Crew List. When someone leaves your crew or joins it, you make a new Crew List.

5.) Fishing Papers. (Mexico only) If you have any fishing gear onboard (fish hook in your life raft?), you are supposed to purchase one **Fishing License** for each person on board from CONAPESCA. (Boat permit is obsolete.) Annual licenses are easier & cheaper (about $45 US). Mexican Navy sometimes checks for fishing licenses, if only as an excuse for a quick inspection.

Download the Application from www.conapescasandiego.org or 50 tackle stores in SoFla, SoCal and AZ hand them out. It contains the current prices, which change. Mail the Applicatin back with your SASE and your money order (no check or cc) for the exact amount made out to **Oficina de Pesca/Conapesca.** Allow 2 weks.

Faster? Come to the Conapesca Office in San Diego, corner of Laurel & 5th; they now accept cash in person. Call for hours (619) 233-4324, fax 233-0344.

CONAPESCA Office
2550 Fifth Ave. Suite 15
San Diego, CA 92103
For questions, email info@conapescasandiego.org

6.) Proof of vessel insurance. All marinas and yacht clubs require proof of liability insurance, especially when you leave your boat there and fly elsewhere. Only Mexico requires a Mexican company policy, so ask your US insurance agent who they work with for down south. Mariners Mexico, Mariners General Ins. Group, Vagabundos del Mar Club are a few that have been recommended by cruisers.

7.) Captain's Letter. If the only captain onboard is other than whomever is listed on the document or registration as the owner, then the captain must carry a notarized letter in Spanish from the documented owner (name, address, phone) giving the captain (name, passport #) authorization to have possession of that vessel (name, doc #, home port, tonnage) from where to where, from a specific date to another specific date. Inhibits theft.

Same is true when the vessel's owner is listed on the document or registration as a corporation, even if the captain/owner is an

*Boardings at sea are common, so have
your paperwork ready for inspection.*

officer of that corporation. In this case, the captain needs the above letter but from another officer of the corporation, plus proof that said other officer is in fact an officer – usually proved by attaching the minutes from the last board meeting on the corporation's letterhead stationery.

8.) Minor's Letter. (Mexico only so far) Children under 18 (minors) can't travel alone in Mexico. If a minor is traveling without either parent, then a notarized letter from both parents is necessary, giving permission for the minor to travel in the custody of the specified adult with whom he or she is traveling. If one parent is present, then the notarized permission letter must be from the absent parent. This letter can be in English. Get the form from a US notary.

9.) Pets. To get your pet back into the US without being quarantined for 6 months (their kennel, you pay), get an International Health Certificate (USDA Form 77-043) showing your name, a legible description of the animal and the rabies vaccination record being up to date for the next 12 months. Get this from your vet before you leave. Some countries also request a stamp from APHIS (Animal & Plant Health Inspection Service), so request APHIS Form 7011. The APHIS form is required if you fly your pet into the US. If your pet needs vaccinations during your trip, any licensed vet can do it and add their notations to your International Health Certificate – or issue a new IHC valid for 12 months. FMI, visit www.aphis.usda.gov

10.) Equipment & Serial Numbers List. Your engine serial number(s) will be needed to get a Temporary Import Permit in Mexico, also for each port clearance in some Central American countries. So, as a security measure, make a list of all valuable equipment on board and the serial

number of each item. Keep copies filed back home, others onboard. Use an engraving tool to add your own numbering system for items without serial numbers. Update it as you replace gear. Engrave your boat name on everything, thus discouraging thieves. If you're ever robbed, this list will help you file the police report and insurance claim.

International Clearance

At your first foreign Port of Entry, you make your International Arrival (*Entrada Internaciónal*), which is the most complex procedure. If you're staying in that port less than 24 or 48 hours, tell the Port Captain and request to exit (*Salida*) at the same time – specifying whether it's to another port in that country (*Salida Naciónal*) or to some other country (*Salida Internaciónal*). All subsequent port clearance

*Mexico's streamlined International
Clearance is handled at CIS offices.*

Cruising Ports: the Central American Route

Puerto Juarez (Cancun & Isla Mujeres) has a CIS office for easy port clearance.

within that country will be much easier.

Mexico is probably the first stop for most yatistas on this route. Mexico streamlined its *Entrada Internaciónal* if you clear in at the CIS office (Puerto Juarez, Ensenada, Cabo San Lucas). Mexico has streamlined its *Salida Naciónal* between subsequent ports even more. You simply notify the Port Captain on VHF of your arrival and departure, unless you have a crew change or must import boat parts.

The basic Paperwork Cha Cha steps outlined below are common throughout Latin America, but they're not carved in stone; each country has its own names for port offices and slightly different procedural requirements for a yacht (*yate, barco de placer*).

The Big Three

The 3 offices normally required for your international arrival are the Port Captain, Immigration and Customs. During subsequent domestic clearances within that country, usually only the Port Captain's office is involved. But expect variations.

For example, in Puerto Quetzal, Guatemala (Pacific side), you'll be at a private marina within a Navy base, and all the officials come to your boat. At Isla San Andrés (Caribbean), you're required to hire a ship's agent, and the agent handles everything for you. In Balboa and Colon, Panama, hiring an agent s optional, but you start with the Maritime Authority of Panama (AMP). In some countries, the routine changes from one port to the next and from year to year.

Port of Entry: Not all ports are Ports of Entry, but only a Port of Entry is able to officially receive vessels arriving from international waters or other countries. In the guide chapters, under the Port Clearance heading, we specify if it's a Port of Entry and where the required offices are located.

For example, on the Yucatan Channel, the first Port of Entry is Puerto Juarez (for Isla Mujeres - Cancun), which has a unique and convenient CIS office (Central Integral de Servicios) for streamlined international port clearance. But the next Port of Entry south is on Isla Cozumel, where you'll find separate offices for the Port Captain, Immigration and Customs scattered around the island.

While approaching your Port of Entry into any country, hoist your yellow Q-flag (quarantine) on your port side and call the Port Captain's office on VHF 16 to inquire how to clear into the country. You'll be told where to "present yourself" and your entire crew and guests and all your paperwork (below) directly upon arrival. Usually the Port Captain's office directs you to start at Migración, but not always.

Take just enough time to get cleaned up before beginning your port clearance – as a sign of respect. Latino officials

Marina Hemingway's port-clearance dock is manned by the Cuban Guard Costa.

are more formal in their business attire and expect guests to reciprocate. Don't present yourself in ragged clothes, short shorts, bare chest or bare feet.

Port Captain: The Port Captain's office is called the *Capitanía*. The Port Captain (*Capitán del Puerto*) has authority close to God within his jurisdiction, which might cover more than 100 n.m. of coastline, lesser ports and dozens of anchorages. The Port Captain commands all vessels in that jurisdiction including cruise ships, freighters, the local Navy battalion – and all yachts, foreign or local. The Port Captain of each jurisdiction determines the exact order in which you'll visit the various port-clearance offices in his port – which might differ from the order required in another jurisdiction.

Some countries rotate their Port Captains every 4 to 5 years, and the next guy may change the order of visits. So far, we haven't heard of a woman Port Captain.

In larger commercial ports, yacht clearance may be handled by the Director of Operations or by overworked secretaries. In some ports, if you don't show up directly (no stopping for a quick *cerveza*), the Navy will track you down and escort you to the proper authorities.

Immigration: The officers from *Migración* will inspect and stamp everyone's passports (and visas from some non-US citizens). Migración will issue blank Tourist Cards for you to fill in. In some countries, they issue a Cruising Permit valid for 90 days, usually renewable.

Customs: Agents of the *Aduana* or Customs may be armed, and they want to know if you have any guns, drugs or other contraband onboard. They inspect the boat very thoroughly.

Other Offices: Some privatized Mexican ports also have an API or the Port Authority inspection and fee for anchoring or using port moorings. George Town, Grand Cayman, puts them all under the Port Department.

Belize relies on local Police chiefs based in town halls, but they have full authority.

What about Fees? In most countries, small port-clearance fees are charged by each branch of port offices, and most can accept payment on the spot, for which you get a receipt recorded on your paperwork.

But where government officials are not allowed to accept money, they'll send you to a bank where payment is accepted; take the bank receipt and paperwork back to the office that requested the fee. Mexico's CIS offices (Puerto Juarez, for example) have bank kiosks for paying all fees at once by credit card. Check www.CentralAmericanBoating.com for Updates as other ports follow suit.

Two Old World legacies still alive here are the *propina* (tip) and the *papaleo* (red tape, multiple layers of official bureaucracy). Gone are the days when you had to bring the Port Captain a bottle of Scotch to clear in or out. "Transparency" being the new credo, only a few port officers still expect a tip for a normal port clearance. But if an official stays open late to help you sift through the *papaleo*, they might not turn down a $5 bill discretely slid onto their desk.

A *mordida* is a bribe, not a tip, and it implies you've done something illegal. Mordida, like blood in the water, attracts more sharks.

Fortunately, during 100s of boardings we've experienced at sea and in port along this route, we've never known of Navy or Marine boarding officers to accept anything beyond a cup of coffee, maybe a sandwich or a cold unopened can of soda.

What about Timing? Port clearance can take 2 to 4 hours if you begin early on a weekday (not

Every regulated port has at least a Capitanía, and they monitor VHF 16.

Officials from Aduana, Migración and Capitán de Puerto come to your boat in Los Sueños Marina, Costa Rica.

a holiday), if all the right offices and banks are not too far apart, not closed for siesta (usually 1400 to 1600 hours) and if everything goes perfectly. With bad luck, it could take 2 days or more.

You may not be aware of "San Lunes," a common Latin American holiday. The Monday after a big Sunday fiesta sometimes turns into another unofficial holiday, satirically called San Lunes (Saint Monday). Many folks fail to show up for work on Monday morning or they arrive a bit hung over and need more time to accomplish less than normal.

Taxi, Gringo? For these reasons, we highly recommend hiring a knowledgeable taxi driver to shuttle you around the dance floor and wait for you at each step. A good *taxista* knows who's out sick this week, which bank has shortest lines and which secretary might slip your paperwork onto the right desk during siesta.

Paperwork Cha Cha

Here are the basic steps for International Arrival, plus some variations to expect. (In some ports, all officials come to your boat.)

Step 1.) Port Captain: Hail *"Capitán del Puerto"* on VHF 16 and ask for instructions to clear into that country for the first time – *Entrada Internaciónal*. Well intentioned fellow yatistas may intercede, wanting to show you the ropes, but follow instructions from the Port Captain. The Port Captain determines whether or not your boat will be boarded and inspected now, later or never.

Step 2.) Immigration: Unless the Port Captain's office or Navy patrol wants to see you in person, you may be directed to take all crew and guests immediately to *Migración*. (Some ports prohibit the crew from stepping ashore until released by Migración.) Present your <u>Crew List</u> (original and 6 copies) and everyone's <u>passports</u> (and <u>visas</u> if required). Present your Zarpe from your previous country (except from US for US citizens). Present a <u>Minor's Letter</u> only if asked.

Migración gives you a blank <u>Tourist Card</u> for each person on board. Fill them in, requesting 180 days or the maximum allowable. Some countries issue a <u>Cruising Permit</u> through Migración, valid for 90 days but renewable once or twice.

If Migración fees are to be paid at a bank, ask which bank is best and what its hours are. After paying, treat the receipt like a port-clearance document. Keep a copy safe until you leave that country.

Keep your validated <u>Tourist Card</u> with you at all times. (Make a copy and stow it for safe keeping.) The Migración officer may also stamp and sign your <u>Crew List</u>.

NOTE: Crew List Changes: When someone on your Crew List wishes to leave, the captain and that person must go to Migración with their Tourist Cards and the original Crew List and a new Crew List showing the person no longer part of the crew. The crew member gets either a new Tourist Card or a notation on his original Tourist Card, enabling him or her to depart the country separately from the boat. If the crew member departs before the new Crew List is validated at Migración, both the captain and the crew member will be in "agua turbia" (troubled waters) when they try to depart the country by air, sea or land. Also, when a new person joins the crew, the captain takes the old and new Crew Lists and the person with passport & Tourist Card to Migración for validation.

Step 3.) Customs: Unless you're directed to go back to the Capitanía, the next step usually is Customs or *Aduana*. Present to the Aduana officers all the papers you've accumulated thus far. Aduana's job is to make sure you don't have anything illegal (guns, stolen items), that you're not smuggling (new boxes of Levis, TVs, medicines) and that the boat is not stolen. They want to see the vessel's document or registration, and they may ask for a list of <u>serial numbers</u> of all your major motors, engines and electronics. If you have a <u>Captain's Letter</u>, present it to Aduana.

In Mexico, you purchase a <u>Temporary Import Permit</u> from Aduana. The TIP option legalizes leaving your boat in a marina when you fly home and lets you fly back with declared boat parts without paying full import duty (requires Bill of Sale).

In Cuba, the Aduana confiscates fire arms and holds them at Marina Hemingway until you depart Cuba at the same port (impossible if you're cruising). But in Mexico possession of fire arms is a serious federal offence, punishable by big fines, confiscation of the boat, prison time, etc. So don't have them on board if you pass through Mexican waters.

Step 4.) Additional: Other inspections may be required, including API (Mexico only), Navy, Health & Sanitation, Agriculture, Police. If in doubt, ask the Port Captain or Port Department. Health officers may spray your scuppers for mosquitoes, especially if Dengue Fever has been reported in that country. Agriculture officers may inspect your refrigerator & freezer looking for Mad Cow beef or poultry with the H5N1 virus. In Belize's outlying cays, the local Police captain may perform all these inspections.

Step 5.) Port Captain: Finish with a sign-off from the Port Captain's office on your Crew List or Cruising Permit.

Most Capitanías post a harbor chart with the latest changes, a list of local marine services with contacts, the latest WX bulletins, a list of VHF channel designations, etc. While researching and updating this guidebook, we always make an appointment with the local Port Captain or Port Operations person to gather the latest data and maritime gossip.

International Departure

When you're ready to exit a country, notify the Port Captain in your last Port of Entry and request a *Salida Internaciónal* procedure, ending with an exit paper known worldwide as a *Zarpe*. It will be required to enter the next country – except into the US if you're all US citizens and your boat is US flagged.

Crew Lists
(1) Mexico Entrance Only
(2.) Spanish-speaking Countries

Please note the differenced in the 2 blank Crew List forms on the following 2 pages.

(1.) If you're visiting Mexico, use the first form for your International Arrival there. Follow the same instructions below for filling in the second form, but on this form obviously you will stop after Part One.

(2.) The second form is for your International Arrival in all other Spanish-speaking countries on this route and for subsequent port clearances there as well. This form has 3 parts, shaded differently. Fill in all 3 parts, ***except*** you'll sign only at the bottom of Part One, the upper section. The signature blanks in the other 2 parts are for the Migración officer and the Port Captain.

Part 1: First paragraph, fill in the blanks with boat captain's name, boat name, document or registration number, home port, country flag, gross tons, net tons.

Second paragraph: destination port & state in that country, intermediate ports. Most Port Captains accept *puertos intermedios* instead of listing them all, but we also list our more important intermediate ports or anchorages just in case.

Third paragraph is the crew list: boat captain's name first, nationality, crew position, age, passport number. Captain is *capitán(a)*; cook is *cocinera(o)*; engineer is *mecanico(a)*; deckhand is *marinero(a)*; guest is *invitado(a)*. Below captain's name, begin the next person. If you run out of lines, write or type their information on a separate sheet and staple it to this Crew List and bring it to the attention of the Port Captain's office so it won't get lost.

Fourth paragraph: number of people on board.

Fifth: fill in today's month, day and year.

Sixth: skipper's signature. (Mexico stops here.)

Part 2: Fill in the blanks with number of people onboard, destination port & state, month, day & year. Don't sign this signature blank.

Part 3: Fill in the blanks with boat name, destination port & state, total number of people onboard, month, day & year. Don't sign the bottom signature blank.

Estimado Capitán de Puerto,

Presente_____ , Capitán del yate de placer "_____"
numero de _____de la matricula de _____ bandera _____
de porte de___tonelados brutas y de___netas de arqueo, siendo la tripulación de este yate
procedente del puerto de_____como sigue: _____
_____

Nombre	*Nacionalidad*	*Cargo Abordo*	*Edad*	*# de Pasaporte*

   Comprende este Rol los asientos de____personas y es de mi satisfación, como Capitán que
soy, manifestar que me obligo al exacto de todo cuanto disponen las Leyes y Reglamentos
actualmente en vigor.

Fecha_____de_____ _____

El Capitán _____

Estimado Capitán de Puerto

Presente_____, Capitán del yate de placer "_____"
numero de_____ de la matricula de_____, bandera de_____, de
porte de_____ tonelados brutas y de_____ tonelados netas de arqueo, declara:

Que el dia de hoy zarpará con destino al puerto de_____con escala en los
siquientes puertos de_____ siendo la tripulación de este yate
como sigue:

Nombre	Nacionalidad	Cargo a bordo	Edad	# de Pasaporte

Comprende este Rol los asientos de____personas y es de mi satisfacción, como Capitán que soy,
manifestar que me obligo al exacto cumplimiento de todo cuanto disponen las Leyes y Reglamentos
actualmente en vigor.

Fecha_____de

El Capitán _____ .

Visada de conformidad por esta Oficina de Migración con____tripulantes inclusive su Capitán; se hace
a la mar con destino a_____escalando puntos intermedios.

Fecha_____de_____ _____

El Jefe de la Oficina de Migración

_____ .

Habiendo cumplido su escala en este puerto, el yate_____ en esta fecha despachese
para_____escalando todos los lugares que se mencionan, con _____
tripulantes inclusive su Capitán.

Fecha_____de _____ _____

El Capitán de Puerto

_____

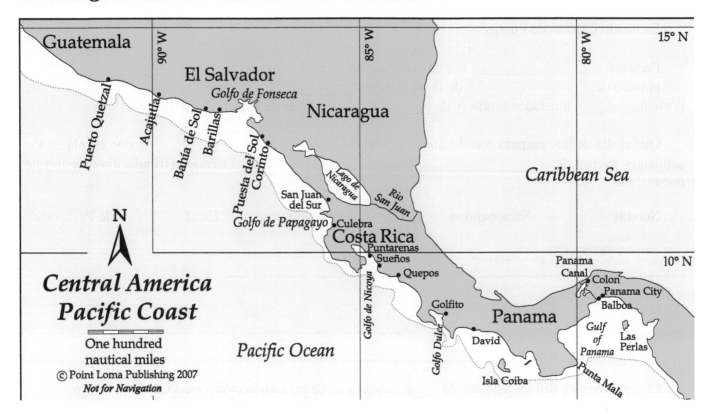

Weather & Routing for Pacific Central America

By Amanda Delany, Meteorologist

Strong local winds, building seas and hurricanes are the main concerns mariners have while traveling between Mexico and Panama. Learning when these scenarios develop and how to avoid them is key to having a safe and enjoyable voyage.

Generally, the weather and sea conditions along the 1,000-mile coast from Puerto Chiapas, Mexico, to the Panama Canal are balmy and benign during winter and spring cruising season. But mariners need to pay close attention to the weather whenever they plan to approach or enter one of this region's major gulfs – Tehuantepec, Papagallo and Panama Bay. Oddly enough, one of the first regions to monitor concerning weather at the gulfs on the Pacific side is the Gulf of Mexico on the Caribbean side.

Strong northerly winds behind cold fronts in the Gulf of Mexico will funnel down the Bay of Campeche and then through a valley north of the Gulf of Tehuantepec. Gale-force northerly winds (known as "Tehuantepeckers") often result across the Gulf of Tehuantepec and can persist for up to a week.

How does this WX event affect Central America? About 24 hours later, NE winds will increase up to gale force across the Gulfs of Fonseca and Papagallo and eventually reach the Gulf of Panama. When the ridge of high pressure weakens in the Gulf of Mexico and Caribbean, these enhanced northerly winds will subside across the Central American gulfs as well.

During these wind events, vessels traveling between southern Mexico and Panama are likely to need to stop before crossing or entering any of these gulfs. Puerto Quetzal, Guatemala; Bahia Jiquilisco, El Salvador; Estero Aserradores, Nicaragua; Bahia Santa Elena or Bahia Portrero, Costa Rica; Benao Cove, Panama, provide shelter for awaiting a weather window to cross the nearest windy gulf. if your vessel can handle gale-force winds, you may be able to travel within 1 or 2 nautical miles from shore in order to avoid or minimize the large northerly seas found off shore. The ham and SSB radio nets are an excellent source of weather information. See appendix.

The eastern Pacific tropical-storm season officially begins on May 15 and lasts through November 30. Tropical waves move off shore from the western Central American coast between 05N and 13N, and they track westward in the area known as the Intertropical Convergence Zone (ITCZ).

Tropical Depressions generally develop west of 90W and track either WNW toward the open Pacific or NW to the Mexican Gold Coast or the southern Baja California coast. Because these hurricanes don't from or move south of 10°N, the coast of Central America south of the ITCZ is usually considered a safe place to summer over. Before hurricane season begins, mariners need to move south or north of hurricane alley. If you head south, be aware that fast-moving squalls, downpours and intense lighting strikes are a normal part of summer in the tropics. The rare water spouts are short-lived but dangerous enough to be avoided.

Many new marinas in Pacific Guatemala, El Salvador, Nicaragua, Costa Rica and Panama are becoming popular year-round destinations for sportfishing enthusiasts, passage-making motoryachts and long-term cruising sailors.

Volcano peaks mark your approach to Pacific Guatemala.

Here on the Pacific side, we begin after crossing Mexico's southern border with Guatemala and move generally SE along the Central American countries of Guatemala, El Salvador, Nicaragua, Costa Rica and Pacific Panama to the Panama Canal.

This book's companion guide, *Mexico Boating Guide* covers all of Pacific Mexico from the US border (Baja, Sea of Cortez, mainland Mexico) to Guatemala. See excerpts and details at www.MexicoBoating.com. The Caribbean coast of Guatemala is covered in a later chapter of *Cruising Ports: the Central American Route.*

Pacific Guatemala

Guatemala's Pacific coast is only 132 n.m. long. A Mexican Navy ship from Puerto Madero (Chiapas) stands picket off the Mexico-Guatemala border at Rio Suchiate to greet travelers in both directions.

If you're southbounding, Guatemala's dramatic volcano peaks welcome you. At 10 to 20 miles inland, the coastal plane rises abruptly to a string of volcano peaks. The active Volcan Fuego (13,000') lies 35 miles NNW of Puerto Quetzal, and nearby Volcan Pocaya and may be seen at night spewing smoke and molten lava.

Between the border and Puerto Quetzal (96 miles SE), we coast 3 to 5 miles off shore. A rocky shoal is reported 5 miles out at 12 to 15 miles SE of Champerico pier (not for yatistas). Fishing nets lie within 2.5 miles of shore as you approach the port.

Puerto Quetzal

This man-made harbor (115 miles SE of Puerto Madero, 150 miles WNW of Bahía Jiquilisco) is Guatemala's main Pacific port. It has a W Basin (Navy, cruise ships, marina) and N Basin (commercial only). Here yatistas have access to a full-service marina with fuel dock, easy port clearance, a Navy base, grocery stores, hospital and the PanAmerican Highway.

Approach: About 2 miles west of the port's lighted breakwaters, avoid coastal freighters moored off where the San Jose pier used to be. The port's lighted jetties open eastward. Iztapa Lagoon has 2 tricky, shoaly entrances: the smaller lies .75 of a mile east of Puerto Quetzal, the larger about 2 miles east; but either or both may be silted closed.

When you reach the Puerto Quetzal sea buoy (See chart), hail "Puerto Quetzal Capitanía" on VHF 16, and tell them (Spanish only) you're a yacht requesting permission to enter, and whether or not you need fuel or other services. The use of a ship's agent is optional here, but if you want to hire one, ask the Port Captain now to contact one for you.

Anchoring is prohibited in this controlled port. You'll be directed to enter the W Basin and take a slip in the marina.

Our GPS position in the jetty entrance to Puerto

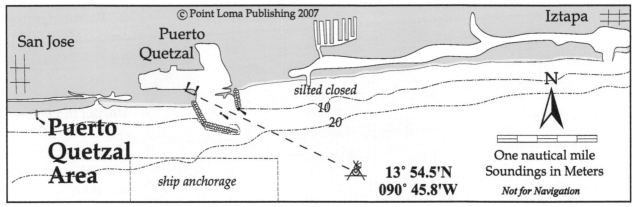

San Jose

Puerto Quetzal

© Point Loma Publishing 2007

Iztapa

silted closed

10

20

Puerto Quetzal Area

ship anchorage

N

13° 54.5'N 090° 45.8'W

One nautical mile
Soundings in Meters
Not for Navigation

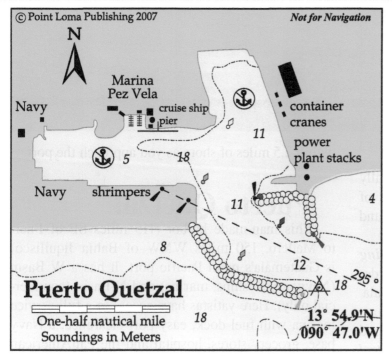

© Point Loma Publishing 2007   *Not for Navigation*

N

Navy

Marina
Pez Vela

cruise ship
pier

container
cranes

power
plant stacks

Navy   shrimpers

5   18   11

11   12   4

8

18   295°

Puerto Quetzal

One-half nautical mile
Soundings in Meters

18   13° 54.9'N
090° 47.0'W

FMI: Until Marina Pez Vela's website is up, for slip & fuel info, email customerservice@marinaguate.com or phone (502) 2379-5778 or 5401-0176. (Don't confuse this marina in Guatemala for one with the same name in Costa Rica that's scheduled to open in 2007.)

Port Clearance: Navy and port officials will board your boat in the marina. Port fees total $150 for simultaneous entry & exit, giving you 5 days; add $10 per additional day.

Hiring an agent is optional. If you need to book flights, tours or find a car and driver, we've used 2 agents. If you speak Spanish, email to Manuel de Jesus Ovalle at tramsmaritimos@intelnett.com or phone (502) 2788-13679 or hail "Miguel Oscar" on VHF 16. Eduardo Perez speaks English but charges more; (502) 2881-1445 or cell (502) 2407-9026 or hail him on VHF 83.

Quetzal is 13°54.90'N, 90°47.03'W. Range lights on the W mole are only for entering the seaward ends of the jetties; they would run you aground if you didn't turn N once inside.

Dockage: The new darsena containing the private marina is in N wall of the W Basin. Just W behind the W end of the cruise-ship landing, you turn N. Marina Pez Vela has room for about 40 yachts; larger ones go to the California-style floating slips; smaller ones continue to the Florida-style slips between dolphins. The dockmaster and staff are very helpful.

The marina has a pleasant restaurant in the big palapa near the local's launch ramp. The adjacent tourist pier has an air-conditioned internet café, bank kiosk and T-shirt shop. Security couldn't be better; you must pass through a guarded gate to get on or off the property, and guards patrol the docks and port entrance.

Local Services: Take diesel or gasoline at the S end of the marina's smaller-boat docks by tying off the dolphins. The pumps are good, fuel is clean, and the marina accepts major credit cards.

Several tournaments are run here and nearby Iztapa Lagoon by Kevin of Great Sailfish Company.

Outside the port's main gate, a taxi or bus can take you W to San Jose where we found 2 tiny markets with scant produce and canned foods. Going E a mile, you'll find a convenience store, then a mile farther behind Iztapa is a larger grocery store with decent produce, provisions, basic tackle, kids' dive masks.

Truck your boat to the Caribbean? Several 35' sailboats have been trucked from Rio Dulce on the Caribbean over the mountains to Puerto Quetzal. Carlos the Yacht Trucker (next to Bruno's Marina) is building a rig for larger boats, and he can pick up boats at Puerto Quetzal. FMI, contact Mariesol rio@guate.net.gt

Marina lies behind a low cruise-ship pier seen in midground. Power plant is visible near harbor entrance.

Dinghy landing at NW corner of Puerto Quetzal's Marina Pez Vela.

Side Trips: Excellent security at Puerto Quetzal makes it a great place from which to explore Guatemala's highlands or *Altiplano* for Mayan market villages, ancient pyramid ruins, historic colonial cities, active volcanoes, coffee plantations and archeological digs. Inform the dockmaster before you depart for overnight ashore. Joining a tour group or hiring a car and driver is safer and more practical than renting a car.

Antigua has dozens of Spanish schools, but we attend and recommend Proyecto Linguistico Francisco Marroquin (PLFM); visit www.langlink. com/guatemala or phone in the US (309) 692-2961. Antigua has an interesting range of small hotels, or you can room & board weekly with a family on PLFM's list (inexpensive).

Beyond Antigua, Guatemala's gringo trail spans Panajachel, Lago Atitlán, Huehuetenango and Chichicastenango. Avoid lingering in Guatemala City; personal security is way bad for gringos. Due to earthquakes, we avoid staying in high-rise hotels.

Iztapa Lagoon

Just east of Puerto Quetzal, a submarine canyon clefts the continental shelf, and the epicenter of many earthquakes lies within 30 miles of here.

Iztapa Lagoon or the Chiquimulilla Canal has 2 shoaly, shallow, surf-prone mouths within 4 miles east of Puerto Quetzal. The narrower

mouth is only .75 of a mile east of Puerto Quetzal breakwaters; it was closed last time we looked, but being dredged. The wider mouth lies about 3 n.m. farther east. Even multihulls and shallow-draft sportfishers shouldn't attempt these zig-zag entrances without calm seas, slack tide and a local guide on board.

In calm conditions, anchorage is possible in the open roadstead outside the lagoon, and it makes an interesting exploration by kayak or dinghy if you can hug the corners of the opening – or follow a local panga going in and out.

Inside, the main channel runs E-W for about 4 n.m. behind the wooded berm. The lagoon's far west end has a guarded, gated community lining a maze of private channels; they don't like visitors. In the middle of the lagoon and at the far east end are two villages with a couple fly-in sportfishing lodges (local boats, marlin & sailfish), fuel docks, shrimper piers and cantinas. Iztapa is the east village flanking Rio Iztapa.

Iztapa Lagoon lies within Monterrico Nature

Laguna Iztapa has a silting problem, but local pangueros know how to get in and out.

Preserve, which protects sea turtles, green iguana, the delicate mangrove iris and other flora and fauna. Kids love the Sea Turtle Center, but hours are irregular.

Iztapa Lagoon is where Juan Rodriguez Cabrillo built the ships he sailed to discover California in 1542. Those local hardwoods are now gone, and his ironworks were forged in Spain and transhipped by mule trains across Guatemala from the Caribbean side – where now a 2-lane highway winds. The lagoon's mouths have been opened and closed many times due to silting from summer rains, pounding south swell and earthquakes (*terremotos*).

El Salvador

The Republic of El Salvador is Central America's smallest nation (about the size of Maryland), yet it is young and densely populated (3.8 million). Since its civil war ended in 1992, El Salvador's emerging economy has been strongly devoted to democracy, fabrication for export, agriculture and international tourism. The Salvadoran currency is the US dollar,

Spanish is the official language, and the capital city of San Salvador has the main international airport.

Geographically, El Salvador is the only Central American nation without a second coast on the Caribbean side. Its Pacific coast is 270 miles long. The Gulf of Fonseca on its SE coast also borders Honduras and Nicaragua.

El Salvador's coastal plane is narrower than Guatemala's, and its Pacific underwater shelf is wider and provides excellent sportfishing (marlin) and commercial shrimping. The coastal range of 20 volcanoes and mountain peaks is divided by the valley of Rio Lempa, which forms the dangerous Lempa Shoals in coastal waters.

El Salvador's 2 yachting destinations lie close on either side of Lempa Shoal: Bahía Jaltepeque and Bahía Jiquilisco.

The Guatemala-El Salvador border at Rio Paz lies about 36 miles ESE from Puerto Quetzal. From Rio Paz, the steep, surf-pounded coastline tends SE for about 20 miles to Puerto Acajutla, on the west flank of the coastal bulge of Punta Remedios.

Puerto Acajutla is a dirty, busy container-ship pier (13°34.4'N, 89°50.5'W). A panga darsena lies a quarter mile north of the pier, and a swell-plagued open roadstead is in between with no shelter from west or SW weather. Acajutla has nada for yatistas.

Punta Remedios: Stay at least 4 miles SSE of Punta Remedios (good radar target) due to detached Sacasa Rock and a collection of wrecks. Mountains reach the coast for the next 29 miles ESE to La Libertad open roadstead and abandoned pier.

Bahía Jaltepeque

Also known as Bahía del Sol, this anchorage and mooring area has a fuel dock, port office and boat yard. It grew popular with long-term sailing cruisers thanks to a free pilot service; see below.

Breakers a quarter mile off shore mark the shoaly mouth of Estero de Jaltepeque (*hahl-tay-PAY-kay*), which lies 57 miles ESE of Punta Remedios, 26 miles west of Bahía Jiquilisco. The prominent double peak of Volcan San

Island Marine
10
5
Bahía Jaltepeque
Hotel del Sol
14
44
Bocana del Cordoncillo
27
© Point Loma Publishing 2007
Half n.m.
Soundings in Feet
migrating shoals
12
breakers
12
Not for Navigation
N
18
30
Rio Lempa Shoal 4 miles
Bahia del Sol
Call for free Pilot Service
13° 15.9'N
088° 53.0'W 43

Vicente cone (7,157') rises 18 miles inland.

Chart 21520 misplaces Jaltepeque's tiny opening, but like at Iztapa Lagoon, natural forces may have changed it many times over the decades. The notorious Lempa Shoal lies within 4 miles ESE, where the massive Rio Lempa empties silt, boulders and snags into the Pacific. If approaching from SE, stay at least 5 miles off to avoid Lempa Shoal.

CAUTION: Do not attempt the shoals-and-breakers entrance to Bahia Jaltepeque without hiring the pilot to lead you in and out, nor without having good sea conditions, a mild incoming tide and plenty of daylight. The tricky area is 100' wide, so the route in may meandering 1-mile. The bar gets up to 3-knot current and has 12' over the bar at MLW (as we go to press). This entrance can range from flat calm to 15' standing waves. At least 1 yacht was destroyed after not waiting for a pilot. But hundreds have no problema.

PILOT SERVICE: Bahia del Sol Resort Hotel & Marina (503) 2327-0300, has taken over operation of this bay's pilot service (from the Barrets of Tarazed who now own Island Marine). Contact the hotel a day in advence, to get the current pilot pickup GPS position, and to let them know you'll be there tomorrow. Boats are normally helped over the bar at near high slack, and almost always only on the incoming tide, but not after dark.

During the hotel's El Salvador Cruisers Rally, registered participants may get their pilot service for free, while other may have to pay about $50US. At times, 2 or 3 boats often wait to enter together.

Hail "Marina del Sol Pilot Service" when you're at the pickup spot. As we go to press, their rendezvous spot is 13°16.6'N, 88°53.6'W – but it changes often, so confirm it by email and voice.

An hour before you arrive there, hail Bahia del Sol Pilot Service on VHF 16. You can jog in place or anchor (36') until the pilot arrives – or until conditions are safe to enter. Their pilot fee includes leading you to the anchorage or moorings and schlepping the port officials out to your boat to clear you in.

If the pilot says conditions are NO GO, you can anchor here or nearby, but be aware of Lempa Shoal. Or try Bahía Jiquilisco; a pilot is also required, but that entrance is wider and sometimes calmer.

Anchorage & Moorings: The free anchorage (15' to 20' over sand, mud, grass patches) is about a mile NW of the entrance along the north side of the peninsula. Holding is not great, yet boats are left unattended. The Navy patrols nearby.

Slips and moorings from the yatista-friendly Hotel Bahía del Sol Marina & Yacht Club are also a mile NE from the entrance, off the hotel's restaurant and fuel dock. Moorings include use of many hotel amenities, WiFi and restaurant discount.

Island Marine has a few at least 23 moorings off the north side of the channel, very reasonable, quieter than off the village. Another smaller marina with slips is planned in Bahía Jaltepeque; check Updates www.CentralAmericanBoating.com.

Port Clearance: Port officials come to your boat. You can get a 90-day visa and international Zarpe here. The pilot fee includes ferrying the officials out to your boat. Clearance ranges from free to about $10, but do have your last international Zarpe.

Local Services: The busy fuel dock (diesel, gas) at Hotel Bahía del Sol is twin pilings, so fender well. The hotel has a sportfishing dock and a waterfront cantina overlooking the anchorage, also a list of local services.

Island Marine boat yard and marina seca has a 30-ton Travelift for boats to 55' and 7.5' draft; on the north side of the channel across from the anchorage. It's owned by the Barretts who provide the pilot service; (503) 7724-8221 or 7947-2132. Island Marine's secure dry-storage yard is becoming a popular place for yatistas to leave their yates on the hard while they explore inland or fly home for the summer. They also have a list of local services.

Bahía Jiquilisco

Bahía Jiquilisco (*hee-kee-LEE-skoh*) is the larger of El Salvador's 2 navigable estuaries; it contains Barillas Marina Club with moorings, fuel dock and posh shore services. Next door is a modern shipyard. Nearby is an old shrimper port and miles of mangrove channels - part of a wildlife preserve.

Jiquilisco Bay lies 26 miles SE of Estero de Jaltepeque, 138 miles SE of Puerto Quetzal, Guatemala, 32 miles west of Punta Ampala in the Gulf of Fonseca and about 70 miles NW of Marina Puesta del Sol in Nicaragua.

Bahía Jiquilisco has a shoal-and-breakers mouth similar to Estero de Jaltepeque, but this

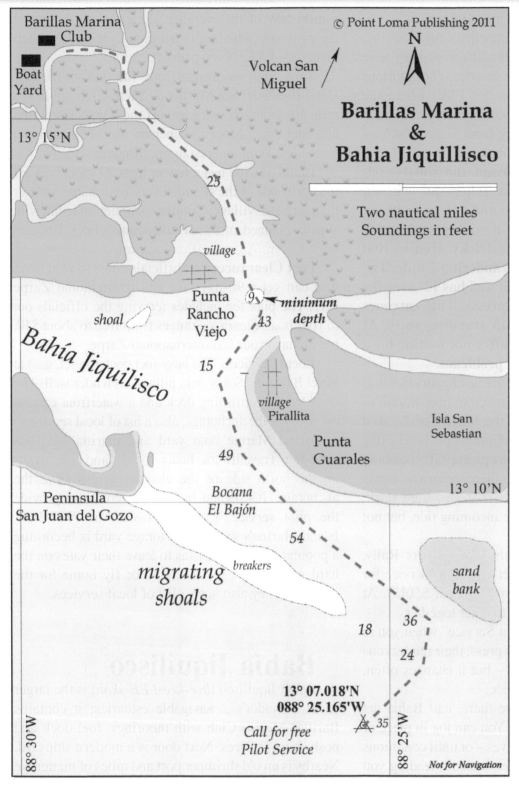

Barillas Marina Club

Boat Yard

© Point Loma Publishing 2011

N

Volcan San Miguel

Barillas Marina & Bahia Jiquillisco

Two nautical miles
Soundings in feet

13° 15'N

25

village

Punta Rancho Viejo

9 ← minimum depth

43

shoal

Bahía Jiquilisco

15

village Pirallita

Isla San Sebastian

Punta Guarales

13° 10'N

49

Peninsula San Juan del Gozo

Bocana El Bajón

54

breakers

migrating shoals

sand bank

18

36

24

13° 07.018'N
088° 25.165'W

Call for free Pilot Service

35

88° 30'W

88° 25'W

Not for Navigation

entrance is wider and deeper, usually less turbulent.

CAUTION: A pilot guide is required for entering the mile-wide breaking-shoal entrance to Bahía Jiquilisco. Do not attempt to enter otherwise. The safe path changes month to month, so even though we have been in and out of here many times, we always use the pilot service. Inside, the

shallowest spot is 9' at MLW; tidal range is 6' at springs, so some fairly deep-draft yachts can enter here by watching the tides. Just the entrance that is tricky.

PILOT SERVICE: Barillas Marina Club provides the free pilot service to guide its guests safely through the entrance to Bahía Jiquilisco and 9 miles up to its marina. Call or email the marina a few days in advance to confirm the pilot pick-up spot; (503) 2675-1131 or info@barillasmarina.com. They monitor SSB 8.1220 from 0700 to 1900 daily. As we go to press the pilot pick-up spot is 13°07.018'N, 88°25.165'W, but it can change seasonally. When you're an hour from the pilot pick-up spot, hail "Barillas Pilot" on VHF 16.

The marina suggests less powerful boats might need to come in with the tide slack and rising. Time your approach, because if you can't clear the entrance and reach the marina (9 miles in) before dark, the pilot won't schedule you to enter until the next day. If that happens, you can anchor outside or cruise off shore overnight.

Marina: Barillas Marina Club has 80 heavy moorings for boats to 200', each anchored by tractor engine blocks embedded in 2.5-ton concrete blocks. Yachts over 145' use 2 moorings. The pilot or a marina launch will hook you up to one of the moorings, and then he'll wait to take you ashore to check in or bring out the officials.

Moorings, club house, fuel dock & boat yard line the sheltered channel at Barillas Marina in El Salvador.

Barillas Marina Club (pronounced "bah-REE-ahz") has no alongside berth, except for the fuel pier, but side-tie fingers are planned. The dinghy landing and work docks are east of the clubhouse. Or a complimentary shore boat comes through the moorings to pick up boaters every 30 to 60 minutes – unless you call them sooner on VHF.

Barillas is a private club, but visiting boaters automatically become members when they rent moorings (very inexpensive). Behind the fountain gardens and pools, you'll see the marina office on the right side of the street. General manager Heriberto Pineda is a former cruiser, and the whole uniformed staff aims to please.

Barillas has more amenities within the huge gated compound than are found in most US marinas. Security guards and a shore boat constantly patrol the moorings; security is excellent. The boat-sitting service keeps an eye on yachts left at the marina while their owners explore inland or fly home.

The clubhouse overlooking the moorings has showers, laundry, patio restaurant, satellite TV and free videos after dark. Nearby are a small air-conditioned gym and a convenience store with refrigerated groceries (ice cream). Plug your laptop into the Web; 20 palapas at the swimming pools have Internet hookups. Or use their PCs and Macs in the air-conditioned Computer Building.

This marina is having a big impact on the migration patterns of East and West coast cruising yachts, because a stop here for fuel and rest allows smaller yachts (or less adventurous folks) to bridge the gap between Pacific Costa Rica and Mexico. After Barillas Marina Club is fully discovered, prices are likely to rise, but it will still be a very good deal. FMI visit www.BarillasMarina.com or call their new phones: (503) 2675-1131 or fax 2675-1134.

Port Clearance: All the offices required for national and international port clearance have an annex on the marina's property. When you call for a pilot, Barillas informs Customs and Immigration officers, so they'll be ready when you arrive. The marina can clear your papers, or you can do it yourself

Heriberto Pineda brings port-clearance officials to handle your paperwork at Barillas Marina Club.

Volcan San Miguel rises 12 miles NE of Barillas moorings.

The marina's heliport is busy, because Salvadoran club members would rather zoom over the mountains than risk the narrow, twisty highways. Barillas Marina Club's heliport handles VIPs, and security is good. A level grass airstrip (5,576' long, 164' wide) handles fixed wing aircraft. You can bring your own, or the club has 2 for charter. Local members keep their boats in covered sheds near the launch ramp, and 2-story bungalows are for rent.

Fuel Dock: Texaco fuel dock in front of Barillas Marina's clubhouse has 18' of water at low tide and has been used by yachts of up to 150' length. The fuel dock has 2 well fendered pier facings, 2 pumps and 12,500 gallons of diesel delivered at high or low speed. Large quantities of oil should be ordered a day before. Credit cards are accepted, and unlike most of Mexico and Central America, no extra fee is tacked on.

Boat Yard: Just west past the marina's fuel dock is Varadero Puerto Barillas, a large new boat yard with 3 marine ways for hauling vessels up to 125' and 200 tons. Other services are marine-electronics sales-installation and service, all kinds of welding, shaft and prop repair, a/c and refrigeration, electrical, carpentry and fiberglass. Parts can be ordered from the US and flown into the marina next door.

The channel past the marina and boat yard has salt pans off its north side, and it curves SW around Isla Madresal then branches into the west end of Bahía Jiquilisco near the old Puerto El Triunfo. When El Salvador's shrimp fleet berths at this boat yard, they enter and leave via the other end of this channel, not past the moored yachts. To contact Varadero Puerto Barillas boat yard, ask Barillas for their new phones.

here. Otherwise, all the offices are in Usulutan, a 45-minute drive inland.

Local Services: Basically, everything this region has to offer is supplied through the marina and its transportation services. The club's beautifully manicured grounds are on a former coconut plantation and family farm enclosed in a high concrete wall, so all visitors must pass through a security gate with armed guards.

Barillas Marina Club is remote, 15 miles from the nearest big town and an hour's drive from the international airport at San Salvador, the capital. But the marina's air-conditioned van shuttles up to 8 guests to the colorful market town of Usulutan for weekly provisioning. Larger groups can use the marina's bus and driver. See Side Trips below.

Nordhavn 57 lays alongside fuel dock at Barillas Marina, seen from club house.

Free pilot service panga meets you at sea, guides you in and helps you get hooked up to a mooring at Barillas Marina Club.

Anchorage: Boaters can anchor off the abandoned port of El Triunfo in the west end of Bahía Jiquilisco. Enter the bay same as for the marina, but quickly turn left before the second village. After 2 miles, take a small channel north then west. The anchorage has many wrecks, and theft was reported by the few yachties who anchored there. A paved road leads through the cane fields and jungle to Ozatlán.

Hurricane Hole: Surrounded by mangrove islands 9 miles inland, the curved mooring channel of Barillas Marina Club makes a good hurricane hole. Storm winds cannot build fetch, and the mangroves absorb waves from Bahía Jiquilisco. El Salvador lies at the southern edge of the hurricane belt; hurricanes are very rare here, but not unheard of. Cruisers use Barillas as a summering-over spot, and their reports have been very favorable.

Side Trips: The marina's moorings are a safe and handy place from which to explore inland. Nearby Usulutan has the regional weekly market. Farther inland are mountain villages that specialize in making miniature pottery figurines; spinning and dyeing cloth; weaving on 300-year-old looms; willow furniture; glassware, etc. Language school in San Salvador and Antigua, Guatemala, are also reasonable side trips from Barillas.

Departure: About 4 miles east of Bahía Jiquilisco's breaking entrance, take care to avoid a smaller breaking shoal outside Rio Grande de San Miguel.

Gulf of Fonseca

The mouth of the gulf is 21 miles wide NW to SE. Inside are 6 islands, 2 tiny ports, 4 sprawling estuaries that have shallow mangrove paddies - plus 3 places near the entrance where yachts can anchor overnight.

The Gulf of Fonseca is patrolled by the Salvadoran, Honduran and Nicaraguan coast guards. In bad weather or emergencies, yachts can anchor temporarily near the entrance in these 3 places without having to clear in.

Punta Ampala

Just inside the west arm of the Gulf of Fonseca, this rolly, fair-weather anchorage is 33 miles east of Bahía Jiquilisco. The point generally gets a light land breeze at night from NE and NNW, and a stronger afternoon sea breeze from south to SW. So Punta Ampala gives marginal shelter only from the sea breeze and Pacific swell. Forget Ampala in Papagallo

Barillas is a gated, guarded compound patrolled 7/24 - a safe place to leave your boat while traveling inland or home.

© Point Loma Publishing 2007

Golfo de Fonseca

Ten nautical miles

N

El Salvador
La Union
Isla Zacatillo
Isla Zacate Grande
Ampala
Volcan Conchagua
Isla Conchaguita
Isla Tigre
Honduras
Isla Meanguera
Punta Ampala
Farallones de Consiguina
Punta San Jose
10 meters

13° 00'N
087° 50'W

Punta Consiguina
Volcan Consiguina
Nicaragua
Estero Real

Not for Navigation

or north winds common October through February.

Punta Ampala's (13°09.5'N by 87°53'W.) eastern tip is low, sparsely wooded and contains Tamarindo village and air strip. Conchagua Volcano rises 4,100' about 8 miles NE of Punta Ampala.

Behind the point is a shallow 1.5-mile wide bay; at its north end an estuary boca forms a migrating shoal with a panga channel. For shelter from Pacific swell, tuck in as far WNW of Punta Ampala as conditions allow. We found 30' of water over sand and mud at 13°10.86'N, 87°54.56'W.

The village has a small grocery, air strip and bus to La Union and Usulutan. A marina may someday be built inside the estuary at the north end of this bay, but for now it is navigable only by pangas and dinghies with local knowledge.

Isla Conchaguita

About 5 miles NW of Isla Meanguera, this 2-mile wide volcanic island rises 1,500' and lies 8 miles NE of Punta Ampala.

In light north wind, anchorage is found in the roadstead off the SW side of Isla Conchaguita, near the Salvadoran Navy patrol's mooring. Anchor in about 30' of water toward the south end of the roadstead, or anchor in 40' off the NW protrusion.

But beware of south swell. The foot of Volcan Conchagua lies only 2 miles from the east side of this island.

The village on the SE side of Isla Conchaguita has panga moorings they pull up on the beach in a Papagallo blow. A *"conchagua"* is a shell used for dipping water, and conchaguita is the diminutive.

Isla Meanguera

Isla Meanguera (*may-ahn-GWAY-rah*), the larger of 2 islands in the mouth of Fonseca, is 4 miles long, 1,626' high. If you must stop in this vicinity during north wind, try the half-mile wide Guerrero cove on this island's south side, which lies about 12 miles east of Punta Ampala. Ridges frame the bay, so in a true gale it might funnel down. Anchor in 20' to 45' within the arms, deeper on its west side. A patrol boat sometimes anchors off the tiny village. Islote Meanguerita is off Isla Meanguera's SE corner.

Departure: Between the east side of Isla Meanguera and the SW tip of Punta Consiguina, avoid the mile-long string of rocks, Farrallones de Consiguina (13°04.73'N, 87°40.78'W), which lie on that track. Punta San Jose at the north tip of Consiguina is surrounded in shoal water.

Nicaragua

Nicaragua's Pacific coast is about 186 miles from Punta Consiguiña on the Gulf of Fonseca tending SE to Bahía de Salinas at the Costa Rican border. Southern swell from South Pacific storms can close this whole coast, and Papagallo winds affect the entire coastline, especially the southern portion along the low isthmus below Lago de Nicaragua, the largest freshwater body in Central America.

Thanks to Marina Puesta del Sol at Estero Aserradores, Nicaragua's first real marina, power & sailing cruisers and long-range sportfishers now have an excellent destination on this country's beautiful Pacific coast. Dozens of times we have bypassed Nicaragua well off shore, because its commercial ports have no services or accommodation for recreational vessels. Now we are delighted to stop.

We hope our readers will visit this marina, find themselves as comfortable and welcomed as we do, and from there explore ashore. However at other ports and in Managua, we hear reports of con artists posing as local guides, pickpockets and petty theft. So please get good recommendations from the folks at Marina Puesta del Sol before hiring guides elsewhere. Nicaragua and Honduras are still struggling to recover economically from Hurricane Mitch. Although Nicaragua's political scene is tranquil as we go to press, avoid demonstrations or don't sound off in public.

Spanish is the language and the currency is the Córdoba, about 17 to 1 US dollar in 2006. Nicaragua's west coast is more densely populated than the lowland Caribbean side. Nine major volcanoes form the Pacific coastal range within 100 miles inland, starting with Volcan Consiguiña (2,755').

Punta Consiguiña (12°54.5'N, 87°41.83'W) is the cliffy NW Pacific point, and 18 miles SE is a large uncharted shoal jutting 1.5 miles off shore from a triple river mouth, so stay at least 2 miles off, preferably 6. Expect larger boca shoals here after hurricane rains hit the highlands.

At 6 miles farther SE, the dangerous Speck Reefs (12°41.27'N, 87°25.47'W) lie 1.5 to 4 miles off shore spanning a 7-mile area, and the west rocks reportedly don't break even in heavy seas. Stay 5 miles off shore for safest approach to Estero Aserradores from north.

Estero Aserradores

The entrance to Estero Aserradores lies 31 miles SE of Punta Consiguiña, 12.5 miles NW of Corinto. The word *aserradores* means sawyers or lumber jacks. *Puesta del sol* means setting of the sun; Marina Puesta del Sol is the reason for stopping. The marina suggests that sailboats or under-powered vessels arrive at high slack water, because the

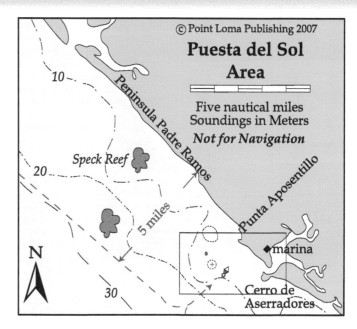

estuary's tidal current (max 7' tides) can reach 5 or 6 knots.

Hail "Marina Puesta del Sol" on VHF 16 when in range. No pilot is required, but they'll guide you in if needed and take your dock lines.

Approach: From north, approach from 5 miles off shore. Our GPS position at the marina's 11' tall red & white sea buoy (white flashing at night) is 12°36.6'N, 87°22.4'W. From there we head 080°M for 1.5 miles and pick up alternating red and green channel buoys at the estero entrance.

On the beach to port is a landmark palapa-roofed building, and the no-longer-detached Cerro Icaco will be to starboard. The 1.5-mile channel has a couple bends but is well marked. The channel might

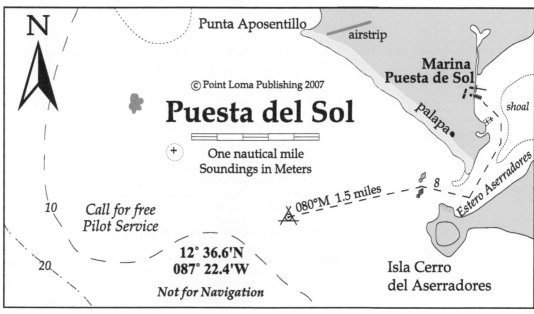

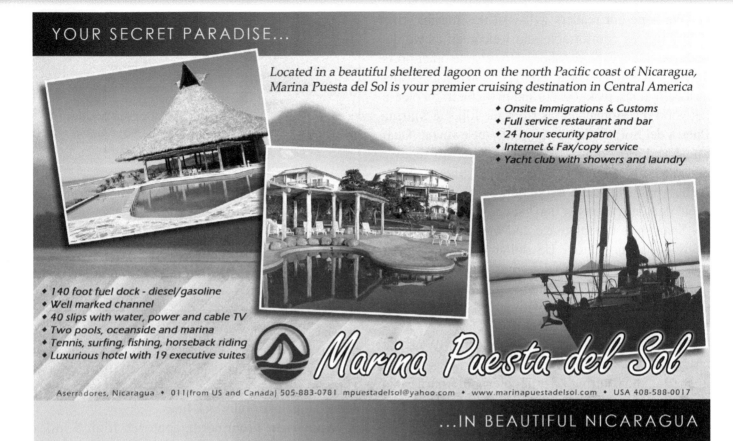
change by the time you arrive here, so use your eyes and sounder, call on VHF. On final approach to the docks, a rock reef juts from the west shore. At low water, we sounded a least depth of 8' near the next to last buoy.

Marina: Marina Puesta del Sol has about 60 full-service slips (30- & 50-amp, single & 3-phase) and end ties for yachts to 100', free mobile pump-out. The marina's guest moorings with landing privileges are in a sheltered area nearby, and they're planning more slips and moorings.

The Clubhouse has showers, laundry, phone service, email & Internet hookups. The 3-story hotel overlooking the docks has a pleasant restaurant, patio bar and pool where yatistas congregate to watch the *puesta del sol* each evening. The landmark palapa on the beach is part of the marina. The docks, moorings and grounds are monitored 24/7 by uniformed guards and patrol pangas, so security has been good. Go along when their van makes provisioning runs to Chinandega or Corinto.

Robert Membreno opened this marina in 2004; he was born in Nicaragua, grew up in San Francisco and, after retiring and cruising his Kelly Peterson 46 along the Central American route, came back to Nicaragua to build Marina Puesta del Sol and a nearby school, to improve his homeland's economy and educational opportunities.

Yatistas are fortunate, because MPdS has become a critical stepping stone that helps us traverse and explore Nicaragua

Entrance to Puesta del Sol is upper right. Marina is center. Village is in foreground.

Modern docks & good fuel at Marina Puesta del Sol, Nicaragua.

and all of Central America in safety and comfort. Bravo! FMI, contact the bilingual dock master; (505) 8883-0781 or 8880-0013 or (cellular, extra digit) 8880-00190; or email info@marinaps

Port Clearance: Marina Puesta del Sol is designated a Port of Entry, so you can get your international entrance and exit Zarpe here. The marina arranges Customs, Immigration and port officials. Part of the CA-4, Nicaragua has no limit on how long yatistas can stay, and the 90-day tourist visa you get upon arrival can be renewed without leaving the country.

Local Services: The marina's floating 110' fuel dock has filtered diesel (up to 7,000 gallons) & gas. Bulk oil & propane are available; ask the marina for its list of local marine services.

For provisioning trips to Chinandega (20 miles), a mini van is available or local bus. Chinandega has banks, Internet and good provisioning at several grocery stores and open-air mercados. It's better here than in Corinto.

Estero Aserradores is a mangrove wonderland, branches 2 miles north and SE, great for dinghy & kayak explorers, but take bug repellant.

Market day at Chinandega near Marina Puesta del Sol, Nicaragua. Farmers haul produce to town in horse-drawn carts.

Side Trips: Nicaragua has 12 national parks & nature preserves, most on the Pacific side. For day trips to Masaya & Catarina volcanoes, working haciendas with horse-riding trails, visit www.centralamerica.com/nicaragua Away from Managua, the hotels, food & guides are generally inexpensive.

Corinto

Corinto's natural harbor entrance (12°28.67'N, 87°11.23'W) is 12.5 miles SE of Puesta del Sol. But since Marina Puesta del Sol opened, yatistas seldom visit this neglected commercial harbor, which isn't set up for their needs. We don't recommend stopping here for cruising pleasure.

Enter NE of Isla El Cordon (south gap shoaled closed), and follow the curving 3-mile ship channel (30' at MLW) to the town's east side wharf area. Anchor anywhere off the beach cantinas but well outside the channel; max 9' tides, bottom is good holding mud. Anchoring off the power plant is reported to be more secure, but it can be noisy and

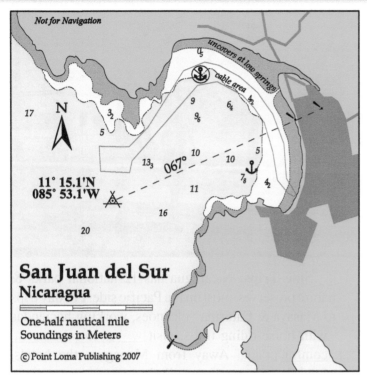

Not for Navigation

uncovers at low springs

cable area

N

11° 15.1'N
085° 53.1'W

067°

San Juan del Sur
Nicaragua

One-half nautical mile
Soundings in Meters

© Point Loma Publishing 2007

has bright lights at night, with no dink landing nearby. The estuary branches north, NW and SE among mangrove islands.

Port Clearance: Corinto is the same jurisdiction as Marina Puesta del Sol, so if you've checked in there, you don't have to do it again here. Otherwise, you'll need to visit the offices of the Port Captain, Customs and Immigration. The Capitanía and Immigration are in the same building in the industrial zone, but Corinto officials seldom see yatistas here, so clearance can be more expensive and time-consuming than normal.

Local Services: We haven't found a secure dink landing or fuel dock for yates in Corinto. Puerto Somoza (30 miles SE of Corinto) also isn't a cruising port.

San Juan del Sur

Amid a half dozen similar pretty little bays, San Juan del Sur lies 105 miles SE of Corinto, 22 miles

north of Costa Rica's Punta Santa Elena. It's a Port of Entry with a boat yard for a small fishing fleet, but it has no berthing or services for yates. Our GPS approach waypoint about .75 of a mile outside Bahía San Juan del Sur is 11°15.1'N, 85°53.1'W.

The entrance is less than a half-mile wide, then the beach-lined bay opens to about .75 of a mile wide NW to SE. But rocky reefs jut in from the north and south arms (south reef sometimes buoyed), so enter between them.

The anchorage and business end of town is in the SE corner of the bay behind the south-arm reef. The bay's north end is shoal. The bottom is good-holding sand, and the max tides are 5' to 8'.

Port Clearance: If the Navy doesn't board you by an hour after you anchor, hail "Capitanía de Puerto" or dink to the rough concrete seawall (fender well) at the south end of the bay and come through the gates to the Capitanía. Inspection by the Navy is part of checking in and out.

As we go to press, the Immigration office is temporarily closed. Boaters checking out of Nicaragua must take a bus or taxi 25 miles to the nearest alternative at the Costa Rica border to get exit papers stamped, then return to the Capitanía to finish. We hope an Immigration office reopens here soon.

Local service: The shrimper boat yard is in remodel mode as we go to press, but it has a concrete fuel dock. San Juan del Sur has 2 small grocers (*pulperias*), but Rivas 20 miles north has supermercados. For more shore details, check out Capt. Eric Blackburn's *Cruising Guide to Central America* – to be released soon.

Papagallo winds blow north, NE, east, SE during cruising season, November – May. Several gaps in the Cerros las Cuestas lie behind this section of coast, and the vast Lago Nicaragua lies only 10 miles inland from this coast. So, this anchorage can be very windy; don't leave a boat unattended. During summer, south swell can turn the whole anchorage into a surf zone.

Departure: From Bahía San Juan del Sur, the Costa Rica border is about 16 miles SE at the north shore of windy Bahía de Salinas, or about 20 miles from excellent shelter in Bahía Santa Elena, Costa Rica.

Concrete landing at south end of Bahía San Juan del Sur is where dinghies land.

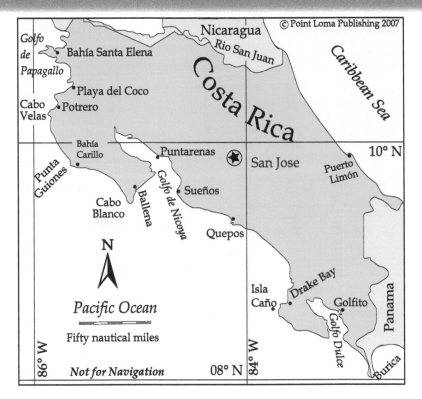

Costa Rica

The Republic of Costa Rica (pop. 4,075,261) is about the size of West Virginia, yet 28% of its land is preserved in national parks, wildlife refuges, forest preserves, wetlands and biosphere reserves – so eco-tourism is one of its biggest industries. Ten major volcano peaks dot the highlands and western half of the country; earthquakes are not uncommon. Costa Rica has an efficient Coast Guard (*Guarda Costa*) with patrol boats to enforce their laws, plus police and rural guards ashore.

Costa Rica is one of the most pleasant countries covered by this guidebook; its people (*ticos, ticas*) are prosperous and well educated, its government is stable, and its sinuous 540-mile Pacific coast has long been popular for yacht cruising, diving and sportfishing. However, petty theft from boats at night or unattended has been reported.

The best time to visit is during dry season (December – April), even if the jungle doesn't look as lush as in summer. Rainy season (May – November) can bring torrential downpours with squalls, lots of lightning and an occasional water spout (*mangera negra*). Hurricanes don't strike this Pacific coast, but after heavy rain in the mountains, expect

dangerous submerged logs in the tide lines well off shore here. The highlands are cooler year-round, inviting us to explore inland.

Cruising Costa Rica: Boaters think of Costa Rica's Pacific coast as three distinct cruising grounds based around its major gulfs; (1.) the Gulf of Papagallo, (2.) the Nicoya Gulf and (3.) the Golfo Dulce.

In the upcoming 7th edition of "Cruising Ports," we will add 12 additional Costa Rican anchorages in the northern Gulf of Papagallo region before reaching Santa Elena, such as Bolanos, Salinas, Jobo, Junquillal, Quajiniquil, Tiny Tom, etc.

Bahía Santa Elena

Although Southbounders are not supposed to stop before clearing in at Playa del Coco, these small stops are good to know about if you have an emergency when the Papagallo winds are blowing - for safety's sake.

Bahía Santa Elena is a beautiful, pristine, nearly land-locked bay found in northern Costa

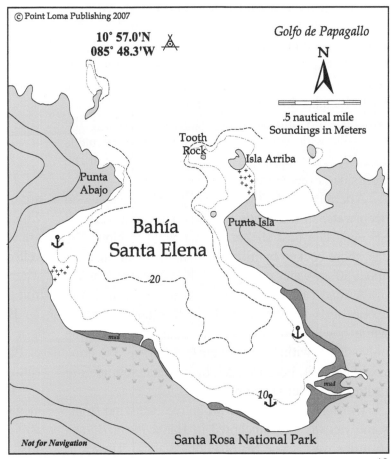

Bahía Santa Elena anchorage is a tranquil stop.

some who anchored in Bahía Juanilla (6 miles east) were asked to leave by the Costa Rican coast guard.

Murcielagos Islands

Scuba diving and snorkeling are excellent along the Islas Murcielagos (Bat Islands), a 6-mile chain that runs almost E-W along the south side of the Santa Elena Peninsula. Divers report big bull sharks, schools of cow-nosed rays and eagle rays, rainbow runners, horse-eyed jacks, spade fish and delicious pompano.

The Guarda Costa patrols the Bat Islands almost daily, but port clearance is done in Playa del Coco. Dive boats and sportfishers frequent the Murcielagos by day – but only when the Papagallo isn't blowing or the south swell is minimal. The Murcielagos are usually too rolly for overnight comfort.

Bahía Culebra

Howler monkeys, big parrots and exotic butterflies are common sights in the lush jungle that surrounds Culebra, Coco and Potrero bays. The coastal waters are teeming with every kind of bill fish, dorado and yellow-fin tuna. We've watched rooster fish tear up the waters right inside the bays. Snorkeling is excellent if you get away from the tourist spots.

Bahía Culebra (23 miles SE of Cabo Santa Elena) is a 3.5-mile long bay entered about 2.5 miles NE of Playa del Coco. Culebra Bay is one of the finest natural harbors in Central America.

The new **Marina Papagayo** (350 slips, some megas) is sheltered in Culebra's north end and has a 200' fuel dock, port clearance, nice shore amenities. Visit **www.MarinaPapagayo.com** Not using the bay's

Rica's Santa Elena National Park, within the state of Guanacaste. Although it has no services, the anchorage is well sheltered even in a Papagallo blow. We stop here when entering or leaving Costa Rica.

Approach: A line of steep peaks (1,250') marks the rugged Santa Elena Peninsula that stretches 15 miles west within the Gulf of Papagallo. Its 3 seaward tips N-S are Punta Blanco (10°56.97'N, 85°53.22'W), Cabo Santa Elena and the west end of the Islas Murcielagos chain. The narrow entrance to Bahía Santa Elena is 4.75 miles east of Cabo Blanco.

Our GPS approach waypoint just north of the half-mile wide opening into Bahía Santa Elena is 10°57.0'N, 85°48.3'W. Avoid tiny Tooth Rock at the west side of the entrance.

Anchorage: As the bay widens SE, we sounded deep water in the center and a shoal estuary off the SE end. The best shelter in east wind is along the east shore backed by hills. We usually anchor here in about 50' of water over good holding sand and mud.

A road runs along the south shore. Parrots and exotic birds twitter close by in the jungle canopy, while howler monkeys wail to nearby tribes – the only sounds within this tranquil anchorage. We hope you'll enjoy it, because such beauty and solitude are rarities on our crowded planet.

During rainy season or when the east wind stops, some yatistas have anchored in Bahía Playa Blanca (6 miles west, close SE of Punta Blanca). However,

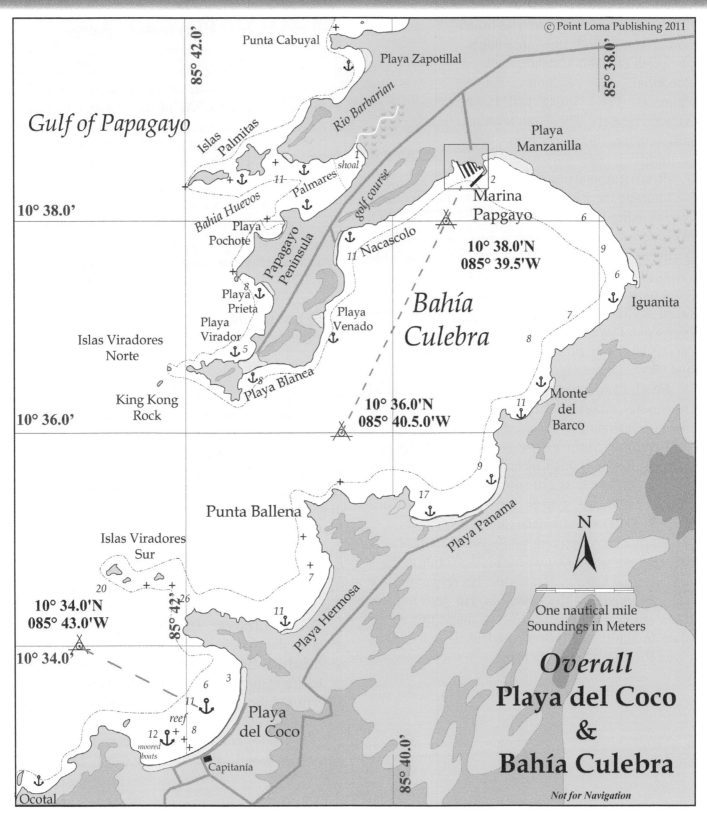

© Point Loma Publishing 2011

Gulf of Papagayo

Punta Cabuyal

Playa Zapotillal

85° 42.0'

85° 38.0'

Rio Barbarian

Islas Palmitas

Playa Manzanilla

golf course

shoal

1

Marina Papgayo

2

6

10° 38.0'

**10° 38.0'N
085° 39.5'W**

9

Palmares

11

Bahía Huevos

Playa Pochote

Papagayo Peninsula

11 Nacascolo

6

*Bahía
Culebra*

Iguanita

Playa Prieta

8

Playa Venado

7

Playa Virador

Islas Viradores Norte

5

8

Monte
del
Barco

10° 36.0'

King Kong Rock

8

Playa Blanea

**10° 36.0'N
085° 40.5.0'W**

11

9

17

Punta Ballena

Playa Panama

N

Islas Viradores Sur

7

**10° 34.0'N
085° 43.0'W**

20

26

85° 42.0'

One nautical mile
Soundings in Meters

11

10° 34.0'

Playa Hermosa

Overall
**Playa del Coco
&
Bahía Culebra**

6

3

11

reef

Playa
del Coco

12

8

moored
boats

Capitanía

85° 40.0'

Not for Navigation

Ocotal

original name (after all, *culebra* means snake), it's now marketed as Peninsula Papagayo Marina. Check for Updates on www.CentralAmericanBoating.com.

When the Papagallo winds blow between southern Nicaragua and Cabo Velas, Bahía Culebra (center is 10°37.14'N, 85°39.41'W) provides shelter at 13 small to medium sized anchorages – each with turquoise waters and a pretty beach. Coral or soft sand beaches range from rosy pink to blazing white or sparkling volcanic black, depending on the geology of the deep reefs off shore. The terrain is steep and the jungle is lush. This is one of Costa Rica's nicest spots.

45

Anchorages: When arriving from north, you'll find tiny anchorages just north of Bahía Culebra, at Playa Zapotillal, Islas Palmitas, Bahía Palmares, Playa Prieta and Playa Virador (resort). The Four Seasons golf course meanders atop this peninsula.

King Kong Rock

To coast around into Bahía Culebra, pass well outside the Islas Viradores Norte and landmark 30' tall King Kong Rock (10°36.52'N, 85°42.28'W). We dubbed it this, because it looks like the giant gorilla's squarish head sticking out of the water and facing NE. But also known as Monkey Head.

Around Bahía Culebra proper, anchorage is taken at Playa Blanca (resort), Playa Venado, Playa Nicascolo, Playa Manzanilla (resort), Playa Iguanita, Monte del Barco, either end of Playa Panama (village) and Playa Hermosa (village).

Beach camping is a Tico tradition, but some of the resorts around Bahía Culebra are prohibiting overnight camping by locals, so it's a controversy.

Berthing: Marina Papagayo (See chart previous page.) is open in Bahía Culebra; 179 full service slips to +220', fuel docks is 220'; dockside pumpout, WiFi, cable, crew lounge, gym & cafe overlooking marina. Dockmaster Don Eaffaldano (506) 2690-3602.

Marina Papagayo can handle your port clearance for a reasonable fee. Or DIY for $120 taxi ride to Playa del Coco and Liberia. The resort's big restaurants are a 3 mile drive out the peninsula, but golf and eco hikes are near the marina. We've found this a safe place to leave your boat secured while you explore Costa Rica, CenAm or fly home.

Playa del Coco

Bahía Playa del Coco (10°33.8'N, 85°42.1'W) is a mile-wide bay about 25 miles SE of the Murcielagos, 2.5 miles SW of the entrance to Bahía Culebra, about 15 miles around Punta Gorda from Flamingo and about 115 miles around the Nicoya Peninsula from Puntarenas.

The town of Playa del Coco is the Port of Entry and service stop for northern Costa Rica cruising. Since closure of the marina, fuel dock and boat yard at nearby Flamingo, this whole region is not as convenient or popular a yachting destination as it once was. We hope at least a new pier will be built in Coco, because shore break on the wide tidal beach discourages landing a dink. We avoid making 2 trips ashore.

Anchorage: Coco Bay has protection from NE winds, but some NW swell enters in summer. Avoid (a) the mostly submerged reef jutting straight out from about the center of the beach and (b) a line of old pier pilings behind the reef that may uncover only at low tide. We hope a new pier will be built. The best anchorage (12' to 34') is in the south half of the bay south of the reef.

Ocotal sportfishing resort on the east side of Punta Zapotal (5 miles SE) has an open roadstead for day-fishing pangas, as do all the hotels around Culebra. But they come back to their moorings in Playa del Coco after work – so don't crowd them.

Port Clearance: The Port Captain's office is about in the middle of the beach, just south of the reef head and largest beach cantina. If you call ahead to the Capitanía on VHF, the Aduana-Immigration folks from Liberia airport might already be here. The Guarda Costa inspects boats, and you may be asked for engine serial numbers. Costa Rica's first female Port Captain began her career here.

Marina Papagayo's entrance (keep red buoy to starboard) is big enough for megayachts.

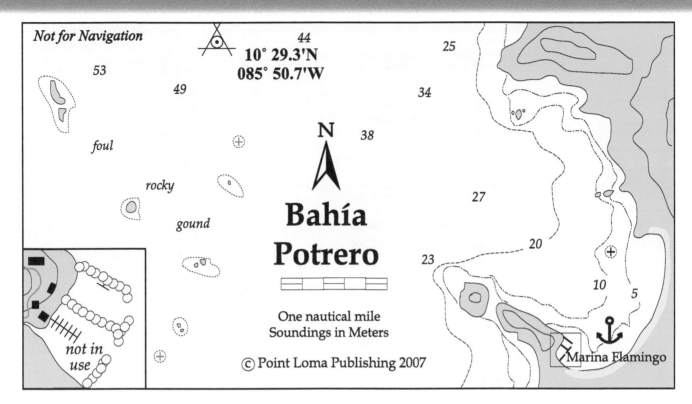

Not for Navigation

44
10° 29.3'N
085° 50.7'W

53
49
25
34

foul
38

rocky
N

gound
Bahía
Potrero

27

20

not in
use

23

One nautical mile
Soundings in Meters

© Point Loma Publishing 2007

10
5

⚓

Marina Flamingo

Local Services: At least 2 small but well-stocked grocers are within 3 blocks of the Capitanía. The closest *gasolinera* is a mile inland on the main road, which starts on the north side of the main park or ball field behind the beach. Taxis wait here. Bikes and scooters are rented at the string of patio cantinas (called "sodas" here) along the beach. Coco has a laundromat, plenty of eateries, 2 nice hotels. When Hotel Itube has empty rooms, and we've paid a couple bucks for long showers before dinner there.

Lots of gringos have retired in Coco and are helpful to visitors. The paved road connects Playa del Coco with the regional capital, Liberia, where there's an airport, and with the rest of the country. You can take a comfortable and inexpensive bus to San Jose, the country's capital. Renting a car has been double what it costs in the US.

Bahía Potrero

Potrero Bay (AKA Flamingo) lies 15 miles around the multi-headed Punta Gorda from Playa del Coco, 125 miles upcoast from Los Sueños Marina.

After Marina Flamingo was closed, the northern part of Costa Rica declined as a sportfishing and cruising destination. Without sheltered slips, fuel dock, boat yard, dinghy landing, chandler and office

services, it's very difficult for mid-sized yachts to stay very long, and many larger yachts simply bypass this corner, moving instead between Barillas and Los Sueños. The breakwaters are still in place, and the municipality plans to build an upscale marina someday. Check for Updates on www. CentralAmericanBoating.com.

Approach: The 231' high Isla Catalina (10°29.2'N, 85°53.0'W) and an extensive reef bed on its SW and west sides lie about 2 miles west and SW of the 1.5-mile wide entrance to Bahía Potrero.

From north, you can enter the wider opening between Isla Catalina (offshore) and Islas Brumel (onshore). From south, stay at least 3 miles off Punta Guiones (09°54'N, 85°41'W) and 1 mile off Cabo Velas (10°22'N, 85°53'W). Then turn NE to enter Bahía Potrero by the smaller passage. It lies between the SE end of the Catalina reef bed (offshore) and the pointed Isla Plata (onshore), which has two small reefs jutting 0.4 of a mile NW and NE respectively.

Anchorage: In the south end of Bahía Potrero, we anchor generally east of the breakwaters in about 18' over firm sand with good holding. In winter, the Papagallo winds blow strongly from the east and a little swell comes in, but you get good protection as close to the lee of the eastern beach as depth will allow, keeping in mind the 10' tide range. Anchoring inside the breakwaters is prohibited as we go to press.

Bahía Potrero anchorage & old marina.

Port Clearance: Playa del Coco's Capitanía governs here, so you can take the bus or taxi there, or pay bus or taxi fare for the port officials to travel 20 miles of winding road to Flamingo. They may ask for engine serial numbers. The tourist card is good for 90 days, then renewable in Costa Rica by application.

Local Services: As we go to press, a few local sportfishing charter boats chip in to order a tanker truck of diesel and use their own pumps and long hoses to get it out to their boats at anchor. The nearest gas station is at Llanos (20-minute ride). The marina docks and dink landing were off limits and deteriorating as we went to press in early 2007.

If the future replacement marina provides real services, not just a hotel-dock, we'll be happy; check Updates at www.CentralAmericanBoating.

Flamingo Corners south of the old marina has a small grocery, 4 cantinas, car rental, several hotels, condos and casino-disco, but things are drying up with no marina. The gringo village of Potrero behind the bay's east beach berm has a gourmet bakery, healthy eateries, take-out pizza, espresso cafe and boutiques.

The Tico town of Brasilito (2.5 miles) has 2 excellent fruterías. Or take a 45-minute taxi or bus ride to Liberia's 2 larger grocery stores, hardware, etc. Santa Cruz, the same distance the other direction, has the region's best produce market and an excellent pharmacy, but only 1 fairly good grocery.

Planes & choppers land at Playa Brasilito, Tamarindo and Liberia; the big airport is at Alajuela near San Jose, a 5-hour cab or bus ride.

Sportfishing along Pacific Costa Rica

Between Cabo Velas and Cabo Blanca, many rivers spout from the jungle clad Cerros de San Blas and Cerros de Habana. At least 5 seamounts or fishing banks lie within 15 miles off shore, so fishing is spectacular year round for a wide variety of eating fish. It's almost as good in the Gulf of Nicoya.

The acrobatic sailfish are the prime catch for the go-fast sportfishing boats, both blue and black marlin and larger yellow-fin tuna. But even on sailboats, we've landed numerous dorado, wahoo and smaller yellow-fin tuna.

Turtle Nesting Grounds

The many small beaches between Cabo Velas and Punta Guiones are the ancient nesting grounds of an estimated 30,000 to 40,000 Olive Ridley and Green Sea Turtles plus a few of the highly endangered Giant Leatherbacks. That's why you see so many turtles bobbing off shore during cruising season. We urge power boaters to pay attention and avoid running over these majestic, slow moving creatures.

But from August to November, the broad beach at Ostional (about 10 miles NW of Punta Guiones) is where more than 300,000 sea turtles come ashore to lay their eggs. Called an "arribada" in Spanish, this mass landing and nest digging may occur twice a month during rainy season.

In 45 to 54 days the tiny hatchlings appear, and volunteers must protect them from vultures and dogs as they scramble toward the waves, and once they are in the water the volunteers wade in as far as possible to scare away osprey and fishy predators.

Volunteers say to never carry a hatchling to the water, because it won't develop its tiny lungs enough to survive in the ocean and it won't learn how to recognize its own home beach. In 10 to 15 years, the surviving females need to return to the beach of their birth to lay their own eggs.

Departure: When rounding the Nicoya Peninsula toward the Gulf of Nicoya, stay at least 5 miles off Punta Guiones (09°53.67'N, 85°40.48'W) due to rocks about 2.75 miles out and strong switching currents.

Bahía Carillo

Bahía Carillo is wide open to the south, so it's dry-season only; even then it's rolly enough to be marginal. At 13.75 miles n.m. ESE of Punta Guiones, Carillo is 1 of 4 tiny indents; the islet-clogged bay close west is Bahía Samara with a village. My GPS approach waypoint just south of the opening (.42 of a mile wide) into Bahía Carillo is 09°51.00'N, 85°29.46'W.

Reefs poke in from both arms, so we stay a mile off shore until abeam the center of the bay, then head straight in the middle. We anchor the middle of the bay in 30' over good sand and mud. The east side has better protection behind the reef, but it's filled with 20 private moorings for the posh fly-in sportfishing lodge, and the western bottom is rocky.

Hail the lodge on VHF 16 for permission to come ashore to enjoy their nice restaurant and pool. (We keep their airstrip in mind for emergencies along this remote coast.) North of the lodge is a public beach and semi-paved road with bus stop (Ballena, Paquera, Naranjo). Samara has a little grocery store and several small hotels and cantinas.

Gulf of Nicoya

Costa Rica's central cruising ground has numerous anchorages, the legendary but decaying Puntarenas

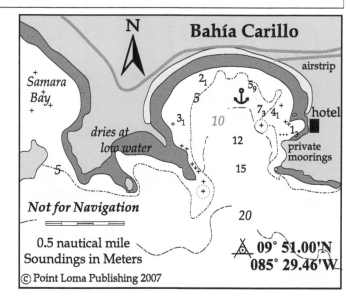

Bahía Carillo

Samara Bay

dries at low water

Not for Navigation

0.5 nautical mile
Soundings in Meters

© Point Loma Publishing 2007

09° 51.00'N
085° 29.46'W

and the nice marina Los Sueños. Avoid traveling this bay at night on an ebb tide; debris in the tide lines can wrap your prop or clog your filters, and dead heads are numerous, especially in rainy season.

Ballena Bay

Entering the Gulf of Nicoya, avoid off-lying rocks by staying 2 n.m. off Isla Blanca when rounding Cabo Blanca (09°33.18'N, 85°06.90'W).

Ballena Bay is 12 miles NE of Cabo Blanco, about 22 miles SW of Puntarenas, 18 miles WNW of Bahía Herradura. My GPS approach waypoint from the south is 9°42.5'N, 84°58.4'W.

Punta Tambor (Drum) is the larger NE arm of this 2-mile wide bay. Punta Piedra Amarilla (Yellow Rock) is the lesser SW arm, but note that the reef

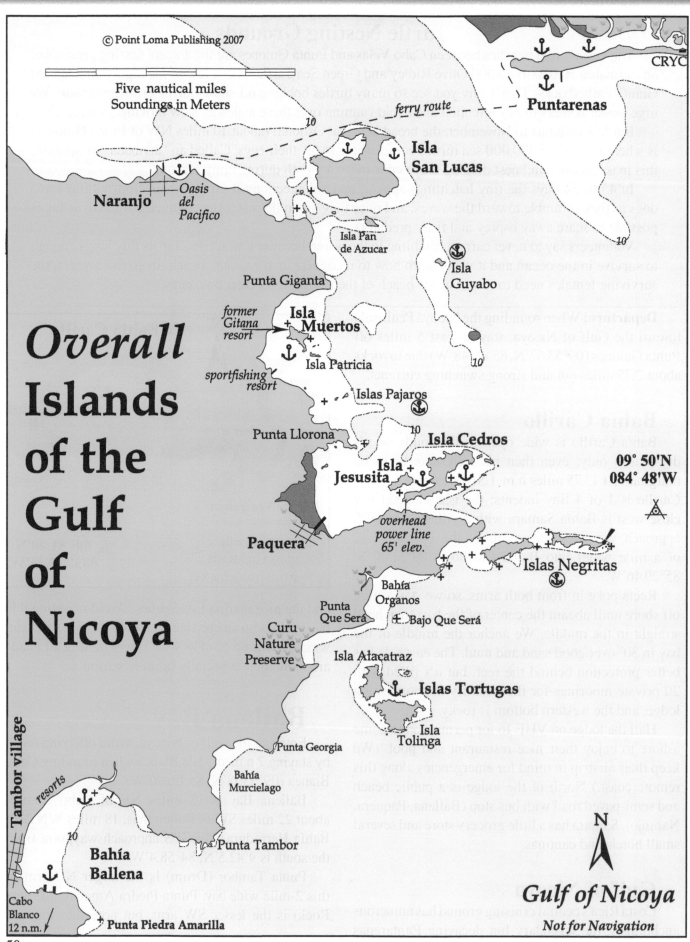

© Point Loma Publishing 2007

Five nautical miles
Soundings in Meters

ferry route

CRYC

Puntarenas

Naranjo

Oasis del Pacifico

Isla San Lucas

Isla Pan de Azucar

Isla Guyabo

Punta Giganta

former Gitana resort

Isla Muertos

Isla Patricia

sportfishing resort

Islas Pajaros

Overall Islands of the Gulf of Nicoya

Punta Llorona

Isla Cedros

Isla Jesusita

09° 50'N
084° 48'W

overhead power line 65' elev.

Paquera

Islas Negritas

Bahía Organos

Punta Que Será

Bajo Que Será

Curu Nature Preserve

Isla Alacatraz

Islas Tortugas

Isla Tolinga

Tambor village

Punta Georgia

Bahía Murcielago

resorts

Punta Tambor

10

Bahía Ballena

Cabo Blanco 12 n.m.

Punta Piedra Amarilla

N

Gulf of Nicoya

Not for Navigation

Bahía Ballena has a popular bar called Bahía Ballena Yacht Club.

off this SW point juts farther east than previously charted, so we keep a good mile off shore until the middle of the bay is abeam before heading into the center of the bay. Once clear of Yellow Rock Reef, we anchor (18' to 25') in the protected SW end of the bay.

Behind the panga moorings in the SW end of the bay, the high concrete pier has landing steps (surgey) for pangas and dinghies, but at low water you might have trouble reaching up to it.

Bahía Ballena Yacht Club: Next door is a similar pier, this one connected with the 5-arch building of Bahía Ballena Yacht Club, a yatista-friendly bar with pool table, juice bar and vegetarian menu. When run by expat gringos, it has rented 5 very inexpensive small-boat moorings out front by the month. But their website and phone were non-op in March 2011.

The Tico village of Tambor has a small but usually well-stocked grocery, internet shop, wash-fold service (not overnight), 4 more cantinas, a sportfishing office and bus stop for going north to the Paquera and Naranjo ferry docks, inland to Curu Vida Silvestre National Park, or south to Moctezuma, which has no reliable anchorage we could find.

Up the beach north of Rio Panica, you'll see a housing tract and several nice resorts. All the resorts have sportfishing boats. Fidelito's Ranch has horseback tours to Lovers Veil falls and a mango finca. Pavas Airline (506-253-6133) flies in from San Jose;

Carillo anchorage is on the outside of the Nicoya Peninsula.

keep it in mind for quick trips to the capital, but don't leave a boat unoccupied at Ballena.

Murcielago Bay (poor holding) is the indent on the north side of Punta Tambor, but better spots line the way toward Puntarenas.

Islas Tortugas

At 6 miles NE of Ballena Bay, these 2 tall, jungle-clad islands lie less than a mile off shore between Punta Georgia and Punta Curu. Isla Tolinga is the larger, 568' high southern island, and Isla Alcatraz is almost adjacent NW.

The sheltered anchorage (09°46.14'N, 84°53.55'W) is off the north side of Isla Tolinga. From Ballena, if you wish to stay inshore, skirt around the west and north sides of Isla Alcatraz to approach the anchorage via the east side of Turtle Rock, which is a reef awash about 1,000 yards off both islands.

Deep water is close to a narrow sand shelf (40' to 50') off Playa Tolinga on the north side of Isla Tolinga. This is a half-mile stretch of brilliant white sand and a stand of tall coco palms backed by the island's peaks. The beach is public, but farther ashore is private property. Turisticas (tour pangas) arrive from Paquera for lunch 3 days/week, but they leave by 1600 and we have it to ourselves overnight.

Besides Turtle Rock, other snorkeling reefs trail off Isla Tolinga's NE and SW corners, and off Isla Alcatraz's NE tip – one forming a rock arch. On tour days, you can hike a trail up through the jungle to a lookout point, then ride a zip line down through the canopy.

Kayaks can explore the mainland estuary of the tiny Curu Vida Silvestre national park where Rio Curu emerges. Donated by the Shutz family whose farm surrounds it, this pristine habitat has white-nosed coati, 9-banded armadillo and, Pat's favorite, the turquoise browed mot-mot bird – among many more exotic species. Ferry tourists swim at Playa Organos.

When departing north, avoid a submerged rock (approx. 09°47.82'N, 84°53.54'W) about half a mile east of Punta Que Será.

Islas Los Negritos Biological Reserve

These 2 islands poke farthest into the Nicoya Gulf, so ships frequently round the lighted east end – but everybody stays at least a mile off that tip due to a reef and erratic current. The eastern side and gap between have hull-eating rocks.

The Negritos are a biological reserve and seabird sanctuary for peregrine falcons, frigates and the Costarican brown pelican. They have no moorings, and stepping ashore is prohibited. They're rather barren isles poking up from fringe reefs.

Don't anchor here; anchor instead at nearby Tortugas, Cedros or Jesusita and tour the Negritos by dinghy or kayak. The snorkeling is pristine, but take only photos.

Isla Jesusita & Isla Cedros

Little Jesus & the Cedars sounds like a band. At 1.5 miles NW of the Negritos, 1.75 miles NE of Paquera village, these 2 small islands fit together like a lock & key, providing popular anchorage areas in rock-studded Cedros Bay (east side of Cedros) and in the narrow but sheltered channel (09°50.31'N, 84°53.57'W) between Jesusita and Cedros.

But come and go via the islands' north sides, because submerged rocks foul the south approach, and a low overhead power line snags masts.

Paquera village

Paquera is the main market town for dozens of tiny villages sprinkled over the Nicoya Peninsula, so it has great produce and staples for a dinky remote spot. The $3 passenger ferry La Lancha runs once daily on weekdays to Puntarenas, departing Paquera at 0730.

Islas Pajaros

When approaching Paquera Bay from north, beware of the reef off the east tip of Punta Llorona and of the small Islas Pajaros, a reefy structure a mile north of Punta Llorona. Nobody got this far without knowing who La Llorona was and what Pajaros are. Another Isla Pajaros lies 10 miles NW of Puntarenas in the shallow upper half of the Gulf of Nicoya.

These Bird Isles are protected as a national biological reserve, so no anchoring or going ashore. We pass outside them.

Isla Muertos

Isla Muertos (3.5 miles NW of Cedros, 3 miles SSW of Isla San Lucas) used to house a cruiser hangout called Isla Gitana (Gypsy), but it's closed and for sale as we go to press. Check www. CentralAmericanBoating.com for Updates.

Isla Patricia is a branching reef patch that juts about half a mile off the SE side of Isla Muertos. A few ancient gravesites were found on this island and

Tico fishermen mend their nets on the beach near Paquero village in the Gulf of Nicoya.

Isla San Marcos has a pier at Prisoners' Bight, the old prison colony.

on the Negritos.

The sheltered anchorage on its south side (09°53.13'N, 84°55.60'W) has 12' to 18' of water over good holding sand & mud; enter from east. Isla Muertos lies half a mile off the yatista-friendly Bahía Luminosa Sportfishing Resort. You can anchor off the resort as well, but don't crowd their sportfishing moorings.

Isla Guayabo

This tiny isolated island (2.8 miles NE of Isla Muertos, 3.5 miles north of Isla Cedros) is part of the national wildlife refuge system, so no anchoring or going ashore. Guayabo (pronounced *wah-YAH-boh*) means guava tree.

Be aware of Isla Guayabo's encircling shoals about .75 of a mile SE to SW, and occasional breakers over the larger shelf of less than 30' of water that reaches a mile north and 3 miles SSE. These are good fishing grounds, and in calm weather we see boats anchored here fishing and diving.

Isla San Marcos

At 2 miles wide, San Marcos is the largest in the lower half of the Gulf of Nicoya. It lies 4 miles north of Muertos, 4 miles SW of Puntarenas. Deeply indented bays on its east and west sides provide good anchorage. The smaller east bay is rollier. The larger west bay is Prisoners' Bight, more protected except from an occasional wake from the ferries.

Isla San Marcos contains a former prison colony. From the dock at the Spanish colonial gates above Prisoners' Bight beach, the caretaker sometimes gives tours of the lush but overgrown gardens and old prison barracks. You can hike trails to the top, possibly from bay to bay – but we haven't done it.

We do avoid the rocky channel off the SW corner of Isla San Marcos.

Naranjo village

The Puntarenas car ferry passes close north of Isla San Marcos and docks 3.5 miles west at the good-sized town of Naranjo (orange tree), which is a good market town, has a few small chandlers and basic outboard parts & service.

My preferred anchorage is just east of Naranjo ferry pier, off the rustic yatista-friendly Oasis del Pacifico resort. Here we get a mooring or anchor off the fishing pier and come ashore (small day fee) to take showers, buy breakfast, lunch or dinner under the huge shady palapa, play on the lawn or soak in the pool. This is a pleasant rendezvous spot, and dinks have been safe. From the Oasis grounds, it's a short walk to Naranjo for provisions (even *naranjas*), and taxi back. Wilhelm, the world-traveling founder of Oasis del Pacifico, has passed away, but his wife Aggie still welcomes yatistas.

At Naranjo village, yatistas can anchor outside the ferry route almost anywhere off the wide tidal beach. Don't leave a boat or dink unattended here; petty theft has been noted.

From Naranjo, you can catch the ferry to Puntarenas; it takes an hour, costs about 710 Colones per person (cheap) and leaves here at 0730, 1230, 1700 and 2100. It departs Puntarenas at 0600, 1000, 1420 and 1900.

Upper Nicoya Gulf

The upper reaches of the Gulf of Nicoya NW of Naranjo and Puntarenas are shoaly, fringed in mangrove estuaries. To cruise here, you need a shallow-draft vessel with lots of power to overcome the strong tidal currents, and a flat bottom with protected props to occasionally spend the night grounded on the mud flats.

Along the shallower west side of the upper gulf, Islas Caballo, Bejuco and Venado are within 9 miles WNW of Naranjo. Caballo and Venado are home to many panga and net fishermen, but Bejuco is private and uninhabited except for a few caretakers.

Deeper water in the center of the gulf runs NNW to Puerto Morelos. Isla Chira (16.5 miles NW of

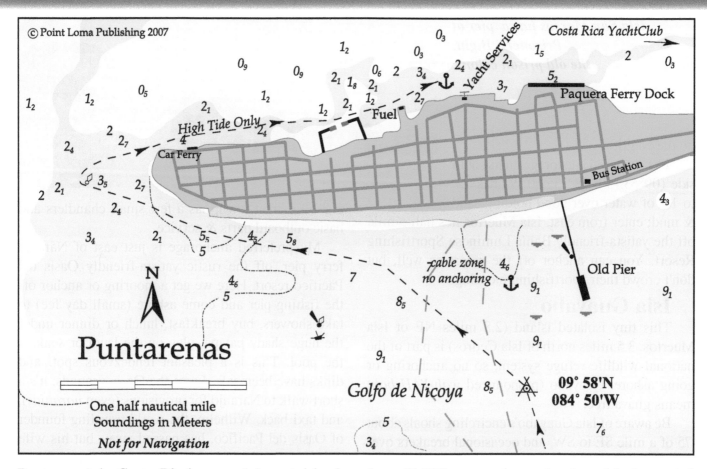

© Point Loma Publishing 2007

0_3 *Costa Rica YachtClub*

1_2 1_5 2 0_3

0_9 0_3

0_9 0_9 2_1 1_8 0_6 2 3_4 2_4 *Yacht Services* 5_2

0_5 2_1 1_8 2_1 3_7 **Paquera Ferry Dock**

1_2 1_2 2_1 1_2 2_7

1_2 2_1 2_1 1_2 *Fuel*

2_1 *High Tide Only* 2_4

2   2_7 4   **Car Ferry**

2_4

2   2_1 3_5 2_7 **Bus Station** 4_3

2_4

3_4 2_1 5_5 4_5 5_8

5   *cable zone* 4_6 **Old Pier**

4_6 *no anchoring* 9_1 9_1

N

5   7 8_5

Puntarenas

9_1 9_1

One half nautical mile
Soundings in Meters

Golfo de Nicoya 8_5 ⚓   **09° 58'N**
   084° 50'W

Not for Navigation

9_1 5 7_6

3_4

Puntarenas) is Costa Rica's second largest island, densely populated with fishermen who live in the mangroves of its eastern bay. Rio Tempesque empties into the gulf's far NW end, but much of that region uncovers at low tide.

Puntarenas

About 3 n.m. NE of Isla San Marcos, the west tip of the 3.5-n.m. long Puntarenas Peninsula juts into the midriff of the Gulf of Nicoya. It lies about 22 n.m. north from Ballena Bay, 22 n.m. NW of Los Sueños Marina at Bahía Herradura. The town of Puntarenas

(pop. 55,500) covers the peninsula and is the capital of the province of Puntarenas.

The old Puntarenas Pier (09°58.10'N, 84°49.81'W) is a good radar target, a quarter mile long and an area landmark on the south side of the peninsula. You can anchor well off to either side of this municipal pier, but you can't come alongside. Cruise ships and cargo go to nearby Caldera.

The small, shallow lagoon (sometimes called the Backside) lining the north shore of the Puntarenas Peninsula is extremely tidal and muddy, but it's a service port for commercial fishing. Fewer yachts come here since fuel and slips are available more easily at Los Sueños.

For yatistas who can manage the channel (8' in the middle at MLW, not well dredged or marked) around to the lagoon, the Costa Rica Yacht Club and Puntarenas waterfront have

Puntarenas docks in the lagoon on the backside of the peninsula.

Costa Rica Yacht Club has moorings, fuel & boat yard in the lagoon.

a few services, hospital, small airport and highway to San Jose. Check here for tides in Costa Rica: http://www.tides.com/tcpred.htm.

Approach & Clear: From Bahía Herradura or Isla Cedros, it's a straight shot to arrival anchorage around Puntarenas Pier on the south beach, where you anchor (20' to 26') and hail the Port Captain on VHF 16, then await clearance instructions. The Capitanía overlooks the pier.

A ship's agent isn't required, but many prefer having an agent provide a pilot to guide them from the big pier around to the backside and having the agent broker the best deal on fuel and bulk oil among the various commercial diesel docks.

We've had good service from English-speaking ship's agents Ernesto Andrade (506) 7661-0948 or eandrade@ice.co.cr or www.paramares.net.

Customs, Immigration and sometimes a Health inspection are required. Even a pet with health certificate is prohibited from national parks and bio reserves. The tourist card is good for 90 days, then renewable in Costa Rica by application. We've sometimes had to wait for officials to drive over from Caldera, and meanwhile nobody can go ashore.

During port clearance, ask about permits for any national parks you wish to visit. After you're cleared in, ask the Port Captain for permission to up anchor and go around to the Backside – depending on the tides.

Backside lagoon: An hour before high tide, up anchor from the arrival anchorage and head around La Punta or the bend into the Backside lagoon. To do this, we head west and parallel the beach – staying off about 100 yards. Once we're past the west end of the spit (La Punta), we look for a single white buoy: head directly toward it and swing around close aboard, keeping it on starboard.

The channel turns nearly 180° and angles toward the north shoreline, then more or less parallels it. Close along shore are many small docks and moored fishing boats; pass just outboard of them, but not too far north or you'll find the unmarked shoals, upon which rest a collection of wrecks. With less dredging, the main channel gets worse each summer.

The yacht anchorage is north of the channel in 8' to 12' of water at MLW. The bottom is soft mud. Allow for strong current and swinging room for the max 9.5' tide range. Farther east, the channel narrows, widens and peters out past the Costa Rica Yacht Club.

Local Services: Every year the city provides a new list of local marine services with street maps, emails, websites, telephone and VHF contacts, so ask the Port Captain when you arrive.

The big INCOPESCA municipal dock about .75 of a mile from the bend is a convenient place to ship water jugs, cases of food, transmission, etc. But fender well and tell the dockmaster you don't want shrimpers rafting outside you. A tank truck can deliver diesel to this pier.

Several smaller diesel docks are in this vicinity, but the one you pick will depend on your draft and state of the tide, LOA and displacement. The heads of some docks are dry at MLW. Some diesel docks also rent moorings. Sportfishing docks run 25' to 56' charter boats.

Costa Rica Yacht Club is a real yacht club with international accreditation, and it accepts guests when there's room, located 3.4 n.m. east along the lagoon channel.

CRYC has 40 good 2-point moorings, a fuel dock, repair yard and nice facilities, CRYC has a launch service to the moorings and a dink landing. The clubhouse has a nice restaurant, laundry, showers, small chandler, pool with shade trees, air-conditioned rooms, car rental, etc. This club has been a safe place to leave a boat while traveling inland, but make

Playa Manta near Punta Leona. Watch out for sting rays.

at least 2 chandlers with diesel and outboard parts and repairs, 2 good grocery stores and lots of little ones, at least 5 internet cafes. A new airport links it to Alajuela, near the nation's capital of San Jose, which otherwise is a 1.5-hour taxi ride, 2.5 hours by fast bus, 4.5 in the chicken bus.

Caldera, the modern port 7.25 n.m. SE of Puntarenas Pier, has lots of ship traffic and anchored freighters, but it prohibits yacht traffic. However, by taxi Caldera yields many chandlers and navigation electronics sales & service.

arrangements with Dockmaster Carlos so they'll keep an eye on everything. FMI on CRYC, visit www. costaricayachtclub.com or phone (506) 6610784.

CRYC's floating fuel platform (6' max at MLW) is off the south side of the channel. Most boats hang off the raft in the strong current. Call the yacht club on VHF 06 for an appointment to take fuel.

CRYC has a 20-ton Travelift, dry storage & work yard reached by a side channel off the north side of the lagoon channel. We've had good report about these services.

Puntarenas also offers a big Mercado Central,

Punta Leona

At 20 n.m. SE of Puntarenas and 4 n.m. north of Bahía Herradura, this half-mile wide bay on the east side of Punta Leona is wide open to the north but has shelter from moderate south wind.

Anchor off the main beach in 22' over mud and sand. If strong south swell wraps the small point, this cove can get too rolly for comfort. Sting rays make getting ashore a bit risky year round, but in December and January the larger and docile manta rays flock to this region to breed and frolic.

Tarcoles wildlife preserve covers the jungle for miles north from here up to almost Caldera. Rumors say a marina may be built at Punta Leona someday, so we'll keep an eye on it; check for Updates at www. CentralAmericanBoating.com

The huge Punta Leona Resort (private membership club) covers the shore. Although the members may enjoy watching a few yachts bob in their view, the management has been charging yatistas $20 to step on the beach, and they have not been welcoming yatistas into their restaurants, bars or pools. This resort has denied charges of dumping raw sewage into the bay, but don't run a watermaker at anchor – just in case.

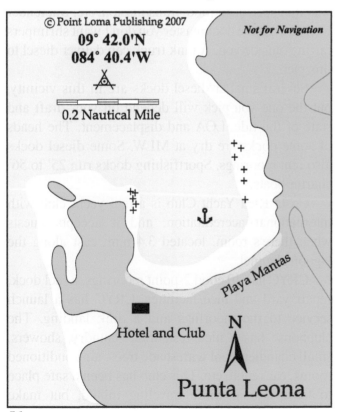

© Point Loma Publishing 2007

09° 42.0'N
084° 40.4'W

Not for Navigation

0.2 Nautical Mile

Playa Mantas

Hotel and Club

N

Punta Leona

Bahía Herradura

Developed for Los Sueños Marina and resort, the 1-mile wide Bahía Herradura (Horse-shoe Bay) on the SE shore of the Gulf of Nicoya lies 26 n.m. ENE of Cabo Blanco and 22 n.m. SE of Puntarenas.

Partly sheltered by Isla Herradura on its south perimeter, this bay is open to west and SW wind and swell. Although Jaco Beach 3 miles SE is a popular weekend getaway for Ticos, the main attraction at Herradura is Los Sueños Marina inside its own breakwaters in the north corner of the bay.

The marina has large, full-service slips, floating fuel dock and yacht services. In good weather, yatistas can anchor outside the marina's breakwaters and dinghy in to use the services for a day fee. Because Bahía Herradura is 22 miles closer to the open ocean, a stop here is more convenient and pleasant than traveling up to Puntarenas – though more costly.

Approach: My GPS approach in the entrance to Bahía Herradura is 09°38.7'N, 84°41'W. Give a 300-yard berth to all sides of Isla Herradura due to reefs. Be careful to spot and avoid a dangerous submerged rock (4' of water) in the middle of Bahía Herradura; it may not be marked by a buoy.

Port Clearance: The commercial port of Caldera has the nearest Capitanía. Port officials arrive by taxi, and you pay the fare. Los Sueños Marina handles yacht clearance for marina guests and also can do it for yatistas anchored out for a small fee. Ask for permits to visit the national parks by boat – Manuel Antonio, Isla del Caño, Corcovado.

Anchorage: After avoiding the dangerous rock pinnacle in the middle of Bahía Herradura, we anchor in Bahía Herradura's south side during south wind, north side in north wind. Don't block access to the marina entrance. Depths range from 11' to 25' in most parts.

Not for Navigation

One nautical mile
Soundings in Meters

N

11

17

25

09° 38.7'N
084° 41.0'W

Bahía Herradura

44

16

16

24

10

7

30

20

Marina Los Sueños
© Point Loma Publishing 2007

Make arrangements with the marina to use their secure dinghy dock and facilities for a day fee.

Berthing: The marina part of Los Sueños Resort & Marina is located inside its own breakwater basin in the north corner of Bahía Herradura, and you enter the basin at its SE corner heading NW. Built in 2001, the marina has 200 slips with all the shore power, security and amenities you could dream of, including access to the Marriott and golf course.

Because of the extraordinary sportfishing in this region and the marina's posh services, many slips are filled with high-dollar sportfishing boats year round, and the few guest slips (40' to 200' LOA) require a reservation especially during tournaments. FMI, visit www.lsrm.com or call (506) 2630-4200 in country,

Los Sueños Marina:
Isla Herradura in background is visible
from inside the breakwater.

Officials from Caldera come to your boat in Los Sueños Marina, Bahía Herradura.

The other half of Los Sueños is a big Marriott resort and 18-hole golf course; marina guests have access to both. The hotel's travel desk books flights and Costa Rica tours. The next community to the south is Jaco Beach, with lots of "sodas," a gas station and bus stop.

Side Trips: This is the safest place to leave your boat and the easiest place from which to explore Costa Rica. To get away from the ocean, try Volcan Poas or Volcan Arenal, both in national parks in the central highlands and NE of here.

Or go all the way up to Monteverde Cloud Forest National Park. Pack your rain gear and warm clothes. On the way up, stop off at one of the jungle canopy tours and ride through the tree tops on a zip line.

San Jose, the capital of Costa Rica, is easily reached by bus or rental car from here. It's up in the cooler mountains. If you're flying in or out of Costa Rica, it's probably through the international airport at Alajuela, which you must pass by on your way to San Jose.

We think the historic downtown and plazas of San Jose are a nice excursion as long as you plan to overnight there. Focus on the main plaza next to the elegantly restored Teatro Naciónal (National Theater) and plan to take coffee on the terraza of Hotel Gran - which is a fine place to stay.

or from the US call toll free (866) 865-9759.

Local Services: Los Suenos' fuel dock is along the north side of the marina basin; diesel, gas, fast pumps, bulk oils, extraction & disposal, major credit cards OK. Skippers of larger vessels may want to call on VHF 16 to see if the fuel dock is clear before heading into this end of the bay.

Los Sueños Marine Supply Store has watermaker, engine, fishing & chandler supplies; FMI call (506) 637-8502.

At the east end of San Jose, the huge Parque Metro La Sabana is like Central Park to NYC - lots to see and do or stroll the gardens.

San Jose is a good place for provisioning and getting boat gear repaired or replaced.

Power & sail boats enjoy the services at Los Sueños Marina.

Quepos

Between the Gulf of Nicoya and the Gulfo Dulce, the cruising port of Quepos (pronounced Kay-pohs) is closest to Manuel Antonio National Park and the Quepos Islands. Located 31 n.m. around the corner from Bahía Herradura and 46 n.m. NW of Drake's Bay, the port lies about 2.5 n.m. north of the Punta Quepos headland.

Quepos (pop. 7,000) was a sleepy village with a high pier built for loading bananas, pineapples and sailfish, but now Quepos is booming. One big marina is in construction and another is planned, plus vacation villas galore.

Quepos pier juts almost east from a headland at the east end of Bahía Vieja or Old Bay. A broad jetty parallels the south side of the pier to break the huge swells of summer storms.

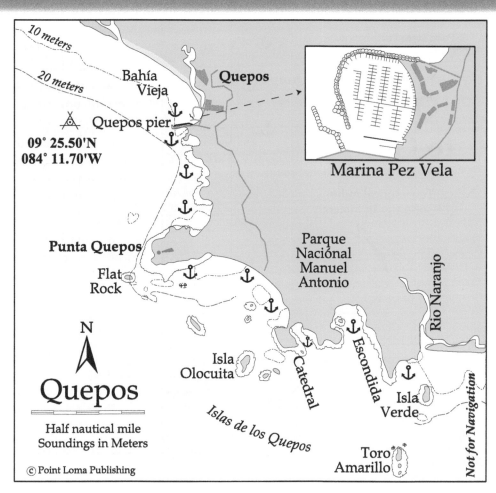

Marina Pez Vela

09° 25.50'N
084° 11.70'W

N

Quepos

Half nautical mile
Soundings in Meters

© Point Loma Publishing

Approach: From the Gulf of Nicoya stay at least 2.5 n.m. off shore to avoid reefs near Punta Guapinol & Punta Judas, also avoid long-liners' nets that

Above: the entrance to Marina Pez Vela at Quepos, CR, is in the center of this photo, and the landmark bridge is visible on the right side.
Right: Downtown Quepos remains a quaint service town for the huge new developments nearby.

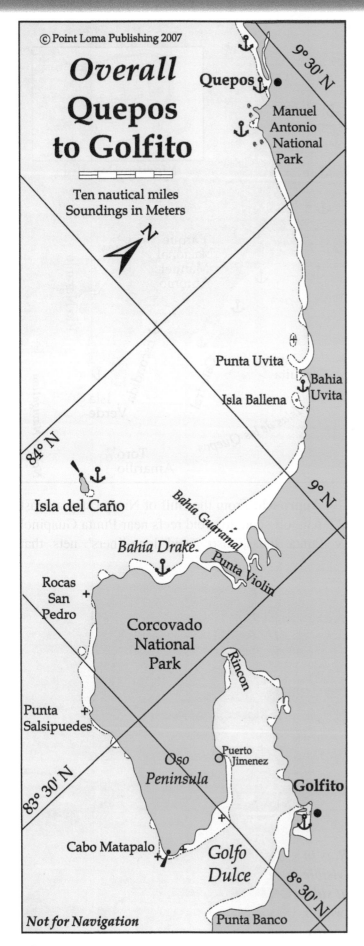

Overall Quepos to Golfito

© Point Loma Publishing 2007

Ten nautical miles
Soundings in Meters

Not for Navigation

sometimes run for miles in this area, but they usually stop as you approach Manuel Antonio park waters extending 14 n.m. south to SW of Punta Catedral.

Anchor & Berth: The primary yacht anchorage is off the north side of Quepos pier in the west end of Bahía Vieja, in 15' to 35' over mud. This anchorage is likely to be affected by marina construction. Another larger but more open anchorage area spreads a mile south of the pier jetty to north of reef-lined Punta Quepos. Depths range from 30' to 60' and current is a factor.

Marina Pez Vela was in construction as we went to press in early 2007, planing to open in fall 2007. They plan about 200 full-service slips, some to 200' LOA, inside a breakwater enclosed basin to be built close NE of Quepos pier. Also planned is a boat yard with 150-ton Travelift and fuel dock. FMI, visit www.MarinaPezVela.com or call (506) 777-4141. When berthing is available at a Quepos marina, it will also be posted on www.CentralAmericaBoating.com.

Port Clearance: The older port administration building (Port Captain and Immigration) is at the head of Quepos pier, but a new office is planned. Quepos is not a Port of Entry for clearing into the country; the nearest is at Caldera or Golfito.

Local Services: Quepos downtown has a couple small grocery stores and pharmacy on the frontage road, a laundry service, central market and lots of eateries and small tourist hotels. The airport is NE of town, and the road to the park goes SE.

Manuel Antonio National Park

This is Costa Rica's most famous biological reserve, and although its beauty is easily accessible to yatistas, almost anywhere you anchor here is going to be rolly even with no wind.

MANP is roughly spread NW to SE across 3 n.m. of small bays, white sand beaches, jungle cliffs, steep islands, detached spires and numerous rocky reefs. The western side has eco-lodges, and the eastern part is totally undeveloped.

MANP generally includes (a.) the 1.5 n.m. wide Bahía Manuel Antonio, which has a long beach called Playa Espadilla north and south, (b.) tiny Caleta Catedral or Cathedral Cove with Manuel Antonio Beach, reported to be the prettiest in Costa Rica, and

Beach anchorage of Manuel Antonio National Park near Quepos.

(c.) the slightly larger Bahía Escondida to the SE. None are free of rocky hazards.

From NW to SE, the more easily identifiable offshore islands are Flat Rock off Punta Quepos, Isla Olocuita off Punta Catedral at the east end of Bahía Manuel Antonio, and the small chain of Islas Toro Amarillo (Yellow Bull) off Punta Serrucho and Isla Verde about a half mile SE of Punta Serrucho. The mouth of Rio Naranjo just north of Isla Verde dumps farm sediment into the Pacific, so that area is often discolored.

Ashore, hiking trails through the jungle reveal the habitat of sloths, iguanas, adorable squirrel monkeys and white-faced howler monkeys, plus zillions of exotic birds, butterflies, insects, flowers, trees, etc.

Permits (about $6 per day per person, children under 12 free) for anchoring within MANP are usually available at the park office in Quepos or at the park's front gate about a mile SE of Quepos. Yatistas already anchored in the park have sometimes been able to get the permits from friendly rangers who patrol the park in skiffs. Regulations prohibit pumping anything into the park waters, even sink drains and bilges.

Manuel Antonio National Park is open to the public from 0700 to 1600, closed Mondays. A bus runs from the park's front gate to Quepos every 30 minutes from 0500 to 2000; fare is about half a buck.

Punta Uvita

About 6.5 n.m. SE of Quepos, Punta Uvita (09°08.55'N, 83°45.85'W) is a natural T-headed point jutting almost a mile out from shore. Punta Uvita and Bahía Uvita off its south side were recently dubbed Ballena National Park. The boundaries extend about 5 n.m. off shore and 5 n.m. south along shore to Punta Piñuela. The park is trying to prevent over fishing by prohibiting it in these waters, but anchoring is fine; no fee so far.

Isla del Caño

Cane Island and Drake Bay lie within 12 n.m. of each other, off the NW end of the huge Osa Peninsula. Cane Island lies about 44 n.m. SE of Quepos, 12 n.m. NW of Punta Llorona and about 65 n.m. up from Golfito.

Cane Island is 300' high, flat-topped and heavily wooded, making a good radar target. Reefs foul the island's east and SE shores, and a nav light stands on the western tip. The island and a roughly 3-mile perimeter comprise the Isla del Caño National Biosphere Preserve, so you need a $6 permit to anchor or step ashore.

Anchorage: Cane Island has no reliable anchorages. Depending on wind and swell, we first try anchoring off the 2-story ranger HQ about half a mile NE of the island's west tip. Two rock spurs poking seaward give some protection from swell.

If you can get ashore here, a trail from the ranger station leads 400 yards SE to a fresh-water lagoon behind the beach.

CAUTION: Isla del Caño is struck by lightning each year more than any other place in Central America. Unplug your electronics when not in use at anchor here.

During thunderstorms in the near coastal waters between Quepos and Golfito, we've experienced almost constant bolt lightning striking the sea surface. A nearby boat's electronics got fried by a direct hit.

Diving Caño: At least 5 plateaus with 10 spectacular dive sites ring the island, ranging from snorkeling beaches and 15' deep coral reefs to 80' volcanic walls. White-tip sharks, sea turtles, manta rays and colorful aquarium species are almost always

Anchorage at Drake Bay is large, often handy for moving between Quepos and Golfito.

seen. The park provides a dive map of the island. Fishing, shelling or collecting anything is prohibited. To protect the island, only 5 dive sites are open each day, and only 10 divers are permitted down at a time.

Culture & History: Cane Island is remarkable for the many pre-Columbian stone spheres discovered scattered around in the jungle, thought to be sacred burial artifacts from an unknown South American culture.

Almost perfectly spherical, the granodiorite stones range in size from a few inches to more than

6' in diameter. They are believed to have been carved between 200 BC and 1600 CE, and nobody knows what they signify. Ask the ranger for directions. (More spheres are found in a valley in Corcovado National Park on the Osa Peninsula.)

Cane Island has already lost so much jungle habitat that many bird, insect and flower species thriving in nearby Corcovado National Park have disappeared here.

Treasure hunters may have damaged Caño's virginity, digging for a pirate treasure that legends say was buried by Sir Francis Drake in the late 1500s on an island off Costa Rica - wonder which one.

Drake Bay

Drake Bay lies 12 n.m. east of Cane Island is a 2.5-mile wide dent into the north side of the Osa Peninsula's mountainous NW corner. Drake Bay, also called Bahía Sierpe, is about 4.25 n.m. south of Rio Sierpe, which is navigable by small craft if you can get over the bar.

Our GPS approach to Drake Bay (08°42.61'N, 83°39.67'W) is from the north, looking into the slightly more protected south corner of the bay. But the anchoring area (20' to 36') below the higher ground in the south end is not well sheltered. Strong south swell can wrap around Punta San Jose and Punta San Pedrillo to drive you out of Drake Bay.

A few eco-adventure lodges are scattered along the dark-sand beach, and most do welcome yatistas. The village at the south end has a panga landing inside a tidal river mouth. About half way up the beach, Rio Aguja crosses the berm, and behind it is a dirt air strip, which is the end of the road. Drake Bay Sportfishing Lodge on the small point at the north

Plaque honoring Sir Francis Drake came from Plymouth, England in 1979. Pirate treasure hunters abound here and at Isla Caño. Photo by Scott Atkins.

Charter sportfishing boats use private docks at Crocodile Bay Lodge at Puerto Jiménez in Golfo Dulce - across from Golfio.

end of the beach keeps a few boats here.

A rough coastal road comes in from Puerto Jiménez in Bahía Dulce. The 2 mountain peaks behind Bahía Drake and Rio Sierpe are the rainiest places in Costa Rica, getting 220" of rain annually. No wonder it's so lush.

Osa Peninsula

The Osa Peninsula covers 500 square miles, most of it within the Corcovado National Park. The south coast stretches 30 n.m. SE from Punta Llorona (08°35.44'N, 83°44.10'W) to Cabo Matapalo at the entrance to Bahía Dulce.

Roca Corcovado: About 7 n.m. SE of Punta Llorona, identify the 60' high Roca Corcovado in order to avoid its dangerous submerged pinnacles that extend almost 1.5 n.m. off the beach called Playa Llorona.

Punta Salsipuedes: At 7 n.m. farther SE, Punta Salsipuedes has rocks a half mile off the point. Give these hazards a berth of at least 2 n.m.

Pay heed to these place names. *"Salsipuedes"* means Leave If You Can. *"Llorona"* literally is She Who Cries, but the term La Llorona refers to a tale of warning, something like the Boogie Man. Better watch out or *La Llorona* will get you!

Golfo Dulce

Southernmost of Costa Rica's cruising grounds, Golfo Dulce (Sweet Gulf) measures 26 n.m. NW to SE and averages 6 n.m across. The entrance to Golfo Dulce is 7.5 n.m. wide, between the multi-pointed Cabo Matapalo on the west shore and the more rounded Cabo Banco on the eastern side.

Cabo Matapalo is a popular surfing destination year round. Round Cabo Matapalo at least a mile off, avoiding detached and conical Roca Matapalo that lies half a mile south of its southernmost point.

Besides surf, the mixing of currents often creates turbulence here. Continue staying at least a mile off the Osa Peninsula side for the next 6 n.m. north heading into Golfo Dulce, due to numerous detached rocks and shoals.

Puerto Jiménez

The SW shore of Golfo Dulce is mangroves backed by low farmlands drained by a dozen tiny rivers. It's 16.5 n.m. from Punta Arenitas to Punta Rincon.

Puerto Jiménez (pronounced *"he-MAY-nayz"*) is the only village on this side of the bay. After its banana loading dock was wrecked by tidal waves and the road flooded out, the nearly abandoned backwater village moved uphill twice. But now it's busy with back-packers, surfers and eco-tourists arriving by ferry 10 n.m. across from Golfito and heading to Corcovado National Park.

Approach: From Cabo Matapalo, it's about 11 n.m. north to shoaly Punta Arenitas. From a GPS approach position (08°32.81'N, 83°17.06'W) about a quarter mile north of Punta Arenitas, the new ferry pier lies about 1.25 ESE. A bridge connects this rebuilt peninsula with "downtown" Puerto Jiménez.

Anchorages at Puerto Jimenez are very tidal. Photo by Scott Atkins.

Jungle bar is called
Puerto Jiménez Yacht Club.

Anchor: Deep water comes close to shore, and charter sportfishers may occupy the prime spots. But you might anchor in about 30' between the west flank of Punta Arenitas and the lighted sportfishing dock at the rather posh Crocodile Bay Lodge. However, don't use their dock or come ashore here without permission.

Another possible anchorage is about a quarter mile NW of the ferry pier on a small shelf off Playa Tigre. Being so tidal, Puerto Jiménez lacks a good dinghy landing. Being marshy, the mosquitoes and no-see-ums are relentless.

Local Services: The Golfito ferry round-trips daily; about $2. The village caters to young eco-tourists, so inexpensive cabins, convenience stores and "sodas" or cantinas abound. But a few fancier resorts dot the hills down to Matapalo. To book a tour, try at Sol de Osa internet café 3 blocks south of the bridge from the ferry pier; the expat owner is very helpful. The airport between town and Crocodile Bay Lodge has daily flights to San Jose.

Continuing around Golfo Dulce

About 15 n.m. NW of Puerto Jiménez, Golfo Dulce National Forest Reserve occupies the NW end of the bay, where the shore terrain changes suddenly to jungle cliffs dropping steeply into the bay.

Bahía Rincon, the enclosed mile-wide bay at the far NW corner of Golfo Dulce, has a tree research station at the south end behind marshy Punta Rincon. Unfortunately, this little bay is 60' deep too close to shore, and mosquitoes are thick.

Along Golfo Dulce's north shore, about 7.5 n.m east of Rincon Bay, the powerful Rio Esquinas deposits a shallow delta with depths of 10' found half a mile off shore. Moving SE from Rio Esquinas, the Piedras Blancas National Park lines the gulf's rugged north shore down of Golfito.

New regulations allow a few eco-lodges to open here, accessible only by boat from Golfito. Except for a few places, deep water comes close to shore and prevents casual anchoring overnight.

Golfito

The only real cruising port in Golfo Dulce, Golfito is a pleasant little town (Port of Entry) at the north end of an enclosed 3-mile long bay

© Point Loma Publishing 2007

N

Golfito

One nautical mile
Soundings in Meters

proposed marina

Pier

Navigation aids are unreliable

dries

5

10

4

10

9

shoal

2 1

9

Punta Voladera

10

047°T

08° 36.5'N
083° 11.5'W

Centro

5

3

6

6

Banana Bay Marina

K&B Marina

Punta El Cabro

5

5

dries

Not for Navigation

Golfito Bay opens off Golfo Dulce. The entrance to Golfito is visible in the right side of this aerial photo.

located 10 n.m. north of the entrance to Golfo Dulce. Golfito has 2 marinas with fuel docks, excellent sportfishing, handy provisioning and other yatista services. Dockwise Express loads and unloads yachts here.

Approach: From a mile east of Cabo Matapalo, lay a course 15 n.m. to our GPS approach waypoint 08°36.5'N, 83°11.5'W, which lies just outside Golfito's entrance channel. If you're approaching from a mile west of Cabo Blanco, a course to this waypoint keeps you just off shoals to port starting 2.5 n.m. south of the waypoint, but avoid getting set east.

Call "Base Naval" on VHF 16 when in range to announce your arrival and request port clearance or a pilot. Don't try entering Golfito harbor after dark or in typical blinding rain, because the buoys along the narrow 2-mile channel NE are unlighted, often missing. Harbor ranges close south of the big commercial pier align on 047°T, but trust your depth sounder.

After the bay widens out, stay mid channel until you're about 400 yards off the shore ahead, thus avoiding shoals on both sides. This arrival anchorage (30' to 40') is normally for port clearance only.

Port Clearance: You called on VHF 16 to announce your arrival, right? If you're being boarded in the anchorage, officials may ask you to pick them up in your dinghy – if it's big enough. Otherwise, a Navy skiff brings them out eventually.

If you're staying at one of the marinas, you may be directed there for boarding, and the marinas will assist or advise with your paperwork.

Yellow buildings mark Banana Bay Marina in Golfito, Costa Rica. Banana Bay has slips, moorings, fuel, cantina, pool, etc.

TIP: Arrive Monday through Friday, 0800 to 1600, to avoid overtime fees.

Former ship's agents Tim and Katie Leechman of Tierra y Mar (Land & Sea) Yacht Services can help you line up repairs, provisions, flights, boat sitting, load onto or off Dockwise, eco tours, etc. They have 3 slips, 5 moorings and dink dock just south of Banana Bay. Hail "Land & Sea Yacht Services" on VHF 16, or phone (506) 2775-1614.

Anchor & Berth: Some yatistas anchor off the big palapa restaurant on the first point of land south of the arrival anchorage. You can also anchor along the west side of the unmarked channel that generally parallels town for about 2 n.m. SE.

Banana Bay Marina has the bright yellow building about 1.2 n.m. SE of the arrival anchorage. Banana Bay has full-service slips for 30 boats to 120' LOA, very popular with sportfishing boats. It also has a long pier for Med-mooring and a few moorings. Shore amenities include showers, laundry and The Bilge bar and grill. The fuel dock is in front of the main

Moorings in Golfito are well sheltered.

and commercial development. Check www.CentralAmericanBoating.com for updates.

Samoa Restaurant (big palapa) has set some moorings; haven't tested them yet.

Local Services: Diesel and gas are pumped at the 2 bigger marinas, and they can boat sit while you're traveling elsewhere. Provisioning for fresh produce is OK here, but not much else. A ferry runs over to Puerto Jimenez daily. Golfito's little airport has 40-minute Sansa flights to San Jose, the capital.

Dockwise Express loads & unloads yachts just outside Golfito harbor. The marina operators can help load or unload your boat, even if you're not here, but better if you are.

building. The marina has a small hotel, handy for guests or getting off the boat for a few days. FMI on Banana Bay Marina, visit www.BananaBayMarina.com or Tel (506) 2775-0838.

Land & Sea Yacht Services has about 5 inexpensive slips and 8 moorings. The owners are former cruisers, former ships agency. Hail Land & Sea or Mar & Tierra on VHF 16 when in range.

Fish Hook Sportfishing Marina is next door to Land & Sea's dock. Fish Hook has 20 full-service slips and a nice restaurant, plus some moorings and dinghy landing dock. They also have a fuel dock and lodge rooms ashore. FMI on Fish Hook Marina call US toll free (888) 535-8832.

Plans are on hold for another larger marina that was to be located just north of the old commercial pier, part of a large Bahía Escondida residential

Dockwise picking up yachts in Golfito.

Pavónes & Playa Zancudo are popular surf spots located in Bahía Pavón between Golfito and Punta Banco, which you pass as you depart Costa Rica for Panama at Punta Burica.

Sportfishing boat fuels up in Golfito before heading out for bill fish. Boats in background are on moorings and at anchor.

WX & Route Planning

Do you want to scoot right along to the Panama Canal? Or do you want to spend some time exploring the jungles and islands of this Pacific coast of Panama? Here are 2 routing options.

Plan A: Direct Route to Panama Canal

Our offshore waypoint (08°00'N, 82°53'W) lies 1 n.m. south of Punta Burica, the peninsula that is half Costa Rica and half Panama. From there, head to waypoint 07°27.3'N, 82°17.3'W, just west of Isla Montuosa avoiding the reef that extends WNW of it.

Pass 1 n.m. south (07°11.5'N, 81°48.0'W) of Isla Jicarita and turn east. You've just passed the most southerly point in this book.

Skirt close along the south shore of the Azuero Peninsula, round 1 n.m. off Punta Mala (07°27.5'N, 79°59.0'W), then head straight to Isla Bona (08°33.8'N, 79°39.2'W), then just east of Isla Taboguilla (08°48.0'N,

Viva Panama

79°29.5'W) and finally to the Panama Canal sea buoy (8°51.5'N, 79°29.0'W) at the Balboa entrance.

Wind and current will generally be against you. If you have the time, take it easy and check out the many stops very close along this pristine and seldom visited paradise for yatistas – sailors and sportfishers alike.

Plan B: Cruising Route to Panama Canal

Below the hurricane belt, this route passes some seldom visited cruising grounds and world-class fishing spots.

The winds in this region are generally light and variable. But in January and February the stronger Caribbean Trade Winds often blow across the Isthmus of Panama – this is the narrowest part – and reach the north side of Coiba Island. This winter wind does not usually reach gale force, but it can make for bumpy and wet travel. During the rainy season the wind and swell tend to be SW.

The tidal range between Punta Burica and Punta Mariato is about 16', but

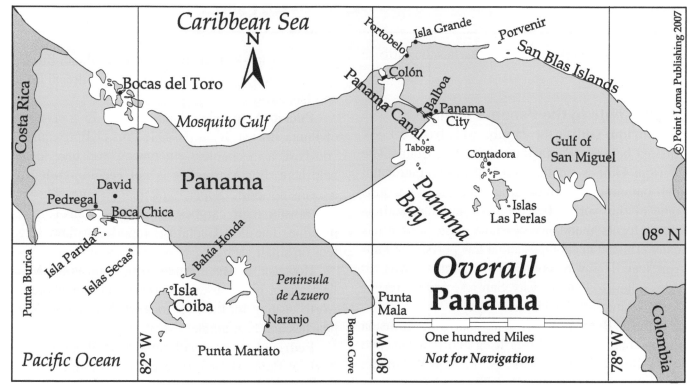

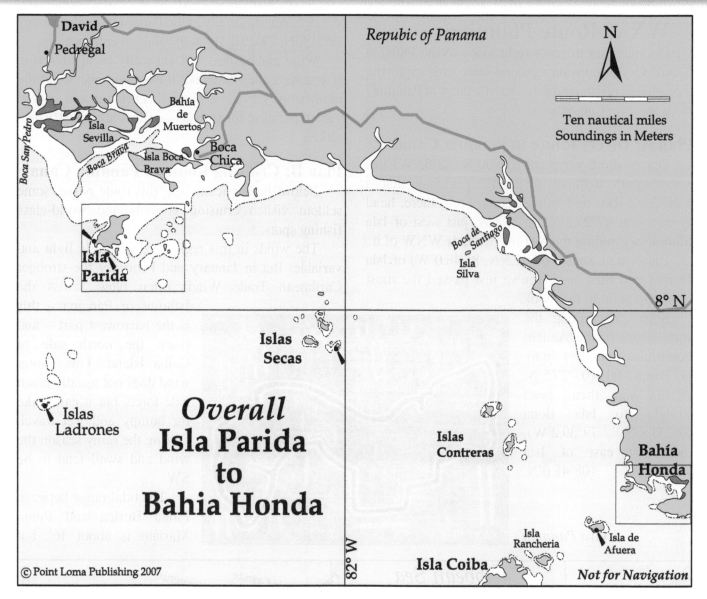

Republic of Panama

David
Pedregal

Bahía de Muertos

Isla Sevilla

Boca Brava

Isla Boca Brava

Boca Chica

Boca San Pedro

N

Ten nautical miles
Soundings in Meters

Boca de Santiago

Isla Silva

8° N

Islas Secas

Islas Ladrones

Overall
Isla Parida to Bahia Honda

Islas Contreras

Bahía Honda

Isla Rancheria

Isla de Afuera

Isla Coiba

82° W

© Point Loma Publishing 2007

Not for Navigation

from Punta Mala up to Balboa it reaches the extreme of 22' on spring tides.

En Route to the Panama Canal

Chiriquí Gulf is the 75-mile wide basin off SW Panama between Punta Burica and Isla Coiba. The Chiriquí Gulf is on the rather shallow continental shelf but close to deep ocean canyons, so it contains some of the world's best sportfishing. This gulf is known for its abundance of island clusters, so it has many cruising anchorages and a few ports. The Pan-American Highway connects the larger towns 10 miles inland to Panama City, San Jose and the rest of Central America's backbone.

Punta Burica is the long, narrow peninsula jutting south between Costa Rica and Panama, and Punta Burica Light (08°01.1'N, 82°52.6'W) marks

the Costa Rica-Panama border. East of Punta Burica, Bahía Charco Azul spreads east to the Pedregal Delta and Isla Parida.

Puerto Armuelles is an oil port 15 n.m. north of Punta Burica. It's a possible Port of Entry, and if you have a mechanical emergency, you may locate help here. But **Armuelles is not recommended** as a cruising port. Super tankers carrying Alaskan oil transfer their cargoes here into a trans-isthmus pipeline. The Port Captain is reported to levy large fees on small yachts.

However, between Punta Burica and Punta Mala lie about a dozen islands and mainland anchorages worth visiting for their seasonal shelter, unpopulated beaches and lush jungle.

Pedregal is the small cargo port about 33 n.m. NNE of Punta Burica, reached by a winding 8-mile

From Playa El Pozo anchorage looking south toward Isla Gamez.

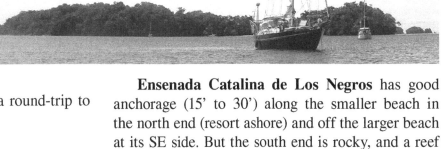

channel between mud flats and mangrove marshes. Pedregal has 3 commercial piers, a few moorings and an anchorage in the small bay. Pedregal has some groceries and a road north to David, the largest town in this area. (A panga service at Isla Parida charges about $80 for a round-trip to Pedregal.)

Isla Parida

Isla Parida (about 4 n.m. long SW to NE) and the cluster of about 100 islets, rocks, pinnacles and reefs off its east and SE sides form a minor cruiser hang-out, located at the south edge of the shallow shelf south of the approaches to Pedregal and David – in SW Panama. The main island of Isla Parida has a few nice homes and clusters of vacation cabins.

From Punta Burica, Isla Parida lies 31 miles WSW. And from Parida, the Ladrones (Thieves Islands) at 07°52.0'N, 82°26.0'W are about 15 miles farther SSW. The SW tip of Isla Parida has a nav light at about 08°06.0'N, 82°22.0'W.

Ensenada Santa Cruz (Bahía Chimo) on the WSW side of Isla Parida is the first anchorage you pass when arriving from Costa Rica. Anchorage is taken in the south end in 15' to 20' of water, as rocks uncover in the north end. This has good protection in moderate south swell, but in strong south conditions, some swell creeps between the south point and Hijo Mocha, the tiny island off the point. A paved trail leads from this beach SE over to Playa Grande, the largest bay on Parida's south side, which has a private home.

Isla Catalina (1 n.m. north) has deep water along its SE side, where you pass to reach Ensenada Catalina de los Negros, which lies about 2 n.m. NE of Santa Cruz or 1 n.m. east of Isla Catalina.

Ensenada Catalina de Los Negros has good anchorage (15' to 30') along the smaller beach in the north end (resort ashore) and off the larger beach at its SE side. But the south end is rocky, and a reef projects NW from the bay's south arm.

NE Parida: Both tiny beach-backed indents on the island's NE arm are anchorable, but give a wide berth to Punta Jurel at the island's extreme NE tip due to a dangerous submerged rock (Roca Jurel) close off that point.

Playa Jurel: Cabañas Parida is a little hotel and anchorage (08°07.8'N, 82°19.0'W) in the northern of the twin coves at Parida's NE arm. This anchorage is slightly deeper (15' to 18') and better N-S sheltered than Playa El Pozo, the next cove south. Cabañas Parida has changed ownership, and it's not as welcoming to yatistas as described in our previous editions. But visitors can still come ashore to buy ice, diesel and propane, and to visit the little restaurant, bar and mini-market store. This is where we found the panga service to Pedregal. If the resort is not accepting drop-ins, you might land a dinghy at the tiny beach along the south arm of the bay or move down to the next cove. FMI on Cabañas Parida (507) 774-8166.

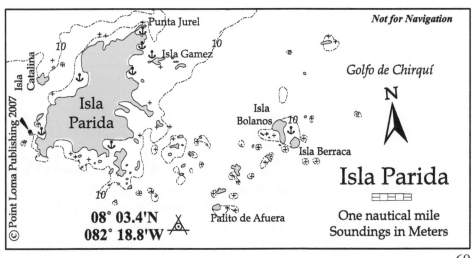

Crew member Scott Atkins explores Isla Parida by dink.

good for snorkeling but not passable. Good anchorage is taken off either of the tiny white-sand beaches on the NW and SW end of Isla Gamez, depending on WX conditions.

Bahía Lanza: Both beach-backed coves within a half mile NW and SW of Isla Gomez are fine anchorages. A 300-yard patch of reef separates the 2 coves, and the eastern edge of the reef lies at 08°07.53'N, 82°19.58'W. At sunset, the northern cove has been visited by no-see-ums from the lagoon behind the beach berm. Mogote el Sepulcro is the tiny islet almost attached off Punta Lanza, the broad wooded headland about .75 of a mile SW of Isla Gamez. Diving is good over the reefs south of Mogote el Sepulcro.

Varadero Bay: Bypassing the shoal bays SW of the Punta Mala ridgeline, enter Varadero Bay via the north side of Isla Paridita (Little Parida) and anchor (12' to 18') off the west end beach with good shelter from north wind. There's an islet and secondary beach in the north end of this enclosed bay. Anchorage is also possible in a small, crescent cove on the north end of Isla Paridita. A deep-water channel leads south along the west side of Isla Paridita.

Playa El Pozo (Socorro): Just south of Punta el Pozo (Well), this tiny cove is a shallower anchorage (10' to 15') and has a rock pile east of its south arm, so use care when moving down to Isla Gamez.

Isla Gamez lies within a mile SE of Parida's NE tip, and the smaller Isla Tintorera lies about .75 of a mile east of Gamez. The reef connecting them is

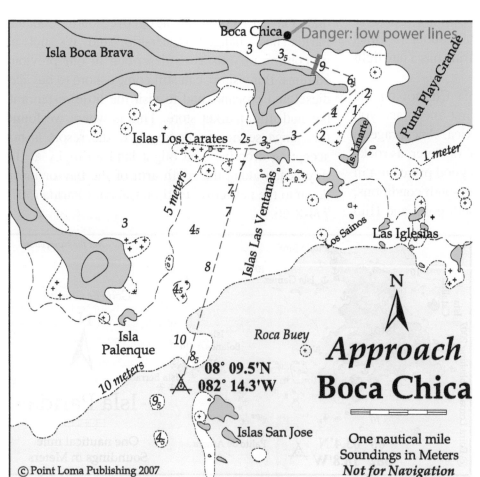

Boca Chica

Boca Chica (village and marina) lies about 10 n.m. NE from the north end of Isla Parida, but due to new overhead power lines, it may best be reached via Boca Brava Channel.

In 2011, Mack Robertson's unfinished Marina Boca Chica dock & cabins were for sale.

The approach waypoint (08°09.5'N, 82°14.3'W) lies along the west side of the Islas

San Jose (5 n.m. ENE of Punta Jurel on Isla Parida). From here, go about 2.5 n.m NNE to the west side of Isla Ventana.

Anchorage is possible on the north side of Isla Ventana in the tidal channel. From the north side of Isla Ventana, go ENE about 1.3 n.m. to the extreme NE tip of Isla Boca Brava, avoiding the shoal off the west side of Isla Linarte. The sandbar off Linarte's north tip forms the east side of this quarter-mile-wide pass.

At the NE tip of Isla Boca Brava, you might decide to turn hard NW and proceed about a mile in the Boca Chica Channel. **But, watch the tides (up to 18' ranges) to see if you can slither safely under the overhead cables, which are about 60' over MLW. Some big sailboats have struck it.**

Alternately, four nice sportfishing resorts and eco lodges on east of Isla Brava have private docks near Boca Chica. They shuttle their fly-in guests from Boca Chica, sportfishing, diving. etc. If a lodge happens to be between guest weeks, maybe you can arrange to rent their dock or dinghy landing for a few days. Hail them on VHF 16 and see what their situation is like at present.

Islas Ladrones

Located about 15 n.m. SSW of Isla Parida or about 27 n.m. SE of Punta Burica, the tiny Ladrones (Thieves) consist of 3 rocky islands in a 1-mile wide U-shape and numerous detached rocks and reefs. Ladrones Light (07°52'N, 82°26'W) stands on the larger middle island.

The Ladrones Bank (18' to 150' patches) extends about 5 n.m. NNE from the islands. These islands and banks provide excellent sportfishing but no anchorage that we know of.

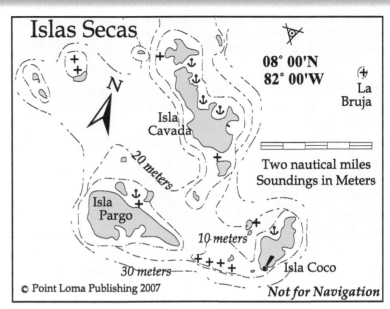

*Two nautical miles
Soundings in Meters*

© Point Loma Publishing 2007   *Not for Navigation*

Islas Secas

About 20 miles SE of Isla Parida are the Islas Secas (Dry Islands). The main group of the Secas consists of 3 high, wooded islands forming a 3.5 n.m. triangle: Isla Pargo (SW), Isla Coco (SE) and Isla Cavada (N). Islas Secas Light (about 07°57'N, 82°01'W) stands on the south corner of Isla Coco.

At least 3 detached features rise within 3 n.m. west, north and east of Isla Cavada. But the most hazardous is La Bruja, a dangerous rock pinnacle rising from 60' depths to only about 2' above the surface (difficult to see), lying 3 n.m. east of the north end of Isla Cavada.

Isla Cavada has 4 picturesque coves along its

Isla Cavada at the Secas is a private island but you can anchor off.

Sunset at Isla Pargo in the Secas.
Photo by Scott Atkins.

side, all fairly shallow (8' to 16') and open to north and east wind. Cavada is a private island with an expensive eco-resort and private dock; visitors prohibited. The resort's yurts overlook the coves, its private dock is in another cove on Cavada's east side, and the resort has a private airstrip on Cavada – which we assume is available in emergency. Otherwise, for security reasons, yatistas are asked not to come ashore.

Isla Pargo's picturesque anchorage (07°57.7'N, 82°02.9'W) is off its north side, between 2 off-lying islets, in 20' to 25' over sand. The western islet has good snorkeling. The beach on Pargo is white sand, and a stream runs out at its west end. A trail runs from the east end of that beach over the island to its easternmost tip.

Isla Coco has a cove on its north side where anchoring may be possible. Numerous rocks and reefs lie within the Secas' triangle, which is rather deep, and a reef blocks the middle third of the mile-wide south opening. Dive charter boats visit the south side of Isla Pargo and the south reef. Cavada means concave or carved out.

Canal de Afuera: Occasional ship traffic between Remedios and Bahía Montijo funnels through the 4-mile wide Canal de Afuera, which is framed by the lighted SW of Isla Canal de Afuera (7°41.8'N, 81°38.4'W) and the NE side of tall Isla Ranchería. Submerged danger La Viuda (the Widow) lies about .75 of a mile NE of Isla Ranchería.

Bahía Honda

Bahía Honda ("*OWN-dah*" or deep) is a well-sheltered bay with good anchorages, a remote village and almost no development. Bahía Honda on the Veraguas peninsula is a popular overnight stop for yatistas and sportfishers, but it has no fuel dock or shore services; 3 bars on Isla Talon.

Approach: In the province of Veraguas, Bahía Honda lies about 33 n.m. SE from Islas Secas, or about 13 n.m. NE from the north tip of Isla Coiba. From the north side of Isla Canal de Afuera (7°41.8'N, 81°38.4'W), the .75-mile-wide entrance to Bahía Honda lies 5.25 n.m. ENE, and you pass south of Isla Canal de Tierra (Isla Medidor, 2 anchorages, science station). Punta Jabali at the south side of the entrance has visible rocks protruding, and Punta de Miel at the north side is steep to, but a shoal spot lies a few 100 yards around the corner to the north.

Anchorage: Isla Talon (.75 n.m. N-W) divides the bay E-W, and east of it the bay shallows into mud flats. The deeper western half (1.5 n.m. by 1.5 n.m.) has 3 coves along the west wall below steep ridges with good protection and holding, including the middle one, Playa del Sol (7°45.9'N, 81°31.7'W), which has become a yatista hangout. The north one is shallowest. Along the north wall of this outer part of Bahía Honda are a few shallower spots beyond a small

Bahía Honda

mud flats

10
1
5
8
Isla 15
Talon
15

Punta de Miel

07° 44.0'N
081° 32.6'W
29

Punta Jabali

N

Two nautical miles
Soundings in Meters
Not for Navigation

© Point Loma Publishing 2007

Village on Isla Talon in Bahía Honda is the only population in miles, no paved road in.

islet, but good anchoring shelter can be found there as well.

If mosquitoes are too bad inside Bahía Honda, some yatistas anchor outside, off the south side of Isla Canal de Tierra (Isla Medidor), but the strong current sometimes makes that spot uncomfortable for overnighting.

A sportfishing lodge in the north end of the bay has opened and closed a couple times. No paved road penetrates the mountains surrounding Bahía Honda, so life moves in small boats. The village is mostly on the east side of Isla Talon, which has deeper water around the south end of the island. The village has almost no supplies, but the natives are friendly and eager to trade their fresh fruits and fish for canned meats or school supplies.

Isla Coiba

Coiba (pronounced "*koh-EE-bah*") is the largest island (25 n.m N-SE) in the Pacific Americas, and it's the core of Coiba National Park & Special Zone of Marine Protection (includes Islas Brincanco, Isla Uvas, Isla Canal de Afuera and the nearby islands Ranchería, Cocos, Jicarón and Jicarita).

Coiba Island's lush mountainous interior rises to 1,372' at Cerro San Juan at the center behind Damas

Bay. Punta Baltazar at Coiba's north tip lies about 14 n.m SW of Bahía Honda via Isla Canal de Afuera. Punta Anegada at Coiba's SE tip lies about 43 n.m. NW of Punta Naranjo on the mainland. Sometimes shrouded in mist, Coiba has many pristine jungle-clad coves, islands and coral reefs.

Coiba National Park: Unfortunately, this last pristine remnant of tropical marine rainforest in the Eastern Pacific (UNESCO World Heritage Site) is facing rapid destruction by tourism, illegal logging and commercial fishing. A law designed to protect Coiba National Park's wider area (including Isla Montuosa, Hannibal Bank and the finger of deep water between them) was changed to shrink the park and to permit hotel developments on shore. After the penal colony and its armed police were removed, nothing now prevents chain-saw theft of the few remaining hardwood trees, long-lining off Coiba's west side, silting, turtle egg hunting, damage to the

Anchorage & beach off north side of Isla Canal de Afuera, off Coiba.

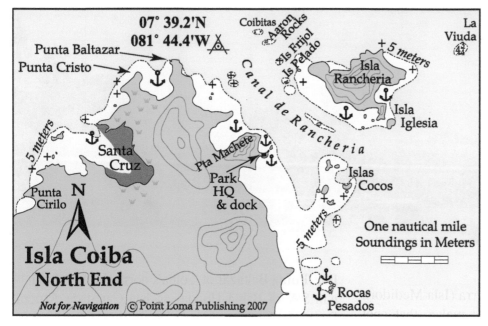

07° 39.2'N
081° 44.4'W

Punta Baltazar
Punta Cristo
Coibitas
Aaron Rocks
Is Frijol
Is Pelado
Canal de Rancheria
Isla Rancheria
La Viuda
+5 meters
Isla Iglesia
5 meters
Santa Cruz
Pta Machete
Islas Cocos
Punta Cirilo
N
Park HQ & dock
5 meters
One nautical mile
Soundings in Meters

Isla Coiba
North End

Rocas Pesados

Not for Navigation © Point Loma Publishing 2007

largest coral reef in the Central Eastern Pacific and rampant poaching of the 1,979 species of exotic or endangered flora and fauna – such as the endemic Coiba agouti and scarlet macaw. It's a hot issue as we go to press - as are huge fees that come and go.

Park rules prohibit pumping your head overboard, taking anything or leaving anything. You can anchor anywhere except near coral. If you wish to step ashore on Coiba, first check in at the park headquarters (and ANAM research station) in the tiny beach-lined bay immediately SE of Punta Machete, where you pay a fee to hike the trails with a researcher.

Anchorages: Coiba has half a dozen anchorages useful for varying wind and sea conditions, but we think the best all-around spots are mostly on the north end. Because this area is only 7° N of the Equator and within the Inter-tropical Convergence Zone, the weather is normally hot and calm. And these are useful in summer south weather as well.

Ensenada Santa Cruz (2 n.m. SW of Punta Baltazar) is large but shallow at its head. We anchor here in flat conditions out by the points. The estuaries around this bay bring bugs.

Machete Bay (07°37.8'N, 81°43.6'W) is a semi-circular bay and anchorage about 2.5 n.m. SE of Punta Baltazar or immediately NW of the steep landmark Punta Machete. We anchor here in 18' to 36' between the points. Ashore, the old fishing lodge used by ANAM may be torn down. A lot of beach uncovers at low tides.

Park Cove is immediately south of Punta Machete. You can anchor here and use the dinghy pier to reach the park headquarters ashore. Or anchor just south of this cove and dink around through the pass inside the islet.

Isla Ranchería (425' high) has shelter off the beach on its SW side, anchoring in 10' to 18' on a shelf off the north side of the very tidal Canal de Ranchería. The island has a SE cove just north of Isla Iglesia where we've seen boats anchor in north winds. Moving south, the Islas Cocos look inviting, but we haven't anchored here.

Rocas Pesadas (Granito de Oro or Gold Nugget) is a delightful dinghy excursion, but avoid anchoring near the coral structures that give this collection of islets its white beach. Local dive boats have set moorings south of the island.

Damas Bay, the 6-mile wide bight into Coiba's east side, contains 324 acres of coral reef. Rocks and reef line the north and south ends of Damas Bay, and the west side is a shallow shelf that likewise prevents good anchorage.

If circumnavigating Isla Coiba, avoid several hazards off its SW side: Logan Rock about 3.5 n.m. SE of Punta Brigida (07°22'N, 81°47'W); Passage Rocks

*Anchorage off Isla Ranchería,
off NE end of Isla Coiba.*

Coiba Island National Park has hikes to interior falls.

about 4.6 n.m. SE of Punta Brigida; Isla Barco Quebrado (you know what that means) and its eastern reef within a mile south of Punta Recimo; the two Hill Rocks at 2.6 n.m. south of Punta Recimo and 5.5 n.m. WSW of Punta Anegada; a patch of foul ground about 2 n.m SSW of Punta Anegada; detached rocks half a mile east of Punta Anegada; a reef patch extending 1.25 n.m. north of Punta Anegada; detached rocks about 2.1 n.m. ESE of Punta Fea – probably a few more yet to be discovered.

History & Culture: Archeologists think the Coiba Chiriquí people lived from about 500 BC onward until the Spanish arrived. English pirates and raiders like Sir Francis Drake and Commodore George Anson evaded Spanish warships by reprovisioning and re-outfitting their vessels here.

After a prison colony was built here in 1919, most of Coiba's 140,000 acres escaped development. Prison camps were in Damas Bay and Ensenada Hermosa (west side). In the 1970s, a fly-in sportfishing resort sprouted in Machete Bay, later down sized and used as a biological research station. Some prisoners escaped, commandeered a cruising sailboat at anchor, killed a man and forced his wife to take them to Bahía Montijo where they fled. When the prison was removed from Coiba in 2005, some cows, dogs and pigs left behind went feral. The island's protected status is endangered. Please tread lightly.

Azuero Peninsula

The vast bulk of the Azuero Peninsula forms the western arm of Panama Bay from Bahía Parida down to Punta Mala, Punta Morro de Puercos and Punta Naranjo. Strong ocean currents run along its south and east shoreline.

The Azuero Peninsula was explored and colonized at the beginning of the Spanish occupation, so its many small hamlets still resemble medieval Spain. Unfortunately, the Azuero is also mostly devoid of forests for that same reason. Along the shores, a few miles of unreachable old-growth trees and impenetrable jungle are visible to passing boats, but the interior mountains are mostly bald. The gently sloping eastern plains of the peninsula are traversed by roads, while the more mountainous western interior is still quite wild. Only one paved road runs along the peninsula's western shore, ending 25 miles north of Naranjo Cove.

Fortunately, Panama has reserved 6 ecological territories of the Azuero in parks: Penon de la Onda Wildlife Preserve near Chitre; Isla Iguana Wildlife Reserve just north of Punta Mala; Isla Cañas Wildlife Preserve near Benao; La Tronosa Forest Reserve near Playa Cambutal at Punta Morro de Puercos Cerro Hoya National Park at Punta Naranjo; Montuosa

Howler monkeys travel in family troops. Photo by Scott Atkins.

Anchorage at Naranjo Cove is the last gunk hole before entering the shipping lanes.

Forest Reserve on the east side of Montijo Bay.

We have not included shallow Montijo Bay but do visit Naranjo and Benao en route to Balboa and the canal. The Montijo Bay is fed by hundreds of rivers draining the province of Veraguas, so debris is a hazard, especially in rainy season. However, the fishing is reported to be excellent and the gulf's shores offer dozens of coves and islands for exploration by shallow-draft vessels.

Naranjo Cove is a small 2-part indent less than 2 n.m. NE of ridge-crested Punta Naranjo and its near-shore mile-long Islote Roncador (someone who snores). The anchorage is open to the west and NW, the bottom has poor holding and swell at high tide can make it rolly. Set bow and stern hooks to keep facing the swell.

No road comes in here, and a boundary of Cerro Hoya National Park is just south of Naranjo Cove. An old logging road across the highlands comes out at Punta Mariato light. Don't mistake Isla Roncador for Islote Restinque on the south side of Punta Naranjo.

Naranjo Cove

This marginal anchorage (about 7°16.49'N, 80°55.6'W) lies about 40 n.m. east of Coiba's south tip (Punta Anegada) and 5 n.m. NW of lighted Punta Mariato on the SW corner of the Azuero Peninsula. Being about 65 n.m. from Punta Mala, it may serve as a staging stop for getting around that bad old point.

The SW tip of Isla Cebaco lies about 23 n.m. NW of here, and the shallow Montijo Bay lies north of Cebaco. Avoid rocks off both ends of Isla Cebaco.

Benao Cove

The steep-to coastline along the south face of the Azuero Peninsula runs generally east-west and is clad in recently logged jungle. From late December through March, the Caribbean Trade Winds blow strongly across the low Isthmus of Panama in a condition similar to that of the Gulfs of Tehuantepec and Papagallo. If you're sailing or powering from the canal toward Costa Rica, it can be fine traveling weather.

But if you're bound toward Balboa and trying to round Punta Mala, it can be rough bashing into head winds and seas. In that case, you can find anchoring shelter at Benao Cove (7°25.5'N, 80°11.3'W), also called Venado on some charts.

NOTE: During rainy season, Benao Cove can be a dangerous lee shore – not an anchorage.

Benao Cove lies 13.5 n.m. WSW of Punta Mala and 4 n.m NW of Roca Fraile del Norte, the northern of the 2 prominent Las Frailes islands.

Crew member Scott Atkins stands watch in typical downpour along south coast of the Azuero Peninsula.

Fraile Sur is smaller and carries a nav light. Both the Frailes are often mistaken for ships.

This crescent cove is less than a mile wide and fairly shallow at the head, but in north wind we anchor in 25' to 30' of sheltered water. The wind blows hard off the hills, but the bottom is good holding. In a long blow, Benao can get crowded. An alternative spot is 5.25 n.m west off Isla de Cañas (Isla Raya).

Several small hotels and palapas on Playa Benao have food and phone, and a bus connects Benao Cove to Las Tablas on the NE shore of the Azuero Peninsula.

Departure: Do not be deceived by the wind in the anchorage. Often it will be blowing hard inside the anchorage but only moderately around Punta Mala.

On the other hand, Punta Mala can generate some "cape effect" wind. If you don't have a reliable WX forecast for Panama Bay, you might want to hail another yacht or ship that has just come down around Punta Mala to ask for their weather observations. Otherwise, you may have to poke your nose around the corner out and give it a try.

Punta Mala

This major headland (Punta Mala Light 7°28.2'N, 80°00.0'W) is aptly named. About 100 miles SSW of Balboa via the east sides of Isla Bona and Isla Taboguilla, Punta Mala is the single most congested turning point for all ships from North America and the Pacific, bound to or from the Panama Canal, including super tankers, small fishing boats, ocean-going tugs towing barges and yachts – all going in both directions. Although you must follow "Rules of the Road," the alternate rule of "Might is Right" takes over here. So stay out of the shipping lanes.

Punta Mala is the more southerly of this 2-pointed cape's protrusions, and it carries a racon M (*dah-dah*) and a reliable 13-mile nav light that's visible from Isla Iguana (9 n.m. north) and from the 2 Los Frailes islands (11.5 n.m. SW). Isla Iguana and Frailes Sur also carry lesser nav lights.

Anchorage off Isla Bono near Isla Otoque is handy for timing your approach to Balboa.

The strong current, an offshoot of the counter-Equatorial current, usually runs from north to south along this side of Panama Bay, and the wind blows at times strongly from the same direction.

Punta Mala does have some "cape effect" winds, so you may not know what's happening in Bahía Panama until you round the corner.

Your radar and visibility can often be blinded for an hour or more by widespread rain squalls, so always keep track of each vessel and be prepared to avoid collision. No boat should go through this area without radar.

Rounding Punta Mala: The main shipping lanes between Punta Mala and the Panama Canal sea buoy (8°51.5'N, 79°29.0'W) are in deep water, so they round Punta Mala about 2.5 to 3 n.m. off shore. You can avoid this intense traffic by rounding it a bit closer to shore – about 2 n.m. out.

When we're northbound, we usually round Punta Mala and lay a straight course for Isla Bona (08°33.8'N, 79°39.2'W). This will give us a course parallel to, but west of, the shipping lanes. Though we'll constantly have shipping on our starboard horizon, rarely will we have to change course for big ships. However, we're always on the lookout for fishing boats doing the same tactic.

Isla Otoque

During daylight hours we may pass between Isla Bona and Isla Otoque (pronounced "*oh-TOE-kay*"), avoiding a rock between the 2 by favoring the passage toward Otoque. A small fishing village is on the north side of Isla Otoque.

A good anchorage in north wind is found on the south side of Otoque, west of tiny Isla Estiva. Another

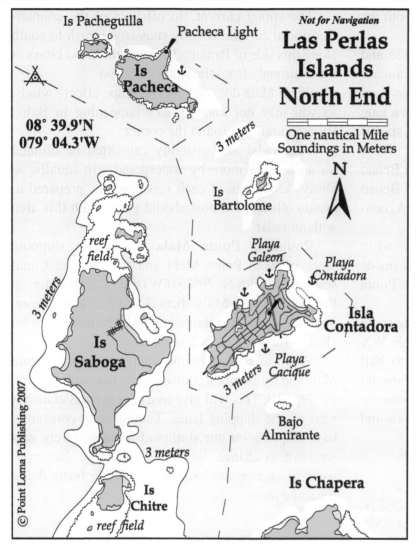

Not for Navigation

Las Perlas Islands North End

Is Pacheguilla
Pacheca Light
Is Pacheca

08° 39.9'N
079° 04.3'W

3 meters

One nautical Mile
Soundings in Meters

N

reef field

3 meters

Is Saboga

Is Bartolome

Playa Galeon

Playa Contadora

Isla Contadora

3 meters

Playa Cacique

Bajo Almirante

3 meters

Is Chapera

Is Chitre

reef field

© Point Loma Publishing 2007

1-boat anchorage is on the west side of Isla Bona, beneath the ruins of a rusting mining relic. Though it's only 17 n.m. from here to the Balboa sea buoy, we've occasionally used these anchorages as a rest stop when fighting a Norther.

Sailing skippers can take advantage of a favorable slant from Punta Mala by reaching out to the Perlas Islands. This puts you in a good position to sail toward Balboa on the other tack with aid from the current.

Las Perlas Islands

Las Perlas Islands in the NE quadrant of Panama Bay are a huge (30 n.m. N-W, 20 n.m. E-W) and increasingly popular cruising ground. They contain about 200 islands big and small and numerous reefs and beaches, but only a few population centers.

Yatistas can spend months cruising the Perlas, because the variety of anchorages are good for different weather directions (basically north wind in

dry season, south in rainy season), and the islands are 40 n.m. to 70 n.m. from Balboa and Panama City. These beaches are almost as lovely as those in the San Blas Islands on the Caribbean side, and the Trade Winds are not as persistent here.

For a complete guide to cruising the Perlas Islands, we highly recommend *The Panama Cruising Guide* by Eric Bauhaus or *The Panama Guide* by the Zydlers. Meanwhile, here are a few Perlas anchorages to get you started.

In the northern half of the Perlas, Isla Contadora was known for the Contadora Peace Process, but in 2006 Contadora and its neighbor Saboga grabbed media attention when the TV show "*Survivor*" was filmed here - spurring resort development and upping land prices in the Perlas.

Dominating the south half of the Perlas, the 3 largest islands are Isla del Rey, Isla San Jose and Isla Pedro Gonzales.

Pacheca, Saboga & Contadora

Pacheca Island is the northernmost of the Perlas. This 150-acre island is marked by Pacheca Light (08°40'N, 79°03'W) on its NE corner. Tiny Pachequilla (Pacheguilla) islet lies close off its NW corner. Pacheca is privately owned.

From Balboa, approach along the SW side of the island (Pacheca Canal). Avoid rocks off Pacheca's SE point. Yachts anchor in the pretty bay forming Pacheca's NE side, 18' to 24' over sand. The dock and island are private property.

Bartolome Shoal (less than 2') is about half a mile SE of Contadora's SE tip. Isla Bartolome (1 n.m. SE of Contadora) makes a good dinghy excursion.

Saboga Island lies 2 n.m. SSW from Pacheca. The wooded mass of Isla Saboga stretches 2 n.m. N-S, about 1 n.m. E-W. But at its north end you must add 1 n.m. to include 9 islets (at least 1 has a house) within a wide patch of rocky shoals jutting north.

On Saboga's south end, Isla Chitre stands in the middle of another 1-mile shoal patch that juts SSW. If approaching Saboga from SW, avoid Isla Santa Catalina (sometimes awash or breaking) about 1.8

n.m. south of reef-ringed Isla Chitre.

Most of Saboga is wild, but Saboga village is found at the north end of the half-mile wide bight on the island's NE side. Rocks and shoals occupy all but the north edge of this bay. Water taxis run the 650-yard channel between Saboga and Contadora.

Contadora Island: Only 1.5 n.m. in length, Contadora has most of the 300 residents of the Perlas, an airport, a shopping center and 2 resorts that have welcomed yatistas - but gated beach mansions do not. Cruise ships anchor off and shuttle passengers ashore with private contracts.

Off Contadora's south side, yatistas can anchor (15' to 40') about anywhere along the middle stretch, or SW of Playa Fea (dark sand) at the south end of the runway, or off Playa Cacique (longest beach on south side). Or, anchor off the nudist beach at Contadora's SE end.

Off the island's north side, the most convenient anchorage is off Playa Galeon (about 08°38.06'N, 79°02.09'W), because you can use the hospitable Punta Galeon Resort (buy food or drinks) for shore access. The shopping center just south of this resort (NW of the airport) caters to tourists. A public dock is below the resort.

Or, anchor well off the prestigious Contadora Resort, outside the shoal shielding Playa Larga. We've anchored a quarter mile east of Punta Bella Vista and north of Punta Verde, then dinked around the north end of the bar. Ask permission to come ashore here.

About 15 small islands and numerous detached reefs spread across the 10-n.m. swath from Isla Contadora SSE to the north end of Isla del Rey, and local knowledge is required.

Bahía del Rey is the 15 n.m. long sound running N-S along the west side of Isla del Rey and east of Isla Pedro Gonzales and Isla San Jose. North Passage is the 3-mile wide entrance (between Isla Bayonet and Isla Señora) to Bahía del Rey from the NW (38 n.m. SE of Balboa), and South Passage is 6-mile wide opening between Isla San Jose and Isla del Rey – most easily approached from Punta Mala.

Isla San Jose

Second-largest island in the Perlas Archipelago, Isla San Jose lies 70 n.m. NE of Punta Mala. Isla San Jose Light (08°12.8'N, 79°07.8'W) marks the hilly SW façade. Privately owned, this 6-mile long island has no town, but 2 bays can provide shelter from north or south weather.

In light southerlies, Bodega Bay on the west side lies about 4 n.m. north of the rocky south end of the island. Shielded behind Isla Bodega, this half-mile wide slot (approach about 08°15.70'N, 79°08.07'W) is open to north wind. And in strong south conditions, swell does wrap the point. Legends say pirates reprovisioned here, hence the name Bodega or Pantry. The stream at the head of the bay pierces the island deeply.

In north wind, Ensenada Playa Grande on San Jose's east side offers several anchoring spots. This 1.2 n.m.-wide bay lies about 3 n.m. NE of the south end of Isla San Jose. Yachts anchor below the cliffs in the north end (33' over sand) and SW end (30') of the bay.

CAUTION: When traversing the SE side of Isla San Jose, stay at least 1.25 n.m. east of Isla Hicaco, which appears as the southernmost point of the island, due to detached rocks east of the 2 detached rocks: Isla Tres Pilas de Arros and Isla Marín.

Isla del Rey

At the SE edge of the archipelago, this largest of

The Perlas are beautiful, but don't you can't ignore the max 20' tides. This was a wide sand beach a couple hours ago.

Nameless stream pours from jungle into Bahía San Telmo on Isla del Rey in the Perlas Islands.

the south beach. The airport was used in 2006 (possibly by real estate developers); keep it in mind for medical emergencies.

Esmeralda village on the SW shore of Bahía San Telmo lies about 2.5 n.m. NW of the Cocos anchorage, but avoid rocks off the intervening point and off the village on approach. In north wind, you may want to move 2.25 n.m. NNE for better shelter in the dramatic cleft at the mouth of Rio Cacique, at about 08°17.75'N, 78°54.19'W. About 3 n.m. SE of Rio Cacique, all of Isla San Telmo is a nature preserve, and the 1.25 n.m. reef connecting it to Isla del Rey makes good snorkeling. Isla Galera (08°11.7'N, 78°46.6'W) lies about 5.5 n.m. SE of Isla San Telmo, but Galera is ringed in reefs and rip currents.

Darien Jungle: The Darien Jungle east of Las Perlas is one of the most pristine tropical rainforests in Central America – much of it a biosphere reserve. But if you plan to venture more than a mile into these maze-like bayous, be sure to hire a local guide. Some will transport you by cayuca or panga up-river to the remote villages, while others will lead your boat in through the tricky spots.

the Perlas rises to 736' in deforested peaks and covers about 400 square miles. Isla del Rey has 2 villages, San Miguel at its north end and Esmeralda at its south end in Bahía San Telmo.

Bahía San Telmo is the 3.5 n.m.-wide bay forming the island's SE side, and it provides shelter from north and south winds in at least 2 anchorages.

From Punta Mala, Isla del Rey lies 80 n.m. NE, and its prominent and curving southern tip, Punta Cocos (08°13'N, 78°54'W), has 2 hazards: a rock islet reported on a shoal about .4 of a mile south; a rock on a shoal about 1 n.m. east of the point.

In south weather, sheltered anchorage is found in the half-mile crescent bay on the north side of Punta Cocos. Anchor west of the cliffs or anywhere off

Tribes live in open thatch-roofed huts on stilts over the water. Tribal men carve tagua nuts and cocobolo wood into delicate sea creatures and jungle birds, while the women weave baskets and bowls so tightly that some can hold water. As with the Kuna of San Blas, some handicrafts are made just for selling to visitors. In recent years, we've found these beautiful Darien handicrafts in the market stalls of Panama City, many of excellent quality and inexpensive.

Yachts anchor north or south of El Morro off Taboga Island's NE side. Note ships anchored upper right.

Dinks anchor off Taboga ferry pier. El Morro is in background.

Taboga Island

In the NW quadrant of Panama Bay, Taboga Island (1,013' high) is the largest of a cluster of small islands near the entrance to the Panama Canal and ship anchorages. The anchorages on Taboga's NE side lie 5 n.m. SW of the Panama Canal sea buoy.

During the week, Taboga's tranquility and rustic ambiance make it an interesting day excursion from the marinas or a handy free anchorage while awaiting transit. On weekends, it's a zoo.

Las Flores (pop. about 950) is the only village on Taboga, and cars are prohibited. (A few high-speed golf carts are used by maintenance crews.)

The village has a municipal dock (ferries & dinks), a grocery store, mini-mart, half a dozen restaurants or beach cafes, 2 or 3 hotels, a few B & Bs, an interesting plaza and historic church and – best of all – 2 passenger ferries to Balboa. Taboga Island National Wildlife Refuge is on the island's undeveloped west side.

Approach: Even in driving rain, Taboga's steep slopes paint a pretty good radar image. Other islands in the Taboga group lie off its east side: El Morro (NE tip), Taboguilla (SW side), Uravá (SSW side) and tiny Tarapa (south tip).

Taboguilla Island (08°48.2'N, 79°30.6'W) carries 2 nav lights on its north and east sides – closest to the big ship approaches to the canal. The processing plant on its NW side is active. The large rock called Isla Tarapa on Taboga's south tip also has a nav light.

TIP: Avoid the dangerous steep-sided reef (6' to 15' of water reported over some pinnacles) that circles Taboguilla's SE side about .25 of a mile off shore. Scuba divers who frequent the large reef may not have flags or buoys.

Moorings: Hail Taboga Island Mooring Service on VHF 74; former cruiser have 11 safe moorings.

Anchorage: In north wind, the preferred anchorage (15' to 30') is close south of tiny El Morro, which is connected at low tides to Taboga's NE tip. This has some north-wind shelter but is shared with excursion boats and the ferry approach. In south wind, yachts anchor north of the sand bar. For a fee, dinghies can be left on the backside of the ferry dock, which has a security guard at the top of the ramp.

The anchorage between Taboga and Taboguilla is better during southerly weather. It is roomier but deeper (50' or more) and visited by small freighters and ACP boats.

History & Culture: Taboga village (Las Flores) has been populated since 1515, and here Francisco Pizarro home-ported his entire fleet of conquest over

Las Flores beach sea wall is a good place to paint your panga. Locals use peeler logs as rollers.

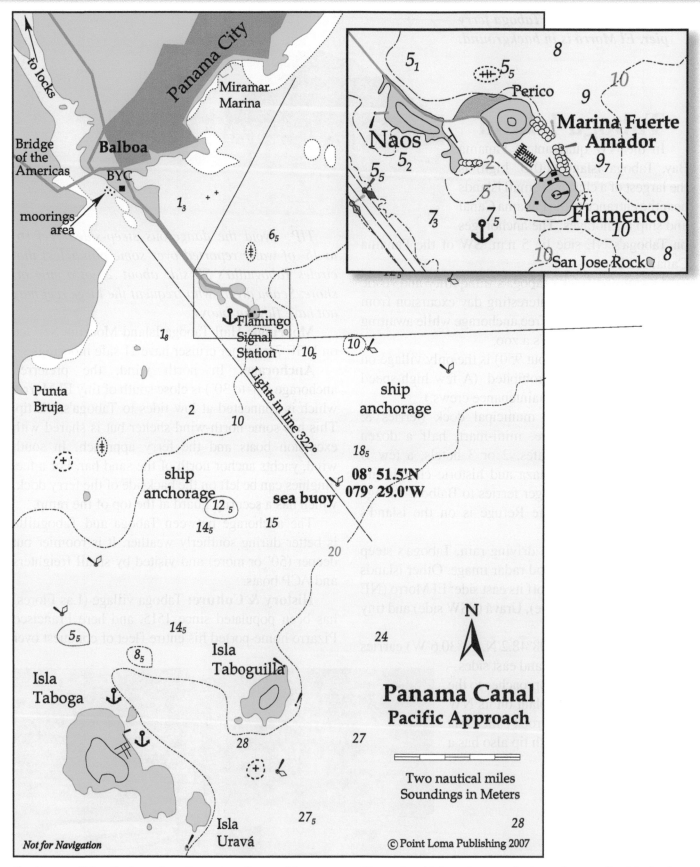

Balboa

BYC

Bridge of the Americas

to locks

moorings area

Punta Bruja

Panama City

Miramar Marina

Flamingo Signal Station

Lights in line 322°

ship anchorage

sea buoy

08° 51.5'N
079° 29.0'W

ship anchorage

ship anchorage

Isla Taboga

Isla Taboguilla

Isla Uravá

Naos

Perico

Marina Fuerte Amador

Flamenco

San Jose Rock

N

Panama Canal
Pacific Approach

Two nautical miles
Soundings in Meters

Not for Navigation

© Point Loma Publishing 2007

the Incas of South America. Savoring the cool breeze, French canal builders put their hospital for yellow-fever victims here, and among the survivors was Paul Gauguin. Taboga's population almost doubled after 2000, and many of the funky little houses are being sold for big balboas. The historic Taboga Hotel is

Looking south into yacht basin of Fuerte Amador Marina & Resort - Flamenco Yacht Club.

being rebuilt; it was sagging dangerously. We hope Taboga Island will remain a pedestrian paradise sans cars, because the narrow paths have public flower gardens, shady benches and foot bridges. Rental bicycles and scooters abound. Trails lead up to Cerro San Pedro (Tres Cruces) and Cerro Vigía above town, or south to Cerro La Cruz. The lush jungle of Taboga Island National Wildlife Refuge covers most of the western slopes except Los Morillos on the SW corner.

Balboa & Panama City

The busy commercial port of Balboa dominates the NE side of the entrance to the Panama Canal. East of Balboa, Panama City has a dramatic downtown skyline.

Balboa is a good staging port when preparing for transit or recovering after transit. Balboa has 2 marinas (Flamenco Yacht Club, Balboa Yacht Club), fuel docks, haul-out facilities, modern shopping centers, chandlers, fishing tackle shops, interesting shore excursions, etc.

NE of the Bridge of the Americas are Balboa's commercial piers and the Taboga ferry terminal, and east of the piers are the ACP Administration Building, Ancon Hill and Albrook Airport. On the west side of the canal, the former Rodman Naval Base is now commercial shipping. Puente Centenario, the ultra-modern bridge is upstream toward Mira Mar.

Panama City has a surprisingly vertical skyline. Marina Miramar is right downtown, and nearby are many marine chandlers, marine services, grocery stores, banks and restaurants. If you're flying in or out of Panama, you'll do so at Panama City's Tocumen international airport well to the east of town.

CAUTION: Yatistas entering the Pacific at Balboa are shocked by the average 18' tidal range (max 22'), because on the Atlantic side it was 3' or less. At non-floating docks use longer dock lines to allow for this huge diurnal rise and fall. Don't let your rail get wedged beneath a dock as the tide rises. If you're gone for long, leave someone aboard to tend lines. Adjust your mental depth sounder too.

Approach: If you're arriving in Balboa from the Pacific Ocean, when you are within VHF range, call "Flamenco Signal Station" on VHF 16 or 12 to request admittance to the Panama Canal region.

Fuerte Amador's marina has big pilings for radical tides, plenty of water depth.

Haul-out yard on Isla Flamenco has big lift. Note the size of the 2 men under the bow. Note size of fenders on same bow.

(*Flamenco* is Spanish for Flamingo, and you'll hear both, but Spanish is the official language here.) Tell the controller your boat name, kind of boat (i.e. 36' sailboat, or 120' motoryacht, whatever) and your speed, and tell them your ETA at the Balboa sea buoy (8°51.5'N, 79° 29.0'W). From here on, you're under their control, much like airline pilots at an international airport. Follow the instructions given.

Balboa ship anchorage (east of the approach line) and south of Flamenco Island (08°54.5'N, 79°31.2'W) may have dozens of ships, some anchored, some underway. Also, north of Taboguilla Island (west of the approach line), ships and tugs may be picking up pilots just before transit. Be sure you know which ships, tugs and pilot boats are underway, which are anchored, before approaching Balboa sea buoy. Use your radar's plot mode.

Call Flamenco Signal again when you're at the sea buoy; it rides about 3 n.m. SSE of Flamenco Island. The east side of the ship channel is backed by 4 small islands connected by a causeway; the islands are (S-N) Isla Flamenco, Isla Perico, Isla Culebra and Isla Naos. You may be directed to La Playita, which is the boarding anchorage close west of Isla Flamenco, just east of the main ship channel.

(If you just finished transiting the Panama Canal,

your Pilot or Transit Advisor will have informed the ACP of your immediate plans by radio, and the ACP will have given you permission to leave the canal and proceed somewhere: to a mooring at the Balboa Yacht Club; a slip at Fuerte Amador Marina on the opposite (east) side of the Flamenco Island peninsula; to Marina Miramar in Panama City; to anchor at Taboga Island – or to proceed directly to sea.)

Port Clearance: Balboa port officers bring all required forms, and you present your ship's papers, everyone's passports and your Panamanian Cruising Permit from your Port of Entry. If Balboa is your first Port of Entry, present your Zarpe from the last country and get your Cruising Permit here.

If you're entering to transit, read the Panama Canal Transit chapter.

If you're leaving after transit, get Flamenco Signal Station's permission (VHF 12 & 16) to proceed to wherever. Don't enter the Main Ship Channel without permission.

Anchorage: La Playita de Amador yacht anchorage is between the Main Ship Channel and the causeway, in the cove NW of Isla Flamenco. A breakwater off tiny Isla Culebra divides this cove, and yachts anchor in the more sheltered NW part east of Isla Culebra. The dock has diesel, a restaurant and shore access. Moorings are available. A marina may be built in La Playita. For canal expansion, the ACP may eliminate La Playita yacht anchorage; no date was released as we go to press.

Naos North is a possible anchorage in south weather, but construction west of Isla Perico may nix it. This area on the NE side of the causeway opposite Isla Naos has depths 13' to

Balboa Yacht Club's moorings, fuel pier to left, Taboga Island upper right.

18' – but it's not an official anchorage.

Berthing: We hope another marina for ocean-going yachts will be built soon to relieve the slip shortage in the Balboa – Panama City region, especially if the ACP eliminates many of Balboa Yacht Club's moorings for canal expansion.

(1.) Fuerte Amador Marina & Resort is on the opposite side of the causeway from the canal. When rounding Isla Flamenco's south side, avoid a shoal .25 of a mile SSW of the island and a lighted rock half a mile SE of the island. Fuerte Amador Marina is a busy harbor behind 2 lighted breakwaters between the NW side of Isla Flamenco and the SE side of Isla Perico. Our GPS approach position is 08°54.7'N, 79°31.3'W.

Inside is Flamenco Yacht Club (VHF 10) (new phone 507-314-1980) has 200 full-service slips for yachts to 135' and moorings with dink-landing service, plus nice shore facilities. Also called Flamenco Marina, it opened in 2005. This same harbor has a busy fuel dock, big boat yard, ferry dock, cruise-ship shuttle landing, shopping center and hotel. FMI, visit Fuerte Amador Marina & Resort's new website www. flamenco-island.com.

(2.) Balboa Yacht Club (VHF 06) has a field of 80 moorings located 2.5 n.m. NW of Isla Flamenco, very close off the east side of the main ship channel but before you reach the Bridge of the Americas. Only the club's skiff shuttles guests to shore and back (free, but we suggest $1/person tip); dinks are prohibited for security. The elevated pier has a floating fuel platform at its SW end, 4 work slips alongside. The historic clubhouse burned down years ago, but BYC has a tent-covered cantina, pool and 2 marine ways for bottom jobs. The public malecon crosses the property, and a new clubhouse is planned. A 5-story Country Inns hotel overlooks the moorings, handy for fly-in guests.

Hail the BYC moorings office (VHF 06) in advance. To avoid shoals, don't turn out of the main ship channel until you're abeam the BYC fuel pier (between red buoys #14-1/2 and #16), then make your 90° turn into the club's fairway (200' wide down the middle of the mooring field) leading to the fuel pier.

BYC shore boat transports you to and from moorings. Dinghies prohibited.

Honk and wait in the fairway until the club skiff comes to lead you to an available mooring. Be prepared for wakes from passing ships and strong tidal current when lock gates are opened. FMI about Balboa Yacht Club, call (507) 228-5794.

(3.) Marina Miramar (VHF 68) has 22 shallow full-service slips, part of the InterContinental Hotel (twin towers) on Panama City's downtown waterfront. At low-low tides, most boats sit on their bottoms in the mud, so it's not for everyone. Check your tide calendar; the north half of this basin dries. Miramar has a fuel barge, and the hotel amenities and location are handy.

Located 3.3 n.m. NNW from Flamenco YC, Marina Miramar shares a breakwater-enclosed basin with the private Club de Yates & Pesca (formerly Club Nautico). The lighted, baffled entrance is half a mile west of Punta Paitilla. Once inside, head east for Marina Miramar. FMI, call (507) 206-8888 or email panama@interconti.com.

4.) Club de Yates y Pesca is an expensive private

Ships on the Panama Canal "approach" run very close to BYC moorings, off the club's big pier & floating fuel dock. Be prepared for ship wakes 24/7.

club with 60 slips in the SW side of the shallow yacht basin shared with Marina Miramar, located half a mile west of Punta Paitilla in downtown Panama City. Get permission before approaching these docks. FMI, call Panama Club de Yates y Pesca (507) 227-0145.

Local Services: Balboa YC's clubhouse is a 2-story with veranda at the head of the big fuel pier and moorings. Diesel & gas are at Balboa Yacht Club, Fuerte Amador Marina (Flamenco Yacht Club), sometimes Marina Miramar.

Haul-out is possible at Flamenco Yacht Club by 150-ton Travelift, or 2 old ways at BYC. Commercial fishing boats haul & repair at Puerto Vacamonte 10 n.m. SW of the Balboa, reached by a buoyed 4.5-mile channel (about 20' depth) from Isla Melones (about 2.4 n.m. NW of Isla Taboga). Vacamonte is a Port of Entry requiring clearance. Some Balboa agents can make arrangements for yachts at Vacamonte.

Islamorada chart store has Central America's best supply of flags, charts & navigation supplies; 808 Balboa Ave in Balboa. FMI on Islamorada, call (507) 228-4348 or email info@islamorada.com.

Balboa & Panama City are good bets for mechanical & electronic repairs and service; ask on the morning VHF net. Both yacht clubs provide street maps and keep lists of chandlers & repair services. Taxis are safer; traffic is chaotic. English-speaking taxistas in Balboa can be gems or hustlers, so get a good referral from BYC or FYC or VHF net.

Provisioning is excellent at Albrook Mall in Balboa and in Panama City at CostCo, Sam's Club, El Rey, etc. This side of the canal is safer and more convenient to provision and run errands than Colón.

Explore Ashore: Hire a recommended taxista for the day. Panama's tourism agency sets up craft markets for the Kuna and Panama's 6 other indigenous peoples (Emberá, Wounaan, Ngobe, Buglé, Teribe or Nazo, Bokotá and Bri Bri) to sell their handicrafts. Besides the Caribbean Kuna women's brightly colored *"molas"* (reverse appliqué collectables), tribes from the Pacific Darien wilderness carve intricate animals from a large *"tagua"* nut that resembles ivory. Others use exotic *"cocobolo"* wood for carvings. Watertight baskets are another worthy souvenir. (If you buy something, your taxista may earn a free soda as a reward for bringing you in.)

Ciudad Viejo (Old City) or Panamá La Vieja on the SE edge of town makes a nice walking tour. In 1542 Spain launched its conquest of the Inca Empire from here, and Henry Morgan loved to sack this port. The Museo del Canal de Panama is housed in a graceful old building of the neoclassical style, adjacent to the Palacio Municipal in the Plaza de la Independencia in Panama City.

A short drive north of Balboa is Parque Soberana, a magnificent preserve of old-growth tropical hardwoods, lush jungle, flowers, birds and waterfalls along hiking paths. Take bug repellant if you hike close to sunset.

Balboa Yacht Club is a good rendezvous, taxi stand, cantina. Puddle Jumpers meet here.

Hey, all you West Coast yatistas! After cruising Panama's Pacific coast, to continue into your Panama Canal Transit, please skip ahead to Chapter 13 beginning on page 232.

Weather & Routing
Gulf of Mexico & Caribbean
by Amanda Delany, Meteorologist

Planning voyages from the Gulf of Mexico to Panama and vice versa requires knowing the main weather factors that affect these regions. Here's a summary of the seasonal weather conditions that occur across the Gulf of Mexico and western Caribbean, plus tips on when to travel during certain times of year.

Gulf of Mexico

The dominant weather features here are cold fronts and high pressure centers moving from the central US to the North Atlantic.

The best time to transit in these regions is from late spring through early autumn (though the tropics must be constantly monitored from June through November. See more on that below). Late spring through early autumn is when fronts remain farther north along the Gulf Coast, and the ridge of high pressure is usually weak across the Gulf of Mexico.

Gentle breezes are usually found across the Gulf during this time of year, and they allow for nonstop voyaging from Texas to Veracruz and across to Chompotón - as well as traveling from southern Florida to Quintana Roo.

Outside of tropical systems, thunderstorms are the main concern across the Gulf of Mexico, because cold fronts pass north of the Gulf and tropical waves move across the Yucatan Channel and Bay of Campeche in the summer and autumn.

Fronts during late autumn through early spring extend southward to the Bay of Campeche and track eastward through the Yucatan Channel and NW Caribbean every 2 to 3 days. Behind the front, arctic air associated with high pressure from the northern Great Plains surges southward, creating gale force northerly winds from off the Texas coast southward along the coasts of Tamiulipas and Veracruz to the western Bay of Campeche.

The worst conditions occur during winter, where storm-force conditions can develop off Veracruz. These conditions usually last 12-24 hours. As high pressure moves from the Great Plains to offshore the southeastern U.S., the associated ridge of high pressure will enhance ENE winds through the Florida Straits and across the Yucatan Channel. These higher winds can last between 3 to 5 days in this region.

It is best to transit ahead of cold fronts in the Gulf of Mexico during this time of year. However, these windows of opportunity are short-lived. Lighter southerly winds develop ahead of the front, allowing for approximately 12 to 36 hours to transit between ports before the front passes through and the strong northerly winds return across the Gulf.

Caribbean

Weather here is chiefly governed by 2 main weather features throughout the year: high pressure in the North Atlantic and the northern Caribbean; and a thermal trough of low pressure in the SW Caribbean and along the NW coast of South America.

These are fairly stationary weather features, showing little overall motion and change in strength over a given time period. But the ridge will tend to be stronger and extend farther west during the summer months than at any point during the year, becoming the "Bermuda Highs" that statesiders know for the warm, humid days synonymous with summer.

Interaction between these features will typically bring NE to easterly Trade Winds across the Caribbean. These winds become somewhat enhanced when one of these features is stronger than normal.

That is certainly the case during the winter months, when large high pressure ridges moving into the Western Atlantic merge and become part of the Atlantic ridge.

Gale force winds, occurring for several weeks at

a time, will develop along the Colombian coast from about Cartagena to Punta Gallinas and extend as far as 150 to 200 nautical miles out from the coast during winter. Conditions will finally ease in this region when the ridge of high pressure weakens across the Western Caribbean and allows about 24 to 48 hours of lighter Trade Winds before the next surge of ENE winds develop offshore Colombia.

Strong northerly winds will funnel through the Yucatan Channel and along the coasts of Quintana Roo and Belize for approximately 24 hours after a frontal passage during late November through March. As high pressure moves off shore the US East Coast, ENE winds will strengthen from Quintana Roo to the northern coast of Honduras, and then spread to the SW Caribbean.

Boat travel during this time of year should be done ahead of cold fronts in the NW Caribbean, and plan to stop frequently in ports such as Cancun, Grand Cayman, Roatán and San Andrés. Be prepared for long delays, particularly in the SW Caribbean, where windows of opportunity to depart may not occur for weeks - depending on what wind and sea conditions the vessel can handle. Vessels with shallow drafts can navigate through the Nicaraguan Banks in order to minimize large ENE seas in the open Caribbean.

The best time to transit in the Caribbean is during the late spring and late autumn, when cold fronts become stationary near Florida and the Bahamas during the spring and early summer, allowing for more breaks in the trades across the Caribbean. Tropical systems are less likely to develop in this region in spring and late autumn. A long-range vessel is more likely to be able to cruise nonstop between the Gulf of Mexico to Panama during these months.

The best route to consider when transiting between these areas is through the Yucatan Channel. It offers more ports to stop in while in transit in the Western Caribbean, and NE winds funnel more often through the Windward Pass than they do through the Yucatan Channel.

Atlantic Tropics

The Atlantic hurricane season officially begins on June 1, reaching a peak in September and ending on November 30. Tropical systems generally develop from tropical waves that track from the West African coast westward to the Caribbean and generally travel between 05N and 20N. This area is known as the Intertropical Convergence Zone (ITCZ).

A tropical wave is usually made up of a large area of disorganized thunderstorms. Approximately 24 hours ahead of a tropical wave, winds will increase from the ENE, and showers and thunderstorms will become more numerous. Once the tropical wave passes, winds will ease and shift to the ESE, and the skies will clear. Tropical waves move through the Caribbean every 2 to 3 days during summer and autumn. When voyaging this time of year, it's best to travel in between tropical waves when Trade Winds and seas are lowest. When a tropical wave approaches, it's best to seek shelter in port - particularly one that is sheltered from ENE winds.

A tropical wave will transition to a Tropical Depression when thunderstorms wrap around a low-level circulation and sustained winds around the low reach 34 kts. During June and early July, Tropical Depressions are more likely to develop in the NW Caribbean or Gulf of Mexico along stationary fronts. These systems generally strengthen and track toward the Yucatan Peninsula and the coast of Belize, or they turn NW and impact the US Gulf Coast or NE Mexico.

By late July through early October, Tropical Depressions generally develop farther east along the ITCZ in the central or eastern Atlantic. These systems then track west or WNE while strengthening and can pass over the northern Caribbean and move into the Gulf of Mexico.

By late October and November, the frequency of these systems diminish but are more likely to develop in the NW Caribbean and Gulf of Mexico again.

Amanda Delany is a Meteorologist with Weather Routing International, Inc. WRI consults with yacht owners who want personalized WX advice while voyaging, delivered to them via HF email or voice reports on a regular or occasional basis – especially while voyaging along the Central American route from one US Coast to the other.

Also see Ms. Delany's planning and traveling advice for the Eastern Pacific from southern Mexico to Panama.

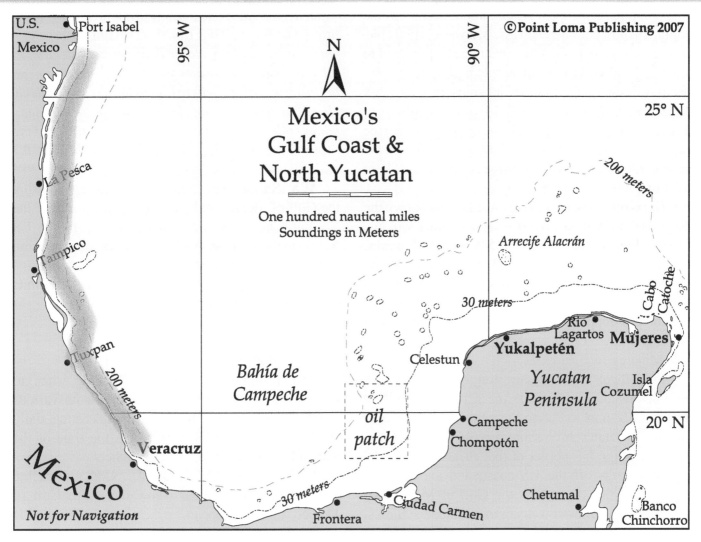

Mexico's Gulf Coast & North Yucatan

One hundred nautical miles
Soundings in Meters

©Point Loma Publishing 2007

Not for Navigation

Gulf Route Planning

The Gulf Coast refers to Mexico's 1,080-mile coastline on the Gulf of Mexico. It traverses the states of Tamaulipas, Veracruz, Tabasco, Campeche and the north coast of the Yucatan Peninsula. (The Yucatan Channel cruising grounds in the next chapter include the rest of the state of Yucatan plus Quintana Roo.)

The Gulf Coast is rich in sea life, but 99% of its boat traffic consists of shrimpers, oil industry vessels running to the many offshore oil platforms, containerized cargo ships and coastal freighters. In this region, when you say recreational boat, most locals think you mean 18' and 22' pangas with *toldos* (sun shades), trailerable catamarans and 24' open day-boats for fishing in the many shallow lagoons.

Private yachts are not a common sight along the Gulf Coast. Of those, long-legged sportfishing boats are most likely, plus a few sailboats racing each year between Galveston and Veracruz Yacht Club.

Most US and Canadian long-range pleasure boats heading to the Yucatan Channel cruising and fishing grounds should head straight across the Gulf of Mexico from their departure ports in and around South Florida, New Orleans or Galveston, paying close attention to weather forecasts. See the section on Gulf Crossing below.

However, for whatever reasons, some pleasure boats cannot cut across the Gulf of Mexico, or their skippers simply intend to explore the Gulf Coast's shallow curving coastline. These folks must be aware of the dangers of traversing a shoal lee shore. They must keep the depth sounder on and always know how much water is under their keel. They must use GPS to constantly monitor their set and drift and use an autopilot that immediately corrects such course errors. Once an hour is not enough.

They must be willing to share the local waters with heavy traffic of shrimpers, commercial fishing and shipping. Shrimpers zig-zag unpredictably in the night. To most commercial vessels, a yacht is invisible. These intrepid explorers by yacht must be prepared to take fuel and water from alongside high concrete pier facings designed for commercial ships, to scale dock ladders never inspected by OSHA and once ashore, to find their way to the limited boat supplies and marine services – where few tourists have gone before. This is not true of most other locations in Mexico, where yachting tourism is flourishing.

(1.) Gulf Crossing: From Florida, travel down the Keys and wait at Key West until a weather window is open for the 325-n.m. hop SW to Isla Mujeres, Mexico. Or, hop 90 n.m. SSW to just off Marina Hemingway, Cuba, and coast 165 n.m. westward along the NW shore of Cuba (staying south of the westbound shipping lanes) before jumping from Cabo San Antonio 103 n.m. (crossing the Gulf Stream) to Isla Mujeres.

From Texas, wait at Galveston for a long enough weather window before starting across the Gulf of Mexico, 560 n.m. to Puerto Yukalpetén near Progreso on the Yucatan's NW shore, or 616 n.m. to Cabo Catoche at the NE corner of the Yucatan Peninsula. Avoid oil rigs off the US coast, and about three-quarters of the way across the Gulf of Mexico, be prepared for shallower water of the Campeche Banks, which can develop steep chop in the normal easterly Trade Winds.

Jellyfish Alert: Provision with plenty of extra filters just for the Gulf Coast – crossing or cruising. Once underway, pay closer than normal attention to all your boat's salt-water intakes and sea strainers, because the sticky jellyfish membranes can quickly clog your filters. Be on the lookout: patties of dead jellies collect debris such as loose line or nets. Having "spurs" on your props might help cut through the additional debris problem.

WX Radio: The best data regarding crossing the Gulf of Mexico and entering the north end of the Yucatan Channel is available by monitoring the US National Weather Service's WX-fax broadcasts from station NMG in New Orleans.

NMG (November Mike Gulf) transmits continuously on frequencies:

4317.9 kHz

8305.9 kHz

12789.9 kHz

The all-important "Schedule" listing when to program your WX-fax machine to run its various weather fax products has been broadcasting daily at 0630 UTC and 1830 UTC – but the time of the Schedule could change. See Appendices.

What products? For example, NMG's "Satellite Images for Map Area 2" show the entire Gulf of Mexico and Caribbean, which are indispensable for all yatistas around the Gulf Coast and Yucatan Channel. Their "24- and 36-hour Forecast" gives

Early Gulf Coast Culture

The Olmec civilizations thrived along Mexico's Gulf Coast from 1200 B.C. to 400 B.C. The earliest alphabetical writing ever found west of the Atlantic was recently unearthed in Veracruz, further evidence of the Olmecs' highly advanced civilization. Some of their most important gifts to future generations were their ideas about government and their religious ceremonies – as evidenced by the many intricate masks and other ceremonial artifacts unearthed by archeologists. The Olmecs were probably the mother culture to the Mayan and Aztec civilizations.

Archeological sites abound inland from the Gulf Coast and on the Yucatan Peninsula, but we've found only a few places for yatistas to leave their vessels (Veracruz, Puerto Yukalpetén and Isla Mujeres) for extensive inland explorations.

In 2006, Mexico approved the ratification of the UNESCO Convention on the Protection of Underwater Cultural Heritage, a key to conserving shipwrecks, coral reefs, fishing grounds, cenotes and any other cultural remains lying under the sea. Mexico's INAH (National Institute of Anthropology & History) oversees the research and preservation. Panama is the only other country in this guidebook to ratify the convention.

ample wind arrows and frontal movements. Their "Tropical Analysis" originates from the National Hurricane Center in Miami – the horse's mouth.

(2.) Coasting Cautions: Paralleling this shallow coastline may be more comfortable, but it's safer during daylight hours than at night. Unfortunately, overnight anchorages are few and far between, and once you get there, you might find them closed out in breaking shoals.

At night, avoid the shrimpers working their back-and-forth patterns close to shore, because they're oblivious of your presence, don't monitor the radar or VHF and are blinded by their own deck lights and machinery noise. Yatistas should be coasting with a depth alarm and well-tuned radar to retain contact with the low-lying coast. In the shallow Gulf Coast waters, a reliable depth sounder is essential.

Fuel stops in intermediate ports are few and unreliable, so carrying deck fuel may extend your range. A collapsible bladder often does the trick without taking up too much space when not in use. However, securing a bladder is difficult unless it's full and taut. So a bladder should be drained completely, not partially, to keep it from flogging around dangerously. The grommets are the first thing to go. PVC barrels with good bungs are the other alternative, more practical for sportfishers and motoryachts. A combination of barrels in the stern and a bladder or two on the well-supported bow may balance out the boat's trim.

The owner of a fiberglass boat should take extraordinary measures to insure that his or her vessel paints a strong radar image to the high bridge of a ship. Hang additional radar reflectors as high as possible. If a collision course develops, turn on your spreader lights.

Before it's too late for a ship to maneuver to avoid you, don't hesitate to hail the ship on VHF 16 and ask them to confirm that they can see you. This simple communication has helped us cheat death hundreds of times. And we often benefit from whatever conversation ensues.

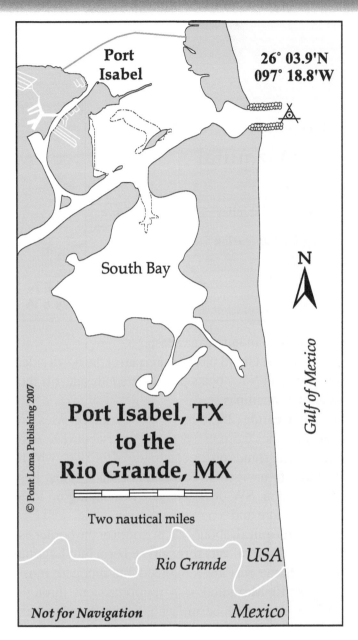

En Route to Tampico

This 240-mile leg from the Rio Grande to the first major port of Tampico should be run at least 5 n.m. off shore (30' to 60' of water), due to rocks and shoals found up to 3 n.m. off the low sandy shoreline. This section of coast has no reliable anchorages, so be prepared to traverse it as a non-stop passage.

Two vast estuaries, Laguna Madre and Laguna San Andres, spread east behind the low coastal berm, and the estuary mouths or *bocas* are usually ringed in breakers. The man-made and natural cuts across the berm often silt closed after heavy rain, sometimes forming a shoal outside the boca. A 1-knot current during winter cruising season generally sets north. Although it reverses in summer, yachts should not be

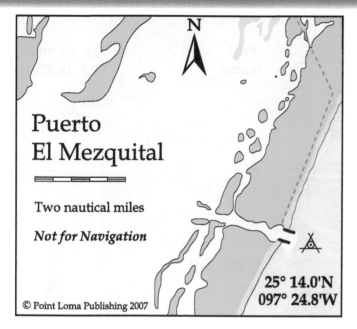

Puerto
El Mezquital

Two nautical miles

Not for Navigation

© Point Loma Publishing 2007

25° 14.0'N
097° 24.8'W

"Capitanía Puerto El Mezquital" on VHF 16 for bar conditions and the least depth in the entrance channel. If the bar is passable, a panguero may be hired (about $15 US) to guide you in. If none is available, don't attempt to enter through the breakers. At the village to starboard, the Port Captain will want to see all your papers, and the Navy will search your boat.

Bocas Ceradas (Closed Mouths) are narrower cuts, usually silted closed, about 12 n.m. (Boca Santa Maria) and 15 (Boca Sandoval) south of El Mezquital.

Boca Jesus Maria, about 47 n.m. south of El Mezquital, is a reinforced but narrow cut through the 0.75-mile wide berm. If it's not shoaled closed, don't try to enter without hiring a local panguero fisherman for pilotage across the bar, in and out. Inside, the fish camp Jesus Maria (no services) is almost 3 n.m. NW across Laguna Madre.

cruising here in hurricane season.

US Coast Guard picket ships patrol the north side, and Mexican Navy boats patrol the south side, off the state of Tamaulipas.

Rio Grande (25°58'N, 97°09'W), the US-Mexico boundary, lies 6.5 n.m. south of Port Isabel, TX. Rio Bravo Light stands on the south side of the river, which is closed to navigation. Rio San Fernando Shoal lies 30 to 35 n.m. SW of Rio Grande, extending up to 3 n.m. off shore and 5 n.m. alongshore.

El Mezquital, about 48 n.m. south of the border, is the first of several cuts through the berm into Laguna Madre. Some cuts are reinforced and dredged; most are not. El Mezquital is a reinforced cut through the 2.5 n.m. wide berm, with lighted breakwaters at 25°14.3'N, 97°25.3'W. Before trying to enter, hail

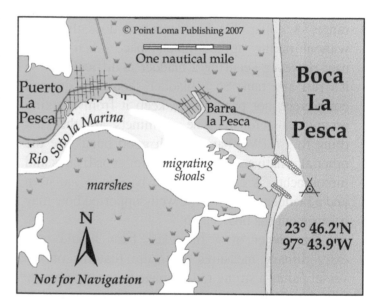

© Point Loma Publishing 2007

One nautical mile

Puerto
La
Pesca

Rio Soto la Marina

Barra
la Pesca

Boca
La
Pesca

migrating shoals

marshes

N

23° 46.2'N
97° 43.9'W

Not for Navigation

Boca La Pesca (Rio Soto la Marina) is about 90 n.m. south of El Mezquital and 90 n.m. north of Tampico. When passable, this reinforced cut through the berm (23°46.2'N, 97°43.9'W) gives local shallow-draft boats access to Puerto La Pesca at the end of Highway 70. The town lies 2.5 n.m. WNW from the entrance. It's also the mouth of Rio Soto la Marina, a canal winding west. Hail "Capitanía Puerto La Pesca" on VHF 16 for bar conditions and the entrance's least depth. Don't try to enter without local assistance.

The La Pesca Port Captain will examine your papers, and his Marines will search your boat. The

Laguna
Madre

N

Boca de
Jesus Maria

24° 28.7'N
97° 40.5'W

Two nautical miles

Not for Navigation

© Point Loma Publishing 2007

La Pesca village is at the mouth of Rio Soto la Marina.

wharf has gasoline, but a local may be hired to truck diesel from 30 miles inland. About 3 n.m. farther up the river (about 8' depth) is La Marina del Rio Lodge, a hunting fishing resort with a T-head pier; when it's not full with fly-in guests, the owners have sometimes welcomed cruisers to the dining room. La Pesca beaches fill up with vacationers during Easter week and Christmas holidays.

By about 15 n.m. south of La Pesca, farmland gradually replaces the sea berm.

Rio Indios Morales and **Barra del Tordo** (Rio Carrizal) are shoaly river mouths at respectively 22 and 44 n.m. south of La Pesca. A tordo is a thrush bird, and Playa del Tordo is a popular beach for fishing and camping. Cerro Jerez is a prominent peak about 18 n.m. SW of the Rio Indios Morales. The Sierra de San Jose de las Rusias may be visible 7 to 12 n.m. inland from Barra el Tardo down to Punta Jerez. Rocks are reported 2 n.m. off between Barra del Tordo and Punta Jerez.

Punta Jerez (about 22°52.8'N, 97°45.44'W) is a gradual SW turn of the low coast at about 70 n.m. south of La Pesca or 35 n.m. north of Tampico. About 13 n.m. SSW, Boca Chevarria (Laguna Rio el Tigre) may have an offshore shoal. From Punta Jerez, Altamira is 14 n.m. and Tampico breakwater is another 14.5 n.m.

Altamira, 14.5 n.m. north of Tampico, may be off limits to yachts when you arrive. Hail "Altamira Port Captain" on VHF 16 before approaching the outer breakwaters to ask permission to enter. If refused entry in NW weather, ask to anchor (25' to 30' sand, mud) just south of the port's south outer breakwater.

If you're allowed to enter Altamira's larger outer breakwaters (22°29.2'N, 97°50.8'W), a narrower set of inner breakwaters may afford anchorage on the north side. Inside, the port runs west for 2.25 n.m. lined in wharfs, one being a Pemex dock where diesel is sold. Anchorage has been permitted around the south bend in the SW corner. The Capitanía is on the seawall by the main pier. The town of Altamira (pop. about 8,000) is 7 miles SW of the port.

Tampico Approach: As you coast past Altamira off the SE corner of the state of Tamaulipas, several lighted oil rigs stand 10 to 18 n.m. east of Tampico. Don't anchor near the pipelines, buoys or submerged cables running between the rigs and the port.

Ciudad Madero covers 1.5 n.m. of the north bank of the mouth of Rio Pánuco, and Tampico covers the rest of both sides of the river. Lumber City is an oil facility.

La Pesca village has small dock along the river.

Tampiqueñas enjoy the many beach cantinas on weekends.

The oil and fishing port of Tampico, state of Veracruz, lies about 230 n.m. SSW of Port Isabel, Texas, 200 n.m. NW of Veracruz and 380 n.m. SW of Progreso, Yucatan. The town (pop. about 400,000) is a Port of Entry, the second-largest port on the Gulf of Mexico after Veracruz. Although Tampico has almost no tourism, it does have some stores with familiar names: Wal-Mart, Burger King, Pizza Hut.

When you're within VHF range, hail "Tampico Port Pilot" on VHF 16, let them know you're a pleasure yacht (*yate de placer*), and ask for pilotage instructions for where you intend to go. You'll eventually enter the lighted breakwaters (heading 257°T) just south of Tampico Light (22°15.9'N, 97°46.3'W), which may appear amber or red due to refinery smog. The seaward end of the north breakwater carries a racon Q (dah, dah, di, dah).

Rio Pánuco: This waterway is navigable for 15 n.m. Because the combined stream around Tampico floods with a current of up to 8.5 knots, or 6 knots in the upper reaches, it's not a good place for smaller or underpowered yachts to spend much time. As you enter the river, it curves SW, and the north side (Ciudad Madero) is tank farms and oil industry wharfs. The south shore is of more interest to recreational boaters. Anchorage may be taken in several places, but only with permission of a Port Pilot or the Capitanía.

Laguna Chijol: About 2.75 n.m. into Rio Pánuco from the start of the breakwaters, the dredged start of the Canal de Chijol (22°14.7'N, 97°49.2'W) exits the south shore of the river and leads SE for about 0.75 of a mile. With permission, yachts can anchor in here to get out of the river current and traffic, but town is on the other side, and you

Tampico

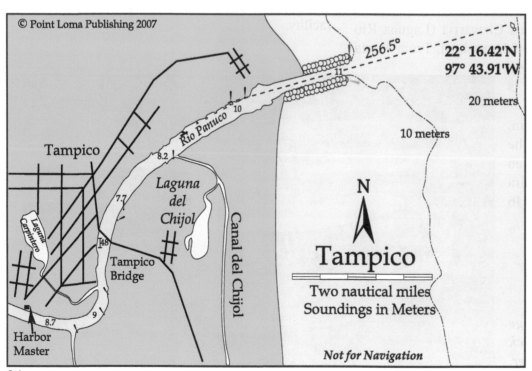

© Point Loma Publishing 2007

256.5°

22° 16.42'N
97° 43.91'W

20 meters

10 meters

Rio Pánuco

Tampico

Laguna del Chijol

Canal del Chijol

Laguna Carpintero

Tampico Bridge

Harbor Master

N

Tampico

Two nautical miles
Soundings in Meters

Not for Navigation

must leave room for small boats to pass in the center channel.

A smaller side channel exits SW into the mile-long Laguna Chijol (pronounced *CHEE-hol*). Anchoring depth in this dead-end lagoon is reported to be 11' but not confirmed. The lagoon and side channel can shoal up after heavy rain.

Canal de Chijol: The Chijol Canal and connected waterways south of it (including the 35-mile long Laguna Tamiahua) used to be called "the Mexican ICW," and small boats formerly traveled 85 n.m. from Tampico to Tuxpan behind the sea berm. But the Chijol Canal has been damaged by many hurricanes. In 2006, the Tampico and Tuxpan Port Captains warned that any navigable channels through the lagoons are not marked, that this system is not dredged or maintained from one end to the other for any minimum depths, and that it does contain unmarked hazards. The Tuxpan end of the Chijol Canal has a low bridge, so it's not useful for ocean-going yachts. But it might make an interesting dinghy adventure.

Laguna Carpintero: Tampico Bridge (159' clearance) over Rio Pánuco is 1.3 n.m. upstream (south) from the Canal de Chijol exit. It's a marvelous suspension bridge, a landmark from off shore. At about 0.75 n.m. beyond the bridge, a commercial channel branches WSW, and the first 750 yards is the general dockage for small boats and yachts visiting Tampico. It's lined in commercial docks, small marinas and fuel docks. This area gives best access to downtown, El Centro.

Carpintero Channel then shrinks, turns north and reaches Laguna Carpintero, but low bridges block access. Parts of Carpintero Lagoon are city park with swim beaches, jet boats and water skiing; other areas are wild habitat for crocodiles and turtles.

Port Clearance: About 5 n.m. in from the breakwaters, the river bends west and WNW. About a mile west of the bend, the modern 5-story Maritime Building (Capitanía, Aduana, Migracion, API) stands on the north bank of Rio Pánuco, just before a side channel goes north toward shoaly Laguna de Chairel. The Capitanía is surrounded by railroad sidings, and the historic red-brick Maritime Building is almost next door.

The river depth drops from 48' to 8.7' upstream of the exit of the channel to Chairel Lagoon – so larger boats are excluded. This area is normally sheltered from easterly Trade Winds by a hill on the east bank of the river bend.

History & Culture: The telephone area code for Tampico is 833.

Beneath the modern city are the remains of a Huasteca village that was plundered and destroyed in the 16th century by Cortez. Mexican Airlines got its start at Tampico in the 1920s by linking the area's oil industry to Mexico City.

One of Tampico's tourist attractions that appeal to yatistas is its historic Maritime Customs House downtown. Tampico is famous for its fine cuisine, which is typically not too spicy and adorned with lots of guacamole, sweet peas and sautéed "*platanos.*" Roasted baby goat is a regional delicacy.

Mexico's recently revived vanilla-bean industry is centered at the rural farming villages of Gutierrez Zamora and Papantla de Olarte. Guided tours of the vanilla vines, drying sheds and extraction process can be arranged by any travel agent in Tampico or Tuxpan, but Tampico may be a better place to leave your boat. Or contact the Veracruz state tourism office in Xalapa; phone (228) 812-8500 or email the tourism office at ambiance_adventure@infosel.net.mx.

In Gutierrez Zamora, the largest vanilla farm is Gaya Via-Mex, and one vanilla grower in Papantla is Heriberto Larios. These family farms or either of these ports are good places to stock up on the world's most pure vanilla extract and freshest vanilla beans – delicious in your galley and excellent gifts or trade items with other yatistas.

El Cielo Biosphere Reserve about 2 hours SW of Tampico by bus is a huge park of nature trails, waterfalls, butterflies and jungle birds.

En route to Tuxpan

Just south of Tampico, you enter the state of Veracruz. From Tampico, the coast runs SE for 49 n.m. to Cabo Rojo. A buoyed wreck lies on a shoal about 3 n.m. SE of the Tampico breakwaters, and an oil rig lies close to shore about 22 n.m. SE of Tampico.

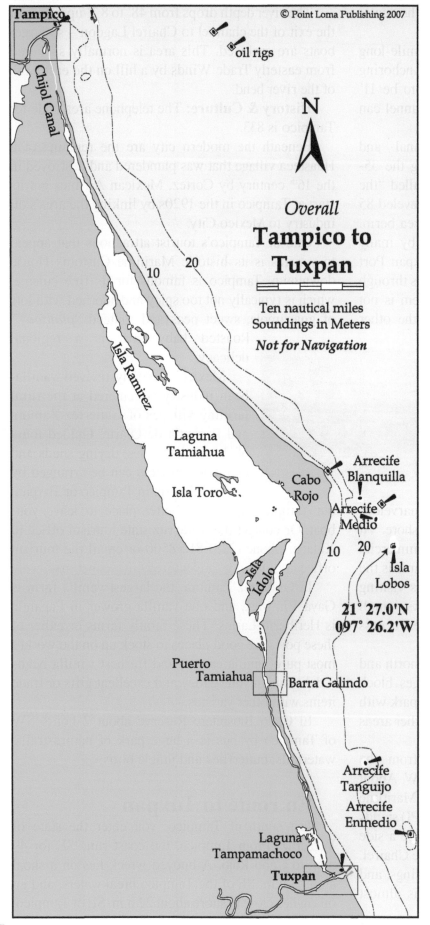

Overall
Tampico to Tuxpan

Ten nautical miles
Soundings in Meters
Not for Navigation

© Point Loma Publishing 2007

Tampico

Chijol Canal

oil rigs

Isla Ramirez

Laguna Tamiahua

Isla Toro

Isla Idolo

Cabo Rojo

Arrecife Blanquilla

Arrecife Medio

Isla Lobos

21° 27.0'N
097° 26.2'W

Puerto Tamiahua

Barra Galindo

Arrecife Tanguijo

Arrecife Enmedio

Laguna Tampamachoco

Tuxpan

This is the northernmost of an oil-rig patch that stretches 60 n.m. southward.

Laguna Tamiahua behind the sea berm spreads to 15 n.m. at its south end, then the berm becomes hilly, 66' to 350' high. This route passes San Sebastian oil fields.

Cabo Rojo: This headland is low (36'), rounded and sandy, but Blanquilla Reef extends 1.8 n.m. east from Cabo Rojo Light (21°33'N, 97° 20'W). Isla Lobos Light (21°28.2'N, 97°13.7'W) is on a small island about 4 n.m. SE of Arrecife Blanquilla. Isla Lobos has a racon O (dah, dah, dah). Isla Lobos is surrounded in extensive reef, but an unmarked channel leads to a small dock. To reach the anchorage of Puerto Lobos, come between the lighted hazards of Blanquilla Reef and Isla Lobos reef.

Puerto Lobos: An 18-n.m. open indentation on the south side of Cabo Rojo provides a welcome lee during the north winds of winter cruising season, for anchoring in 15' to 30' over sand. But it's wide open to the NE, east and south.

Barra Corazones: At 18 n.m. SW of Cabo Rojo, shoals sometimes foul this breakwater reinforced cut (21°15.52'N, 97°24.82'W) that drains Laguna Tamiahua. But if passable, a small anchoring basin lies about 600 yards inside. About a mile west, this cut joins a small-boat canal from the south end of Laguna Tamiahua. The town of Tamiahua lies a mile north of the cut on the west side of the canal.

Oil platforms lie 12 n.m. ENE of Tuxpan.

Barra Galindo (10 n.m. south of Barra Corazones) is a break in Isla Galindo, the barrier island. This small breakwater cut (21°05.88'N, 97°21.61'W) opens NE and is less likely to be dredged or passable. About 400 yards inside is a baffle groin. The panga canal another 600 yards west runs north to Tamiahua, south to Tuxpan, but it hasn't been dredged in years, and the south canal disappears into Laguna Tampamochaco, which has a low bridge at its south end.

Tuxpan Reefs: About 5 n.m. off shore north of Tuxpan are 3 lighted reefs: Tanguijo (Banquillo on some charts), En Medio and Tuxpan (21°01.7'N, 97°11.7'W). Arrecife Tuxpan has a racon X (dah, di, di, dah). Ships and oil gear anchor nearby. The Port Captain says the safer route is east of these reefs, then south. But cruising boats have reported sailing inside the reefs before entering Tuxpan.

CAUTION: About 3 n.m. NNW of Tuxpan harbor, don't try to enter the breakwaters of the thermo-electric plant and its outflow canals.

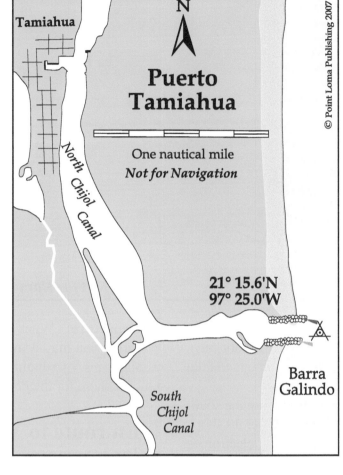

Tamiahua

N

Puerto Tamiahua

One nautical mile
Not for Navigation

North Chijol Canal

21° 15.6'N
97° 25.0'W

South Chijol Canal

Barra Galindo

© Point Loma Publishing 2007

If you come inside, enter the breakwaters heading WSW. La Barra is a prohibited wharf area on the north shore just in from the entrance. Yachts can anchor (a.) most easily in the mud basin immediately to port, but it's rolly. Or (b.) anchor about 1500 yards farther in and to starboard off the west side of Canal de Mojardes – as long as you don't block traffic. Mojardes Canal is the south end of the Chijol Canal as it exits Laguna Tampamochaco. Pemex ships occupy the east side of this canal mouth, and a low bridge crosses it 200 yards farther north. Or (c.) 2.5 n.m. upstream from the breakwater, the yacht-friendly Hotel Rio Paraiso (bright yellow) on the north shore has a small dock (5' alongside) and anchoring area just before you reach the Navy base. Set bow and stern anchors to keep you headed upstream.

If you need to come ashore, first ask permission from "Tuxpan Capitanía" on VHF 16. You will be directed to the appropriate anchorage to await boarding and inspection before beginning your port clearance.

Port Clearance: Unless you plan to stay in Tuxpan more than 48 hours, be sure to ask to perform your *entrada* and *salida* paperwork at the same time.

After you've been inspected, start your round of port clearances with Immigration near the bridge's north end; (783) 834-0987. Hire a taxi, because none of the offices are close. The Capitanía (873-0250) is back near the Navy base on the north side of the river. API (873-0015) is east of the Capitanía on the road to La Barra, and the Aduana (873-5052) is in the old port building downtown.

Local Services: Although Tuxpan has no marina and yacht visitors are rare, it's a pleasant river town

Tuxpan

Tuxpan (pop. approx. 7,500) is the Armada de Mexico's Gulf Coast HQ and an important oil industry and grain shipping port on Rio Tuxpan (Tuxpam on some charts). Tuxpan is the closest port to Mexico City and the Valle de Mexico. But in a strong easterly blow, huge breakers can close the harbor entrance.

Arrival: Because Tuxpan has river current and ship traffic, pilotage is required even for yachts – but they may simply direct you where to go over VHF. Contact "Tuxpan Pilot" on VHF 16 when within range, and have your ETA ready. (It's pronounced *TOOSH-pahn.*) Depths in the marked channel are 36' for 5 n.m. upstream to the town of Tuxpan.

Anchorages: If you merely want to anchor for the night without coming ashore, you may be instructed to anchor outside the lighted breakwaters, where there's 15' to 30' of water over mud outside the shore break SE of the breakwaters.

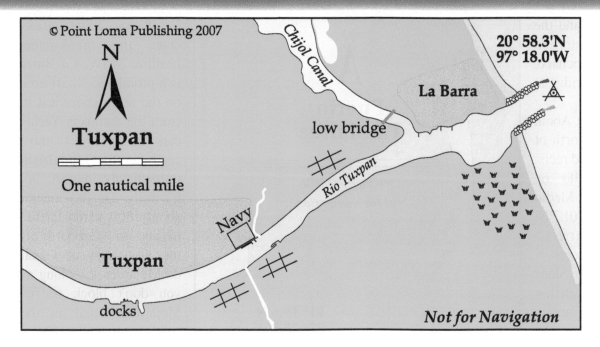

© Point Loma Publishing 2007

N

Tuxpan

One nautical mile

Tuxpan

docks

Chijol Canal

low bridge

La Barra

20° 58.3'N
97° 18.0'W

Rio Tuxpan

Navy

Not for Navigation

with lots of small commercial docks where, if you speak Spanish, you can get at least overnight dockage, and at some docks they will help you arrange to take fuel there.

Tuxpan has at least 2 repair yards along the south shore, and both sides of the river have numerous shops that service marine engines and bridge electronics found on commercial ships. Tuxpan has grocery stores, Internet cafes, banks, restaurants, hotels, an airport and hospital. The main street through the town of Tuxpan is Avenida Juarez.

More shipyards are found at Santiago de la Peña, past Tuxpan Bridge (high clearance). Boats with draft of 7' or less can travel Rio Tuxpan 30 n.m. above the entrance, but beware of river current and unmarked shoals formed by recent heavy rains.

Departure: When departing Tuxpan toward Veracruz, you may want to stay inside (west of) the oil platforms, by running the 10-fathom line about 5 n.m. off shore for the next 65 n.m. SE.

En route to Veracruz

This 125 n.m. coast from Tuxpan to Veracruz can be run 3 to 5 n.m. off shore.

Rio Cazones, marked by 2 lights, is 16 n.m. SE of Tuxpan. The river opens SE about a mile SW of Punta Cazones (20°43.5'N, 97°12.0'W), and a rock lies in the center of the stream. Pangas ford the bar and moor upstream of the rock.

Barra de Tecolutla (20°28.63'N, 97°59.58'W) about 35 n.m. down the coast from Tuxpan has a small lighted breakwater on the north side of the river bar. The town of Tecolutla (Owl) on the north side of the river has a panga fishing fleet pulled up on the beach. From here to Veracruz, a highway runs along the coast serving the inland oil fields, farming communities and broad flat swimming beaches, but no sheltered anchorage is known.

Cerro de los Metates near Isla Bernal Chica has many exquisite Toltec tombs made of stone, like tiny temples. It's a good side trip in calm weather.

Isla Bernal Grande (center left) and Isla Bernal Chica (far right) mark the remarkable Toltec artifacts (foreground) at Quianhuiztlan.

Rio Nautla (20°14.53'N, 96°46.84'W) about 52 miles SE of Tuxpan is marked by a light. This is the mouth of 2 rivers; south is a small breakwater, and north half a mile is a village. Canon from the Spanish conquest are seen at Palmar de Guadalupe. About 6 n.m. south, pangas ford the bar at Barra de Palmas, which has no light.

Punta Delgado (Punta del Morro) 30 n.m. down from Tecolutla shows a light on the hilly point, the first of several small points in the next 10 n.m. Near Punta Delgado, the 10-fathom line moves in to 3 n.m off the beach. Pico Dos Atriscos may be visible 5 n.m. SW, the start of the Sierra de Tezihtlan.

Punta Laguna Verde: (Punta Villa Rica) Laguna Verde nuclear facility lies on the south side of this point, about 10 n.m. down from Punta Delgado. Don't approach within 0.5 n.m. of the breakwater on the south side of Punta Laguna Verde.

Isla Bernal Chica

This island (19°40.27'N, 96°22.95'W) lies 3 n.m. south of Punta Laguna Verde. This 144' tall rock rises about 1,000 yards SE of Isla Bernal Grande, a cupcake of an island that is attached to shore at low tide. Marginal anchorage can be taken within half a mile south or SE of the cupcake. In fact, this is the historic Villa Rica de la Vera Cruz anchorage where Hernán Cortez moored and burned his ships in 1519. But open to NE wind.

Quianhuiztlan: About 700 yards SW of Isla Bernal Grande, a path leads up this hillside (Cerro de los Metates) through hundreds of exquisite stone temples and tombs of the Toltec, Totonac and Mexica people from 900 to 1519 A.D. Among the temples is the landmark Penon de Bernal, a towering basalt plug with sheer sides seaward. Walking tours of Quianhuiztlan (*Place of Rain* in Nahuatl) start at a visitor center half a mile up from the beach.

Punta Zempoala (13 n.m. SSE of Isla Bernal Chica) is low and 2-headed; stay at least a mile off (19°28.54'N, 96°17.69'W) due to shoals. Zempoala is another archeological site. Chachalaca Light (19°24.8'N, 96°19.3'W) at the mouth of Rio Actopan is about 3 n.m. south of Zempoala. A *chachalaca* is a small song bird of the Gulf Coast.

Punta Gorda: This low rounded headland lies 15 n.m. SE of Punta Zempoala and 3.3 n.m. NW of Castillo de San Juan Ulua that guards Veracruz. Due to shoals, from at least .35 of a mile off Punta Gorda (19°15.15'N, 96°10.53'W), get your bearings

Oil rigs like this are a common offshore landmark along Mexico's Gulf Coast.

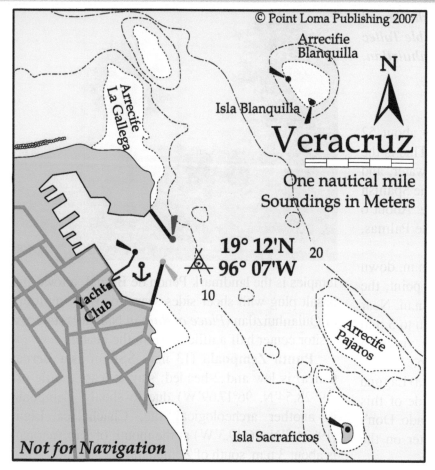

© Point Loma Publishing 2007

Arrecifie Blanquilla

Isla Blanquilla

N

Veracruz

One nautical mile
Soundings in Meters

19° 12'N
96° 07'W

20

10

Arrecife Pajaros

Yachts Club

Isla Sacraficios

Not for Navigation

before entering the maze of reefs that complicate the approaches to the harbor entrance.

Bahía Veragua is the indent between Punta Gorda and Arrecife Gallega at the north side of Veracruz. A huge new riprap wave baffle laid off Veragua's SE shore usually prevents anchoring, due to depth and wave refraction.

Veracruz

Mexico's largest commercial port on the Gulf Coast, Veracruz lies about 415 n.m. south of the US border at Rio Grande, 275 n.m. west of Ciudad del Carmen and 320 n.m. WSW of Campeche.

Veracruz has a small yacht club, a cruise ship or two, plus lots of regional tourism, so it's likely to be the primary destination for those few yatistas venturing this far south into Mexico's Gulf Coast. However, Veracruz is the heart of Mexico's oil industry and a major container port, so expect big tankers and freighters maneuvering off shore. Ashore, the historic center of Veracruz shines through the industrial fringes.

Caution: *Coral reefs abound in the Veracruz*

area, surrounding every shoal and land feature. Before entering the area or receiving directions from the port pilot or *Capitanía*, be familiar with the names and locations of the reefs and land features.

Caution: A strong or prolonged Norther may cause water to temporarily pile up around Veracruz reefs and shoals, vexing depth readings.

NOTE: *The anchorage at Bahía Veraguas is no longer useable by small boats, due to a huge riprap wave barrier completed since the previous edition of "Cruising Ports."*

Approach from North: Pilotage is required, so call "Piloto Veracruz" on VHF 16 when you're in range. Inform them of your size and nature (*yate de placer*) and that you're arriving from the north. And if you want pilotage safely through the reefs and ship traffic all the way into the yacht anchorage inside the harbor, then give them your ETA at the north side of Arrecife Galleguilla (19°14.39'N, 96°07.37'W). This deep-water GPS position is a quarter mile north of the Arrecife Galleguilla, which is the smaller reef immediately north of Arrecife Gallega. You may see pangas zipping through the slot between these two reefs, but it requires local knowledge.

Approach from East: If you're arriving from the east, the racon Z (da-dah di-dit) on Isla Sacraficios 1.4 n.m. north of Punta Mocambo can guide you to an ETA about a quarter mile south of Isla Sacraficios Reef (19°10.17'N, 96°05.57'W). The deep-water slot between the reef off Punta Mocambo and the reef around Isla Sacraficios provides a straight shot NW for about 2.5 n.m. to the harbor breakwaters, but avoid Arrecife La Lavandera that extends almost half a mile SE from the root of the south breakwater.

Caution: *Veracruz has a TSS or Traffic Separation Scheme, bringing ships in from 2 ship anchorages: SE of Islas Verde and Sacraficios; and north of Punta Antón Lizardo – both of which must be passed when approaching from the ESE or south.*

Veracruz Harbor: The harbor's north breakwater overlaps the south one a bit. Yachts must anchor or take a mooring in the outer basin, SE of the huge Muro de Pescadores that separates it from the industrial inner harbor. Yachts are not allowed to come alongside the Muro de Pescadores. Minimum depth in the ship channel is 26' at low tide, but the yacht basin's south end shoals and can dry at LLW.

Inside Anchorages: Yachts should anchor off the Veracruz Yacht Club in the SW corner of the outer basin, at the root of the Muro de Pescadores. Club de Yates is a sportfishing club with no berths, only a dinghy dock and a few moorings for its members. On weekends they may monitor VHF 16 or 68.

Visiting yachts usually anchor in 6' to 18' over mud and coral sand near the club's mooring area, immediately north and NE of the dink dock and clubhouse. When anchored here, you pay a daily fee to use the club's dinghy landing, toilet, shower, picnic tables and clubhouse. Taxis come to the front door. If you're an affiliated club member and plan to be in Veracruz long, you might ask about renting a mooring from one of the members who plans to be gone.

When VYC hosts the semi-annual Regatta de Amigos (Lakewood YC and Galveston Bay YC) in spring (2008, 2010), visiting sailboats get special permission to Med-moor off the malecon in the inner harbor, below Hotel Emporio. Same for its big Tarpon Tournament.

Even if you're anchored outside the harbor, the yacht club's dinghy landing is the safest way to get ashore, so request permission and pay the small fee. The yacht club is on Blvd. Comacho (the malecon) near the downtown zocalo. FMI, phone Club de Yates de Veracruz at (229) 932-0917.

Outside Anchorages: Port officials tell yatistas to anchor off the yacht club inside the harbor, but if it's totally packed they refer you to 3 lighted features within 3 n.m. SE of the harbor that are designated small-boat anchorages: Isla Sacraficios Reef, Isla Pajaros Reef and Isla Verde. Isla Sacraficios carries a racon Z (dah, dah, di, dit). All 3 islands are entirely surrounded in coral reefs that usually break.

Club de Yates de Veracruz hosts several sailing regattas and sportfishing tournaments that draw US yatistas. The malecon is then used for visiting boats to Med-moor.

NOTE: Please use care when anchoring near living corals, so you don't damage their delicate structures.

Ships anchor at least half a mile SE of Sacraficios, Pajaros and Verde - and on down to Arrecife Chopas off Punta Coyol (Lizardo). Smaller ships and pilot boats steam around the yacht anchorage on their way in and out of the harbor.

Reefs and islands SE of the harbor or off Punta Coyol are A. Blanca, A. Chopas, I. Los Bajitos, A. Polo, Bajo Aviso, A. and I. Enmedio, A. Rizo, then the outer A. Cabeza, A. Anagada de Afuera, I. Tapitillo, I. Santiaguilla and A. Anagadilla. Rio Jamapa south of Punta Mocambo has a lighted breakwater, but is primarily a drainage canal.

Those reefs and islands NE of the harbor are Arrecife La Gallega, A. Galleguilla, A. Blanquilla, Isla Sacraficios, A. and I. Pajaros, A. and I. Verde, Bajo Paducah and A. Anagada de Adentro.

Port Clearance: Veracruz is a Port of Entry, but a ship's agent is no longer required for clearance of recreational boats (unless you're documented commercial). The Capitanía is located on the seawall between Muelle Fiscal #1 and #2, which are on the SW side of the inner harbor. You can come by dinghy or land.

El Castillo de San Juan de Ulua is the historic stone fort guarding the north approach to Veracruz harbor. A foot bridge leads across.

The Port Captain will direct you to Migración. Aduana clearance is not mandatory here, but if you're arriving here from the US, we recommend that you go to the Aduana's office to get your Temporary Import Permit (TIP), which is required before importing boat parts or leaving your boat in Mexico while you head home.

For details on the International Arrival port clearance, see the Paperwork chapter.

Ship's Agent: If you have paperwork problems, crew changes or need help importing boat parts, or if you don't have enough Spanish to carry out your regular port clearance, the Port Captain can connect you with a local ship's agent. Agent services include providing a car and driver to take you around town for provisioning and shagging parts and repair services.

WX-fax charts are posted on the Capitanía, and local weather is broadcast in Spanish at 0800 local time on VHF 12. For emergency information, call the Veracruz Port Captain (in Spanish) at (229) 931-4342.

Local Services: Veracruz area code is 229; Anton Lizardo is 297; Boca del Rio is 228.

Fuel Barge: Request a fueling *Permiso* from the Port Captain's office when you begin port clearance in. Veracruz doesn't presently have a fuel dock for yachts, you can take any quantity of centrifuged diesel and gasoline and other petroleum products such as bulk oil from one of several fuel barges that operate at various docks inside the north end of the harbor. Or, a fuel barge may come to you off the yacht club.

The fuel barge comes alongside a concrete seawall or another docked commercial vessel, then you raft or tie up to its outer side. Fender yourself well, and don't use your cleanest lines. If their nozzle is too big for your deck fills, you'll need a reducer. Be prepared for a fast flow.

Haul Out: Astilleros de Veracruz is a shipyard on the NE side of the inner harbor that has numerous marine ways, cranes used for cargo and engines, also the familiar Travelifts with flexible straps for hauling all size vessels. According to the Port Captain, this yard has the most experience handling yachts. A ship's agent can make haul-out arrangements and negotiations for you.

In case of an emergency situation, haul-out can be arranged through the Port Captain or the Navy base at

Holidays are big fiestas in the streets of El Centro Veracruz.

Canon that once fired on pirates have more peaceful uses in romantic Veracruz.

Veracruz. Across the street from the yacht club is an inexpensive Hotel Mar y Tierra, but we haven't stayed there.

Provisioning: Veracruz is the best place in the Gulf Coast to provision. Hire one of the small collective taxis in front of the VYC, but you may need a bigger taxi to haul your provisions back. The huge municipal market is about 2 blocks SW of the zocalo, for everything from vanilla beans to Viagra; this is where to buy pure Papantla vanilla in handy 1- and 2-liter plastic bottles. Veracruz also has a WalMart, Sam's Club, CostCo, a good Comercial Mexicana and many excellent fruterías.

Explore Ashore: Dive the many wrecks on the spectacularly beautiful coral reefs around Veracruz harbor, which were Mexico's first underwater park. In June 2006, Mexico ratified the UNESCO Convention on the Protection of Underwater Cultural Heritage, so these reefs and the spot at Isla Bernal Chica or Villa Rica should benefit.

If your boat is secure in Veracruz, rent a car and drive 2 hours NW to Papantla's vanilla-bean market, then 30 minutes south to Zanath Ecological Park to see the world's only stingless bees (Melipona) pollinate the vanilla orchid flowers. FMI, phone (784) 842-3311 for park curator Jose Luis Hernandez Decuir; 16 Sept # 902 in Papantla.

Veracruz has Mexico's only Museum of Naval History, and the Veracruz Aquarium helps young yatistas appreciate the fantastic world below their hull.

As we go to press, the car and passenger ferry between Corpus Christi and Veracruz is still delayed, but when it happens, it will be a handy method to check out this region before deciding to bring your boat down.

History & Culture: Hernán Cortez came here from Cuba in 1519 when it was the village of Chalchihuecan. He named the town site Villa Rica de Vera Cruz, and he named the nearest reef La Gallega

Traditional plazas of smaller pueblos are within touring distance of Veracruz harbor, like this one at Yanga.

(pronounced "gah-yAY-gah"), meaning a woman or ship from the Spanish province Galicia.

El Castillo de San Juan Ulua is the picturesque castle built on the south side of Arrecife La Gallega starting in 1582, completed in 1799. From this castle, Veracruz has fended off attacks from the Spanish, French and twice from American warships (1847 and 1914).

Veracruz's artificial bay was constructed by connecting Gallega Reef to land via a north breakwater, which was eventually improved by President Porfirio Diaz to form the sheltered harbor with wharfs, shipyard and tank farms you see today. The landmark castle is still surrounded by water, which floods the dungeon cells at high tide.

Veracruz Naval Institute is the Mexican equivalent to Annapolis, MD, in the US, because the Navy and Marine training schools are at Arrecife Hornos and Punta Coyol.

Veracruzano is the region's unique style of cuisine that's popular across Mexico.

Departing Veracruz: Contact the Port Pilot before departing Veracruz harbor. Numerous reef hazards lie within 7 n.m. of Punta Anton Lizardo, so take care to clear these reefs before laying a course across the Bay of Campeche to the Yucatan side.

Satellilte image shows reefs surrounding the Veracruz area from Punta Gorda down to Punta Anton Lizardo and well east - so use caution on your departure.

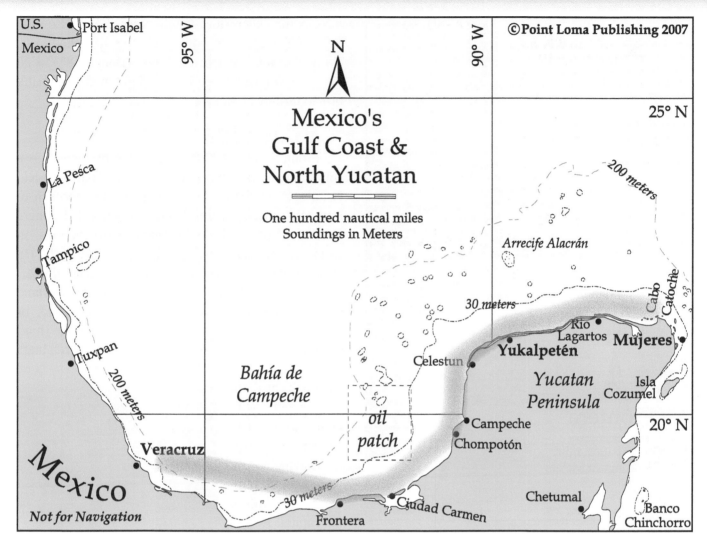

Route Planning:
Veracruz to Campeche

Plan A: From Veracruz, cut across Bay of Campeche either to the deep-water port of Ciudad del Carmen (about 245 n.m.) or the shallow-draft basin at Campeche (about 315 n.m.) or to some point in between – as opposed to coasting the south shores of Bahía Campeche.

No Plan B: From Veracruz, we recommend that yatistas do not cruise the south shores of the Bay of Campeche. Why? It's not a place for pleasure boating. Unmarked shoals form 0.5 to 1 n.m. off shore, and extensive shallow waters of the lower gulf are plagued with strong currents and frequent gale-force winds – the north side of the dreaded *Tehuantepeckers* on Mexico's Pacific coast. (See the chapters on the Gulf of Tehuantepec in *MexWX: Mexico Weather for Boaters* and *Mexico Boating Guide*.) During winter and spring cruising season, north winds frequently

closed out the shallow south end in rough chop and breakers up to 10 n.m. off shore.

Yatistas should not be cruising in the lower Bay of Campeche between mid-June and mid-November, due to the frequency of hurricanes and severe thunderstorms. After heavy rains, the bars across the river bocas silt up with soft mud and rocky debris, thus clouding visual navigation and making depth soundings inaccurate.

However, emergency help is available at Coatzacoalcos (approach 18°10.17'N, 94°24.86'W), Dos Bocas (approach 18°27.25'N, 93°12.33'W) and Frontera just upstream from Punta Buey (approach 18°38.8'N, 92°43.2'W).

CAUTION: Yachts should avoid the 300-square mile oil fields around (a.) Cayos Triangulas, Los Obispos and Cayos Arcas, and (b.) about the Ku, Cantarell, Akal, and Abkatun rig systems rising 35 to 65 n.m. NNW of Ciudad del Carmen. These two areas

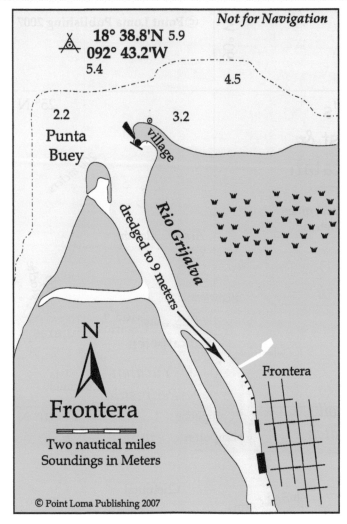

Not for Navigation

18° 38.8'N 5.9
092° 43.2'W
5.4

4.5

2.2
Punta
Buey

3.2

village

Rio Grijalva

dredged to 9 meters

N

Frontera

Two nautical miles
Soundings in Meters

© Point Loma Publishing 2007

Frontera

On the other side, you'll cross 2 Ship Routing System corridors as you reach the 10-fathom line about 12 n.m. north of Punta Buey (18°32.1'N, 92°41.33'W), which is a 14-mile light on the NE bank of Rio Grijalva.

Frontera

Frontera (pop. 6,800) in the state of Tabasco is a small banana port 6.5 n.m. upstream (south) on Rio Grijalva's east bank. Shoals plague the approach to Punta Buey, so if you must come in here, hail "Frontera Capitanía" on VHF 16 for pilotage instructions. In calms, if you merely want to anchor for the night, try close SE of Punta Buey Light off El Bosque village.

At 3.5 n.m. farther in, the east side of the island has been passable. Anchor south of the island, or come alongside the 300-yard commercial mole (high rough concrete). Shrimpers and small freighters own this dock, but don't let them raft outside you. Don't block traffic on Rio Grijalva; it's navigable by barges for 70 n.m. to Villahermosa, the capital. A high bridge lies a mile past the town.

The port's historic Capitania and Aduana building may still be in renovation. See photo above. Frontera has a small grocery and a big farmers' market in the plaza on weekends, when it's packed with pickups. The Museo de Navegación Rio Grijalva is open 9 to 7 Tuesday through Sunday. The Capitanía phone is (913) 933-2046.

Manatees, crocodiles and a flat-billed fish called *pejelagarto* live in the river mangroves and surrounding Biosphere Pantanos de Centla.

are actively being developed and have uncharted rigs, pilings, mooring buoys, storage tankers and heavy industrial traffic. This is now an **Area to be Avoided** under the mandatory Marine Traffic Control System and strictly enforced in Campeche Bay.

After Veracruz, if your plans call for a stop at Celestún Biosphere or the marinas of Puerto Yukalpetén near Progreso, it's safer to cross Campeche Bay to the deep-water port of Ciudad del Carmen or toward Campeche pier and then coast hop northward – rather than lay a course from Veracruz directly to Punta Boxcohuo (Celestún) on the NW corner of the Yucatan Peninsula.

En route to Carmen

Bahía Campeche: After departing the Veracruz reef area, look for a tidal current 20 to 30 n.m. out that sets you north from 1 to 1.5 knots. Expect 24-hour ship traffic while crossing Bahía Campeche. Don't set the autopilot and go below.

Continuing toward Carme, if weather and traffic permit, come to about 6 n.m. north of Punta Buey and coast generally east at 4 to 6 n.m. off shore for 46 n.m., which keeps you in or near the eastbound lane. About 20 miles east of Rio Grijalva (Punta Buey), you cross the border into the state of Campeche.

Shrimping traffic increases as you close with the shallow coastline and port. Be aware of shrimpers

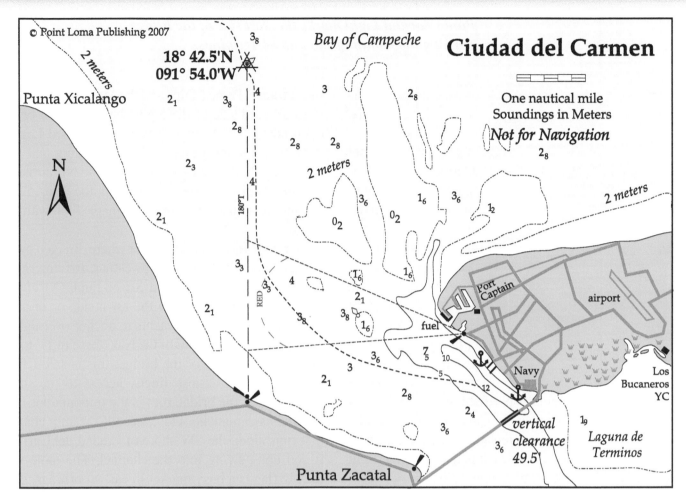

© Point Loma Publishing 2007

18° 42.5'N
091° 54.0'W

Punta Xicalango

N

2 meters

RED

Bay of Campeche

Ciudad del Carmen

One nautical mile
Soundings in Meters
Not for Navigation

Port Captain

fuel

airport

Navy

Los Bucaneros YC

vertical clearance 49.5'

Laguna de Terminos

Punta Zacatal

working at night, because they do not notice your approach, being blinded by their own lights and noise. They change direction often and seemingly erratically.

Approach to Carmen: Punta Xicalango (This X is pronounced "Sh.") is the west corner (low, wooded) of the entrance bay. The lighted sea buoy (18°42.5'N, 91°54.0'W) lies about 2.75 n.m. NE of this point. The town covers the opposite point, which is recessed about 6 n.m. SE of Punta Xicalango.

Ciudad del Carmen has a traffic pattern for all vessels, and pilotage is compulsory, so call "Carmen Port Captain" on VHF 16 when you're in range, and tell them your ETA at 1.5 n.m. NE of Punta Xicalango, plus your intentions as a "*yate de placer.*"

The 2-mile wide entrance (10' depths) to Ciudad del Carmen, and the lagoon is called Barra Principal. This passage runs between Punta Zacatal (18°36.7'N, 91°51.4'W) on the mainland and Punta Vigia on the SW corner of Isla del Carmen. From the sea buoy line up on the range marker on the west bank and proceed on 180°T. However, several 5.25' shoals foul the approaches from NE, but they are usually buoyed

and marked by a red sector on Punta Atalaya Light (18°38.7'N, 91°51.7'W) on Punta Vigia. When abeam of the north side of the island to port, begin a slow turn to port keeping the buoyed shoal markers to port. A buoyed channel leads to the docks along the SW shore of Ciudad del Carmen.

Carmen Bridge: The low 2-mile long bridge from Punta Zacatal to the south end of Carmen Island has a passable section (elevation 49.5' at MLW, channel depth 12') near the east end, at 18°37.26'N, 91°50.68'W.

Ciudad del Carmen

Ciudad del Carmen (pop. 132,400) in the state of Campeche is a deep-water Port of Entry serving the oil industry, fishing & shrimping fleets and the Navy and Marines. The port lies along the west shore of this pleasant city, which covers 8 square miles of the west end of 20-mile long Isla del Carmen, the barrier island north of the vast Laguna de Terminos estuary. Access to Puerto Real at the NE end of Isla del Carmen has shoaled up beneath the high bridge and

Punta Zacatal Light marks the west side of the bridge crossing the mouth of Laguna de Terminos.

is useful for pangas and trailerable skiffs. Family-oriented hotels dot Isla del Carmen's north-shore beaches, not to be confused with the nightclubs at Playa del Carmen on the Yucatan Channel.

Carmen is not a yatista destination; seldom do 15 cruising boats stop in a year. Buccaneros Yacht Club is a private facility for small sportfishing boats (5' depth approach). But at Ciudad del Carmen you can make emergency hull repairs, replace bridge electronics fried by lightning, seek medical help or catch a flight to Miami, Los Angeles or Mexico City.

NOTE: Tell the Port Captain why you're stopping here, and his office will tell you where to anchor, may find you a spot on one of the commercial docks (not cheap) or will definitely make arrangements for an emergency haul out.

Puerto Pesquero: Two fuel docks (Orsan Pemex, FUVA Shell) occupy the high seawall (18°38.89'N, 91°50.99'W) corner close SE of the island's lighted western point. This corner is the entrance to Puerto Pesquero, Carmen's big commercial darsena. Across

the entrance, Pemex ships and the Marines' docks line the starboard side of the main channel, and 3 basins open north. The farthest NE basin is called Laguna Azul, but it's not a lagoon. The Capitanía and port offices are half a block inland from the NE corner of Laguna Azul. Past Puerto Pesquero, the next inlet is a panga cove that turns into a drainage ditch with low bridges.

Anchorages: Yachts anchor where directed by the Capitanía or pilot boat. In flat weather, arriving yachts can use the open roadstead SE of Punta Xicalango or off the range lights. On the town side or in north wind, the best place for yachts to anchor overnight is called Puntilla, close SE of the Navy base in 17' to 46' of water, just north of the bridge; this is safest from thieves and has easiest dinghy access to the shore. (Just south of the bridge root is the impound lot.)

Yachts can anchor close west of the ship channel that runs along the SW shore of Ciudad del Carmen, if you don't swing into the channel. The mole with the big flag is a busy market in early mornings, good place for breakfast.

Another anchorage is found half a mile beyond the bridge (See Carmen Bridge above.) at the mouth of Arroyo Grande commercial basin, but theft is reported. Shallow draft boats anchor almost anywhere off the mangroves SW of Punta Maniagua. Tides range about 4' at springs, but the lagoon flow is considerable.

Port Clearance: Ciudad del Carmen is a Port of Entry. The Capitanía is on the corner of Calle 1 Sur and Calle 4 Oriente, at the NE corner of Puerto Pesquero. Yachts need to clear Aduana and Migración as well, and both offices are located at the airport on the east side of town.

Local Services: Pemex (Orsan) and Shell (FUVA) are found at the 500' long fuel

Ciudad del Carmen has 2 fuel docks at the entrance to the Puerto Pesquero commercial basin.

High section in Carmen Bridge.

docks (4' high concrete) on either side of the light tower at the entrance to Puerto Pesquero. We sounded 11' of water at the first fuel dock, and the next one is deeper.

Carmen has a shipyard, marine hardware stores, repair shops for diesels, pumps, radar and sounders and at least 2 supermercados with good canned and fresh foods. The regional fruteria mercado (fresh produce) takes place at Puntilla, the old zocalo SE of the Navy base and across from the bridge ramp. Leather goods are produced here, sometimes from iguana and shark skin.

Buccaneros Yacht Club lies 2.18 n.m. beyond the bridge, but ask a member (VHF 16) to guide your dinghy in, because there's no marked or dredged channel (5' at MLW). Go past Maniagua and angle NE toward the far side of the biggest mangrove forest. The narrow entrance channel is hidden north of a mangrove finger. At the dock, our GPS is 18°38.33'N, 91°47.58'W. This is a friendly club, focused on fast boats and corbina tournaments.

History & Culture: In 1517, the Spanish explorer Grijalva left Isla Mujeres and sailed around the north side of the enormous Yucatan Peninsula. Convinced it was really a large island, he searched for the south passage around it, and when he reached this large lagoon, he named it Laguna de Términos, meaning the end. Grijalva was wrong.

For the next 200 years, this lagoon and islands were a pirate lair, so stories of buried treasure are still told. In the 18th Century, Spanish colonists and naval patrols chased out the pirates and built Fort San Felipe on Playa Norte to fend off further incursions.

One legacy of the English pirates is the fair skin and blue eyes still seen around town. After Empress Carlotta of Spain visited Isla de Carmen, she was reported to have regretted not picking some 'ladies in waiting' for her court, because their fair features would have caused pride for the crown of Mexico.

En route to Campeche

From Ciudad del Carmen to Campeche is a 100-n.m. straight shot, but the coast curves NE and can be run 3 to 4 n.m. off shore. Use caution or avoid traveling at night when shrimpers work this wide shallow shelf. The low coastal berm is backed by marshes until Chompotón, and you may see traffic on Highway 180.

Sabancuy Banks (patches of 14' to 30' depth) start about 35 n.m. NE of Carmen City, lie 4 to 12 n.m. off shore, extending for about 8 n.m. NE. Shrimpers anchor around them.

Sabancuy Light 40 n.m. NE of Carmen City marks a small-boat channel (blocked by low bridge) into Estero Sabancuy. A shallow 10-mile waterway behind the berm reaches the NE end of Laguna de Terminos.

Buccaneros Yacht Club has a rescue boat and helpful members.

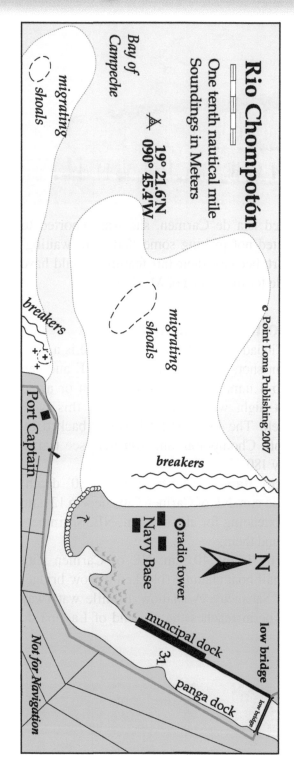

Top: Entrance to Rio Chompotón runs along a pleasant malecon.
Above: Municipal dock is OK for yatistas.

Rio Chompotón

The mouth of Rio Chompotón (19°21.6'N, 90°45.4'W) is guarded by lighted 20' tall rock about .2 n.m. off the south lip of the entrance and by migrating shoals, and the boca's north lip is recessed about 300 yards. But once past these hazards, the buoyed river channel (10'

depth) is navigable for half a mile to a low bridge. A Navy base occupies the mouth's north side, and upstream on the north bank is a municipal seawall and apron providing good shelter and secure shore access. Most of the town is south of the river.

Hail the Capitanía (VHF 16) or a navy skiff for guidance into the river channel. Taxis at the seawall can take you to the Aduana 2 n.m. south on the malecon, next to a big hospital.

Once you're cleared in, diesel can be arranged by tank truck at the seawall. Rio Chompotón is a panga port with basic marine hardware and outboard repairs, grocery stores, a big regional farmers' market next to the bus station, a fishing school and weekend beach tourists. After Rio the Campeche coast turns north for the next 20 n.m.

Chompotón Banks: Another area of shoals (14' to 27') starts about 8.5 n.m. WNW of Chompotón and extends 5 n.m. NW, showing depths of 14' to 27'.

Playa Sihoplaya (7 to 12 n.m. north of Rio Chompotón) is an open roadstead off a regular sandy beach south of Punta Sihoplaya. Locals say the English pirate Henry Morgan used this anchorage regularly, gathering wood and water ashore, leaving mementos in the fishing villages from Sihoplaya 5 n.m. north to Sebaplaya on the south side of Punta Morro.

A landmark fort, Castillo San Bartolo, stands above the shore about a mile NE of Punta Maxtun Grande, and new power transmission towers run along the hills behind the castle.

Campeche Approach: Cerro San Bartolo is the highest of the town's unique limestone outcroppings behind the coastal berm; it's marked by San Bartolo Light (19°49'N, 90°35'W), the most powerful nav light (26 n.m.) in the region.

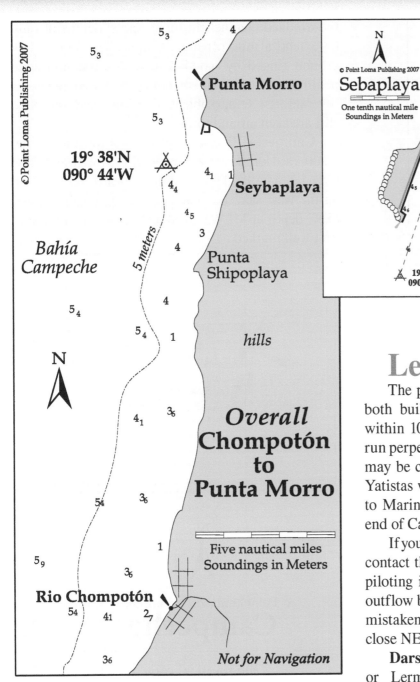

Lerma - Campeche

The ports of Lerma and Campeche are adjacent, both built for the commercial vessels that anchor within 10 n.m. west on 21' shoals. Several channels run perpendicular to shore. After storms, the channels may be closed, or dredges may be working in them. Yatistas who wish to stop here are normally directed to Marina Bahía Azul at Campeche Pier at the NE end of Campeche.

If you must enter Lerma or elsewhere in Campeche, contact the Campeche Port Pilot for permission and piloting instructions. Lerma power plant intake and outflow breakwaters at the SW end of town are often mistaken for harbors. A shallow panga harbor opens close NE of the curved outflow jetty.

Darsena de Pesqueros (19°49'N, 90°36.6'W) or Lerma's Fishermen's Basin has a 300-yard approach channel. The enclosed basin has room for a 72' motoryacht to turn around, 13' depth at MLW alongside, a diesel dock and a commercial ways for possible emergency haul-out.

Muelle Castillo Breton: Half a mile past the darsena, the older Breton Castle Pier juts farther out into the shallow shelf than does the darsena, and ships (max 13' at ML) use range lights (139°) to reach it. The Capitanía at the head of this pier also has Immigration and Customs.

Campeche (pop. 150,000) is the Port of Entry and capital of the state of Campeche. This city is pleasant and modern. The public malecon has a tiny ski-boat

Sebaplaya: Yachts are prohibited from entering this new container port off the south side of Punta Sebaplaya, except in an emergency. Our approach waypoint just off the lighted south-opening entrance is 19°39.0'N, 90°42.5'W.

Punta Morro: Another large pier is in construction off this lighted headland a mile north of the container port. From 3 n.m. off Punta Morro, you may see Campeche Pier about 16 n.m. NE. The coast here turns NE for 6 n.m. to Punta Maxtun Grande (426' high, wooded). A small private breakwater (9' depth) lies between this point and lesser Punta Maxtun Chica a quarter mile farther.

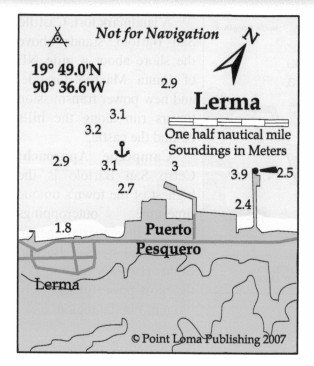

the dredged channel. In many spots, depths of only 6" extend a mile offshore. Campeche occupies low ground ringed by wooded hills. Natural limestone pediments gave Spanish colonists foundations for several forts. Remarkable walls of quarried limestone still are seen around town.

Campeche Pier at the NE end of town is a wide, 1,200-yard long breakwater carrying a roadway, with a large rectangular darsena at the seaward end, opening on the west side. Use caution; the approach channel (5'9" depth at MLW) is subject to storm silting and isn't well marked.

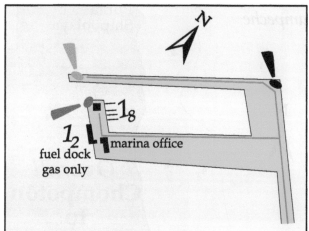

darsena about 1.4 n.m. NE of Lerma's Muelle Castillo Breton, but it's very shallow and not secure.

Campeche is Mayan for "place of savage ticks." We think it's a place of savage shoals, because everything is surrounded in less than 4' of water – except for

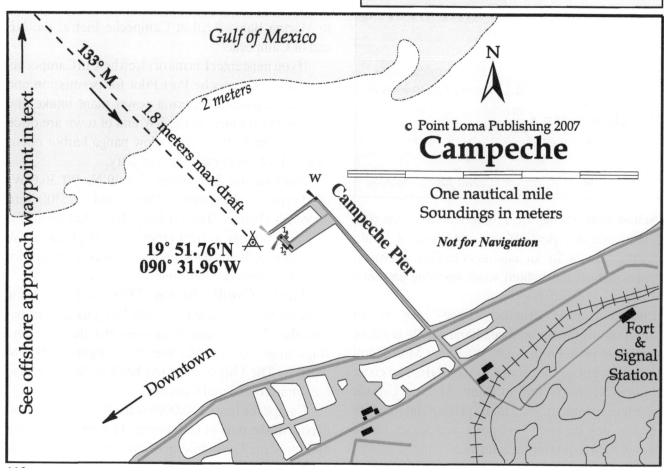

Fishing boat heads out entrance to Marina Bahía Azul at end of Campeche Pier.

Just inside the darsena, Marina Bahía Azul has 6 slips (depth 5' 9" at MLW), reportedly unreliable 110-volt power, a cold shower and washing machine ashore, though improvements are planned. Some boats here are tide-bound and sit on the bottom at low water. Shallow-draft yachts can find acres of side-tie room elsewhere in the large darsena. The pier has ample lighted parking and a part-time café.

If you draw less than 4' of water, a gas pump (no diesel at press time) and short dock are outside the darsena, just past the entrance.

Port Clearance: This region's Capitanía is in Lerma, at the head of the Darsena de Pesqueros or Fishermen's Basin, and it houses Immigration, Aduana and Navy offices as well. If the Aduana is closed, try the airport SE of town.

Local Services: Outside the Marina Bahía Azul yacht basin is a gas dock; see Campeche Pier above. Lerma's Fishermen's Basin has diesel on the dock and a marine ways. In Campeche, jerry jug gas or diesel from the Pemex across the highway from the marina pier, or from 2 other gas stations down the road about half a mile and 2.5 miles. Or ask the marina or Port Captain to arrange for a tank truck delivery at the marina.

Provision for food in Campeche's Sam's Club, Mercado Barrand and ComMex, plus many fruterías in the residential side of town. Most of the fishing & outboard supplies are found in small chandlers lining Highway 180 going through Lerma. The airport and train depot are SE of Campeche.

History & Culture: Campeche has an archeological museum displaying ancient cultural artifacts from the many Mayan digs around the Yucatan Peninsula.

The Mayan chieftain Moch-Couch who ruled this region successfully repelled the early incursions of Europeans. Hernandez de Cordoba was so roundly defeated that he labeled this area Bahía de la Mala Pelea (Bay of the Bad Fight). Plaza Monumental de Moch-Couch is a lasting reminder of the Mayan victory.

Campeche's 6 forts date from the 16th Century when the Spanish began kicking out pirates. Hernán Cortez's grandson was born in Campeche's Convent of San Francisco in 1562, and this church is still operating in town. Just north of town, the Spanish developed the San Ramon area as a ship-building center. It produced the world's first single-masted sloop in 1580, and for more than 200 years many skilled shipbuilders at Campeche and San Ramon continued producing the wooden naval vessels.

The Mayan culture is one of the most amazing of the New World. They inhabited a region encompassing today's Guatemala, Belize, Honduras and El Salvador, and parts of southern Mexico (the states of Yucatan, Campeche, Quintana Roo, Tabasco and Chiapas). Today this area is occupied by the descendants of

Marina Bahía Azul is shallow but pleasant and handy to Campeche.

the ancient Maya, the vast majority of whom have to some extent preserved their cultural heritage and still speak the many Mayan languages.

By 5000 BC, the Maya had settled along the Caribbean and Pacific coasts, in fishing communities. By 2000 BC the Maya had also moved inland and adopted agriculture for their subsistence.

For yatistas arriving from Veracruz or the US, Campeche may be their first encounter with Mayan people, often characterized by short stature, straight black hair, rounded or broad faces and slightly flat noses. These people are proud of both their rich Mayan ancestry and their Mexican citizenship.

Chicxulub Meteorite Crater

You're about to transit Earth's third-largest impact crater. The crater's east and west walls span from about Punta El Palmar to Puerto Telchac. But the area still measurably affected by the buried meteorite includes everything from Celestún to Punta Yalkubul and encompasses the many reefs and islands off the NW coast of the Yucatan Peninsula.

This was the big one, smashing into Earth about 65 million years ago near what today is Progreso. The impact of the Chicxulub meteorite marks the K-T Boundary, meaning the devastation it caused to the environment quickly ended the Cretaceous period and ushered in the modern Tertiary period. Chicxulub's havoc is believed to have zapped the dinosaurs into an early extinction – but it opened a niche for mammals.

The crater's horizontal limestone geology gave the Mayans building material for their great pyramids. Despite 36" annual rainfall, this region has no surface streams; instead, fresh water seeps into a vast labyrinth of caverns within the bedrock, which the Mayans used as reservoirs. Today we yatistas can explore and swim in the Yucatan's unique cenotes, grottos and blue holes.

En route to Puerto Yukalpetén

Campeche (state of Campeche) to Celestún (state of Yucatan) is about 75 n.m. and Puerto Yukalpetén is another 45 or 50 n.m., depending on how far off shore you travel.

North of Campeche, the bottom's 5-meter curve extends 15 n.m. off shore, and the coast drops to marshes (invisible to radar), so we depart the

Campeche Pier channel and continue NW for at least 15 n.m., then stay about 18 n.m. off shore or run in no less than 15' of water. Highway 180 and the train track run east of the marshes. At night, lights to the east are probably boats.

No-Go Area

Cayos Arcas (20°13'N, 91°58'W) are the southernmost of the oil-field cays about 90 n.m west of the Yucatan Peninsula, but they are off limits to yachts and have a no-anchoring zone of about 5 n.m. The Arcas, Obispos and Triangles are an "Area to Avoid;" Navy gunboats have prohibited yachts from approaching.

Obispo Shoals about 95 n.m. west of Isla Piedras stretch about 6 n.m. SW to NE with 2 drying bars at the north (20°29'N, 92°12'W) and south ends; a wreck is reported in between.

Cayos Triangulas: These 2 large lighted reefs, east and south (20°54'N, 92°14'W) lie about 25 and 30 n.m. NNW of Obispo Shoals and are also No-Go zones for yatistas.

Isla de Jaina, about 20 n.m. up from Campeche at the edge of the marshes, is a Mayan ruin from about 200 A.D., but it's accessible only to shallow-draft craft.

The Campeche Shelf begins to close with land, so in fair weather you may be able to travel in 15' to 20' of water over the sand bottom about 5 to 7 n.m. off the low coastline. Isla Piedras (30' high) may show on radar about 30 n.m. north of Campeche.

Isla Arena Light (20°36'N, 90°28'W) is a 14-mile light about 22 n.m. up from Isla Piedras and 14 n.m. down from Celestún's lighted wharf. Isla Arena Light marks a migrating shoal south of Punta Desconocido (Unknown Point) and La Costa panga village. Don't confuse this with the similarly shoal entrance to Real de Las Salinas (Salt Flats) about 10 n.m. farther north.

Petenes Ecological Reserve fronts the coast from Isla Arena up to the Celestún Reserve. A *peten* is an island of foliage centered around a fresh-water cenote. Petenes provide habitat for many exotic flora and fauna species.

Real de Las Salinas (20°45'N by 90°26'W) is the shoal mouth of Laguna de Las Salinas (Estero Celestún), an 18-mile estuary of Celestún Biosphere

Reserve, but no access to Celestún harbor. The state of Yucatan border runs down the middle of this lagoon mouth. Uncharted since recent hurricanes, the estuary is navigable by local pangas within unmarked channels.

Ria Celestún Special Biosphere Reserve: Pontoon boats and pangas drawing less than 3' ferry tourists through this 146,000-acre eco-park. Its 30,000 pink flamingoes are the big attraction, but many endangered sea turtles nest here as well. *Ojos de agua* (eyes of water) or fresh-water springs are welcome swimming holes amid so much salt water. This park is similar to Rio Lagartos farther east.

Yachts are no longer permitted to enter this biosphere, so yatistas need to hire one of the park's certified naturalist guides with a registered park vessel to enjoy this eco-adventure. Guides are booked most easily at Celestún harbor, and they provide transportation to the tour boats. A Celestún park guide we know of is Bacab Ortiz Jesus David; phone (988) 916-2049. A tour provider we recommend is hotel Eco Paraiso Xixim on the north side of town; phone (988) 916-2100, or www.ecoparaiso.com. They can also get you tours of the area's cenotes, Mayan ruins & Spanish haciendas.

Map:
Not for Navigation
Gulf of Mexico
old pier
estuary
panga docks
N
Celestún
20° 50.9'N
090° 24.4'W
One half nautical mile
Soundings in Meters
© Point Loma Publishing 2007

From the turning basin, the narrowed channel angles NE into a shallower north basin.

Celestun

Celestún, state of Yucatan, has a small fishing harbor or *puerto abrigo* with a Pemex diesel dock. The harbor shoals up after heavy rains; a dredge may be working in the narrow channel, so call the Celestún Port Captain on VHF 16 when you're within range to confirm the depths.

Yatistas can come into the harbor (about 4' in channel at MLW), the entrance to which is marked by Celestún lighted breakwaters (20°50.9'N, 90°24.5'W) opening west. The channel runs east half a mile, then north half a mile with a seawall on the west side.

Thousands of pink flamingos delight visitors to Celestun Biosphere.

Eco-Tourism in the Gulf Coast

Eco-tourism is a blossoming industry in Mexico's Gulf Coast states, and it's more developed in the Yucatan Peninsula. Hiking a jungle trail to ancient ruins, touring a vanilla-bean plantation with stingless bees, kayaking white-water rapids or tranquil lagoons, exploring blue holes and cenotes – they're all part of Mexico's Gulf Coast and Yucatan Peninsula.

Cenotes are ancient limestone caverns that formed near the coast but are now submerged and filled with fresh or salt water. Swimming or scuba diving in a cenote is a unique experience. Some cenote systems are vast, linking inland cenotes to the open ocean through underground channels.

Visiting yatistas can easily join up the day before with hotel-based groups that are planning to explore environmental delights in that area. Some biospheres and wildlife preserves limit the number of visitors allowed inside each day, and rules are enforced by rangers to prevent damage to the environment. Some coastal biospheres allow yatistas to enter in their own dinghies, but we suggest that you first join one of the many licensed excursion groups that provide an experienced naturalist guide – then come back in your own dinghy or boat after you've got the lay of the land.

The Rains Guides and Point Loma Publishing support Mexico's robust form of eco-tourism that preserves and protects the natural environment while educating all visitors to these delicate places.

The Capitanía overlooks the harbor entrance, and he directs yachts where to anchor inside, or he'll make docking arrangements and issue you a fuel permit.

Larger boats can anchor off the town's seaside wharf (8' to 10' at MLW) about half a mile north of the breakwaters. Celestún is not a Port of Entry, but the Navy patrol usually boards and inspects vessels anchored near the wharf or in the harbor.

Celestún town has a propane distributor, a few small grocery stores, lots of seafood restaurants and small hotels for eco-park visitors. This harbor doesn't connect to the estuary part of Celestún Biosphere Reserve. Guides will find you. For hiking or biking into the edge of the park, dink across to the east

seawall or take the dead-end beach road north of Celestún. From the center of town, Highway 281 runs east about 60 miles to Merida, the capital of Yucatan state. Departing Celestún, head NW off shore until you find deep enough water (15' to 25') before turning NE and paralleling the low coastline about 6 n.m. off.

El Palmar Eco-Reserve spreads behind Celestún park and up the coast almost to Sisal, and although from off shore you can't see where one park ends and the other begins, the coast is higher (radar visible), carrying a 1-lane beach road that washes out in spots and has horse-riders.

Punta Boxcohuo is the low sandy NW corner of the Yucatan Peninsula. A detached shoal (8.9' of water) was reported 3 n.m. north of Punta Boxcohuo. From here eastward, the Campeche Shelf narrows toward shore, and the coast begins tending more E-W, and the Gulf Stream's west-setting current is felt more strongly.

Las Palmas Light (21°03.7'N, 90°15.2'W) has a racon Q (dah, dah, di, dah) on the low sandy shore about 15 n.m. west of Sisal harbor. Deeper water

Tunnels through the mangrove forests lead to flamingo playgrounds and provide habitat for 100s of protected species.

comes closer to shore, so most yachts can travel about 3 to 5 n.m. off.

Sisal & Madagascar Reefs lie about 13 and 22 n.m. offshore respectively, outside the 20-fathom curve, each with about 8.9' of water over coral heads. Sisal Reef (21°21'N, 90°09'W) has a light.

Arrecife Alacran (Scorpion Reef): This offshore coral reef system (13 n.m. N-S, 10 n.m. wide) lies about 65 n.m. north of Sisal. The whole reef area is a national park created to protect the delicate corals. If you stop here, use the park's moorings – don't anchor within the corals or you'll damage the reef habitat. Or anchor half a mile west of the reef's west perimeter.

Alacran's 3 nav lights: tiny Isla Pajaro and largest Isla Perez (racon Z, lighthouse) near the south end and Isla Desterada near the north end. The east wall breaks heavily and is littered with wrecks, some reported as 16th Century galleons. During normal Trade Winds the current is 1-knot westerly. From the west, small sand channels lead between coral heads. From the south, our approach is 22°20.14'N, 89°42.64'W.

Puerto Sisal: Back on the mainland, this tiny harbor where henequen fiber used to be exported is reported shoaled closed, so we pass about 4 n.m. off (21°13.63'N, 90°04.84'W). Chuburna panga harbor about 13 n.m. east is being dredged for ocean-going boats. Beyond its low bridge, the estuary spreads behind the berm eastward.

From here, Puerto Yukalpetén lies about 8.5 n.m. east, and the big seaward end of Progreso Pier is visible 12 n.m. ENE.

Puerto Chuberna is found at 21°10.00'N, 90°03.00'W, popular for jet boats and skis.

Puerto Yukalpetén

Puerto Yukalpetén is about 125 n.m. around from Campeche, 42 n.m. east of Punta Boxcohuo, 150 n.m. WSW of Cabo Catoche and 190 n.m. around from Isla Mujeres, Quintana Roo, in the Yucatan Channel.

Since this man-made harbor opened in 1990, many sportfishers and cruising boats from Galveston and New Orleans plan for fuel and weather stop here en route to the Yucatan Channel cruising and fishing grounds.

Puerto Yukalpetén shelters several small marinas (the only yacht slips between Veracruz and Isla Mujeres), boat yards, a ship yard, the Navy base, Pemex docks, plus commercial fishing sea walls with ice and diesel. Around the harbor you'll find chandlers, electronics sales & service, etc. The city of Progreso (pop. 32,000) about 3 n.m. east has ample provisions and shore services and is home to many retired Canadians.

Approach: Puerto Yukalpetén lies 4 n.m. SW of the large commercial darsena at the north end of Progreso Pier (21°20'N by 89°40.8'W), lighted and

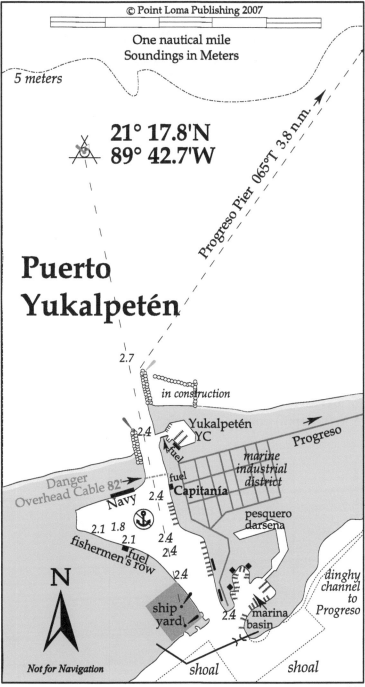

© Point Loma Publishing 2007

One nautical mile
Soundings in Meters

5 meters

21° 17.8'N
89° 42.7'W

Progreso Pier 065°T 3.8 n.m.

Puerto Yukalpetén

2.7

in construction

Yukalpetén YC

2.4

Progreso

marine industrial district

fuel

Danger Overhead Cable 82'

fuel

Capitanía

Navy   2.4

pesquero darsena

2.1 1.8

2.1   2.4

fishermen's row   fuel   2.4

N

2.4

ship yard

2.4   marina basin

dinghy channel to Progreso

Not for Navigation

shoal   shoal

Note 82' overhead clearance into Puerto Yukalpetén.

marked with a racon Y (dah, di, dah, dah). Up to 5 cruise ships cluster around this deep-water darsena, so stay clear of traffic.

Our GPS approach waypoint just off Puerto Yukalpetén's lighted breakwaters is 21°17.8'N, 89°42.7'W. Range lights (169°T) bring you in the breakwaters to the ship yard. But overhead power lines (See photo & chart above.) allow 82' clearance, so larger sailboats may not get in. The east breakwater projects farther than does the west. This entrance can get closed out in Northers; don't wait too long.

Lay of the Land: The main channel minimum dredged depth is 7'11" at MLW. The yacht club's side basin opens east just past the stubby west breakwater. A quarter mile in from the west breakwater, overhead power cables (82' elevation) restrict access to taller masted sailboats. Beyond the overhead cables, the most accessible marina has a depth of 7' at MLW. Smaller marinas are found in another side lobe. New bridge has only 75' elevation. The west basin is all commercial and Navy, but the ship yard handles large yachts. Anchoring is no longer allowed in Puerto Yukalpetén. Not part of the port, Laguna Frago is mostly shoal, but a panga channel reaches the south side of Progreso, by going under the new bridge.

Berthing: Make an 80° left to enter the side basin (5 to 7' depth) containing Marina Yukalpetén (Club de Yates de Yukalpetén). With 100 full-service slips to 70' LOA, the yacht club has an occasional guest slip. The yacht club's 70' fuel dock (centrifuged diesel) lies to starboard as you enter their basin. FMI, contact Eduardo Ponce (969) 935-2969. Hail "Marina Yukalpetén" on VHF 74.

Marina Tortuga (7.9' depth) past the Capitanía has about 90 slips, with end ties to about 65'. Inside the marina basin, clockwise around the north shore are Marina Torre, Chabeta's Marina, Marina Johnson and Marina Rohano (dry storage only). Chabeta's and Johnson have about 15 slips each, to about 40' LOA. A narrow channel leads NE to the Darsena de Pesqueros. On the marina basin's south corner is Marina Alacranes, then a boat yard and 2 smaller marinas. Sportfishers occupy most of these slips.

Anchorage: Shallow-draft yachts can anchor in the north side of Estero Yukalpetén, which is mostly shoal but spreads 2 n.m. east and 3 n.m. west. A flamingo sanctuary covers the estuary's south shore, so no anchoring there.

Port Clearance: No fuel permit is required, but you must clear in before taking fuel. Notify "Capitanía Yukalpetén" on VHF 16 or come to the Capitanía on the east seawall overlooking the harbor. Until more streamlined procedures are implemented, if you have a crew change or need to import parts with your TIP, a full port clearance may be required.

Local Services: Yatistas are encouraged to use the 70' diesel & gas dock just inside the yacht club's basin. For larger boats, we found 2 larger diesel docks: adjacent to the Capitanía on the harbor's east side, and across the harbor at the south end of fishermen's seawall.

A small chandlery store is part of Marina Yukalpetén. The area east of the

This Capitanía in Puerto Yukalpetén handles yatistas, not the one on Progreso Pier.

Marinas, chandlers, repair yards & services surround this harbor.

harbor is mostly marine industrial shops, a great place to get boat stuff fixed. Chabeta's Marina has a workshop, and Pabco handles hull & rigging. Zema ship yard handles big yachts.

Estero Yukalpetén is mostly shoal; an unmarked panga-dinghy channel (may be dredged in the future to 12') runs about 3 n.m. east to small public docks (not secure) at the south side of Progreso, where odd numbered streets run E-W, even ones N-S. Spanish classes are at Casa Isadora, 117 Calle 21; (969) 935-5473. Taxis don't hang out inside Puerto Yukalpetén, so if you find one you like, get his VHF call or cell number. Cell phones work Progreso

to Merida. A regular high-speed ferry service between the US and Progreso is planned. Merida (20 miles south on divided highway) is the capital of Yucatan, has CostCo, Sam's Club and Carrefour, plus grocery chains ComMex, Gigante and Chedruai. Merida has welders, electricians, travel agents and tour providers.

Side Trips: Puerto Yukalpetén is the most practical place to leave your boat in a secure marina, while you explore Yucatan's world-famous Mayan ruins, cenotes and grottos. Next

best is from Isla Mujeres. Put together a group of 6 and hire your own guide; EcoTurismo Yucatan (999) 920-2772 or www.ecoyuc.com. Or ride the Expreso Maya, a private train tour between Chichén Itzá and Palenque; www.expresomaya.com.

Chichén Itzá was the Mayan center: Watch sunrise on the vernal equinox (March 21) at *Castillo* pyramid dedicated to Kukulcan. In the Astronomical Observatory, Mayan priests accurately charted the planets' movements and developed the Mayan calendar still in use. In the Ball Court the game Pelote was played to the death – sometimes kicking around the losers' heads. Check out the Sacred Well of Sacrifices. Nearby are 2 blue holes: Cenote Sagrado (Sacred) and Cenote Dzitnup with iridescent fresh waters that are reached by descending into the cavern.

Merida (20 n.m. south) is a lovely state capital, has a large Museum of Anthropology & History, gracious haciendas and henequen works to tour. En route to Merida, you'll transit a national park of the D'zibil Chaltum Mayan ruins 5 miles east of the toll road. Other Mayan ruins south and east of Merida are Ake, Mayapan, Ux-mal, Kabah, Sayil, Labna, Kom, Kihuic, Chac Multun, Salpacal, Mul and X-Hasil.

Club de Yates de Yukalpetén lies inside the first basin off the entrance channel.

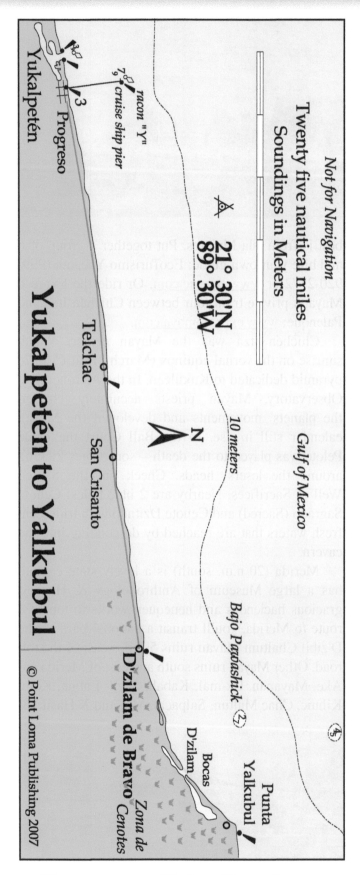

Not for Navigation

Twenty five nautical miles
Soundings in Meters

21° 30'N
89° 30'W

Gulf of Mexico

N

10 meters

Tacon "Y"
cruise ship pier

Progreso

Yukalpetén

Telchac

San Crisanto

Yukalpetén to Yalkubul

D'zilam de Bravo

Bocas D'zilam

Zona de Cenotes

Bajo Pawashick

Punta Yalkubul

© Point Loma Publishing 2007

En route to Cabo Catoche

Clear the seaward end of Progreso Pier and find deep water. This 150 n.m. leg is mostly ENE, often straight into the Trade Winds and against the Gulf Stream (half to 1-knot out to 30 n.m.). If you don't need to stop, travel 5 n.m. off the low but tree-lined shoreline and stay in about 20' of water to avoid shoals. Inside 15' many shifting shoals and recent wrecks are found. However, Bajo Pawaschick rises from about 25' of water about 8 n.m. west of Punta Yalkubul. Plan to round Cabo Catoche at least 10 miles off.

If you do have a problem and need to stop en route, here are some small harbors along the north coast of the Yucatan Peninsula that may offer shelter and assistance. With caution, most boats can travel about 3 n.m. off shore in 15' to 20' of water.

Puerto Telchac

This small fishing harbor (21°20.7'N, 89°18.7'W) about 25 n.m. east of Progreso Pier has lighted breakwaters, but the west one is much larger and has a dog leg, so you must enter from the east. Depth in the entrance channel is about 6', but it is being dredged and improved in 2011. If in doubt, hail "Telchac Harbormaster" on VHF 16.

A quarter mile in, the main basin opens east. Yachts can anchor in a side basin off the north side of the main basin. The NW corner of this yacht spot is shoal. A seawall lines this area, and a taxi may come out from town to see if you need anything.

A fuel dock with diesel and gas (5.28' of water alongside) is on the harbor's SE seawall, and the Puerto Telchac municipal harbormaster's office is next door.

Cannery docks line the SW side of the main basin. The east end is shoal and in construction. An abandoned beach hotel half a mile west is a good landmark. Pangas zoom under the low bridge and into the estuary south of Highway 27, which runs from Progreso to D'zilam de Bravo.

Tiny Puerto Crisanto is for shallow-draft fishing boats.

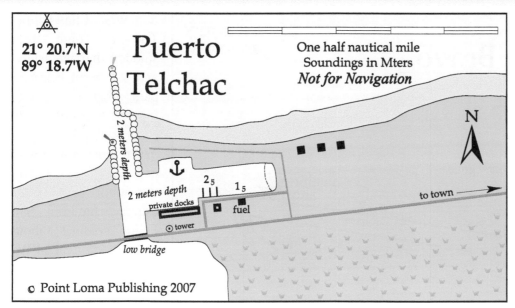

panguero guide) to lead you in and point out the high spots in the channel.

The lighted breakwaters have a wave baffle at the seaward end, so approach from NW. The narrow channel runs south for about 300 yards, but then you need to angle WSW to reach the main basin, avoiding a shoal side channel that disappears into the marshes.

Come alongside a vacant spot on the seawall in the west channel, as long as you don't block the ice house or fuel dock, or Medmoor in the slightly larger basin at the west end.

The Capitanía overlooks the west basin; office upstairs on the east side. The Port Captain says they get only a few yatistas each year (one January we were the third to stop in 3 months), but that the port welcomes yates and makes all services available. Be sure to use the port's whole name, because several other D'zilam towns exist.

Diesel and gas are pumped on either side of the west channel. The largest building near the entrance is a machine shop that can weld aluminum and fabricate steel. Nearby are other repair shops, batteries, fishing supplies. The town of D'zilam de Bravo to the west has a grocery, small hotels, several restaurants behind the beach and a bus station (60 miles to Merida).

San Crisanto: About 11 n.m. east of Telchac, there's no approach channel through the 2 n.m of shoals to reach this very tiny harbor. It's often silted to less than 4' of water – unless a dredge arrives. Shallow-draft craft may enter the unlighted breakwaters and anchor off the beach in the south end of the entrance channel. The beach is used for careening local fishing boats. San Crisanto has no services.

The low tree-lined coast tends NE for about 17 n.m., and the 5-meter curve begins moving farther off shore. By D'zilam de Bravo, 3 n.m. off shore puts you in about 16' of water.

D'zilam de Bravo

This small harbor (6' depth at MLW) is the best of these small hopes along Yucatan's north coast, because you can come alongside to get diesel and access a good machine shop. Hail "Capitan de Puerto" on VHF 16 when in range to confirm the channel is open. If in doubt, ask for a *piloto* (local

Lighted entrance channel into D'zilam de Bravo harbor has crook at north end.

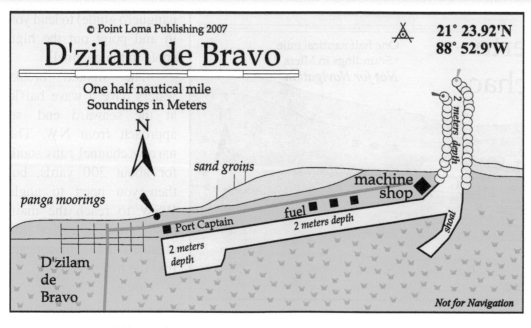

© Point Loma Publishing 2007

D'zilam de Bravo

One half nautical mile
Soundings in Meters

N

21° 23.92'N
88° 52.9'W

sand groins

panga moorings

machine shop

2 meters depth

Port Captain

fuel

2 meters depth

2 meters depth

D'zilam de Bravo

2 meters depth

shoal

Not for Navigation

n.m. west of San Felipe. The 10' high tree-studded barrier island and sea berm begin to paint a better shoreline, but the half-mile wide estuary mouth is shoal. You might see the lights of San Felipe village on the south side of the estuary, but the San Felipe channel (about 21°35'N, 88°14'W) into the west end of Rio Lagartos Estuary has been closed by hurricanes.

Departing D'zilam de Bravo, head due north for about 3 n.m before turning NE. You won't see a beach road again until past Rio Lagartos. The mouths of Estero Arenas and Bocas D'zilam have been silted closed.

Bajo Pawaschick (reported 8.91') lies about 21°31.5'N, 88°46.2'W, which is about 5 n.m. north of the coast and about 8 n.m. west of lighted Punta Yalkubul.

Punta Yalkubul (21°31.2'N, 88°36.7'W) is low, tree-studded. Pass 3 to 5 n.m off (about 22' depth). In strong Trades, the current may accelerate around this point.

From here, 22 n.m. ENE to about San Felipe Light, the marsh coastline disappears from radar. We stay 5 n.m. off to avoid Bajo Antonieta (2' depth) about 4

Instead, we suggest yatistas proceed 4 n.m. farther NE to the safer entrance channel just SW of Punta Holchit.

Rio Lagartos

According to local legend, *lagartos* were dangerous man-eating crocodiles that the Mayan natives convinced the Spanish explorers were found everywhere within this estuary – so they'd go away. Rio Lagartos Biosphere is a special reserve and the largest pink flamingo habitat in North America, and like Celestún Biosphere, it houses many species of sea turtle and other marine fauna and flora.

From about 3 n.m. off shore, approach the NW side of the wave-baffled lighted breakwaters. Our approach waypoint about a mile off the entrance is 21°37'N, 88°11'W. The east breakwater extends farther than does the west, but unlike most entrance channels in this region, Rio Lagartos entrance runs SE.

Inside the fairway at D'zilam de Bravo are a machine shop, fuel dock & Capitanía.

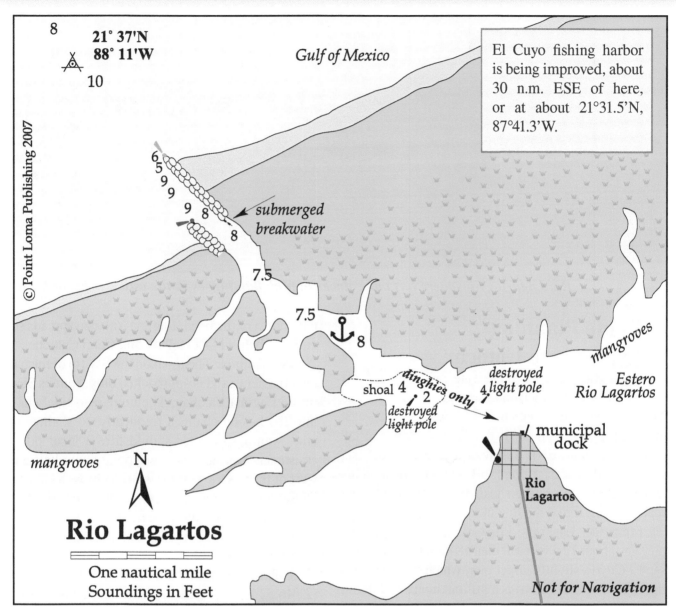

8

21° 37'N
88° 11'W

10

Gulf of Mexico

El Cuyo fishing harbor is being improved, about 30 n.m. ESE of here, or at about 21°31.5'N, 87°41.3'W.

© Point Loma Publishing 2007

6
5
9
9
9
8
8

submerged breakwater

7.5

7.5
8

mangroves

shoal 4
2
dinghies only
4 *destroyed light pole*
Estero Rio Lagartos

destroyed light pole

municipal dock

mangroves

N

Rio Lagartos

One nautical mile
Soundings in Feet

Rio Lagartos

Not for Navigation

This breakwater has been the best maintained of the small ports in this region, but one big hurricane can change everything. If in doubt, hail "Capitanía Rio Lagartos" on VHF 16 and ask the channel depth, or request a piloto (local panga guide) to get you safely in.

The first natural side channel to starboard shoals in about 100 yards. Yachts drawing less than 8' can anchor about a mile inside the sheltered main entrance channel, while dinghies and boats drawing less than 4' can cross the estuary (look for stakes marking the channel) and dock at the town of Rio Lagartos.

The Capitanía is next to the rectangular lighthouse on the west side of the town's delta peninsula, where most pangas moor. The municipal fuel dock is on the east side, where most excursion boats berth. El Mirador, a tourist tower on the point is for viewing

flamingos, but you may spot a resident flock just west of the channel anchorage. The town has minor provisions, weekend tourist hotels and lots of seafood restaurants. By bus, the nearest city is Valladolid, about 50 miles south.

Rio Lagartos Biosphere is off limits to yates, so hire one of the many licensed panga guides to take you around. Don't worry, they'll find you. One tour provider who focuses on Rio Lagartos bird-watching and wildlife photography by kayak or panga is Rio Lagartos Eco Tours; email bebemariam@yahoo.com. The biosphere encompasses everything east of the entrance channel for 20 n.m. If you fancy a freshwater swim in the jungle, a small cenote is on the edge of town.

Rio Lagartos Biosphere has more flocks of pink flamingoes in the estuary east of the town.

Route Planning
Lagartos to Catoche

From Rio Lagartos breakwater, we stay at least 4 n.m. off the northernmost rounded point of the Yucatan Peninsula, which lies about 2.5 n.m. east and isn't always lighted. If the Trades allow, we lay a course 60 n.m. ENE to stay at least 8 n.m. off Isla Holbox and at least 10 n.m. off Cabo Catoche. This avoids several migrating shoals (max 10' depth) that reach at least 6 and 8 n.m. out.

From Rio Lagartos, Los Colorados small panga pier lies about 12 n.m. east, then 18 n.m. ESE you may see El Cuyo's slightly larger pier, which is sometimes lighted. Monte del Cuyo is a 40' landmark hill about 30 n.m. east of Rio Lagartos. The state waters of Quintana Roo begin about 5 n.m. east of Monte del Cuyo.

Boca de Conil: From El Cuyo, the low north edge of Isla Holbox lies another 15 n.m. NE, but the indent between is Boca de Conil, the mostly sand-barred entrance to Laguna Yalahau. A bar with about 4.5' depth crosses the entrance, and a 12' deep shoal lies 5 n.m. north of the boca. Laguna Yalahau spreads south and east behind Isla Holbox and Cabo Catoche.

Isla Holbox: The town on the SW tip of the 6 n.m. long barrier island is approached only from its SE side inside Laguna Yalahau. The unmarked tidal channel into the lagoon changes frequently, so shallow-draft craft wanting to enter should hire a local pilot for assistance. Our approach waypoint about half a mile west of the town's west tip is 21°30.19'N, 87°23.77'W. Diesel and gas may be jerry-jugged from the Pemex station (cash only) on the east side of Isla Holbox. A ferry runs SE across the lagoon to Chiquila, which is the nearest road link.

Cabo Catoche: Stay at least 10 n.m. north (21°46.52'N, 87°06.29'W) of Cabo Catoche to stay in deep water and avoid the migrating shoals that reach about 7 n.m. NE of the point. Cabo Catoche Light has been very reliable, a 25-n.m. light and excellent landmark on low Isla Boca Iglesias. From this offshore waypoint, it's another 38 n.m. to Isla Mujeres by staying well outside Isla Contoy and Isla Blanca with reefs off its east side.

NOTE: Please skip ahead one chapter, if you're going around Cabo Catoche and down the Yucatan Channel to Isla Mujeres, Cancun, Puerto Morelos, Cozumel and other destinations.

NOTE: If you're arriving from or returning to the Key West by way of the Florida Straits, please continue with the next chapter on NW Cuba. It starts at Marina Heminway near Havana and moves west to join the Central American route at the north end of the Yucatan Channel.

About the Cuba Chapter

This chapter is unique. It includes emergency approach information and closer details for Marina Hemingway only, because it's the most fully developed recreational boating facility in Cuba. But for all Cuba's 12 smaller marinas scattered around the island, we can provide only the basic emergency contact and approach information about whatever emergency assistance or services they might have.

The problem is not Cuba's reception of yatistas, which has been hospitable and helpful in recent years (not always so). The problem is US Customs officials' reception of U.S. citizens who have visited Cuba in violation of the US economic embargo.

Logistically, it's almost impossible for a recreational vessel to travel from Miami toward the Yucatan Channel without passing close to more than 200 n.m. of Cuba's NW coastline. Traveling generally westward, slow-moving yachts are safer staying south of the heavily traveled eastbound shipping lanes, and that almost requires coast-hopping Cuba.

Despite the US economic embargo against Cuba, we believe that omitting nautical facts about Cuba from a nautical guidebook of this region would not only be a disservice to our readers, it would also be an act of negligence on our parts. As a matter of safety and good seamanship, the prudent mariner should always have access to the latest information that would allow him or her to seek the nearest refuge in case of dangerous weather or disabling mechanical or medical problems.

Most of the research in this chapter was performed by the Rainses in Cuba as journalists during 2003, but it has been updated with fresh information from several trusted contributors in Cuba through early 2007. We hope that future editions will be able to include all the marinas, a dozen all-weather anchorages and some of the fishing, diving and cruising grounds around Cuba – just as this guide does in Mexico, Belize, Guatemala, El Salvador, Honduras, Nicaragua, Costa Rica and Panama. Please check for Updates on www.CentralAmericanBoating.com.

Meanwhile, for boaters who wish to cruise here we recommend Nigel Calder's excellent *CUBA: A Cruising Guide* published in England by Imray Laurie Norie & Wilson, Ltd. www.Imray.com.

Nobeltec has vector charts of inshore Cuba in its Caribbean package.

WARNING!

As we go to press with this 6th edition, our main concern about Cuba is that US citizens who stop at Cuba are still being prosecuted by the US State Department. Visit the US Treasury Department's Office of Foreign Asset Control (OFAC) to get the official picture http://www.treas.gov/offices/eotffc/ofac/. We hope that by the time you read this, the US economic embargo against Cuba will have been lifted.

But if it has not, then US citizens who visit Cuba should be prepared upon their return to the US (1.) to be interviewed in person by a US Customs Officer, and (2.) to state in writing (a.) why they went to Cuba, (b.) whether they spent any money there, and (c.) what they brought back from Cuba. US citizens have been fined thousands of dollars per person and, in extreme cases, faced federal imprisonment for "trading with the enemy."

US Customs officers patrol the approaches to Key West.

What's a mariner to do?

Severe weather, serious medical emergency or disabling mechanical failure are justifiable reasons for stopping in Cuba, according to US Customs. Before going to Cuba, accredited journalists should obtain a Letter of Intent from their publishers and then apply to US Customs for one of two types of licenses to visit Cuba.

We're told that cash receipts left in drawers or waste baskets onboard are the most common ways inspecting officers prove money was spent in Cuba. Electronic records of credit-card transactions are readily available to US Customs inquiries. Anchoring out each night helps boaters avoid spending money, but the Cuban Guarda Frontera (Coast Guard) usually prohibits anchoring outside Marina Hemingway overnight.

Tourism in Cuba

Many political and economic pundits predict that US tourism with Cuba will soon be reopened. Tourists who fly in or arrive by cruise ship from Europe, Mexico, Central America and South America are fairly common in Havana.

As we go to press with the 6th edition, US cruise-ship lines and tour companies have spent millions and are standing ready in Florida and Mexico. When the floodgates finally do open, we hope the Cuban people won't be overwhelmed or jaded by large-scale tourism. As yet, the ordinary folks we met are genuinely friendly, blatantly honest and adore anyone from the US. Brave individual entrepreneurs are bucking their country's system to learn conversational English and gringo manners, hoping to shake hands with "real Americans" and earn a few greenbacks.

"Bring it on!" they say. Yet we wonder if they can imagine the many ways our tourist presence will change their lives – hopefully all in positive directions. The Cuban Coast Guard, port officials and marina operators who we met welcomed us as tourists and journalists, and they were extremely helpful in all matters.

Route Planning: Key West to the Yucatan Channel

1.) The direct non-stop route SW from Key West to Isla Mujeres is about 330 n.m. This passage is complicated by strong adverse Gulf Stream current and heavy ship traffic. If the easterly Trade Winds are blowing, they'll be generally against the current, developing large seas. The CPA Cuba would be about 20 miles off Santa Lucia Light at the north end of Los Colorados Reef.

This offshore route avoids traffic rounding Cabo San Antonio, but it crosses ships heading up the Yucatan Channel toward US Gulf Coast ports. This route should be attempted only by experienced mariners in a very seaworthy vessel, with a large enough window of good weather to complete the passage. (Expect current turbulence as you approach Isla Mujeres.)

2.) Alternately, from Key West toward Marina Hemingway is about 90 n.m., approximately 205°T, and from there the coastal route allows you to point hop about 175 n.m. WSW along Cuba's NW coast to Cabo San Antonio, then jump off for the 100 n.m. passage to Isla Mujeres. (Expect current turbulence as you approach Isla Mujeres.)

This approach course to Marina Hemingway is almost perpendicular to the Gulf Stream, the Trade

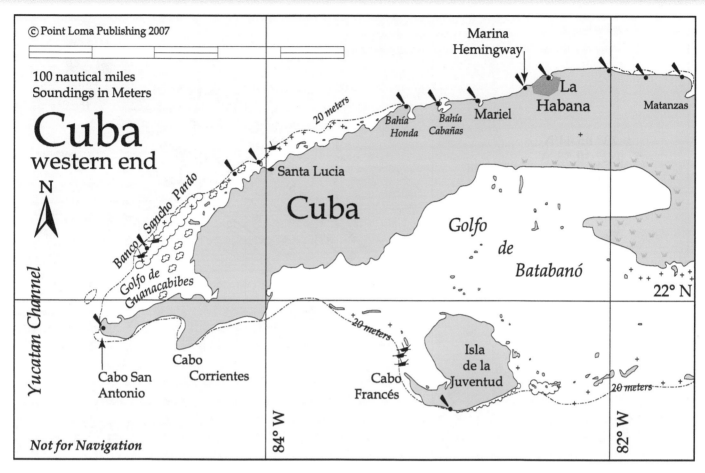

© Point Loma Publishing 2007

100 nautical miles
Soundings in Meters

Cuba
western end

N

Not for Navigation

Yucatan Channel

84° W

82° W

22° N

20 meters

Banco Sancho Pardo

Golfo de Guanacabibes

Santa Lucia

Cuba

Bahía Honda

Bahía Cabañas

Mariel

Marina Hemingway

La Habana

Matanzas

Golfo de Batabanó

Cabo San Antonio

Cabo Corrientes

Cabo Francés

20 meters

Isla de la Juventud

20 meters

Winds and shipping lanes. Stand a 2-person watch and use your radar and radios continuously, especially if you make this passage overnight when winds may be lighter.

If you can average 8 knots, you might opt for a nighttime crossing from Key West. By leaving just before sunset, you'll have daylight both for departing Key West's notorious dog-leg channel and for negotiating coral reefs on the Havana entrance. The strongest current of the Gulf Stream (3 kts) is usually encountered about 25 miles north of Havana.

Marina Hemingway, Havana

Except in an emergency, Cuba asks visiting yachts to officially clear into the country at Marina Hemingway before approaching other locations.

Yatistas drawing no more than 13' will find good shelter from the Gulf Stream and the Trade Winds inside this man-made small-boat harbor, which is lighted, buoyed, staked, dredged, gated, guarded and operated by the government. Other amenities on premises are alongside berthing, a fuel dock, a small boat yard for hauling out and minor emergency repairs, a small ship chandlery, a convenience store, an English-speaking doctor, a pharmacy and taxis. Nearby is a hospital and Havana's international airport.

Approaches: At 12 miles out of Havana, you're in Cuban territorial waters, so call the Cuban Coast Guard (*"Guarda Frontera"*) on VHF 16 to inform them of your intentions to enter the Marina Hemingway breakwater. At this time, hoist your Cuban flag (tip of star pointing up) and your yellow Q-flag.

When approaching Havana from Key West, you see the lighthouse (23°09.0'N, 82°21.4'W) on Castillo El Morro, the historic Spanish fort marking the east side of the entrance to Havana Harbor. El Morro is a 25-n.m. light on the east headland forming Havana Harbor. Yachts are not allowed into this harbor patrolled by armed Navy vessels. Prominent downtown buildings create a dramatic skyline.

Marina Hemingway lies inside Laguna Barlovento, meaning windward. The marina's entrance lies 9.25 n.m. SW of downtown Havana. At least 2 small inlets with panga traffic may be seen in between, so don't

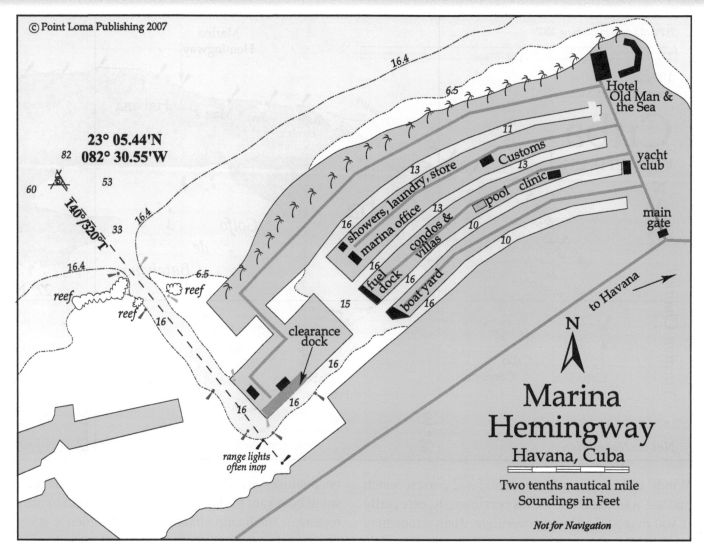

© Point Loma Publishing 2007

23° 05.44'N
082° 30.55'W

140° 320'T

reef
reef
reef

clearance
dock

range lights
often inop

16.4
6.5
Hotel
Old Man &
the Sea

11
yacht
club

Customs
13
13
showers, laundry, store
marina office
condos &
villas
pool clinic
main
gate
16
fuel
dock
13
10
16
16
10
boat yard
16
15

to Havana

N

Marina Hemingway
Havana, Cuba

Two tenths nautical mile
Soundings in Feet

Not for Navigation

aim for the wrong one. The Marina Hemingway sea buoy is 23°05.44'N, 82°30.55'W – about a quarter mile off shore.

When you're 5 n.m. out from the marina, call "Marina Hemingway" on VHF 72 to repeat your intentions to enter the breakwater. Don't attempt this approach at night, because of all the background lights.

Take the sea buoy close aboard on either side (16' depth), then come to a course of 140°T. (To the east of the entrance, you can see the masts of dozens of sailboats showing over the top of the riprap enclosing the north side of the marina, but don't aim for the masts.)

On this course, you're lined up on 3 sets of red and green posts marking the edges of the narrow gap through the dangerous reef that runs for miles on either side. This narrow channel has 16.5' of water depth between the posts. See chartlet. The third green post is on the east side of the entrance sea wall.

You pass close to this 175-yard-long sea wall (10' to 15' depth), and at the far corner of the sea wall you turn hard to port (NE), then immediately come to the clearance dock on your port side – marked by red cleats and the words "AREA DE DESPACHO" painted in red on the dock. Stop and tie up here; do not continue farther. This dock is vertical concrete with good cleats; use large fenders.

Port Clearance: To make it easier, call ahead on VHF and arrive during business hours. If you don't speak Spanish, they may have to locate a translator for you. Federal port officials handle your port clearance, then hand you off to Marina Hemingway.

Cuba's clearance procedure is protracted, standard in Latin America. Fortunately, the boarding officials all come to your boat to clear you in. The Coast Guard (*Guarda Frontera*) may be your primary inspectors, because they sometimes wear the hats of Customs (*Aduana*) and Immigration (*Migración*). If you are coming from the US, as far as the Guarda

Arrival dock is labeled Dispachos and has red bollards.

is concerned, you need only your passports and the vessel's document or registration. If you're coming from another country, present your passports and your Zarpe from there. The boarding officers bring the clearance forms and fill them out for you while asking you questions. They may bring a sniffer dog as well.

The Cuban Aduana and Migración stamp only a slip of paper, which they collect as you depart, so no permanent record of your visit is stamped in your passport. Other inspections may be done by the Ministry of Health and Agriculture (checking your provisions and health of all onboard) and the Ministry of Transportation (check your boat's safety gear, look for mosquito larvae in your bilges, mark the level of your holding tank, etc.).

If you intend to clear in and out of Marina Hemingway within a 24- to 72-hour period, inform the Guarda right at the start. As in all countries, clearing in and out at the same time saves lots of time and effort. Let them know what your needs are while you're here –fix injectors, take fuel, find a doctor, visit Old Havana, etc.

Cruising Permit: If you intend to proceed elsewhere in Cuba, give them a typed list of *puntos intermedios* – all the possible ports or anchorages where you could possibly hope to stop before departing Cuba. You'll receive your Cuban Cruising Permit (fee about $30 US) before pressing on toward other points after Marina Hemingway.

So far, Cuba allows visiting yachts to arrive with firearms and ammunition, but they must be declared to the Guarda and are taken off the boat

while it's in Cuba. Reportedly, you get a receipt for them, and they are kept in storage and returned when you are ready to depart. However, Mexico and most other countries in this guidebook strictly regulate possession of firearms, so we recommend not having them onboard.

Castro's Cuba was said to be *mordida* free. In fact, we have had more than 20 different inspectors on board, and only one official whispered and gestured that he'd like a tip as we were clearing out. In other Caribbean ports, almost every official would have had his hand out for a $20 US.

After an hour juggling papers, you get a slip assignment in the marina based on your draft, length and beam, on how long you're staying, on where they have power and water for your needs, etc.

Anchoring Restrictions: Visiting yachts are prohibited from anchoring in Cuba until they have cleared into a Port of Entry such as Marina Hemingway.

Looking west at arrival dock.
Note red bollards.
Photo by Larry Benvenuti.

Alongside berthing in Marina Hemingway.

Within this 100 n.m. vicinity, no anchoring is permitted. Foreign yachts are not permitted to even enter Havana Harbor, let alone anchor there. These rules are posted in Marina Hemingway and enforced by the Cuban Navy.

Don't approach anywhere not already approved on your *puntos intermedios* list on your Cruising

Permit. Before you do anchor, contact the nearest *Guarda Frontera* on VHF 16 to inform them of your approach. They will come in a patrol boat to inspect your papers and guide you in.

Berthing: This marina is built around 4 man-made channels curving less than a mile NE from the entrance. The channels form 3 peninsulas. The marina has 100 numbered berths alongside the non-floating concrete sea walls on both sides of the 4 channels. If you don't enjoy listening to someone else's Salsa selection cranked up to 90 decibels, then ask to be assigned a slip far from the marina's disco (goes all night) or swimming pool (quiets down after 1800).

The marina's uniformed electricians and security guards stand by to wave you toward your slip, then help get you tied up and plugged in. The berth cleats are strong, the tidal range is 2' and the shore-power hub has standard 50-amp connections. During cruising season, the Trade Winds keeps the marina cool and bug free. Electricity is metered and expensive; the electric bill can easily be higher than the slip rent. Water is also metered, though inexpensive, and you pay for just what you use.

FMI about Marina Hemingway near Havana, Cuba: (537) 209-7270 or 7928 or 7201, fax (537) 204-5280 or hail them on VHF 16 or 72. Or email Sergio Ameneiro at rpublicas@prto.mh.cyt.cu or Ing. Isuara Oraz Perez at comercial@prto.mh.cyt.cu.

Yacht Services: The end of the first peninsula contains a small boat yard. On the end of the second peninsula is the large fuel dock. The third peninsula's end contains a children's park, the disco and the marina office buildings.

Fuel dock (foreground) and boat yard (background) at Marina Hemingway.

*Power hookups in
alongside berthing.*

Scattered all along the three peninsulas you'll see 5 or 6 small, colorful hotels and time-share villas with restaurants, convenience stores and trinket shops. Coconut palms line the streets, sidewalks and grassy lawns between the channels.

NOTE: All the "Capitalistic luxuries" within the gated marina grounds are available only to people who (a.) are citizen of other countries and arrived on foreign yachts or (b.) are Cubans who work for the government in this marina. If you work here, you have passed a security clearance and wear a photo ID tag at all times. Any Cuban actually stepping foot aboard a yacht in its slip first had to get an even more specific pass from the marina office, and a guard stood by on the dock until that person disembarked. The Cuban government is trying to prevent yacht visitors from bringing gifts to the Cuban people, so don't try it. Big Brother Is Watching.

Fuel: The marina's fuel dock is easy in, easy out. From the east end of the Despachos dock where you clear in and out, the fuel dock is about 200 yards north, covering the west end of the middle peninsula. Depth at the outer end of this concrete structure is about 13'. They have diesel and gasoline from nozzle pumps. Unless a sportfishing tournament or sailing regatta is going on, you don't need to reserve fuel in advance. Early morning is hectic at the fuel dock, when dozens of hotel boats are topping off. Prices are similar to Miami. Payment is by cash, not credit card. Greenbacks are accepted.

Chandlery: A small chandlery adjacent to the marina office contains limited Cuban charts, used dive gear, some marine hardware, outboard engine oil and spark plugs, small anchors, fish nets, lobster floats and spools of fishing line and yellow polypro. Because many Havana hotel boats operate bill-fishing and sight-seeing charters out of this marina, the chandlery regularly stocks huge bags of frozen shrimp – and lots of Havana Club Rum.

Boat yard: The marina's small boatyard may use a crane to haul boats to about 30 tons and 40' in length. They specialize in propellers and shafts, rigging, gas and diesel engines, fiberglass and steel, carpentry, welding, painting and electrical, and they handle some electronics (slim on electronic parts). Make arrangements through the marina office.

Dock helpers: At your slip, you can hire an independent dock helper – such as to wash down the boat, polish the stainless – but first you have to go to the marina office with the worker and make out an Employment Contract with him. The government collects $20 per day for his labor, and you pay the worker directly whatever deal you work out. He has to be licensed to enter the marina, but ask the office which person is best for which jobs.

The marina's laundry service is in the recreation

*Hemingway International
Yacht Club office has dock.*

June it's the Ernest Hemingway International Billfishing Tournament, begun in the 1950s. In late September it's the Internat'l Blue Marlin Tournament, begun in the 1980s. The Internat'l Wahoo Tournament is in November. Fishers who fly into Cuba for these week-long tournies stay at the marina hotels. FMI, contact HIYC Commodore Jose Escrich: yachtclub@cnih.mh.cyt.cu or tel (537) 204-6653, fax (537) 204-1689 or VHF 16 or 68.

Provisions: Don't plan to provision here. Groceries in the marina's chandlery and convenience store are meager, and the 4 small grocery stores on and near Fifth Avenue, the highway leading NE to downtown Havana, have slim pickings.

Taxi: Guards and uniformed staffers circulate through the marina in extended golf carts, offering boaters free rides anywhere within the grounds. Small orange taxis also appear on weekends. At the marina's guarded entry gate, a regular city taxi may be found or hailed while it's passing on the highway out front on Fifth Avenue. Be careful, there's no stop sign there.

Local Services: Licensed English-speaking guides with or without their own cars can be hired through the marina office. They can help you rent a car or air-conditioned van and a licensed guide for longer expeditions. If you plan to leave the marina grounds, we recommend hiring one of the marina's licensed guides, because they know where foreigners are allowed and where not. We had good service from Alex Rodriguez Muñoz, who was recommended by other cruisers and reached through the marina office.

Charts: Aside from the few GeoCuba overall charts found in the marina's chandlery, the best selection of Cuban charts (Departamento Hidrográfico de Cuba) is found at El Navegante (The Navigator), a

hall north of the chandlery. Because they have propane dryers and Trade Winds breezes, a normal load needs only a 2-hour turnaround.

Medical: The marina's 24-hour First Aid office is in a small hotel on the east end of the middle peninsula. A nurse is on duty 24/7, and an English-speaking doctor has regular hours. Medical care is free for Cuban citizens, but foreigners pay about $25 for an exam. The pharmacy across the street has lots of baby lotion but almost no OTC remedies for common ailments. Prescription medicines are much higher in Cuba due to the embargo. We understand a hospital nearby has treated US yatistas.

Hemingway International Yacht Club: With a nice clubhouse in the marina's SE corner, Hemingway International Yacht Club (HIYC) has strong ties to European and South American yacht club groups. HIYC sponsors regattas and teaches sailing and sportfishing on its 24' boats Club Nautico I and II.

HIYC's Power Boating Club is very active in sportfishing, honoring Ernest Hemingway by hosting with 3 annual sportfishing tournaments. In early

Hotel view of Marina Hemingway's curving channels. Photo by Larry Benvenuti.

Havana Harbor Light photo by Larry Benvenuti. Below: Coco Taxi serves the marina.

full-service chart store at 115 Mercaderos, between Obispo and Obrapia in Old Havana. They have the *Cartas de Yates* series covering the entire coastline, each about 15" by 24" size in albums. You can hail El Navegante on VHF 16 or phone from the marina 61-3625 or 62-3466 or fax 33-8754.

Eateries: Restaurants are either "government" or "underground." Government restaurants are plagued with poor service, so many families turn their homes' inner courtyards or garden patios into "underground" restaurants. The government frowns on non-gov enterprise, but ignores it as long as no more than 12 or 15 people can be seated at a time. The best underground eateries have a line around the block for lunch and dinner.

One place we recommend highly is Arte Y Hospedaje (Art and Hospitality), a private home and restaurant owned and run by Italian master chef Jose Saivane, his lovely wife and large family. Dinner is an elegant all-evening affair in their garden patio, everything fresh and from scratch, all delicious and reasonably priced. The Saivane's home, decorated in paintings by local artists (for sale), is in a nice residential neighborhood not far from the marina, and they also rent rooms. The address is 1903 Calle 208 in the Atabey Playa neighborhood; phone (53) 271-9669. Jose Saivane and his brother also work as fishing and diving guides.

Other eateries popular with marina visitors are (a.) El Buganvil in the Playa Siboney neighborhood and (b.) El Laurel on Fifth Avenue about 4 blocks west of the marina. El Laurel's backyard fronts the marina entrance and Guarda station, and it has a shallow dinghy dock.

Sight-seeing: The street outside Marina

Hemingway's guard gate is Fifth Avenue, and it runs NE into downtown Havana. Various embassies have preserved many of the wonderful old homes on both sides. The "US Interest" berths with the Swiss Embassy, we're told. Many community gardens used to be private parks. The crumbling Russian embassy

is unmistakable – a 15-story edifice that looks like a monster robot made of Lego blocks, surrounded by a vast compound. The Russian robot is visible from 15 n.m. off shore.

Vintage American cars from the 1950s ply Havana's downtown streets, kept alive as tourist taxis by mechanical magicians, painted bright colors after their original paint wore away. Check the lineup in front of the National Capital building. Other taxis

US cars from the 1950s and earlier are preserved in Cuba, favored as luxury taxis.

Old Havana's streets are mostly pedestrian walkways along quaint shops & apartments with frilly wrought-iron balconies.

are boxy 1980s Russian cars. Giant portraits of Ernest Hemingway are almost as common around Havana as are those of Che Guevara and Jose Marti.

Old Havana is Numero Uno. About 4 square miles, it's a step into the 16th Century. Narrow streets are filled with flowering balconies, quaint hand-made shops and tapas restaurants reminiscent of modern Spain. Plaza de las Armas, the gardens and the flea market are popular tourist sights. International groups are restoring some original Spanish colonial architecture, but much is crumbling away. Storm surge from recent hurricanes damaged some 1880s buildings along the malecon.

Two historic castles guard the Havana harbor entrance: Castillo el Morro and Castillo de la Fuerza. If you enjoy romantic sculpture, the downtown cemetery has 10,000 angels; massive monuments are carved of white marble and quarried coral. Check out the Firemen's Monument. In the suburbs and rural areas, you may see a few horse-drawn carts and teams of oxen hauling sugar cane.

statue of Papa Hemingway was set there. La Floridita invented the daiquiri, but Hemingway's favorite drink was the *"mojito"* (a little moistener) made of fresh lime juice, raw sugar, crushed fresh mint leaves, Havana Club Rum and sparkling water. La Floridita is also a nice restaurant with dress code.

Hemingway's beautiful *finca* or farm (Finca Vigia) is a 90-minute drive east of Havana, but it has a view down to the harbor. His heirs donated the home and grounds to Cuba if nothing would be changed and if they would be preserved and maintained as a museum honoring Hemingway. The main house

Hemingway's Cuba

La Floridita is the corner bar in downtown Havana where Ernest Hemingway often hung out. His favorite bar stool, far left from the entrance, was so coveted that fights broke out to occupy it, so recently a

was built for entertaining, and it still contains all his furniture, clothing, books and hunting trophies. The typewriter upon which he always wrote standing up still waits atop his bedroom bookcase – exactly where he used it each morning. His Key West studio has a similar stand-up typing arrangement.

Hemingway's beloved 1934 Wheeler sportfisher "Pilar" is displayed under a shed on the tennis courts. Mystic Seaport Museum curators are evaluating and

Hemingway's home in Cuba was Finca Vigia, now preserved as a museum displaying his main house (above) and writing studio.

Fighting chair on Pilar, Hemingway's beloved Wheeler sportfisher at Finca Vigia.

possibly restoring this historic craft, one of only two remaining 1934 Wheeler Playmate sportfishers. Yatistas will appreciate the fighting chair, home-made fly bridge and upper steering station that Hemingway added. Nearby, the pool where Eva Gardner and other Hollywood stars once skinny dipped is now empty.

Marina Hemingway would be a good place to read some of Hemingway's most famous works: "The Sun Also Rises" (1926), "A Farewell to Arms" (1929), "To Have and Have Not" (1937) and "For Whom the Bell Tolls" (1940).

Hemingway moved to Cuba in 1940, and it's the locale of his Pulitzer Prize-winning novella "The Old Man and the Sea" (1952). He was awarded the Nobel Prize for Literature in 1954. Shortly after the 1959 revolution, he left Cuba and moved to his hunting lodge in Idaho. Suffering depression and bad health, Hemingway shot himself within a year of leaving Cuba. His Paris memoir "A Moveable Feast" (1964) was published posthumously. Hemingway's style of concise wording and sentence impact are proverbial examples for budding writers, and he still influences American and British authors.

Diving Cuba

Excellent visibility and spectacular scenery are found while snorkeling and scuba diving almost all around Cuba, thanks to its broad northern reef and the shallow waters and cays off its SW coast.

Centro de Buceo dive shop in Marina Hemingway rents scuba gear for about $5 per day when you go out on its boats, but the gear package may not include everything you're used to. Take your own gear.

Someone loaned us *"Recreational Diving Guide CUBA,"* an excellent underwater guidebook, and then we met the author, Gustavo

G. Gotera, who lives in Havana. You can hire the handsome young Gustavo Gotera himself as your dive guide, or buy his 120-page full-color dive guidebook. It's written in English and Spanish, crammed full of excellent underwater charts and photos all around Cuba. Contact his US book-sales agent, Larry Benvenuti at Post Office Box 501403 in Marathon, FL 33050. It sells for about $25 – well worth it.

For example, along the 16-n.m. coastline between Playa Baracoa (7 n.m. east of the marina) and Havana Harbor (9 n.m. west), Gotera identifies 23 magnificent dive sites. He must have 1,000 spots around Cuba. Just outside Marina Hemingway, Gotera says the living coral reef is well preserved, because it has very few predators, and in some places it's 2 n.m. wide. Visibility is 30 meters (98') throughout the year. He describes the 39' and 66' stair pattern on the reef's north side and what's found on the more protected inside.

"The sessile fauna in this area is very attractive, colorful, well developed and diverse. Sea fan prairies, more than 20 species of gorgonians, big sponges like

Reefs just outside Marina Hemingway are pristine habitat and contain lots of ship wrecks. Photo by Gustavo Gotera.

Castles of coral and colorful sponges rise behind diver off Marina Hemingway. Photo by Gustavo Gotera.

the Venus Basket are abundant. Massive or flat corals (brain, mountainous star), leaf or finger, also flower corals and the cavernous star corals are seen."

"… Coral fish are abundant everywhere here, giving a special charm to this area populated by big schools of blue and gray chromis, squirrelfish, bigeyes, fairy basslets, grunts, goatfish, damselfish, butterflies, wrasses, small parrotfish and surgeonfish. It is also frequented by green and spotted morays, cornetfish, scorpionfish, the dancing drum, filefish and porcupine fish."

Gotera advises our readers to bring along all their own dive gear, because (at least until the embargo is over) Cuba has no specialized dive-gear stores or repair service. Bring plenty of O-rings, silicone oil, masks, straps, hoses, underwater camera cases, film, batteries, DIN or INT connectors and an INT converting yolk – because you won't find them here.

Cuba's Other Marinas

Not all Cuba's other marinas have guest facilities, and they are often filled with local hotel boats. All Cuban recreational boating areas have Customs, Immigration and Port Authority services, plus 24-hour security. During 2005, some of these marinas were in the process of dredging their entrance channels deeper, marking their approaches with lights and buoys, building more slips or deeper slips, expanding their shore facilities and developing basic yacht services. Don't assume they're all as comfortable as Marina Hemingway. Don't show up unannounced.

The information below comes primarily from publications by Edimar, the nautical charting agency of GeoCuba, provided by the Marina Hemingway's public relations department. We have added only what we can verify by personal observation.

1.) **Marina Puertosol Tarará:** 23°10.5'N, 82°13'W. Located in La Habana province about 8 n.m. east of Havana Harbor, this marina has 40 stern-to berths for boats drawing no more than 4.9' of water. They monitor VHF 16 & 19. Their fuel dock has diesel & gasoline. Berths have water, phone and 110- and 220-volt power. The marina has a pool, restaurant & snack bar. Nearby are groceries, ice, taxi, parking & shopping center. The dive shop has a hyperbaric chamber. FMI, phone (53) 797-1462, fax (53) 797-1333 or email comercial@tarara.mit.tur.cu.

2.) **Marina Darsena de Varadero:** 23°08'N, 81°19'W. Located about 18 n.m. east of Bahia Matanzas, this attractive marina (See photo next page.) has 112 stern-to and alongside berths for boats up to 62.5' in length and drawing no more than 16.5' of water. They monitor VHF 16 & 19A. Their fuel dock has diesel & gas. The berths have water, phone, cable TV and 110- and 220-volt power. The marina has a chandlery, restaurant & snack bar. Nearby are groceries, fishing supplies & ice. Near the dive is a hyperbaric chamber. FMI, phone (53) 566-8060 to 63, or fax (53) 566-7456 or email darsena@psolvar.get.cma.net.

3.) **Marina Chapelín:** 23°10.9'N, 81°10.7'W. Located in Matanzas province about 5 n.m. inside the mangrove estuary on the south side of the Varadero Peninsula, this small marina offers 20 stern-to & alongside

Marina Varadero at the SE end of the Varadero Peninsula is shallow.

Marina Darsena de Varadero has 16.5' depths and hosts sailing regattas.

berths for boats drawing no more than 9' of water. They monitor VHF 16 & 72. Their fuel dock has diesel & gas. The berths have water, phone and 110- and 220-volt power. The marina has a chandlery, restaurant & snack bar. The dive shop offers rentals, sales, air, lessons & dive charter trips. FMI, phone (53) 566-7550 or 566-7566, or fax (53) 566-7093.

4.) **Marina Varadero:** 23°11.7'N, 81°07.7'W. Located in the Matanzas province at the east tip of the Varadero Peninsula, this small marina (See photos this page & next.) has 10 stern-to berths for boats drawing no more than 9' of water. They monitor VHF 16. Their fuel dock has diesel & gas. The berths have water, phone and 110- and 220-volt power. The marina has a marine ways, restaurant & parking. The dive shop has a hyperbaric chamber nearby. FMI, phone (53) 566-7755 or 566-7756, or fax (53) 566-7756.

5.) **Marina Cayo Guillermo:** 22°25'N, 78°28'W. Located on the south side of Cayo Coco in the Archipelago de Sabana Camaguey in the province of Ciego de Avila, this tiny and remote facility has 6 stern-to berths for boats to 66' length and drawing no more than 6.5' of water. They monitor VHF 16 & 19. The fuel dock has diesel. Berths have water and 110- and 220-volt power. The marina has a restaurant & dive shop; groceries & ice are nearby. FMI, phone (53-33) 30-1738 or 30-1637, or fax (53-33) 30-1737, or email psol@cayo.cco.tur.cu.

6.) **Marina Vita:** 21°05'N, 75°53'W. Located in the Holguin province about 100 n.m. NW of Punta Maisi (20°14.5'N, 74°08.8'W), Cuba's SE tip, this tiny facility has 9 moorings for boats drawing no more than 6.5' of water. They monitor VHF 16 & 72. The fuel dock has diesel & gas. The dock has water, phone and

110- and 220-volt power. The marina has a restaurant & dive shop. FMI, phone (53) 243-0132, or fax 243-0126.

7.) **Marina Santiago de Cuba:** 19°58'N, 75°52'W. Located on Cuba's south coast in the province of Santiago de Cuba about 35 n.m. west of Guantanamo Bay, this marina has 30 stern-to & alongside berths for boats up to 165' and 26.5' beam, drawing as much as 29' of water. They monitor VHF 16 & 72. The fuel dock has diesel & gas. Berths have water, phone, cable TV and 110- & 220-volt power. The chandlery has repair services for props, rigging, gas & diesel engines, wood carpentry, fiberglass & electronics. The marina clubhouse has a restaurant & snack bar, rental cars & taxis. Near the dive shop is a hyperbaric chamber. Nearby are groceries, fishing supplies, bait & ice. FMI, phone (53) 226-91446, or fax 226-86108.

8.) **Marina Puertosol Trinidad:** 21°48'N,

Slips at concrete docks at Marina Varadero.

80°02'W. Located on the south shore of the Sancti Spiritus province, this marina has 25 stern-to berths for boats drawing no more than 5.9' of water. They monitor VHF 16 & 19. The fuel dock has diesel. Berths have water and 110- & 220-volt power. The marina has a restaurant & snack bar. Nearby are groceries & ice. FMI, phone or fax (53) 419-6205, or email marinastdad@ip.etecsa.cu.

9.) **Marina Puertosol Cienfuegos:** 22°02'N, 80°28'W. Located inside Bahia Cienfuegos on the south shore. This small marina has 16 stern-to & alongside berths for boats to 200' in length drawing as much as 11.5' of water. They monitor VHF 16 & 19A. Berths have water and 110- & 220-volt power. The fuel dock has diesel. The marina has a restaurant, dive shop & snack bar. Nearby are groceries & ice. FMI, phone (53-43) 245-1241, fax (53-43) 245-1275 or email mpsolcfg@ip.etecsa.cu.

10.) **Marina Cayo Largo del Sur:** 21°37'N, 81°34'W. Located near the NE end of the Canarreos Archipelago, this large marina has 90 stern-to & alongside berths for boats drawing no more than 11.5' of water. They monitor VHF 16 & 19A. The fuel dock has diesel & gas. Berths have water and 110- & 220-volt power. The chandlery has repair services for

diesel engines, props & fiberglass. The marina has a hotel, restaurant, dive shop & snack bar. Nearby are groceries and ice. FMI, phone (53) 548-213 or 548-133, fax (53) 548-212 or email gcom@psol.cls.tur.cu.

11.) **Marina El Colony:** 21°37'N, 82°59'N. Located in the bay on west side of the Isla de la Juventud, this small marina has 15 stern-to & alongside berths for boats drawing no more than 4.3' of water. They monitor VHF 16. The fuel dock has diesel & repairs diesel engines. Berths have water and 110- & 220-volt power. The marina has a hotel, restaurant & snack bar. Near the dive shop is a hyperbaric chamber. Another hyperbaric chamber is found on the island's north shore. FMI, phone (53) 619-8181 or 82, fax (53) 619-8420 or email carpeta.colony@gerona.inf.cu.

12.) **Maria La Gorda:** 21°49'N, 84°29'W. Located about 25 miles ESE of Cabo San Antonio, along the NE end of Fat Maria Bay, this small & remote anchorage has about 6.9' of water and a dinghy landing. Previous facilities were silted over. Ashore are fresh water, phones, diesel, ice & a small shopping center with restaurant. FMI, phone (53) 827-1306, fax (53) 827-8131.

Top left & right: Emergency dock at Cabo San Antonio, west end of Cuba.
Left: Roncali Light on Cabo San Antonio.
Photos this page by Larry Benvenuti.

Where is the Yucatan Channel?

That depends.

If you're checking today's Gulf Stream predictions, you may be interested primarily in the coastal waters off eastern Mexico. If you're monitoring Yucatan Channel shipping traffic, you're probably focused on what's rounding Cabo San Antonio at Cuba's west end. If you're planning a route from Panama up toward Texas, then for you the Yucatan Channel runs about 400 n.m. SE to NW from Cabo Gracias a Dios (Honduras) to the Yucatan Gap.

The Yucatan Gap is the narrow neck of ocean at the north end of the Yucatan Channel, between the pointy Cabo San Antonio at the west end of Cuba and the blunt NE corner of Mexico's huge Yucatan Peninsula. This 100 n.m. constriction is the only sea link between the Gulf of Mexico and the NW Caribbean. That's why huge variances in the Gulf Stream current, the Trade Winds, continental weather and heavy shipping all affect the yatista's experience while either crossing or transiting the Yucatan Channel and the Yucatan Gap.

Stop or Pass Through?

The western shore of the Yucatan Channel (Mexico's state of Quintana Roo) is one big cruising ground with lots of destinations and activities, yet it's conveniently en route to the turquoise cays off Belize and the hurricane hole up Guatemala's Rio Dulce.

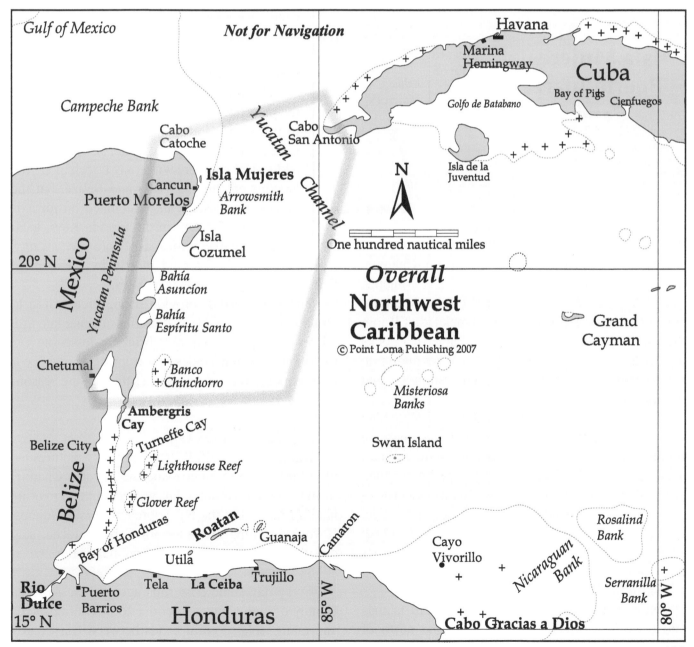

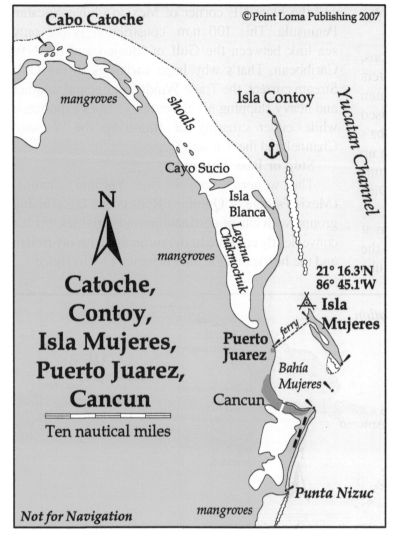

Cabo Catoche

© Point Loma Publishing 2007

mangroves

shoals

Isla Contoy

Yucatan Channel

⚓

Cayo Sucio

Isla Blanca

N

Laguna Chakmochuk

mangroves

21° 16.3'N
86° 45.1'W

△ Isla Mujeres

Catoche, Contoy, Isla Mujeres, Puerto Juarez, Cancun

Puerto Juarez

ferry

Bahía Mujeres

Cancun

Ten nautical miles

Punta Nizuc

Not for Navigation

mangroves

Along the western side of the Yucatan Channel, the popular yatista destinations are Isla Mujeres, Puerto Morelos, Isla Cozumel and Puerto Aventura. When Cancun's yacht marina is completed, it'll join the list. They offer marina slips, reliable fuel docks and shelter from the Trades, also excellent diving on the outer barrier reef and good sportfishing on and outside the reef.

Smaller stops are at Sian Ka'an and Xcalac. Sian Ka'an is a fairly new Biosphere Reserve encompassing Bahía Asención and Bahía Espíritu Santo. Small anchorages here will never be developed more than perhaps a few overnight moorings. Xcalac is a cruise-ship pier, but it's handy for clearing out of Mexico. However, after the new Zaragoza Channel is opened, south-bounders might be able to pick up their Zarpes there.

Skipping Through?

West of the Yucatan Channel, Cayman Islands and Cayo Vivario lie well off shore and north of

Honduras' north coast, so if you don't intend to stop in Mexico, Belize or Guatemala, then you might lay a course from the Yucatan Gap SE toward Cabo Gracias de Dios, thereby skipping through the NW Caribbean. If so, skip ahead to the Grand Cayman and Cayo Vivario chapters.

The Yucatan Channel cruising grounds run from Isla Contoy on the Mexico side extending south for about 300 n.m. to the border with Belize. Between Isla Contoy and Punta San Antonio on the west end of Cuba, the Yucatan Channel is only about 100 miles wide.

The two major destinations for boaters are Isla Mujeres and Isla Cozumel, but dozens of small anchorages are found along the reefs, coastal lagoons and offshore banks. Cruise-ship passengers visit Cancun, but it has no true marina for ocean-going yachts.

The warm-blooded Gulf Stream is one of the most powerful and reliable oceanic currents in the world, and along the Yucatan Channel it runs generally south to north. A few back eddies and counter swirls may be felt along the lagoons of Quintana Roo and Belize, but the deep stream itself can be counted on for a 1- to 6-knot effect. As in the Florida Keys, local marine weather broadcasts note the velocity, but here it's reported mostly by commercial fishing boats and the Mexican Navy.

The Trade Winds provide strong breezes (25 to 35 knots) from all easterly directions during late fall, winter and spring. Summer brings a lessening (15 to 20 knots) in the Trades, but tropical storms occur often enough to bring an end to safe cruising season.

Isla Contoy

Dangerous Landfall: Isla Contoy is a picturesque visual reference when crossing the Yucatan Channel from Cabo San Antonio, but we recommend making landfall instead at the NE approach to Isla Mujeres. If you're coming around from Cabo Catoche, stay outside Isla Contoy if possible and make your arrival at Isla Mujeres.

Every day some boat runs aground west of Isla Contoy or onto Contoy Reef due to migrating shoals and many isolated coral heads between Isla Contoy

Isla Contoy rises steeply from Yucatan Channel depth. Photo by Larry Dunmire.

and Isla Blanca to its west, to deceptively strong currents and to very shallow channels (average depth 6') along Contoy's west side. Better to come here by dinghy or hire a local guide for your first few visits to the west side of Isla Contoy.

Isla Contoy Biosphere Reserve: *NOTE: Boaters are not supposed to enter the waters of the Isla Contoy Biosphere Reserve without first clearing in with the Port Captain at Isla Mujeres and getting a permit from the SEMARNAT or SEDESOL office there. With a permit, anchoring is permitted only during the day – no overnight anchoring.*

This exquisite little isle is only about 600 yards wide and 4.5 n.m. long NW to SE. Isla Contoy Light (21°30'N, 86°49'W) is about .25 n.m. south of the island's north tip. But a line of rocks juts .25 n.m. NW of its north tip, and a line of ship-killer coral reef stretches almost 8 n.m. SSE from the island's south tip – called Contoy Reef, a great snorkeling spot.

Composed of brilliant white sand and coral heads, dotted with welcoming palms and lush mangroves, Isla Contoy's windward east side presents a coral face rising abruptly from deep water. But the island's leeward east side is riddled with 3 lagoons, only 1 of them accessible to shallow-draft boats.

Isla Contoy's visitors center and oceanographic research center employ solar power, water reclamation and sustainable methods, but they struggle to keep up with so many visitors daily. Dozens of excursion boats come out from Cancun and Isla Mujeres throughout the day.

North Anchorage: You may enter the anchorage west of the lighthouse from the NE by giving a 500-yard berth to the 500-yard long string of rock off the island's north tip. Anchor about 300 yards west of the lighthouse in 6' to 9' of water over sand and coral gravel. Avoid the Navy mooring buoy. Landing is possible on the shingle south of the lighthouse. From here you can snorkel the rocky reef, which has a popular wreck, or walk half a mile south to the pretty crescent beach. The lighthouse keeper may give tours, and rangers may check for permits.

South Lagoon Anchorage: The dock, research center, visitor's center and observation tower for wildlife researchers are visible at the south end of South Lagoon, which lies about .75 n.m. NW of the south end of Isla Contoy.

You can anchor either inside (6') or west of (10' to 12') the South Lagoon. The easiest approach has a least depth of about 8'. From the North Anchorage by the lighthouse, head SW for about 1.25 n.m., staying outside (west of) a 5' deep breaking sand bar that juts 1 n.m. west from the island, this bar starting about 1.25 n.m. south of the lighthouse. Then head SE toward the observation tower. Avoid the sandbar forming the lagoon's south arm.

From here you can explore the sea bird rookeries on the south end of the island, and snorkel the rocky north part of Contoy Reef, as well as the whole reef. The remnants of a Spanish galleon lies in snorkel depths where the rocks join the coral. We suggest exploring Puerto Viejo and another smaller lagoon by kayak.

Isla Blanca: This low curving sand spit forms the west side of the unmarked channel behind Contoy Reef. Only shallow-draft craft can enter the lagoon west of Isla Blanca's north end. Isla Blanca runs 12 n.m. south to Puerto Juarez.

Contoy Reef: This 8-n.m. long line of coral reefs (submerged and awash) runs from the south tip of Isla Contoy SE toward Isla Mujeres. Contoy Reef is a dangerous ship killer. With local knowledge, sheltered passage is found in the narrow channel (half n.m.

wide) between Isla Blanca and Contoy Reef system. Also with local knowledge, you can snorkel the west side or scuba the east side.

The 3.5 n.m. gap between the south end of Contoy Reef and the north end of the reef north of Isla Mujeres is the safest approach to Isla Mujeres.

Isla Mujeres

Isla Mujeres lies about 330 n.m. SW of Key West, Florida; 490 n.m. SE of the Mississippi River mouth; or 650 n.m. ESE of the Rio Grande at the US border. This low island runs 4.2 n.m. long (NW to SE) and lies about 3 n.m off the mainland state of Quintana Roo, 6 n.m. NE of Cancun.

The Isle of Women was named by Hernán Córdoba in 1517, when he visited the uninhabited island and the Mayan temple on its south end. Inside were many statues of their goddess Ixchel and her female court; hence he named it Isla Mujeres (pronounced "moo-HAY-rayz"). She slept in Mayan tranquility for centuries. Today, tiny Isla Mujeres is still beautiful, but she has WIFI, street drugs and is working hard to catch up to her glitzy sister, Cancun.

If your boat draws 8' or less, Isla Mujeres offers 3 marina with slips and services for yachts to 185', 2 fuel docks, anchorage, provisioning, plenty of shore diversions and ferry access to Cancun and the mainland.

Approaches: The south end of Contoy Reef (mostly breaking) is 3.5 n.m. north of El Yunque (Anvil Rock Light), which stands about 400 yards off the north tip of Isla Mujeres. Between these lies a submerged reef (about 9' to 14') that deep-draft craft must be aware of.

Isla Mujeres is so low that when arriving from the NE, you first see large hotels on the north tip. The windward east side of the island is steep coral cliffs with no inlets. Garrafón and Manchones are reefs extending .75 n.m. south from the island's SW end. The leeward west side is more hospitable, and the anchorage and lagoon entrance is on the NW side.

From the NE, our GPS approach waypoint (21°16.3'N, 86°45.1'W) is about .4 n.m. north of El Yunque (Anvil Rock Light). From there, turn to 190°M and head for the buoy marking the harbor entrance (min. 8' depth), putting it on your starboard bow. Be careful of a brownish shoal on starboard, visible with high sun. Keeping the entrance buoy to starboard, turn to port while keeping the low white sandy point on your port side. Pass close along shore. You'll pass another buoy on your starboard marking a shoal, so stay close to shore to avoid it.

From the SE, pass between Roca La Bandera, also called Becket Rock (21°10'N, 86°44'W) and the south end of Isla Mujeres, heading to just west of Bajo Pepito buoy (21°12.5'N, 86°45.3'W). Manchones and Garrafón reefs lie between this buoy and the island, and a very strong current sets you toward the reefs, so give them a wide berth. Round Pepito Shoal in 18' of water, and you'll see range lights marking the harbor entrance. Keep these off your starboard bow at about 2.2 n.m. until you see the channel buoys. Stay north of the channel buoys as you enter the harbor, to avoid an uncharted shoal in the center.

Harbor: Continuing south close to shore, we count 24 docks lining the beach-fringed east side of the harbor. Enrique's Marina & Fuel Dock, Marina Paraiso and tiny Milagro Marina are here, and the 2 biggest docks are for 3 ferries, plus the Navy's the Navy's concrete T-head pier and some commercial fishing docks.

At the south end of the harbor, mangroves line the narrow 500-yard long channel (max. 10' depth) into sheltered Laguna Makax, which spreads half a mile SE filling the south half of the island. Puerto Isla Mujeres' larger fuel dock is along the east side of the

Isla Mujeres: Looking north from Makax Lagoon (lower left), note canal and town anchorage (upper right).
Photo next page by Larry Dunmire.

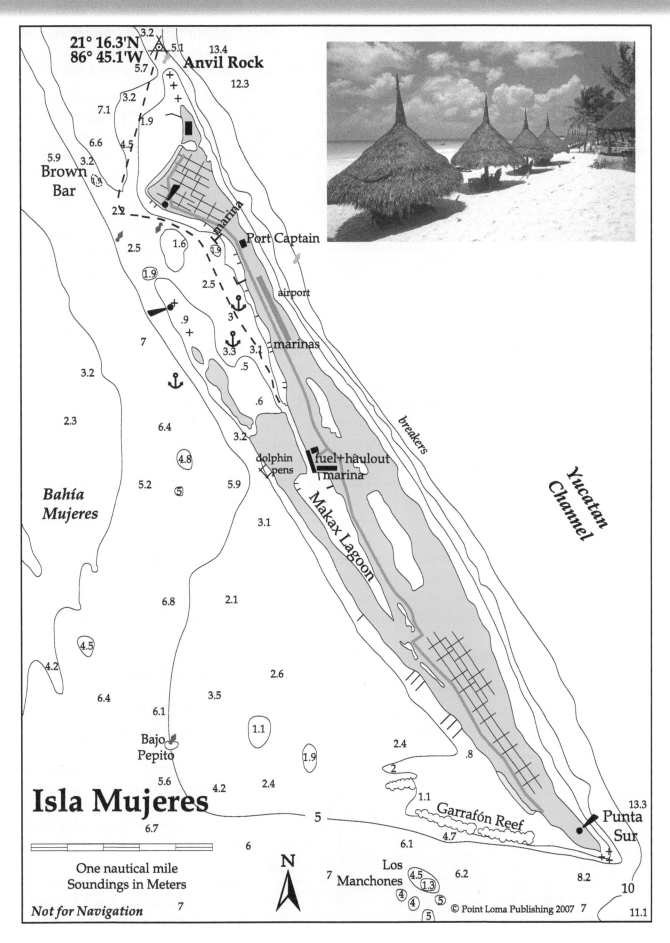

21° 16.3'N
86° 45.1'W

3.2
5.1
13.4
Anvil Rock
5.7
12.3

+
+
+
3.2

7.1
1.9

6.6
4.5

5.9
3.2
**Brown
Bar**
1.9

2.2

marina

2.5
1.6
● **Port Captain**
1.9

1.9
2.5
airport

.9
+
3'
+

7
3.3
3.1
marinas

3.2
.5

2.3
.6

6.4
3.2

4.8
dolphin
pens
**fuel+haulout
marina**

*Bahía
Mujeres*
5.2
5
5.9

3.1

breakers

*Yucatan
Channel*

Makax Lagoon

6.8
2.1

4.5

4.2

6.4
3.5

6.1
2.6

2.4
.8

1.1
**Bajo
Pepito**
1.9

2
5.6
4.2
2.4
1.1

Isla Mujeres
Garrafón Reef
13.3
**Punta
Sur**

5
4.7

6.7

6
6.1

N

One nautical mile
Soundings in Meters
7
**Los
Manchones**
4.5
1.3
6.2
8.2

Not for Navigation
7
4
4
5
© Point Loma Publishing 2007
7
10

7
5
11.1

channel, and their largest marinas slips are farther inside the lagoon, which is a hurricane hole.

Anchorages: Isla Mujeres' municipal anchorage (10' to 12' over sand and mud) parallels the west side of the harbor channel, from Roca La Carbonera along the inside of Chico and Tiburon islands, to a shoal opposite Paradise Marina at the south end of the harbor. This anchorage has wakes and petty theft.

Berthing: Isla Mujeres has 4 full-service marinas and 4 new smaller marinas. Check UPDATES.

Enrique's Marina was the island's original yacht facility, built by Enrique Lima in the north end of the harbor, so it's the first one you see after entering. It has about 15 slips with 110-volt power, and it is handy to the middle of town. It's rarely used by visiting yachts unless all other slips are taken, such as during Semana Santa, because it is exposed to boat wakes and south to SE winds. However, it has a serviceable non-floating fuel dock on the south side of the dock. FMI, call (998) 877-0211.

Marina Paraiso (Paradise) is farther SE in the

Marina Paraiso (Paradise) is one of several marinas in the harbor at the north end of Isla Mujeres.

harbor, a bit more exposed to north winds. It has 24 non-floating slips (7' depth) with shore power, guards, showers, laundry, pool and office with phone. FMI, call Paradise Marina (998) 877-0252 or marinaparaiso@yahoo.com.mx.

Milagro (Miracle) Marina is next door to Paradise, a couple full-service docks (15' at seaward end) for Med-mooring a dozen boats or 4 big ones. Milagro's homey atmosphere includes 24-hr security and a pleasant palapa with Internet, showers and BBQ patio. Owner Eric Chott also rents apartments out front. FMI, call (988) 877-1708 or in the US (805) 698-8165.

The largest and best sheltered is Puerto Isla Mujeres, with 61 full-service slips in the north end of Laguna Makax, reached via a narrow channel (10' depth). The docks have reliable shore power, and the gated compound has a pool, showers and laundry service, small hotel and secure parking. The marina office has phone, fax, copier, email and port clearance assistance if you need it. Sportfishing tournaments bring dozens of mega-sportfishers, but it's popular with cruising sailboats. FMI, call Puerto Isla Mujeres (998) 287-3340 or email marina@puertoislamujeres.com.

Port Clearance: The Capitanía (VHF 16) is on Rueda Medina, the malecon, just south of the ferry docks. This is a Port of Entry; Migración and Aduana are side by side about 3 blocks up the street. When you check in on VHF, don't hesitate to ask the Port Capitanía or Navy for a pilot or local guide to lead you safely into the harbor.

The Port Captain and Navy close this port when hurricanes threaten during the summer and fall. That means boats already here cannot depart, due to unsafe conditions over the shoals or dangerously heavy seas

Marina Puerto Isla Mujeres is the largest on the island, has a big fuel dock (left) and slips in Makax Lagoon, which serves as storm shelter.

as you enter the Gulf Stream. Of course, if you make it here, you can come in.

Hurricane Hole: Laguna Makax serves as a hurricane hole, but the grass bottom makes poor holding. We found 12' in the middle of the north end, but it shallows to 5' at the south end. The NW corner is shoal. Mangroves and mud line the lagoon, and a raised road runs around all sides. A slip in Puerto Isla Mujeres is a reasonable option, but during a hurricane watch, the marina gets packed and accepts vessels only on a first come, first served basis.

Local Services: Fuel docks: (1.) Enrique's is to port as you turn into the north end of the harbor. Boats to 50' Med-moor and hang over while fueling, and the Pemex station is nearby. (2.) Larger yachts use the 200' side tie at Puerto Isla Mujeres on the east side of the channel (max 10' depth) into Laguna Makax.

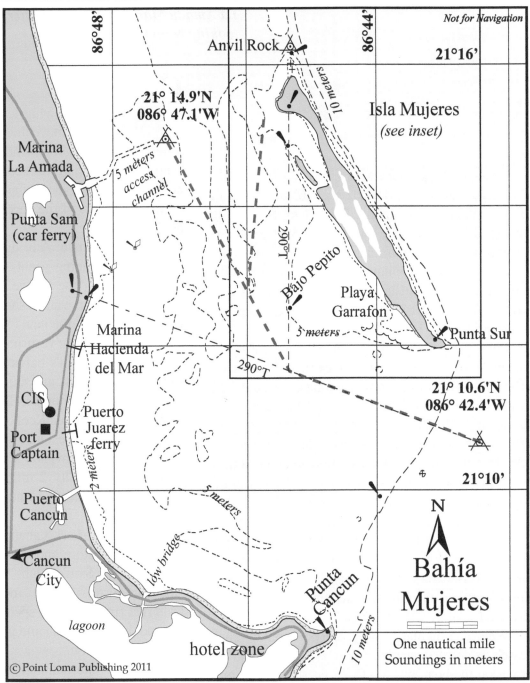

Not for Navigation

© Point Loma Publishing 2011

The only haul-out on the island is at Puerto Isla Mujeres; 150-ton Travelift, reached on the east side of the channel (10') into the lagoon, just past the fuel dock. Their "marina seca" or dry storage space is limited. (La Amada Marina also has a Travelift.)

Street maps of Isla Mujeres are free in many shops. Centro and the main plaza fills the whole north end, and locals live in the south end. Between are the airport, Marine base and light industry.

Provisions: Super Benito is Isla Mujeres' largest grocery store on the main plaza, and the Mercado Municipal (open 0600) is at the north end of Matamoros. For a major provisioning, take the ferry to Cancun and try the WalMart store. Ferries go to 2 different docks in Puerto Juarez, and the car ferry goes to Punta Sam.

Visit the Mayan observatory on the south tip of Isla Mujeres, or the pink flamingo ponds along the SE flank. Garrafón Reef is sadly picked over.

Emergency medical: English-speaking Dr. Antonio Salas (998) 877-0021.

La Amada Marina is just N of Puerto Juarez. Here we're looking N into their N basin.

Puerto Juarez

Puerto Juarez (21°11.02'N, 86°48.26'W) on the Quintana Roo mainland lies 5 n.m. SW of Isla Mujeres harbor entrance and about 2.5. n.m. NW of the entrance to Cancun's lagoon. Puerto Juarez is an open roadstead with a huge new T-head pier that has limited space for gueists – so call the Capitanía (VHF 16) for anchoring or landing instructions on your way in toward this port in flux.

Port Clearance: Puerto Juarez has Caribbean Mexico's first CIS (Centro Integral de Servicios) office for streamlined port clearance, located next to the new Capitanía building overlooking the pier. Inside are officials representing the Port Captain's office, Migración (Immigration), Aduana (Customs), API, Health-Agriculture, plus a Banejercito (Bank of the Army) booth where you can pay all fees by credit card. See the chapter on official paperwork.

This CIS streamlined port-clearance service (sometimes called *Ventanilla Unica* or Single Window) works beautifully on Mexico's Pacific coast at Ensenada and Cabo San Lucas, so we hope East Coast yatistas will take advantage of it as well. Eventually, more CIS offices will be created.

When a yacht marina with plenty of room for guest vessels is located nearby, we'll be able to clear in, provision the boat, pick up fly-in guests and do some sight-seeing all from one location. Meanwhile, taxis near the pier can whisk you down to Cancun.

New Marinas: Punta Sam is the car-ferry dock, located 3 n.m. north of Puerto Juarez and 2.5 WSW of the entrance to Isla Mujeres harbor.

La Amada Marina (21°14.00'N 86°47.96'W) is open, 100 slips, has a fuel dock & Travelift, interior basin, very nice. www.LaAmada.com

Marina Hacienda del Mar has 75 slips on exterior docks about a mile north of Puerto Juarez, lighted wave baffles, chandlery, hotel & cafe. Puerto Cancun residential-marina complex should open soon a mile south of Puerto Juarez pier. Check our UPDATES.

Cancun

Only vessels drawing less than 6' and with less than 15' clearance above the water can enter Cancun's inner Nichupte Lagoon, which is surrounded by a low, sandy barrier island marked by 300 tall hotels – the hotel zone. The lagoon's narrow entrance channel is on the north side of the barrier island, at 21°08.73'N, 86°47.22'W.

Port Clearance: A bridge 15' high blocks access to most ocean-going yachts, but the Capitanía is on the NW side of the bridge. In calm weather, some boats anchor off the north shore for port clearance, but Puerto Juarez has the new CIS office, much easier.

Anchoring: We've usually found the north and east side of Cancun's barrier islands too exposed to sudden north winds and shifting easterly Trades for safe overnight anchorage. The south side is mostly shallow behind Nizuc Reef.

Local Services: Once you're ashore, Cancun is a good place to provision and party. For real prices, shop in Cancun City 2 miles SW of Puerto Juarez, inland from the glitzy Cancun known to cruise-ship passengers.

Near the Eco Park Kubah, the Comercial Mexicana mega grocery store and CostCo are adjacent, as are WalMart and Sam's Club. We found Home Depot, Ace Hardware, Sears, movies, restaurants, etc. Fruterias (markets that specialize in fresh produce) abound, but they come and go, so ask your taxista for a recommendation.

Cancun's international airport is 10 miles south of the hotel zone. Cancun generally has Mexico's cheapest direct flights to US hubs. Highway 180 from Merida circles Laguna Nichupte. Lush landscaping is returning after devastation by hurricanes.

Explore Ashore: Almost the entire coast of Quintana Roo is marketed as Riviera Maya, emphasizing the ancient culture, history and natural environment. Playa del Carmen is ground zero.

The protected marinas at Isla Mujeres, Puerto Morelos and Isla Cozumel are a good place to leave your boat, to travel to the Yucatan Peninsula's many biosphere reserves, flamingo & turtle nurseries and fresh-water cenote wells scattered all over the states of Quintana Roo, Yucatan and Campeche. Check out www. ecoyuc.com. Form a group of boaters, or join an air-conditioned bus tour that picks up at one of the hotels, or rent a car from Cancun.

Mayan ruins are still being excavated and have quality educational tours. Some favorites are Chichén Itzá, Palenque, Cobá, Xixum, Xelha and Uxmal to name a few. Unless you're going to Rio Dulce, Guatemala, this region is handy to take off for a land excursion to Tikal in Guatemala.

Although on the coast, Tulum and Xcarat don't have good anchorages. Sian Ka'an is easily visited by boat at Punta Allen. Celestun and Rio Lagartos have marginal anchorages near where you pick up your guide panga, so you may want to see them by land.

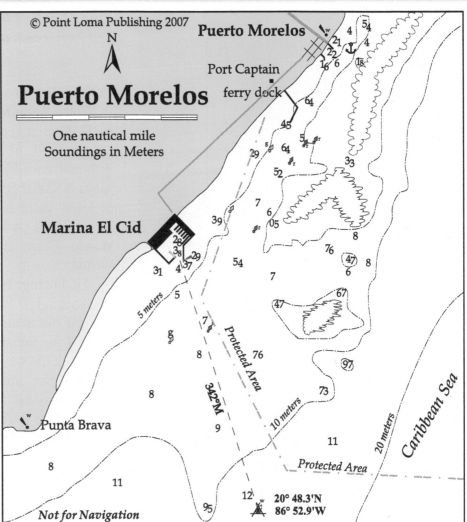

© Point Loma Publishing 2007

Puerto Morelos

N

Port Captain

ferry dock

Puerto Morelos

One nautical mile
Soundings in Meters

Marina El Cid

Punta Brava

342°M

5 meters

10 meters

20 meters

Protected Area

Protected Area

Caribbean Sea

20° 48.3'N
86° 52.9'W

Not for Navigation

En Route to Puerto Morelos

Punta Cancun Light (21°08'N, 86°44.8'W) is on the NE tip of Isla Cancun, the 10-mile barrier island forming Laguna Nichupte. Punta Nizuc Light is on the south corner of Isla Cancun. From Punta Nizuc the coast tends SW for about 75 miles to Tulum.

Nizuc Reef (usually breaking, coral) starts 400 yards off Punta Nizuc near Cancun (see previous chartlet) and parallels the receding coastline 1 to 2 n.m. off, with only small cuts. Expect north current. The

first good pass is 14 n.m. SE. at Puerto Morelos.

Arrowsmith Bank, a popular sportfishing destination, lies about 25 n.m. east of Puerto Morales. This bank is about 30 n.m. long, 6' wide, and has depths from 27' to 150' and generally NNE current from 2- to 3-knot current. Rips have been reported off the south end of Arrowsmith Bank.

Puerto Morelos

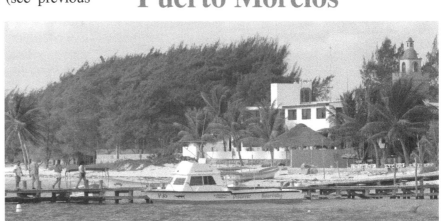

Excursion-boat docks on Puerto Morelos' waterfront usually allow dinghies to tie up for a small fee when they're not too crowded.

Puerto Morelos Light (old & new) is a reminder about hurricanes along the Yucatan Channel.

The new marina with fuel dock recently put Puerto Morelos on the yatista route, and the artsy village is a nice contrast to Cancun's bustle. Provisioning and picking up fly-in guests is even easier here than at Isla Mujeres.

Approaches: Puerto Morelos Light (20°51.7'N, 86°53.0'W) is visible for 18 miles, located about 1.5 n.m. NE of the deepwater opening at the south end of Nizuc Reef. This light and the older one (still tilted by hurricanes) mark the town's panga pier. NIMA Chart 28201 of Puerto Morelos is out of date.

Come down to the lighted sea buoy (20°48.3'N, 86°52.9'W) at the south end of Nizuc Reef (about 1.5 n.m. ENE of Punta Brava Light), then enter the sheltered corridor behind the reef and follow the buoys NNW about a mile to the lighted breakwater-enclosed yacht harbor, a rectangular "outie" type basin. Yachts no longer can approach the big Puerto Morelos-Cozumel car ferry pier, a mile NE of the marina.

Anchoring: From the marina, go about 1.5 n.m. north behind the reef to anchor (9' of water, 1.7' tides) well off the town pier near the light towers. Inside the reef we found strong current and isolated coral heads, but the water is inviting. Dinghies can land on the town pier amid excursion pangas. The "jefe del muelle" may ask for a $1 security fee to guard your dinghy while you're ashore; good service.

Berthing: Marina El Cid Cancun built this huge breakwater enclosure (9' to 12' depth) for its 300 full-service floating slips 40' to 120' with big-boat power, filtered water from the resort's private wells, 24/7 security. The first slips are in the north end, and anchoring (day fee) is permitted in the south end until construction begins there. Mooring buoys may be available inside the reef.

Marina El Cid Cancun has showers, coin laundry, chandler, tackle shop, quick market and cantina restaurant. Marina guests do potluck BBQ under the shady palapa. Better yet, you're welcome to walk next door and use El Cid Hotel's pools, spa, restaurants, golf course, concierge, travel agent, shuttle bus to Cancun airport, etc. FMI, call Marina El Cid Cancun (998) 871-0184 or email the dockmaster at elcidcaribe@prodigy.net.mx.

Port Clearance: The Capitanía (VHF 16) is behind the car ferry pier on the road from the marina to town, so if you need to clear in

Marina El Cid Cancun has nice slips inside a hefty breakwater, nice shore amenities, nice location.

Easiest fuel dock along the Yucatan
Channel is Marina El Cid
at south end of Purto Morelos.

person, ask the marina to drive you there. Yachts cannot approach the car ferry pier.

Local Services: Marina El Cid Cancun has an 80' fuel dock (fast-flow diesel, gas, pumpout) just to starboard from the entrance to their yacht harbor. Bulk oil can be delivered from the Pemex in town.

Want to check out Isla Cozumel before taking your boat there? Take the ferry from here.

Puerto Morelos town has a central plaza behind the wooden panga pier (dinghies only) and light towers, and 3 streets parallel the beach. We found Super Casa Martin grocery store, Alma Libre bookstore (English), a pharmacy, 3 money changers, dive gear rentals and lots of eateries (vegan to German). Taxis hang out at the marina and on the plaza; it's 20 miles to Cancun airport, 30 miles to Cancun provisioning.

This break in Nizuc Reef provides excellent diving. In calm seas, several divable shipwrecks lie outside the reef. Botanical Gardens (orchids, butterflies) are south of town. Crocodile Zoo is just north.

Fishing: Sportfishers come here for amberjack, dorado, barracuda, grouper, jewfish, mackerel, marlin, sailfish, shark, snapper, tuna.

En route to Cozumel

From Puerto Morelos sea buoy, the Cozumel Banks lie 12 to 15 n.m. ESE to SSW, and the island's yacht harbor is about 20 n.m. south. Current races at 3 to 5 knots up the deep 10-n.m. wide channel west of the island. Expect ferries and cruise ships.

Punta Hut (Punta Maroma) (20°43.5'N, 86°58.0'W) is a sandy point 7 n.m. SW of Puerto Morelos yacht harbor. In moderate north wind and easterlies, anchorage is possible (6' to 10') south of the point, behind Maroma Reef.

To get in, go about 1.75 n.m. SW of Punta Hut and find the 300-yard wide

pass (6' depth) through the breaking reef, giving wide berth to the rocky edges. Then turn NE and inch along in 10' of water behind the reef until you find a comfy spot. Grass bottom has been reported some years. Many yatistas love Punta Hut; others say "*No vale la pena.*"

We'll look at the mainland side of Cozumel Channel (Playa del Carmen, Xcarat and Puerto Aventuras) right after Cozumel.

Isla Cozumel

Isla Cozumel (say "koh-zoo-MELL") lies about 375 n.m. SW of Key West, about 85 n.m. down the coast from Cabo Catoche, and about 44 n.m. south of Isla Mujeres. Yatistas find 2 small yacht basins, fuel and a few services.

The island is 24 n.m. long NE to SW, 8 n.m. wide but only about 60' above sea level, so it suffers saltwater inundation from hurricanes. Trade Winds batter

Ferry brings a few tourists from
Cancun & Cozumel, but Puerto
Morelos is quaint & tranquil.

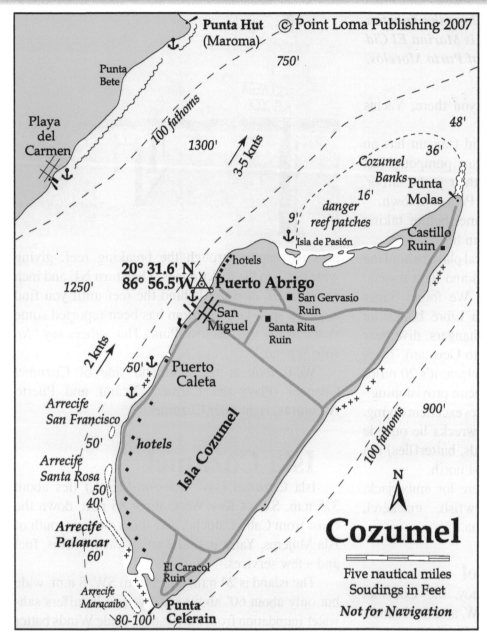

Punta Hut
(Maroma) © Point Loma Publishing 2007

Punta Bete

Playa del Carmen

750'

1300'

100 fathoms

3-5 knts

48'

36'

Cozumel Banks

16'

Punta Molas

danger reef patches

9'

Isla de Pasión

Castillo Ruin

hotels

1250'

**20° 31.6' N
86° 56.5' W** **Puerto Abrigo**

San Gervasio Ruin

San Miguel

Santa Rita Ruin

2 knts

50'

Puerto Caleta

Arrecife San Francisco

50'

hotels

Isla Cozumel

100 fathoms

900'

Arrecife Santa Rosa

50'

40'

N

Arrecife Palancar

60'

El Caracol Ruin

Cozumel

Five nautical miles
Soudings in Feet

Not for Navigation

Arrecife Maracaibo

Punta Celerain

80-100'

Approach: Avoid the shoaly, current-ripping Cozumel Banks that extend up to 13 n.m. off the island's NE corner. The first time John let me drive a big sportfisher into Puerto Abrigo's narrow entrance channel, I didn't use enough power; the current grabbed my bow and had me going in sideways.

From south, give Punta Celerain (20°16.17'N, 86°59.39'W) a good 2-n.m. berth due to divers down.

Berthing: Just north of San Miguel and next to the airport, Puerto Abrigo yacht basin (approach 21°31.68'N, 86°56.47'W) has a narrow entrance channel carved out of the ancient coral and limestone bedrock. Inside, the 400-yard long municipal basin opens NE with 100 full-service Med-mooring slots.

Come alongside in front of the office (just past the fuel dock to starboard). After registering, move to your Med-moor slot. Sometimes a buoyed "muerto" is provided in the center of the basin. If not, the 12' bottom is slippery gravel over hardpan. Set fenders and lines for surge. The marina has a fuel dock, tackle shop; gets full during tournaments. FMI call Cozumel Club Nautico (919) 872-1113 or 1118.

If Club Nautico is full, try Bahía Caleta, a tiny natural basin half a mile south the cruise-ship piers. The lighted 30' wide entrance channel (6.5' depth) runs along the north side of a big El Presidente Hotel, but as you reach the spot where the basin opens, jog to the north to avoid a large submerged rock. Caleta has no real docks; boats Med-moor to the shoreline. Even so, Caleta is usually filled with local sportfishing charter boats. Many local boats are out working during the day, so before you take someone's permanent spot, ask people on other boats where an

the east shore, starting at Punta Molas on the NE tip down to Punta Celerain. Even on the more hospitable west shore, a current rips up to 3.5 knots.

Cozumel is a major cruise-ship destination and locus of billfishing tournaments. Up to 4 cruise ships anchor off Cozumel's 3 west side piers at San Miguel (pop. 15,000), the island's only real town. Shore boats shuttle throngs ashore for T-shirts, handicrafts, margaritas. VW taxis putt around the island to see Mayan ruins and beaches.

Anchoring is prohibited near the coral reefs on Cozumel's SW side, but sadly, prop wash and silt from all the cruise ships have already damaged them. Bigger sportfishing marinas have sprung up nearby, so Cozumel now shares the bounty.

Cozumel: Puerto Abrigo basin, fuel dock is to starboard as you enter.

available spot is.

Anchorage: The island's best anchoring roadstead (20°28.996'N, 86°56.829'W) is right in front of the Capitania, in 15' to 30' over sand, between Puerto Abrigo and the older ferry pier. It's sheltered from Trades, but open to Northers and wakes from cattle boats. Ask to land your dinks on the N side of the N-most ferry pier (not on the pier itself) and pay the guard for security.

Port Clearance: Cozumel is a Port of Entry very occupied with cruise ships, but this is a good place to clear out of Mexico southbound. The Capitanía (VHF 16) is on the road between Puerto Abrigo and town. Immigration & Aduana have reps on the cruise-ship piers and offices at the airport. If you get your Zarpe here, you can still stop anywhere without another full-scale exit clearance – except Xcalac or Chetumal, which are rather difficult stops to make anyway.

Local Services: Puerto Abrigo has the only public fuel dock. (But ask at the fast ferry pier.)

To provision, take a ferry to Playa del Carmen and taxi to the Mega CoMex grocery store at 30th and Constituyentes. A big frutería is nearby. The ferry does 10 round-trips daily 0400 to 2100.

San Miguel has 2 grocery stores, bakery, 3 Internet cafes, lots of ice cream parlors and cerveza depositos. Bottled water is sold in gallons. Downtown San Miguel has 4 banks, 2 laundromats, 3 long distance phone offices, a dozen dive shops with air, and a post office. Eateries abound along San Miguel's waterfront and most hotels. The airport is NE of the Capitanía, and Marines are based there.

History & Culture: Explore 14 Mayan ruins around the island, mostly on the NE and south ends. Closer to town, San Gervasio ruins are very interesting and beautiful, and the Temple Suhuykak was the Mayan Sanctuary to the Goddess of Fertility. Hire a VW taxista or rent scooters and a guide.

Dive Cozumel: South of the cruise ship piers,

the coral reefs from north to south are Chankanaab, Yucab, Santa Rosa, world-famous Palancar, Colombia and Maracaibo or Celerain west of the lighthouse. Hire a local guide for at least your first dive. The whole south end of Isla Cozumel is an underwater park, so no anchoring (certified local excursion boats only), no fishing, spear guns or taking of flora or fauna are allowed.

For exotic yet sheltered snorkeling, Laguna Chankanaab is fed by underground tunnels from the sea, now almost collapsed, and the crystalline lagoon is surrounded in jungle garden.

En route to Puerto Aventura

Playa del Carmen: Originally named Mocché for the Mayan god, this busy tourist development of Playa del Carmen is 8 n.m. SW of Punta Hut (Maroma). It has no reef shield and at least 2 very busy ferry piers often in repair. Hotels line Highway 307 and the beach.

In rare flat conditions, yatistas may anchor (marginal, 10') behind stubby Zubel Reef (approach 20°37.9'N, 87°03.5'W), which lies north of town, but it's often full of snorkelers and not good overnight.

It's safer and more practical to come to Playa del Carmen by ferry from Cozumel, so you can (a.) provision at the Mega CoMex grocery store at 30th and Constituyentes, or (b.) tour the string of Mayan Riviera ecological parks down the coast.

Mayan land tour: You can't see all the sites, but take at least a day and get to Tulum. Off Highway

Yellow range markers are in line 345°M to enter Puerto Aventuras.

307 south of Playa del Carmen are Xcarat park and Pa'amul. Then after Puerto Aventuras are Chac Mool, Xpu-ha, Kentenah, Akumal lagoon, Aktun Chen, Chemuyil, Xcacel, Xel-Ha lagoon, Tan Kah and finally Tulum. It's hard to pay to see dolphins and sea life you've just been swimming with off your own boat, but the Mayan sites, shady jungles and cenotes are inviting.

Xcarat Lagoon Ecological Preserve: This harbor 5 n.m. SW of Playa del Carmen is not yet open to visiting yates, and reefs block close anchorage.

Puerto Aventuras

This gated resort is most useful to yatistas for its large sheltered marina and fuel dock, but it's a fun stop for families and a good place to leave your boat while traveling elsewhere.

Puerto Aventuras (20°29.35'N, 87°13.34'W) is about 28 n.m. down the coast from Puerto Juarez and 16 n.m. across the channel from Puerto Abrigo on Cozumel. Deep enough (8' entrance) for sailboats, megayachts and sportfishing tournaments, Marina Puerto Aventuras has excellent shelter from the Trades, an easy access fuel dock and is in the middle of the Mayan Riviera eco-parks.

Approaches: Fátima Bay is blocked by 3 small reefs, and at the north end of this indent is the lighted entrance channel (8.5' to 9' depths) leading north into the darsena. Don't try this entrance for the first time in heavy easterly wind, because the approach will be beam onto the swell, which could make you bottom out, and the entrance gets hidden by breakers. If you'd like the marina's pilot panga to lead you in, hail them on VHF 16 when you're in range.

From our approach waypoint to Puerto Aventuras (20°29.77'N, 87°13.479'W), you'll see (a.) 4-story buildings on both sides of the breakwater, and (b.) 2 yellow range-maker posts on the south side of the channel. Line up on the range and keep the 3 green buoys to port and then enter between the breakwaters.

Immediately to port, come alongside the non-floating check-in dock. Walk 200 yards NW on the malecon to the marina office.

Berthing: You'll be assigned a spot. Full service non-floating slips & Med-moor slots for 200 yachts line the marina's 3 basins: Ice Station Zebra (10' depth) straight ahead, turn left for Park Avenue (5' to 7'), then Skid Row (5' to 6' depth) is beyond. Some yatistas report over-standard voltage, but upgrades are ongoing and service here has been great. Around the marina, guests enjoy the gated resort's dolphin pond, swimming pools, restaurants, shops, nicely landscaped hotels, condos and shady parks. FMI, call Marina Puerto Aventuras (984) 873-5110 or 5180 or

Puerto Aventuras

One tenth nautical mile
Soundings in Feet

6

5.5

9

10

Harbor Master

Guest dock

10

Range 345°M

fuel dock

Fatima Bay

9.5

10 feet

Not for Navigation

8

N

reef

20° 29.757'N
87° 13.479'W   14

© Point Loma Publishing 2007

Puerto Aventuras is closest place to berth safely and travel to Tulum by land.

marina@puertoaventuras.com.mx.

Port Clearance: The marina office handles your domestic port clearance, but Puerto Aventuras is not a Port of Entry.

Local Services: The marina's diesel dock is hard to starboard after you enter the harbor. We sounded 13' alongside. Major credit cards are accepted. Dockmaster Gerry Segrove keeps a list of recommended local services and is most helpful.

Tulum National Park

Our favorite land exploration is the dramatic temple city of Tulum - The Wall – the only site the Mayans built on the coast, 20 n.m. down the coast from Puerto Aventuras. Many of the ruins are still being excavated and studied, but what's open to the public is awesome. Arriving by land, you pay upon entrance near the trinket shops, so grab a free walking map of Tulum's layout.

Early one morning as we drove a rental car down to Belize, we happened to glimpse a tiny road sign for Tulum and – on a whim – we turned in. Although it was still quite early in the day, we were surprised to find tour buses and swarms of shutter bugs already climbing all over the temples. After jostling with crowds for 30 minutes, we left in a huff.

On our way down the coast, we realized this was the Vernal Equinox, THE only sunrise when the serpent's head finally connects to his body and tail, which is what the Temple of the Descending God was created for. We'd missed the mystical shadow show by less than an hour. Mark your cruising calendar for Tulum before sunrise on April 21.

Anchor: Unfortunately, as we go to press, Tulum National Park offers no moorings behind the barrier reef, which runs about 8 n.m. up and down the coast,

Tulum's great castle overlooks the huge reefs shielding it from approach by sea. Photo by Larry Dunmire.

very close in. And the park doesn't permit visitors to arrive by climbing up the cliff paths from the ocean side. Maybe someday they'll add yacht moorings and a seaside park entrance.

Meanwhile, the owners of shallow-draft vessels have told us that, in flat calm weather, they negotiated a narrow break in the reef (about 1.5 n.m. south of the landmark El Castillo temple) by following a local catamaran tour boat. Once inside the reef, they anchored just south of the broad sandy point visible 0.6 of a mile south of El Castillo, staying for a few hours of daylight. But most of the potential anchoring area behind the reef is fouled by isolated coral heads and depths of less than 4' over sand. During typical Trade Wind days, this wouldn't be possible.

Sian Ka'an
National Biosphere Reserve

On the mainland between Isla Cozumel and Banco Chinchorro, this huge preserve encompasses

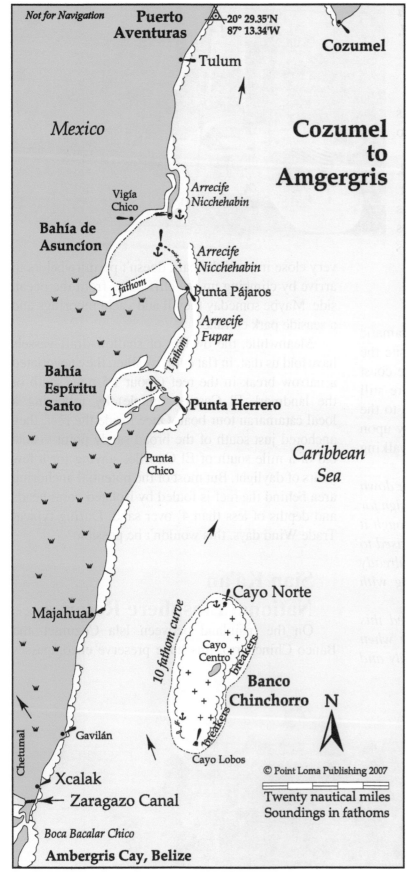

Not for Navigation

Puerto Aventuras

20° 29.35'N
87° 13.34'W

Cozumel

Tulum

Mexico

Cozumel to Amgergris

Vigía Chico

Arrecife Nicchehabin

Bahía de Asuncíon

1 fathom

Punta Pájaros

Arrecife Nicchehabin

Arrecife Fupar

Bahía Espíritu Santo

1 fathom

Punta Herrero

Punta Chico

Caribbean Sea

Majahual

Cayo Norte

10 fathom curve

Cayo Centro

breakers

Banco Chinchorro

N

Cayo Lobos

breakers

Chetumal

Gavilán

© Point Loma Publishing 2007

Xcalak

Zaragazo Canal

Twenty nautical miles
Soundings in fathoms

Boca Bacalar Chico

Ambergris Cay, Belize

Espiritu Santos. Sian Ka'an is a UNESCO World Heritage Site.

If you stop here, arrive fully provisioned and empty headed (pumped out), because the preserve has no services or supplies. Unescorted visitors are limited to anchoring in the outer reaches of the bays. To really check it out, link up with a park guide at Punta Allen in Asunción Bay.

Sian Ka'an was the Mayan name for this region, meaning *Where the Sky is Born*. The unusually high level of biodiversity has been shielded from development. Within Sian Ka'an are 318 species of butterflies, 325 species of birds (roseate spoonbills, white-fronted parrots, belted kingfishers, blue & boat-billed heron, frigates and the Jabiru stork – the world's largest flighted bird. Endangered species: jaguar, puma, tapir, manatee and spider monkey. Loggerheads, hawksbills and green turtles nest here in summer. Of the 230 tree species within Sian Ka'an, 14% are endemic to the Yucatan Peninsula.

NOTE: If you hike ashore, avoid the toxic Chechen trees that look like Ficus trees but ooze black sap, stronger than poison ivy.

Surprisingly, catch & release fishing for bonefish, tarpon and permit fish is allowed in some spots, but a certified park guide must show you where. Otherwise, all flora, fauna and habitats are protected. Aquaculture nurseries hatch several species of turtle, shrimp and lobster within the pristine park.

Bahía Asunción

Asunción Bay covers 130 square miles, but most of it is mud shoals. In prevailing Trades, boats drawing less than 8' find marginally sheltered anchorage behind the barrier reef, or SW of Punta Allen peninsula or west of Isla Culebra.

Nicchehaben Reef runs N-S, is dry or breaking, thus preventing direct approach to Asunción Bay. But a 2-n.m. wide gap in the reef allows careful entrance starting about 2 n.m. SE of Punta Allen Lighthouse (19°46.9'N, 87°28.0'W), which stands about 2 n.m

87 n.m. of the coastline, and it reaches about 25 n.m. inland, including all of Bahía Asunción and Bahía

Reef shields along Quintana Roo create nice beaches.

inside the reef on the north arm of the bay. Strong current sets north across the reef opening. The easiest anchoring spot is just inside and north of this reef break, in about 10' over sand patches and sea grass.

Punta Allen settlement on the point is surrounded by 3' shoal water, but a dredged boat channel leads to an anchorage just inside the point. The village has a park office, several small cafes and hotels, but no other services, and the dirt road runs 20 n.m. north, where it joins a 10-mile paved road to Highway 307 near Tulum.

As eco-tourism expands in the Yucatan region, more kayakers and bird watchers arrive here each year – in air-conditioned vans – and new little hotels pop up along the jungle shores. But so far, no yacht services are found.

Cayos Culebra (Snake Keys) are a curving string of mangrove islands at the bay's south arm of land, located about 4.25 n.m. south of Punta Allen. Anchorage is possible (8' over sand and grass) behind the north cay, which has a lighthouse. Approach by the NW end of Cayo Culebra, because the south end is connected to lighted Punta Nohku by a rocky shoal. Nicchehaben Reef begins again about 3 n.m. ENE of Cayos Culebra (19°41.7'N, 87°28.0'W).

In the SW end of Bahía Asunción, another shallower lagoon goes 5 n.m. west, providing good dinghy exploration and bird watching amid marshes.

Punta Pajaros Light (19°35.8'N, 87°24.8'W) marks the SE end of Bahía Asunción, still barred by Nicchehaben Reef, which dries to a rocky ledge as it runs SSE.

Bahía Espíritu Santo

Punta Tupac (about 19°28.4'N, 87°26'W) about 8 n.m. SSE of Isla Pajaros Light is kind of the divider between Asunción and Holy Spirit, and from here the land drops away SW. Tupac Reef extends about 5 n.m. south of Punta Tupac, thus shielding the NE approach to Bahía Espíritu Santo.

Punta Herrero (19°18.7'N, 87°26.8'W) forms the south land arm of Espíritu Santo Bay, but it too has a detached reef curving north for about 3.25 n.m. So the deep-water opening between Tupac and Herrero (aka Noja) reefs is about 1.25 n.m. wide.

Like at Asunción, the easiest anchoring area during prevailing Trades is up inside the northern Tupac Reef, in 6' to 10' of water over sand and sea grass, but this whole triangular area has isolated coral heads.

Another spot is off the NW tip of Isla Chal (aka Owen) in about 10' over sand and grass. Isla Chal (3 n.m. NW to SE) is the NW extension of Punta Herrero headland. The navigable pass (12' depths) between the north end of Isla Chal and the south end of rounded Punta Hochecat (aka Punta Lawrence) is about 1.2 n.m. wide.

Mud shoals and mangroves ring the rest of the 6' to 12' deep bay, and El Porvenir (Fortune) is a collection of shacks in the south end of the inner bay. In Holy Spirit Bay, only the village on Punta Herrero is connected by road.

Chinchorro Bank north end lies 33 n.m. SSE from outside Punta Herrero. (See below.)

Majahual cruise ship dock lies 35 n.m. SSW of Punta Herrero. It has no facilities for yatistas, and Highway 307 lies 35 miles inland.

Xcalac, about 65 n.m. down from Punta Herrero, has a very narrow cut (min 7' depth) through the breaking reef. Attempt to enter only in flat conditions. Several yatistas report banging bottom and getting pooped here. Line up the white lighthouse and the yellow-black light tower at about 283°, time your dash between breaking sets, favor the north side and then turn north just behind the reef to avoid coral heads close south. Ashore is a Port of Entry Capitanía where you can clear out of Mexico. A cruise ship pier is slated for construction, so a larger reef cut may appear.

Club Nautico de Chetumal welcomes all yatistas, but max depth is 6' at end tie.

Zaragosa Channel: At 70 n.m. down the coast from Punta Herrero, this newly excavated ship canal (10' depth) into Chetumal Bay was slated to open in early 2007, replacing the nearby Canal Bacalar Chico that was destroyed by hurricanes.

A sea buoy is supposed to mark the reef cut (outside approach 18°13.05'N, 87°49.48'W), which lies .65 of a mile east of the actual land opening of the Zaragosa Channel. Operated by the Mexican Marines, this shortcut into Chetumal Bay runs .75 of a mile through land, then winds 3 n.m. in a series of staked channels through mangrove cays. From there it's about 30 n.m. across the open bay to Chetumal. See below. We hope a Capitanía will open at the entrance to the Zaragoza Channel, so yatistas can clear in and out of Mexico here.

Chetumal

This Port of Entry at Quintana Roo's south end was not approachable by yacht through most of 2006, due to hurricane damage and heavy silting. By press time, we hope both approaches (from sea via the new Zaragaso Channel, or from behind Ambergris Cay via the old Bulkhead Reef channel) will be dredged, marked and reopened for pleasure-boat traffic.

After either approach, the magic spot about 1.75 n.m. NE of Rocky Point in Chetumal Bay lies at 18°23.90'N, 88°04.89'W. Post a "manatee watch" on the bow to avoid these slow-moving creatures living all over Chetumal Bay. From here, it's 13.5 n.m. WNW in about 11' of water to the docks along the south side of Chetumal, which covers the north banks of the mouth of Rio Honda, the border between Mexico and Belize.

If you get lost, you can request a pilot service from the Club de Yates de Chetumal on VHF 16 or 68. With a good sense of humor, they say the cost depends on time of day and whether or not you already ran aground. See below.

Anchor & Berth: The east side of the big concrete Muelle Fiscal is foul with rocks. Along the west side we found 8' of water near its south end (18°29.41'N, 88°17.96'W). You share the pier with the Navy and small commercial fishing boats. Next door, the oft full Club Nautico de Chetumal (VHF 16 & 68) dock has 6' of water at the 40' long end tie, less toward shore.

As long as you don't block access to Muelle Fiscal, anchorage is possible off Club Nautico; pay a small day fee for secure dinghy landing privileges. This fishing club is very friendly to visiting yatistas, has a palapa and BBQ barrel, weekend parties, gated parking and offers pilot service in or back out. The pilot fee depends on time of day and whether or not you're aground.

TERMINAL MARITIMA CHETUMAL

Muelle Fiscal is guarded by Navy, but it's a popular paseo at sunrise & sunset.

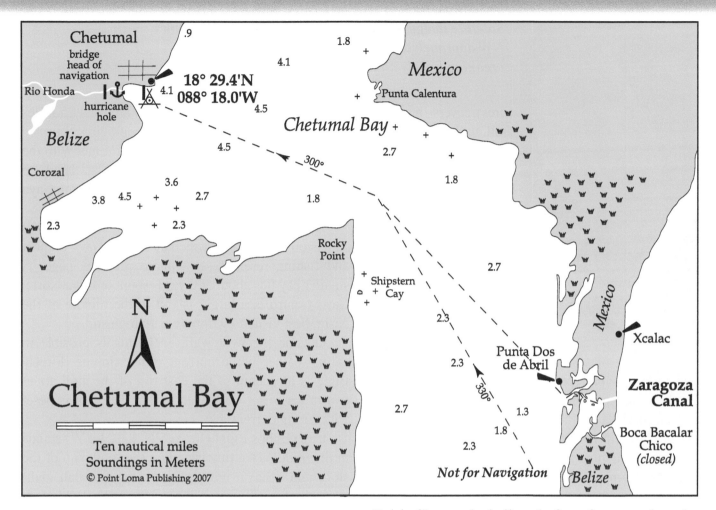

Chetumal
bridge
head of
navigation
Rio Honda
hurricane
hole
Belize
Corozal

18° 29.4'N
088° 18.0'W

.9
4.1
1.8
4.1
4.5
4.5
3.6
3.8 4.5 2.7
2.3 2.3
2.3

Mexico
Punta Calentura

Chetumal Bay

2.7
1.8

Rocky
Point

Shipstern
Cay

2.7

2.3

2.3

Punta Dos
de Abril

2.3

2.7

1.3

1.8

2.3

N

Chetumal Bay

Ten nautical miles
Soundings in Meters
© Point Loma Publishing 2007

Mexico

Xcalac

**Zaragoza
Canal**

Boca Bacalar
Chico
(*closed*)

Belize

Not for Navigation

300°

330°

Port Clearance: The Capitanía (VHF 16), Aduana and Navy have a booth at the head of the Muelle Fiscal, and they will call Migración from the airport if you need to clear in or out of Mexico here with your international Zarpe.

The Port Captain said very few yatistas visit Chetumal except for international clearance, and he thinks most clear in or out at Puerto Morelos, Isla Mujeres or Puerto Juarez at the north end of the Yucatan Channel. Perhaps after the approaches to Chetumal are improved, that will change.

Chetumal has a SEMARNAT office on the Malecon where you can purchase day permits to visit Banco Chinchorro. As we go to press, the Navy also sells permits once you arrive - but ask here.

Local Services: Fuel can be arranged by tank truck to the Muelle Fiscal or Club Nautico dock. Chetumal has large grocery stores, fruterías and marine hardware. The airport is 2 miles west; the bus station is 2 miles north.

West of the Club's docks to the Rio Honda is a manatee park, so no motors. At the north end of

Bahía Chetumal, shallow-draft craft can explore the Uaymil & Laguna Bacalar Nature Reserves, but the bay develops lots of Trade Wind chop.

Banco Chinchorro

NOTE: As we go to press on 6.5 edition in March, 2011, Banco Chinchorro is closed to private yachts, hopefully only temporarily, due to security measures and damage to the biosphere reserve. Yachts have been turned away by the Navy, so please check its status before planning even a brief rest stop here.

Chinchorro Bank (33 n.m. SSE of Punta Herrero) is Mexico's only coral atoll, and the largest one in the western hemisphere, measuring 23 n.m. N-S, 11 n.m. E-W at the wider northern half. Yatistas come here (a.) for spectacular diving along the sheer walls and coral gardens, or to observe the abundant marine wildlife; or (b.) as an overnight rest stop sheltered from the Trade Winds while they travel south from Mexico's Yucatan Channel cruising grounds to those in Belize, Guatemala and Honduras.

Chinchorro Bank Biosphere Reserve (324,000

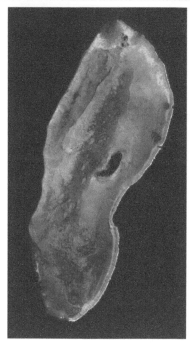

Satellite image of Mexico's Bancho Chinchorro shows NW approach to Cayo Norte, also Trade Wind seas breaking hugely along the eastern side.

acres) covers the coral atoll and surrounding waters, regulated by SEMARNAT and other agencies including fishing coops. To protect the habitat, yachts are not allowed to stay here more than about 48 hours (1 or 2 overnights). Park rangers will come to inform you of the complex regulations and collect the park permit fee for SEMARNAT. Ask for their map or chart of Banco Chinchorro.

No services are found in the park, but in an emergency Cayo Norte has a new lighthouse, Navy patrol outpost and fishing research station. The nearest hyperbaric chamber is on Ambergris Cay.

The steep-to east side gets pummeled by Trades and the Gulf Stream, and it's radar conspicuous with 200 shipwrecks and spuming breakers. The west side fares much better, but a southbound counter current can occur. Inside the reef walls, most of the basin contains coral heads that are awash only at some spring tides, but depths between the hazards are from 5' to 18'.

Anchorages: NOTE: these anchorages may be closed. The primary access through the reef wall is a 1.25-n.m. wide break (10' depth) just west of the north end of the bank. Our approach waypoint just outside the opening is 18°46.69'N, 87°19.63'W. Shipwreck debris marks the SW edge of the opening in the reef, but dangerous foul ground extends almost 1.25 miles NE from that tip of the reef, encouraging entrance closer to the north side of the opening. Enter with the nav light bearing about 132°T. Most boats head 1.5 n.m. farther SE to anchor (6' to 10') west of Cayo Norte (low sand, mangroves & palms).

Banco Chinchorro Light (18°45.8'N, 87°18.9'W) stands on Cayo Norte, which also has a Navy outpost and fishing research. See photo previous page. A smaller cay lies about 500 yards south of Cayo Norte. Cayo Centro is a larger island in the middle of the basin, best visited by dinghy with high sun.

Outside the west wall, anchoring is possible in calm weather while current is not ripping. Firefly Bight is an indent of the east rim of the atoll about two miles SE of Cayo Centro, but the bight is beset with strong current.

Cayo Lobos Light (18°23.5'N, 87°23.2'W) stands in the middle of a tiny island on the south rim of the atoll, and it has a new racon C (dah, di, dah, dah) readable for 20 miles when operational. Skylark Ledge is a dry rocky ledge about half a mile WNW of Cayo Lobos, and Blackford Ledge is another awash area about half a mile farther NW.

Entrance to the SW side of Chinchorro's interior can reportedly be made through Blackford Gap, a large break in the reef immediately north of Blackford Ledge. Depths inside between coral heads and sand bars are from 6' to 10' over white sand and dark sea grass.

Chinchorro refers to a cinch-type fishing net used on early Spanish ships that first named this beautiful atoll.

Bancho Chinchorro is our last cruising stop in Mexico. From here, we continue south into Central America.

Research station next to Bancho Chinchorro Light on Cayo Norte is popular stop for yatistas en route to Central America.

Belize

The tiny country of Belize (pop. approx. 201,500) is loved by yatistas for many reasons: 130-mile barrier reef of living coral, 130 turquoise and sand cays inside the reef, 3 huge offshore atolls and the charming Caribe soul of its people.

English is the official language, but Spanish is common on the coast; Garifuna, Creole and Mayan tongues are spoken inland. One US dollar (US$1) equals 2 Belize dollars (BZ$2), and US dollars are accepted everywhere. The capital Belmopan is 40 miles inland from Belize City.

For yatistas summering over in Guatemala's Rio Dulce, Belize is a quickie getaway, because the south entrance to the Inner Passage behind the reef is only 35 n.m. north of Livingston. But Belize is not a hurricane hole, nor does the barrier reef knock down the Trade Winds of winter cruising season – just most of the big seas. And when the Trades are hooting, the reef cuts can be treacherous.

Belize is world-renowned for colorful, comfortable snorkeling and scuba diving, so in some spots it's overdone. The old wind-jammer cruises first chartered out of Belize decades ago, and scuba diving magazines and organized dive tours entice tourists to visit the region's Mom 'n Pop dive hotels. Cruise ships stop here with non-diving passengers.

Belize is on Central Standard Time (like Chicago) but has no Daylight Saving Time. Firearms are not allowed in Belize; see Port Clearance for Ambergris Caye.

Route Planning

Getting inside: For a cruising destination, we recommend the Belize chapters of Capt. Freya Rauscher's comprehensive *"Belize & Mexico's Caribbean Coast."* Also NIMA charts 28167 and 28168. Belize's vast cruising grounds are complex, fraught with shoals, isolated coral heads, unmaintained channels and unsurveyed expanses, which is beyond the scope of *"Cruising Ports"* – but we will cover 3 popular access paths behind the reef:

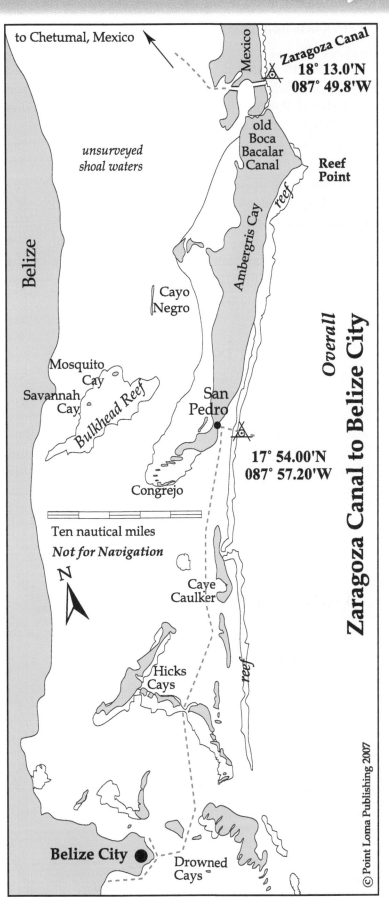

to Chetumal, Mexico

Mexico

Zaragoza Canal
18° 13.0'N
087° 49.8'W

old Boca Bacalar Canal

Reef Point

unsurveyed shoal waters

Belize

Ambergris Cay

reef

Cayo Negro

Mosquito Cay

Savannah Cay

Bulkhead Reef

San Pedro

17° 54.00'N
087° 57.20'W

Congrejo

Ten nautical miles
Not for Navigation

N

Caye Caulker

reef

Hicks Cays

Overall

Zaragoza Canal to Belize City

Belize City

Drowned Cays

© Point Loma Publishing 2007

(1.) San Pedro Cut at Ambergris Caye and vicinity (6' in spots).

(2.) Eastern Channel deep water to the Inner Passage near Belize City.

(3.) Inner Passage (deep water) from Sapodilla Cays north to Belize City.

San Pedro and Belize City are Ports of Entry, as are Dangriga (formerly North Stann Creek) and Punta Gorda both south of Belize City.

Staying outside: If you are just passing through the NW Caribbean en route to Rio Dulce (155 n.m. from Ambergris) or Roatan (135 n.m. from Ambergris), you may only wish to shelter at Belize's offshore atolls (Turneffe Islands, Glovers Reef, Lighthouse Reef), and we'll look at Turneffe.

Ambergris Caye

Coming down the Yucatan Channel, most yatistas enter Belize at San Pedro on Ambergris Caye, where you can clear into the country and also reach the Inner Passage if you can travel in 6' of water.

Largest of the cays behind the reef, Ambergris is 21 n.m. long from the abandoned Bacalcar Channel border with Mexico down to the Hol Chan Marine Reserve. The easiest access is San Pedro Cut. San Pedro (pop. 2,000) is where Port Authorities handle your Port of Entry clearance into Belize. It has a fuel dock, yacht club marina, anchorages, dinghy docks, groceries, some marine supplies, an airport and more than 40 small tourist hotels aimed at divers.

San Pedro Cut: A counter current to the Gulf Stream sometimes runs south along the west sides of Chinchorro Bank and Turneffe Islands Atoll. San Pedro Cut has a 9' least depth, and the anchorage has 6' to 9' of water. Enter the cut with high sun and only in moderate seas. Time your entrance between the wave trains so you don't slam the bottom.

San Pedro Cut is about 44 n.m. SW of the south end of Chinchorro or 16.5 n.m. down from prominent Reef Point. In this vicinity, the barrier reef runs generally NNE to SSW. Our GPS approach position about a quarter mile outside San Pedro Cut is 17°54.0'N, 87°57.2'W.

The 300' wide gap is usually visible between breakers, but about 120' inside and to port is a taller stubby reef that angles north for about a quarter mile – creating a narrower channel that starts off heading NW but then quickly dog-legs north. We enter on a NW course about 320°T, and as soon as our starboard quarter is well clear of the outer reef and rubble around it, we start turning our dog-leg north.

If in doubt, hail "any boat with local knowledge" on VHF 16 or 68, and ask for pilot service getting in. Some charge, some don't.

Anchor & Berth: Within .75 of a mile NW of San Pedro Cut you can anchor in 6' to 9' of water starting about 250 yards off San Pedro town. More than 2 dozen docks line the anchorage, and some of them rent space to yatistas. Town Hall and Police Department where officials hang out are just north of the busy water taxi dock. Central Park runs north to Island Ferry

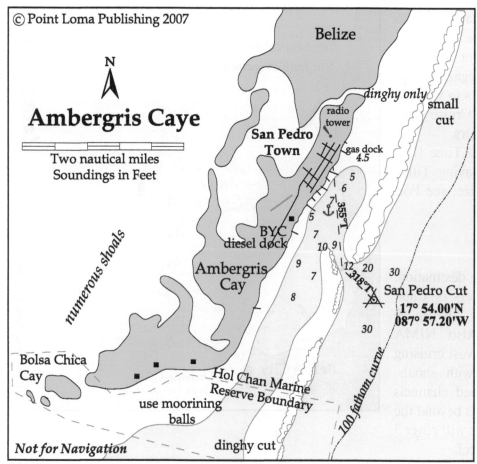

© Point Loma Publishing 2007

Ambergris Caye

Two nautical miles
Soundings in Feet

N

Belize

dinghy only

radio tower

small cut

San Pedro Town

gas dock 4.5

5

6

7

355°T

5

BYC diesel dock

7

10 9

9

7

12 20

318°T

30

San Pedro Cut
17° 54.00'N
087° 57.20'W

30

Ambergris Cay

8

numerous shoals

Bolsa Chica Cay

Hol Chan Marine Reserve Boundary

use moorining balls

100 fathom curve

Not for Navigation

dinghy cut

Belize Yacht Club Marina guest dock.

docks. North of there is only dinghy depth.

Port Clearance: Call "San Pedro Customs" on VHF 16 with your ETA when you're within range. Fly your Q-flag and remain in quarantine until you're officially cleared in. Customs and Immigration officers (501)-422-3869 come out to inspect the boat and help you fill in Belize entrance papers. If this is your first Port of Entry into Belize, present your Zarpe from your last country, along with all your other ship's documents and passports.

If you're docked, only the captain is allowed to come ashore directly to Customs and Immigration at the airport. All others must stay aboard until Customs and Immigration are done with you. (They may bring you a *San Pedro Sun* newspaper with all local services information.)

Recreational boats can stay in Belize up to 90 days without further paperwork. Passports are stamped for an initial 30-day visit, extended monthly for a small fee. Visas are not required for citizens of the US, Mexico, Canada or other British Commonwealth countries, Belgium, Denmark, Finland, Greece, Iceland, Italy, Liechtenstein, Luxembourg, Spain, Switzerland, Tunisia, Turkey or Uruguay.

NOTE: Guns larger than 9 mm are prohibited. Declare any weapons toBelize Customs and Immigration right away. They'll be locked up until your departure. If undeclared weapons or ammunition are discovered during the inspection (which might go on while you're busy filling in papers) or any time later, we're told that all persons onboard will be sent directly to Hattieville Prison for 3 years and the boat will be confiscated. Period.

Yachts may also clear Customs and Immigration at

Belize City, Dangriga (formerly North Stann Creek), Big Creek and Punta Gorda.

Local Services: Belize Yacht Club Marina near the reef cut has 20 non-floating slips to 60'LOA, about 4.5' of water at low tide, 6' at high. So far the only true marina in town, it has power, water, WiFi, phone & TV and security. The marina office can assist with port clearance. It's part of a pretty resort with bar, restaurant, gym, nice services; this marina often fills with charter boats. FMI, contact BYC at new phone (501) 226-4338 or new website BelizeYachtClub.com

Belize Yacht Club Marina has a diesel dock with gas and lube oil. Another fuel depot up the beach had gas only.

San Pedro Town has plenty of grocery stores, dive shops, restaurants, Nellie's laundry service (501) 226-2454, golf-cart rentals 226-3262, tackle shops and a small boat yard past the airport. The ferry 226-3231 runs to Caye Caulker and Belize City from here. The water taxi is on VHF 11. A bank with ATM is at the

Anchorage inside reef at San Pedro, Ambergris Cay. Photo by Dave Humphries.

Hol Chan Marine Refuge

Hol Chan starts about 3 n.m. south of San Pedro town, covers 4 square miles: Boca Chica Cay on the east, to Shark Ray Alley and Hol Chan Cut dinghy pass through the barrier reef. On the park's north shore is Boca Ciega, a collapsed blue hole, maybe the most easily accessible of the dozen or so in Belize. A permit is required for Hol Chan (call 501-226-2247 or dive shops), and anchoring of non-excursion craft may be prohibited. Snorkelers and scuba divers also enjoy 100 other spots along the inside and outside of Belize's barrier reef where no permit is required. Congrejo Cay appears connected to the south end of Ambergris Cay.

South of Hol Chan Marine Refuge and Congrejo Cay, several unmarked channels with least depths of about 6' can take you to Caye Caulker, Chapel Cay and Long Cay.

Caulker Caye: Located 7.5 n.m. south of San Pedro on Ambergris Caye, this smaller island with the British spelling is known for being laid-back. Reach the village anchorage by following the channel SSW from San Pedro. Old charts call this Corker Cay.

Cay Chapel: The next cay south on the same inside channel (6' to 10' depths) is even smaller. Cay Chapel has a marina basin carved out to 6' depths on its west side, and an airstrip runs N-S on the north end. Pyramid Island Marina has about 40 slips, power and water. The fuel dock is on the starboard side of the entrance channel (6').

water taxi is on VHF 11. A bank with ATM is at the foot of Buccaneer Street, but there are others.

For medical emergencies, Lion Hospital is (501) 226-2073 is west of the airport terminal. Call for the region's only hyperbaric chamber 226-2851, or the air ambulance is 223-3292.

For the 15 n.m. route onward to Long Cay, Puerto Stuck and Belize City we recommend Freya Rauscher's excellent *Belize Cruising Guide*.

South Chetumal Bay: Recent hurricanes closed this route, but by the time you arrive it may be dredged open and marked – or not.

Overlooking the anchorage at San Pedro, Captain Morgan's pool welcomes yatistas.

Wonder why it's called Brain Coral? Hol Chan Marine Refuge is a good spot for snorkelers. Photo by Tony Rath.

From Cay Caulker's west side, a course NNW for 10.75 n.m. arrives at a position about 2.5 n.m. west of Congrejo Cay. Going about 6.5 n.m. NNE (staying east of Bulkhead Reef) you may see a lighted marker and a casually staked channel (5.5' depth if dredged) leading 3.5 n.m. NW between mudflats that uncover at LLW.

Now you're in Chetumal Bay, part of the bi-national Bacalar Chico Marine Park. A course of about 024°M or midway between mudflats for 15 n.m. should keep you west of shoals west of Cayo Negro and bring you to a position about 4 n.m. west of Punta Dos de Abril, the bayside entrance to the Zaragoza Canal. For information on Chetumal, see the previous chapter on Mexico.

Eastern Channel to Belize City

About 35 n.m. south of San Pedro Cut into Ambergris Caye, you'll find the entrance to Eastern Channel, the 60' deep ship channel that zig-zags to the Inner Passage (12' depths) and to Belize City. Providing some wind shelter, the west wall of Turneffe Atoll lies only 4 n.m. east of the Eastern Channel's opening in the barrier reef, but expect current on approach. Enter with high sun to help read the bottoms.

Goff's Cay Sandbore (17°20.3'N, 88°02.2'W) at the north edge of the barrier cut overhangs the 850-yard wide opening about half a mile farther east than does the south edge, which is English Cay (17°19.6'N, 88°03.0'W). Both cays are lighted and edged by isolated coral heads, but English Cay has range markers (300°T) and a pilot station.

Enter the middle of Eastern Channel

heading WNW while keeping Water Cay Split Light to starboard, then turn NW for about 1.75 n.m. to take North East Split Light (17°22.8'N, 88°05.5'W) close to port.

Here the Eastern Channel bends WSW for about 1.5 n.m., keeping White Grounds Split Light (yellow concrete pile) to starboard. Then angle WNW for 1.25 n.m. while keeping Spanish Cay Split Light (green concrete pile) to port. After Spanish Cay, turn SW and continue for about 3.5 n.m. between the Grennel Cays (starboard) and the Spanish Cays (starboard).

Entering the broad Inner Passage, turn NW while keeping the Grennels and Robins Point Light to

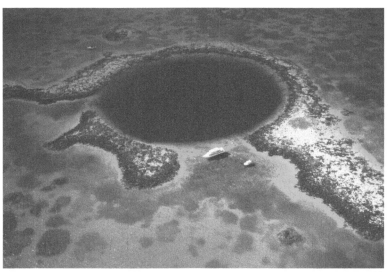

Note sailboat anchored outside Blue Hole rim - it's in the photo's upper left quadrant. Photo by Tony Rath.

Cucumber Beach Marina is the most protected of the marinas near Belize City.

starboard. Belize City lies about 8 n.m. NNE. Please note that along either side of Eastern Channel, you may find several anchorages and side channels.

Belize City

Belize City (pop. 48,000) is the country's largest city and a Port of Entry. Yatistas find at least 3 small marinas with fuel, good provisioning and international flights. But it's an uncomfortable open roadstead, and security ashore at night isn't great.

Belize City covers a 3-mile long peninsula. The new commercial port on the peninsula's south side has a half-mile long causeway jutting south to its offshore island, which gets cruise ships and freighters. Old Belize River (about 4' deep) splits the peninsula and forms a shallow half-mile wide bight on its SE side. On the north point of the river bight, Barron Bliss monument (about 17°29.59'N, 88°10.99'W) and Fort George Light overlook the historic approaches. The water taxi and several small docks line the river bight, and local fishing boats moor in the middle of the river, leaving scant room on either side for dinghies. About 200 yards upstream, the low swing bridge opens twice daily.

Anchor & Berth: Staying at least 500 yards off, you can anchor (10' t 18') in the open roadstead east or SE of the commercial port's lighted offshore island, as long as you don't block ship traffic. What we call Port Island lies at about 17°28.38'N, 88°12.03'W. Or off the east side of Belize City, you can anchor (5' to 8') in the open roadstead off the Fort George Radisson hotel's marina dock. Or anywhere in between.

Belize City has a slip shortage, but we think more are being built. The marinas for ocean-going yates are Cucumber Beach Marina SW of town, the small marina dock in front of the Fort George Radisson Hotel at the SE corner of town, or another small marina about a mile NW of the Fort George marina. For details, see local services below.

Port Clearance: It's possible to clear into

Call ahead to Cucumber Beach Marina for the latest depths.

Map

yard

dockmaster

© Point Loma Publishing 2013

Cucumber Beach Marina

Port Authority

N

restaurant

tower

water slide

330°T

One tenth nautical mile
Soundings in Feet at MLW

17° 28.10'N
088° 14.75'W

12

Not for Navigation

Belize City while at anchor or dockside, but either way yatistas must fly the Q-flag and hail "Port Authority" on VHF 16 immediately on arrival to request clearance.

A Customs boat boards you in the roadstead, and they'll bring their forms and inspect your boat. Then the captain is directed ashore for a taxi to Immigration (501-282-2423) near the Police Station. When done, lower the Q-flag and everybody can go ashore.

Marinas will call the Port Authority to arrange your dockside clearance. Customs is 227-3510.

Local Services: Cucumber Beach Marina (about 2.65 n.m. west of Belize City's Port Island) has a red buoy and lighted 300-yard twin-jetty entrance channel (6' at MLW) leading NNW. Inside the sheltered basins are about 40 full-service finger slips and side ties (6' depth). Diesel and gas can be brought to the slips, which have 24/7 security. Within the compound are showers, coin laundry, cantina with WiFi, sheds and dry marina.

The Cisco Woods family built this marina around a historic dock that loaded produce – including cucumbers – hence the name. CBM is often full, so make a reservation, and hail them on VHF 16 and 68 before entering. Cucumber Beach Marina (501) 222-4153 or marina@oldbelize.com.

Cucumber Beach Marina also has the region's only boat yard for yachts. Contact info@oldbelize.com.

Fort George Radisson Hotel & Marina is on the SE shore of Belize City. It's single dock juts 500' east, and behind its T-head are half a dozen full-service slips (6' to 10' depth) to about 60' LOA. The hotel has a laundry, gym and eateries, plus walking access to downtown. This dock also has a diesel and gas service. Fort George Radisson Marina (501) 223-3333 or visit www.radissonbelize.com.

Belize City has marine supplies, bulk oil, groceries, propane, a hospital, international flights, charter yachts, etc. For a better rate, hire a taxi by the day or half day, but pick one with a good vehicle, big enough trunk for your provisioning and agree on the rate before you set off.

Visit the Maritime Museum just SE of the swing bridge, then walk across and down Regent and Albert streets to the market stalls for fresh produce. On Market Square, the beautiful colonial Supreme Court building has a landmark clock tower, but don't set your chronometer by it.

For local arts and crafts, the biggest selection has moved out to the new commercial port with tables set up for the cruise ship passengers.

Turneffe Islands

The Turneffe Islands group is a massive (300 sq.mi.) coral atoll containing nearly 200 islands, cays and reefs. Including its outer reef wall, Turneffe (pronounced *TURN-ef* by locals) measures 30 n.m. NNE to SSW, max 10 n.m. across, but only 3.5 n.m. across its narrow neck 8 n.m. south of the north tip. Turneffe (like Lighthouse Reef and Glovers Reef) is

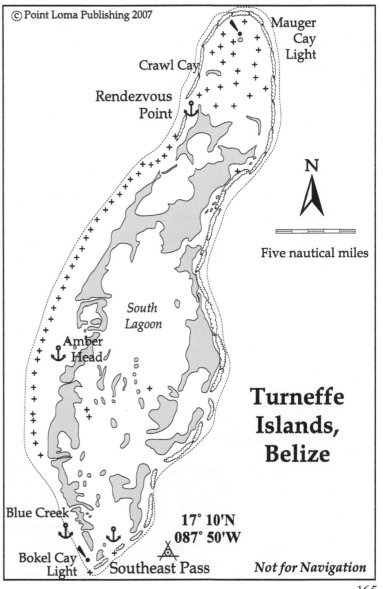

© Point Loma Publishing 2007

Mauger Cay Light

Crawl Cay

Rendezvous Point

N

Five nautical miles

South Lagoon

Amber Head

Turneffe Islands, Belize

Blue Creek

17° 10'N
087° 50'W

Bokel Cay Light · Southeast Pass

Not for Navigation

Delicate corals thrive in center of Turneffe Islands and Belize's offshore atolls. Photo by Tony Rath.

nearly encircled by reefs, but unlike the others it has much more land and visible mangrove forests within its reef walls. Deep water rises sharply on all sides.

The north end of Turneffe's outer reef (about 17°37.5'N, 87°45.3'W) is about 20 n.m. SE of San Pedro Cut. Mauger Cay Light stands about 1.5 n.m inside the north end of the lagoon, which is full of coral patches.

Turneffe's eastern side is usually bashed by Trade Winds, littered with shipwrecks and goes from deep to dry in a flash.

The west side is partially submerged reef up to half a mile off the land line. The coral reef has a sand fringe a few hundred yards wide, and in some places you can anchor just outside the west wall or sail right over it in 10' of water. The westernmost place in Turneffe's west side lies only 8 n.m. east of the Eastern Channel Cut, so expect strong current in that area – sometimes counter to the Gulf Stream.

Rendezvous Point

This popular anchorage is on Turneffe's NW side about 7 n.m. SW of the atoll's north tip and 20 n.m. NE of the Eastern Channel Cut through Belize Reef.

The 100-yard wide navigable break (9' to 10' deep) in the reef wall lies less than a mile west of north tip of the large northern island. Approaching the Rendezvous Point break (17°32.68'N, 87°49.80'W), avoid the darker reef ends on both edges and head toward just south of the north tip of the low island. From the anchorage (8' to 9' sand, some grass), dinks can explore the inside of the reef wall and the area north to Crawl Cay between coral patches.

Blue Creek

Along the SW side of Turneffe, the approach to Blue Creek (17°12.39'N, 87°55.83'W) lies about 3 n.m. NW of the atoll's south tip. If you can get in over the 5' bar, this narrow but usually well-marked channel (8' at MLW) runs about 0.8 of a mile through the mangroves. Avoid speeding dive boats in the blind curve. You emerge inside the open lagoon, which contains several 6' deep channels through the coral patches and sand bars. About 2 n.m. SE you reach Turneffe Island Lodge on Big Bokel. Recent hurricanes might have changed the bottom since we went to press.

Southeast Pass

On the SE corner of Turneffe, this break in the reef is open to easterly swell, so you may decide to avoid it during strong Trades. Bokel Cay Light (17°09.8'N, 87°54.4'W) stands about half a mile north of the southernmost reef point of Turneffe. Bokel means Elbow, named for the acute angle. But give a quarter-mile berth to the SW quadrant of this light tower due to rocks and debris from the former lighthouse that was destroyed by hurricanes.

About a mile NE of the south tip of Turneffe, a gap in the reef shield (10' deep, less than 200 yards wide) gives access to a fairly large and sheltered anchorage (6' to

[Map:]

Blue Creek 5

coral patches & sand bars

mangrove islands

mangrove islands

2

7

sand mud flats

Turneffe Island Lodge

6

2

5

10

Southeast Pass

N

Bokel Cay Light

One nautical mile
Soundings in Feet

17° 09.8'N
087° 53.0'W

© Point Loma Publishing 2007   *Not for Navigation*

Yatista lounges on coco palm bent toward dock at Turneffe Island Lodge. Photo by Dave Humphries.

8' depths) east of Turneffe Island Lodge. (See below.) Locals call this gap Southeast Pass.

Enter the middle of the gap by keeping Bokel Cay Reef about 100 yards to port, keeping clear of submerged rocks on the NE side of the gap as well. Aim north for the eastern shore of the small palm-studded island with lodge buildings, offshore breakwaters and private boat dock. Shallows surround the island, so turn NE for the best shelter behind the eastern reef shield. Anchor in 6' to 8' of water over sand.

If you approach without enough daylight for safe entrance, you might try anchoring off the atoll's steep shelf about 500 yards WNW of the Bokel Cay Light tower in 12' to 20' over coral scrabble and sand. Take into consideration the constant 1-knot ocean current flowing from the south end.

Turneffe Island Lodge is a private resort (bone fishing, scuba diving) on a private island. Do not anchor too near, and don't dinghy over. However, if you reserve a cabaña 2 weeks in advance, you can use the lodge's facilities, which might be nice for a big batch of fly-in guests. FMI call them in Houston (713) 313-4670.

Departures: From Southeast Pass on Turneffe, the south tip of Lighthouse Reef is 16 n.m. ESE. Glovers Reef is the most remote of Belize's offshore atolls. Its wide north end is about 16 n.m. SSW of the Turneffe's Southeast Pass.

Inner Passage via Sapodilla Cay

From the south end of Belize's barrier reef, it's relatively easy to reach Belize City and dozens of prime cruising anchorages en route.

Sapodilla Corners: The Sapodilla Cays and Seal Cays form the SW end of the barrier reef, but isolated reef patches curve NW from the south end like a scorpion tail, so unless you're stopping in, give them at least 1.5 n.m. berth. The only light in the Sapodillas is on Hunter Cay, more than 3 n.m. north of the south end.

We pass south of 16°02.19'N, 87°17.00'W (or about 1.5 n.m. south of the Sapodillas) before turning WNW for about 8 n.m. and then head north (about 2 n.m. west of Lawrence Rock), thus heading up the middle of the Inner Passage in no less than 18' of water. East Snake Cay Light on the mainland side of the Inner Passage lies about 10.25 n.m. west of Seal Cays on the east side, so to avoid the shoals around Lawrence Rock (about 4' depth), favor the west side of the pass.

Big Creek is a banana shipping port 2 n.m. SW of Placentia, reached by a dredged (22') and well-marked 4 n.m. channel that starts at the Inner Passage north of Harvest Island and eventually curves a mile between mangroves, providing good all-weather shelter. See "Hurricanes" below.

Placentia Narrows: About 20 n.m. NNE (about 020°T), you thread the needle (2.5 n.m. wide) between the lighted Bugle Cays and Placentia Cay. Placencia Cay has a popular anchorage on its SW side, and the town has a fuel dock, small marina, dive shop, groceries, hotel and restaurants. More anchorages are found among the cays east of Bugle Cay.

The 30 n.m. straight line route from Placencia Cay to Dangriga (formerly North Stann Creek) is done in deep water by staying about 3 n.m. east of

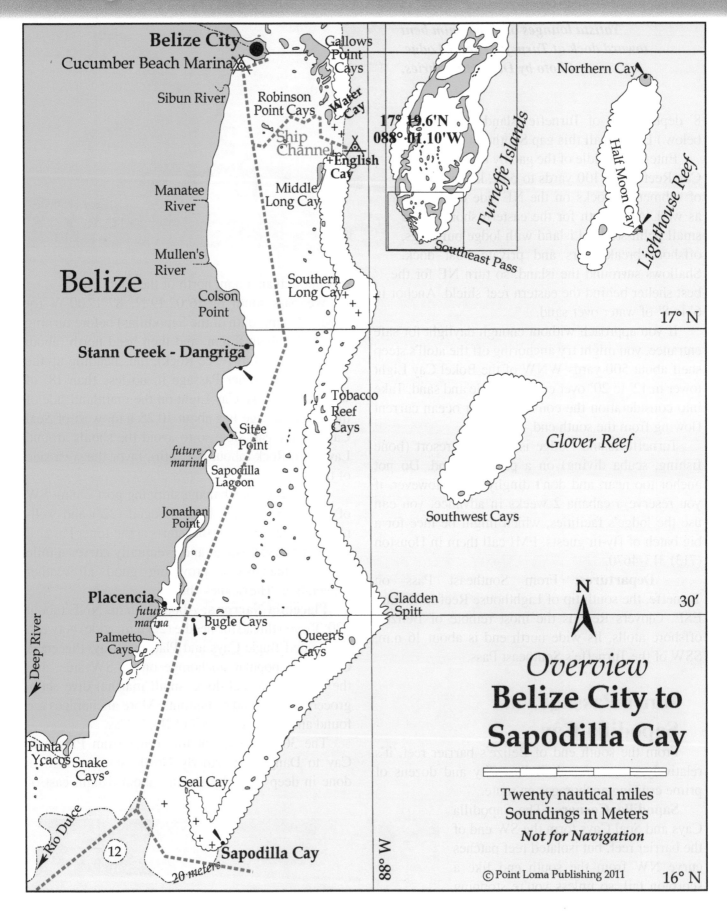

Belize City
Cucumber Beach Marina

Gallows Point Cays

Northern Cay

Sibun River

Robinson Point Cays

Water Cay

17° 19.6'N
088° 01.10'W

Turneffe Islands

Half Moon Cay

Lighthouse Reef

Ship Channel

English Cay

Manatee River

Middle Long Cay

Southeast Pass

Belize

Mullen's River

Southern Long Cay

17° N

Colson Point

Stann Creek - Dangriga

Glover Reef

Tobacco Reef Cays

Sitee Point

future marina

Sapodilla Lagoon

Southwest Cays

Jonathan Point

Placencia
future marina

Gladden Spitt

30'

Bugle Cays

Queen's Cays

N

Palmetto Cays

Deep River

Punta Ycacos Snake Cays

Seal Cay

Overview
Belize City to Sapodilla Cay

Twenty nautical miles
Soundings in Meters
Not for Navigation

12

Sapodilla Cay

20 meters

Rio Dulce

88° W

© Point Loma Publishing 2011

16° N

Coral sand forms the beaches of Belize.
Photo by Dave Humphries

Rum Point, False Cay, Jonathan Point and Sitee Point. This brings you to a turning point (about 16°57.75'N, 88°08.96'W) about 4 n.m. east of the mouth of North Stann Creek at the N point of the Dangriga settlement.

Dangriga

Dangriga or Stann Creek is the second largest town in Belize and a Port of Entry, sometimes said to be an easier place to clear into the country than Belize City.

The new Commerce Bight port is on the south side of the point. Hail the "Port Authority" on VHF 16 for instructions. Dangriga has fuel, groceries and general supplies. Yatistas come here on November 19 for the big Garifuna Settlement Day festivities.

From the Dangriga turning point, it's 27 n.m. NNW to a point one mile west of Robinson Point Cays. This is generally where the Eastern Channel merges with the Inner Passage. From here Cucumber Beach Marina lies 7.5 n.m. NNW and Fort George Light at Belize City lies 8.5 n.m. NNE. See the section on Belize City above.

Sitee River Lighthouse marks the point, and a small marina seawall lies 1.75 n.m. upriver, on the backside of the Sitee settlement.

Sapodilla Lagoon and Placencia

About 4 n.m. SW of Sitee Point Light, a new marina is planned inside the N end of Sanctuary Bay.

Placencia's 12-mile peninsula has a dozen small resort docks. Most of the town is on the mainland W of Bugle Cays. Within Placencia Lagoon and Seine Bight, shallow-draft craft can enjoy about 6 new marina channels in construction. The Moorings berths a catamaran fleet at Roberts Grove Beach Resort about 3.5 n.m. up the lagoon side of the Placencia peninsula. For online Updates on these marinas, please check **www.CentralAmericanBoating.com**

Big Creek: The nearest true hurricane hole is up the Rio Dulce in Guatemala, described in the next chapter. But yatistas have used the 22' deep channel at Big Creek, entered about 4 n.m. SW of Placencia Cay. It curves a mile between mangroves.

History & Culture: Mayan civilization flourished for more than 2,500 years in what we today know as Belize – from about 1000 BC to about 1500 AD. Archeologists are still unearthing evidence of their highly developed astronomy, agriculture, social structure and religion – along with wars, social

Garifuna Settlement Days festival is big in Dangriga. Photo by Tony Rath

The people of Belize are among its natural wonders. Photo by Tony Rath.

and religious upheavals, plagues and famine. No one knows for sure what caused the sudden demise of the Mayan world. Only a few thousand Mayan descendants, mostly Kekchi and Mopan, were still around when Columbus showed up in 1502 to name this region Bahía de Honduras.

The first European colonists were English Puritans who settled the coastal plains and built small farms. They later moved to the highland rainforests and began logging the vast hardwood forests for mast timbers and other ship-building woods. Pretty soon, pirates were drawn to the cays of Belize's barrier reef to lie in wait for the hundreds of Spanish treasure ships loaded with gold, silver and hardwoods. Calling themselves "Los Hombres de la Bahía" for Honduras Bay, these polyglot corsairs resisted all Spain's attacks. But in 1763 and 1786, the hardwood foresters made treaties with the Spanish navy to protect their exports.

By 1840, England declared British Honduras part of its empire and began shipping over colonists. Creole is a term for the beautiful blend of English and

native people. Many Kekchi and Mopan migrated to the Punta Gorda region, and those Maya who settled in the coastal areas became known as Garifuna. British Honduras became a delightful blend of classic European architecture graced with palm trees and parrots. Life was good for several generations.

But British Honduras and the rest of the British Empire's more distant colonies eventually began shriveling due to neglect, and by 1930 British Honduras was so stressed its poorer citizens were starving. When the vote was extended to all Belizeans in 1954, they voted to cut the apron strings. It was a slow process. In 1961, resources were nationalized and the country became Free Belize. The name became Belize in 1973, and on September 21, 1981 Belize, declared its Independence Day.

Today, we yatistas are fortunate to be able to explore not only Belize's incredibly beautiful barrier reef and cays, but also the many Mayan ruins and protected rainforest parks. Among the many Mayan sites open to tourism are Altun Ha, Caracol (See photo under Belize City.), Cerros, Lamanai, Lubaantun and Xunantunich. For details of these and other historic and cultural sites in the interior, visit www.travelbelize.org.

Natural Wonders of Belize

Coral Atolls: Blue Hole, Half Moon Caye and Turneffe Islands are the only 3 coral atolls in the western hemisphere.

Marine Reserves: Bacalar Chico, Glovers Reef, Hol Chan off Ambergris Caye, Sapodillo Cayes, South Water Caye, Port Honduras, Caulker Caye, Gladden Split and Silk Cayes.

National Parks: Aguas Tibias, Bacalar Chico, Blue Hole, Chiquibil, Five Blues Lake, Guanacaste, Laughing Bird Caye, Monkey Bay, Paynes Creek, Rio Blanco, Sarstoon Temash and Honey Camp.

National Monuments: Blue Hole, Half Moon Caye and Victoria Peak.

The Rio Dulce region of Guatemala's Caribbean coast is one of the most popular cruising grounds found along the entire 5,000-mile route covered in this book. Thanks to the sheltering topography and the many marinas found up river, Rio Dulce is popular year round – even during hurricane season.

The Rio Dulce (sweet river) cruising region is more than just one river. The navigable portions of this river open up a huge expanse of the country's interior to exploration by yacht – places where no roads exist. Just inside the river's mouth at Livingston, the lower 7.6-n.m. portion of river carves a sinuous Rio Dulce Gorge between 300' high limestone cliffs that are draped with lush jungle foliage. Continuing upstream, the Rio Dulce leads you into the 9-n.m. long El Golfete Bay, and it has lots of islands and tributaries with anchorages. As you proceed upstream, the main channel compresses and twists between 2 towns where most of the marinas and boating services are found. Above the 5-n.m. marina region, an ancient Spanish fort guards the narrow approach to the Lake Izabal, which spreads 24 n.m. long and 10 n.m. wide, and tributaries afford getaway anchorages.

Waterfalls, hot springs, Mayan villages, beautiful jungle scenery, friendly locals, and many miles of inland waterways protected from tropical storms are just some of the attractions. Several marinas, fuel docks, a haul-out yard, marine supply stores and dingy-up restaurants accommodate about 400 cruising yachts each year. Many long-term cruisers and retirees from the US, Canada and Europe have made Rio Dulce their home port. So you'll find a large community of friendly yatistas – as well as friendly locals.

Rio Dulce hasn't been overrun by jet-set tourists, because, remember, we're talking wild monkeys, vast jungle-covered mountains with no roads and the developing nation of Guatemala. The indigenous Mayan tribes usually welcome a chance to sell their native foods, colorful "*huipiles*" (hand-woven and embroidered blouses) or carvings to the yatistas, who are still somewhat a novelty.

Hurricane Hole: Because the inner reaches of the cruising grounds are relatively protected by mountain ranges (Sierra de Santa Cruz and Montañas del Mico) and the entrance lies behind Cabo Tres Puntas, the inner reaches have long been considered a hurricane hole. During the devastating Hurricanes Mitch and Iris, 100s of yatistas fled into Rio Dulce, using it as an effective hurricane hole. Many plan their itineraries to spend the summer here – or at least to leave the boat at a marina here.

However, this region does lie slightly within the latitudes that can be raked by tropical storms and hurricanes. If you are visiting the many islands, reefs and cays of Belize or Roatan when tropical storms threaten, we recommend that you scoot up river here for protection. Exactly where depends on the direction, speed and intensity of the storm.

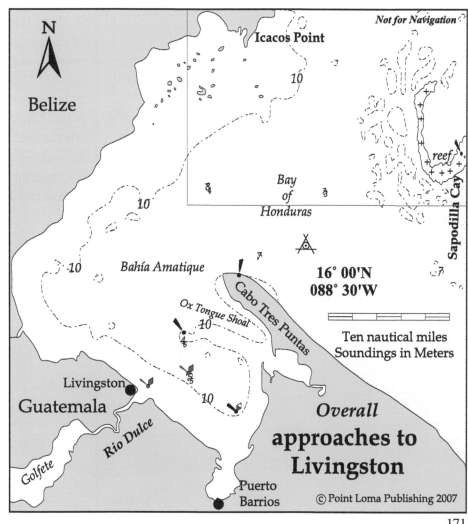

Livingston

In Bahía Amatique about 10 n.m. SW of Cabo Tres Puntas, the small port of Livingston (pop. 2,000) covers the north bank of the mouth of Rio Dulce. Livingston is so remote that it is reachable only by boat – the few cars you see were ferried by barge from Puerto Barrios. The entrance to Rio Dulce is difficult to spot among the backdrop of hills, but Livingston's red roofs stand out from the green vegetation.

To enter Rio Dulce, boats must first cross the bar outside the mouth (See below.). Then, before visiting the Rio Dulce cruising grounds, boaters officially clear in here at Livingston, because it's a Port of Entry into Guatemala and the nearest Port Captain's office. Boaters going up the Rio Dulce for the first time should plan to give half a day or more to clearing in, then spend their first night off Livingston, giving themselves an early start into the gorge.

Approaches: From Punta Gorda, Belize,

Buoy at Rio Dulce Bar off Livingston, Guatemala.

use a course of 166°M to the Rio Dulce sea buoy (15°50.25'N, 88°43.70'W). This 17-n.m. approach is free of hazards.

From Sapodilla Cays or from Honduras, round Cabo Tres Puntas and head 218°T for the sea buoy 10 n.m. SW. This course clears the lighted west end of lighted Ox Tongue Shoal (10' deep) by a quarter mile.

Rio Dulce Bar

This one is a sphincter-tightener. The bar is about half a mile wide, and the 'sweet spot' where you cross is about 300' wide. Generally a maximum 7' draft boat is the deepest you can get across at high tide. But you'll hear stories of captains who plow across with 8' draft by powering through the soft bottom, or of intrepid sailboats being towed across while another launch with a line attached to the mast heels them over to lift the keel over the bar. (If needed, a tug from Livingston can assist your vessel over the bar.)

Synchronizing with the tides is critical here. If you don't have a tide calendar, you can call the Livingston Port Captain's office on VHF16 for the tide status. Ideally you should cross at a spring high tide with the afternoon onshore sea breeze at your back. The push of the wind against the river current will tend to raise the level of the water across the bar. On the other hand, if too big a swell is running you might ground at the bottom of a trough.

Our GPS position of the Rio Dulce sea buoy is 15°50.25'N, 88°43.70'W and lying in 17' of water a little over a mile off shore. The water color is usually murky gray-green to brown – worse after heavy rains. At the sea buoy, hoist your yellow Q-flag to port and your Guatemalan courtesy flag (pale blue & white) to starboard.

From the sea buoy inward, take a heading

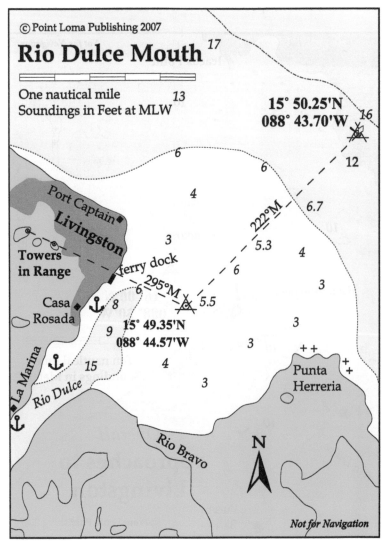

© Point Loma Publishing 2007

Rio Dulce Mouth 17

One nautical mile 13
Soundings in Feet at MLW

15° 50.25'N
088° 43.70'W

Port Captain
Livingston
Towers in Range
ferry dock
Casa Rosada
La Marina
Rio Dulce
15° 49.35'N
088° 44.57'W
Punta Herreria
Rio Bravo

222°M
295°M

N

Not for Navigation

*L-R: Texaco dock,
Hotel Berrisford,
Livingston Pier.*

of 222°M to cross the bar. Directly ahead you see high land (Pico Montebica) and a bluff dropping off to the notch of the river. You head for the high point above the edge of the bluff.

Livingston on the right shows 2 distinctive red and white cellular telephone towers with square platforms near their tops. Keep on heading 222°M until you have these 2 towers lined up in a range (295°M). That position is 15°49.347'N, 88°44.571'W. Don't deviate from this heading or you can hit some shoal spots. Directly along this line we sounded a minimum of 5.3' over the bar, taking into account the state of the tide. With a max high tide of 1.9' at springs that would give you 7.2' of water. After heavy summer rains, the bar may be higher or lower, but it normalizes soon.

At this position, you turn starboard onto the range and head into Livingston's big concrete municipal dock (7' alongside), just off your port bow, just downstream from the landmark 5-story white Hotel Henry Berrisford. Once you've identified the concrete dock, come to port and anchor 50 yards out. Wait at anchor here for the officials to board for clearance. (Downstream of here, you may notice a beach with stairs going up to the Capitanía, but unfortunately that's not a very good anchorage.)

Port Clearance: Livingston is by far the easiest, fastest and cheapest place for yachts to clear into Guatemala, but you can also do it in Puerto Barrios and Puerto Santo Tomas.

Hail "Livingston Port Captain" on VHF 16 as soon as you clear the bar to start the ball rolling. The Port Captain's office (502-7947-0029) is on

a bluff overlooking the river entrance, so he knows all. If he doesn't respond or no one shows up at the anchorage in an hour or so, the captain – and only the captain – may go ashore to initiate clearance.

Five different offices may send someone to board you, and they'll bring you a map of Livingston with all the required offices marked. Customs takes your last Zarpe, crew lists and ship's papers. Immigration takes all your passports. The Port Captain will ask for any firearms; he will give you a receipt and take them away for now. The police or Navy are likely to give your boat a good search, and finally, the health inspectors or doctor may pay you a visit.

When your papers are ready, the captain is called to go ashore with the Livingston map. (Get at least 450Q at the bank on your way, if possible.) From Customs you need your Boat Permit. Immigration returns your stamped passports and issues you Guatemalan visas (good for 90 days). From the Port Captain you need a Guatemalan Cruising Permit (good for 3 or 9 months). All this amounts to about 450Q. After that, you can apply for a 12-month extension. Total stay without leaving is normally 2 years.

The Cruising Permit issued on the Pacific coast

*Yatistas on Livingston
Pier after clearing into
Rio Dulce area.*

Hilly streets in Livingston give everyone a view.

of Guatemala is not valid on the Caribbean side and vice versa, because your boat has probably exited the country in between. (However, what if you truck your boat across?)

If you began your port clearance process in the early morning, you may be able to get all your papers back the same day. But not likely. Instead, enjoy an overnight stay in Livingston – where marina dwellers upstream come for a change of scenery. Anchor or go to La Marina upstream.

Ship's Agent: To extend visas or Cruising Permits, or to get your Zarpe from Guatemala with a week's notice, you can hire ship's agent M.E. ("Emy") Langdon, a gringa lady who lives aboard in Fronteras. We know her and recommend her. You can reach her on VHF 11 when within range, or phone (502) 5612-1415. Also, "Raul the Customs Agent" on VHF 16 has also earned good reports (502) 7947-0083.

Anchorage: After officially clearing into Guatemala and the Rio Dulce region at Livingston, you might want to shift anchorages, as the holding is not good off the municipal pier. The normal wind pattern is from the west in the mornings, from the east and stronger after 1200, and it may die at sunset – when 'no-see-ums' appear.

To be within walking distance of Livingston, anchor in the good holding just outside the small pier of the hotel Casa Rosada – about 200 yards upstream of the municipal pier. This nice little hotel (pink, 2-story) and patio restaurant is owned by the same boater-friendly folks who own La Marina (See below.).

Casa Rosada's pier (4.2' of water at the end) has 6 Med-mooring slots. It's also the only place where you can safely leave your dinghy while you go ashore, but you must show your appreciation by eating in their restaurant. Casa Rosada has great Caribbean lunch, dinner, snacks and cold beer. They have showers near the patio. From Casa Rosada, it's 5 or 6 blocks up and down the hilly streets to Livingston's quaint "downtown" area.

Or move your boat farther up the river anywhere between Casa Rosada's small pier and La Marina about half a mile up river, right at the start of Rio Dulce's famous gorge.

Local Services: La Marina is the only yacht marina in Livingston. Their stationary wooden pier (See photo 2 pages below.) has 11.7' of water and full service for 8 cruising boats Med-moored. Being located almost in the gorge, this area has better shelter from Trades. La Marina (15°48.673'N, 88°45.504'W). If there's room, make arrangements to anchor off the marina and use the shore facilities – a pleasant, shady restaurant café and bar. No road cuts through the jungle from La Marina to town, so you need to use your skiff. FMI call (502) 974-0303.

The Capitanía in Puerto de Livingston has nice patio with view of all approaches to Rio Dulce.

Casa Rosada is a yatista hang out in Livingston with handy dock and good food.

Livingston's diesel dock (15°49.148'N, 88°45.043'W) below the Hotel Berrisford has 5.4' of water at the end. Boatmen around the piers try to sell visitors open-boat trips up to Fronteras or over to Puerto Barrios. Diesel and gas are also available about 20 miles up-river in the marina zone.

Two banks in Livingston change your money for Quetzales, pronounced "*kayt-ZAH-layz*" – often shortened to "Q." ($7.6Q to $1US) US dollars are not always accepted in Guatemala, definitely not for port clearance. The Livingston Bank on top of the hill has been slightly better for currency exchange than elsewhere in the Rio Dulce area. Outside, a tiny outside ATM booth has no air-conditioning (i.e. sweltering). Inside the air-conditioned bank itself, you can get a cash advance using your credit card. An armed and uniformed guard stands watch over customers inside the bank.

Reports of robbery at night have increased in Livingston. It's never been a tourist town, just a service center for remote villages. Keep track of your wallet and camera.

A grocery store with a modest selection of staples is near the bank. We found 4 other small grocery stores (but Frontera-Relleno up river usually has better provisioning). Small stands selling fresh local produce are scattered around Livingston with tropical fruits, a few local vegetables and delicious unrefrigerated eggs.

Livingston has many cantinas, "comedores" and small hotels. Bromeliads sprout from wooden telephone poles and anywhere they lodge. Chickens and goats wander the side streets, and flocks of parrots cruise overheads. Bicycles and bike carts are more common than cars. But people mostly walk. Much of Livingston's businesses are built on the steep hillsides – so everyone gets a nice view of the entrance to Rio Dulce.

A ferry chugs between Livingston and Puerto Barrios (1.5 hours), but the water taxi launches are faster – about 30 minutes.

History & Culture: Livingston's residents are primarily Garifuna. Descendents of African slaves brought to the New World, they trace their roots to Isla Roatan where they were resettled by their British masters after a revolt on the island of St. Vincent in 1795. From Roatan, they settled all along the east coast of Central American, where they intermarried with indigenous Mayans and Spanish settlers. Most Livingstonians speak the Garifuna dialect as well as English and Spanish.

Livingston's Anglo name came from a Louisiana lawyer who wrote Guatemala's penal code and helped introduce the democratic trial-by-jury process, at the request of Guatemala's President Morazan in 1823.

However, by Guatemalan law you're guilty until proven innocent, and some yatistas have been swept into legal problems with local business owners, so take care.

The remote villages scattered miles inland from the Rio Dulce are mostly Kek'chi Mayan. Stuck in the spiral of poverty, illiteracy and pregnancy, most of the natives who survived decades of war and

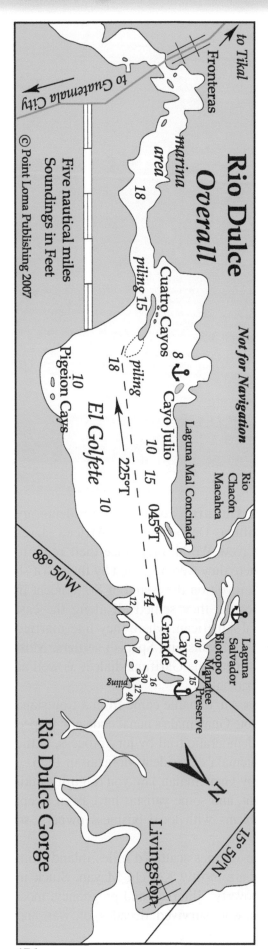

Five nautical miles
Soundings in Feet

Not for Navigation

**Rio Dulce
Overall**

to Tikal
Fronteras

to Guatemala City

marina
area

18

piling 15

Cuatro Cayos

piling 15

8

Cayo Julio

piling

18

18

Pigeon Cays

10

El Golfete

10

225°T

10

045°T

15

Laguna Mal Concinada

Rio
Chacon
Macahca

Cayo
Grande

Laguna
Salvador

Biotopo
Manatee
Preserve

10

15

16

30

40

12

piling

12

14

88° 50'W

N

15° 50'N

Rio Dulce Gorge

Livingston

discrimination fear contact with visitors. (See Ak-Tenamit below.)

But each year, more Mayans intermarry with their Spanish, Mexican and Garifuna neighbors. These are the ones you sometimes spot paddling carved-log cayucas up and down the Rio Dulce.

Rio Dulce Gorge

NOTE: Ask in Livingston if banditos are active in the Gorge. Rarely, robbers in pangas hide out in the Gorge under overhanging foliage or up tiny streams, lying in wait for unsuspecting yachts or dinghies coming around blind turns in the river. Time your trip to get through the Gorge and El Golfete before dusk, and stay alert to all traffic. Travel with other boats if possible.

It's comforting to know that deep-draft vessels have been navigating this river for 300 years – with frequent soundings and peeled eyeballs. Spanish explorers called this dramatic gorge *"el cañon."*

The 7.6-n.m. long jungle-lined gorge of the Rio Dulce is spectacular kingdom where Johnny Weissmuller once swung through the trees playing Tarzan for movie cameras. Several

sections of 300' high limestone cliffs pierce the green drapery on either side of the river. Some old graffiti has been found, but please don't contribute to it.

Expect a constant half- to 1-knot river current, more during rainy season when you should watch for floating or partially submerged logs. Some salt-water organisms attached to your hull's bottom and in your head plumbing may die after a few days in this fresh-water environment. They may be replaced by fresh-water algae and scum, but that's easier to clean.

NOTE: Hanging wires crossing the gorge near La Marina are reported to give a 120' overhead clearance. However, ask the Livingston Port Captain about those wires. Things that normally are stationary can change during storms or earthquakes.

Starting near La Marina (15°48.673'N, 88°45.504'W) (See photo previous page.), as the river bends right and left, you'll generally stay toward the outside, because the river tends to shoal on the inner sides. The exception is a particular hairpin turn (at about 15°46.59'N, 88°56.65'W) where you favor the outside of the turn. But then cut across toward the north bank immediately after the turn to avoid the shoal on the south bank. The edge of this shoal may be marked with stakes – or not. This is the only place where both sides of the river have the white cliffs.

Most of the habited places are on the south side (to port going upstream) of the river. You'll pass a couple small anchorages, a tiny wooden store selling rice and beans, a brightly painted Nazarene church, a handicrafts shop and a small boat-up restaurant (15°46.828'N, 88°47.867'W) called El Viajero.

Toward the upper end of the gorge, several shallow tributaries feed in from both sides, and you'll see natives paddling cayucas along the edges, casting nets, swimming and zooming by in fast pangas. Just after El Viajero restaurant on the south side you'll see Rio Lámpara (Lightning) joining at the village of El Remanso.

Coming in from the right (north) side is Rio Tiatin, the largest tributary entering the gorge almost to the upper end. A short dinghy trip up Rio Tiatin goes to some low waterfalls. Kayaks and light boats can be portaged around the falls and continue to the village of Rio Tiatin.

Near the junction of the Dulce and the Tiatin is Ak-Tenamit, a non-profit NGO outpost giving basic health service and vocational education to more than

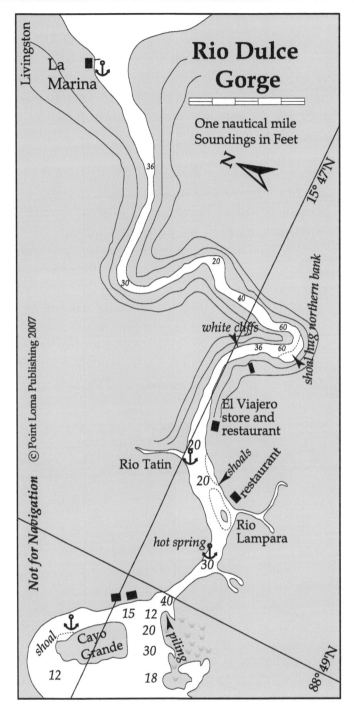

6,000 Kek'chi Mayas living in Rio Dulce's remote villages. They bring handicrafts to sell to tourists brought up by boat from Livingston or down from Fronteras. Ak-Tenamit has a small dock, school and visitor center on the west bank of Rio Tiatin. The newer handicraft store is next to El Viajero. Many cruisers donate to this worthy effort started in 1992. For details, visit www.aktenamit.org.

Just past the Rio Tiatin junction, on the north bank you'll pass the most popular hot-springs swimming hole (15°46.443'N, 88°48.373'W) in the gorge, and a

Manatees in Rio Dulce

Manatees are thought to have descended from elephants before Africa and Central America separated. Hunted for their ivory-like bones and juicy meat – called "bucan" by the Mayan natives – the gentle and slow-moving manatees once formed enormous herds in all the western Caribbean lagoons, munching away on the watery plants. The Mayan natives used simple spears and arrows to hunt just what they needed to survive, and they held solemn ceremonies before eating any bucan.

The first European explorers to see manatees thought they had human facial features, so they were called "sirenas" or mermaids. Pirates hiding out in coastal lagoons began slaughtering manatees en masse with guns and coconut bombs, in order to fill their holds. Pirates who lived on the free manatee meat were called "bucaneros," a negative term indicating they didn't earn enough to pay for decent provisions. By 1930, manatees were almost extinct, and the Rio Dulce was one of their last refuges.

The manatee female and her nursing calf shown below had learned to sip fresh water from the hose left to dribble for them at one of the Rio's many marinas, but these nearly domesticated creatures are an exceptional case, photographed by fellow yatista Monty Navarre.

Most manatees that survive have learned to be extremely fearful of humans and will startle at the slightest noise. Unfortunately, they're too slow to be able to flee from a speeding dinghy or fishing boat, so many manatees die either directly from prop wounds or from starvation after they are too severely wounded to eat. Please pay attention and look out for these helpless creatures – in the Rio Dulce gorge, El Golfete, around the marinas and throughout Lago Izabal.

Manatee mom takes on water while her calf has lunch.

small anchorage is adjacent. Pick your temperature by moving closer to the scalding sulfur springs – or farther away as it mixes with cold river water. From here you can see El Golfete opening upstream.

El Golfete

The upper end of the gorge opens directly into El Golfete, the 9-n.m. long lake. Depths in the middle average 11' to 15', so you could anchor almost anywhere. But the afternoon wind blows down the length of this bay, creating nasty chop.

Several routes through El Golfete all begin by passing an ancient wooden marker (15°46.642'N, 88°49.349'W) to port. Behind it are kayak marshes.

Direct Route: To reach the marina zone of Rio Dulce from here, curve around the series of islets on port. (In the last inlet to port, Gringo Bay restaurant and anchorage monitors VHF 68, in case dark overtakes you.) After passing the inlets, aim about 225°T for a few hundred yards south of the SE end of Cayo Largo, the largest of the 4 cays at the far end of El Golfete. The SW shore of this lake is shoal, and the boathouses there have private channels through the muck.

Take Cayo Largo to starboard, and give the shoaling SE end of Cayo Largo a berth of about 200 yards. Our waypoint is 15°42.378'N, 88°55.506'W. The SW side of the island is steeper to, with about 12' of water. A well-marked dog-leg channel takes you into the Rio Dulce marina zone – obvious by all the antennas, docks and houses.

Cayo Grande Route: The large island of Cayo Grande lies about half a mile to starboard (north) of the marker, and a mud shelf extends from the

Barge gets pushed upstream across El Golfete.

island's south tip. A good anchorage area is found off the east and NE side of Cayo Grande, at about 15°47.18'N, 88°49.71'W.

This anchorage can be used overnight to let you enter the gorge downstream with good daylight tomorrow, or as a fall-back position if a chubasco rolls down from the mountains to the south as you're about to cross El Golfete going upstream. Several homes and the restaurant Los Palafitos with boat house are visible on the east side of this channel behind Cayo Grande, and new homes are springing up on Cayo Grande itself.

Watch out for manatees throughout El Golfete. El Biotopo Chocón Machacas cover about 4 n.m. of El Golfete's low north shoreline and 100s of acres inland. The parks have hiking trails through the rainforest back to Livingston, and kayakers love exploring the small creeks and lagoons.

From the north end of Cayo Grande, aim for 200 yards south of the SE end of Cayo Largo, the largest of 4 cays at the far end of El Golfete. A heading of about 220°T will bring you to 15°44.92'N, 88°52.39'W, the deeper edge of a shelf fringing Mal Cocida (Badly-cooked), a mangrove peninsula forming Laguna Mal Cocida on the north shore of El Golfete. (We found a dangerous unmarked stump at 15°44.452'N, 88°53.013'W.) The village of Cuatro Cayos is along the shallow north shore behind Cayo Largo – also many dangerous waterline stumps and dozing manatees.

Take Cayo Largo to starboard, and give the shoal SE end of Cayo Largo a berth of about 200 yards. Our waypoint is 15°42.378'N, 88°55.506'W. The SW side of the island is steeper to, with about 12' of water. A narrow but well-marked dog-leg channel takes you into the Rio Dulce marina zone – obvious by all the antennas, docks, houses and small-boat traffic.

Many restaurants and cantinas overhang Rio Dulce and a few in El Golfete.

NOTE: All phone numbers in Rio Dulce have added a digit before the 7-digit local number. Usually, if it's on the Fronteras side, the added number is a 7, or if on the Relleno side, add a 5 before the regular number. The newest marinas are also listed in our UPDATES on www. CentralAmericanBoating.com

Rio Dulce Marina Zone

The next 5.5 n.m. of the river contain 2 towns and at least 11 marinas; more soon. Depths in the middle are no less than 12' – and shallower areas along both shores are normally marked by pylons or flags.

You can anchor just about anywhere out of the traffic flow and where you find shelter from the diurnal winds, but don't anchor near the "cable crossing" signs. You'll see lots of small-boat traffic shuttling people and supplies back and forth between the town docks and the marinas, many of which run water taxi service. Do plan on using your dinghy daily.

Tune in the Cruisers' Net on VHF 69 at 0730 Mon-Sat, get welcomed, find out everything.

Layout: Bahía Nana Juana is a large side basin off the river's east side; entered about 600 yards before the bridge. Bird Island is in front of the bridge, and Bahía Redonda is the small natural basin NW of the bridge or SW of Bird Island. The water taxi docks are in Bahía Redonda. Almost everything here is referenced by before or after the bridge and east or

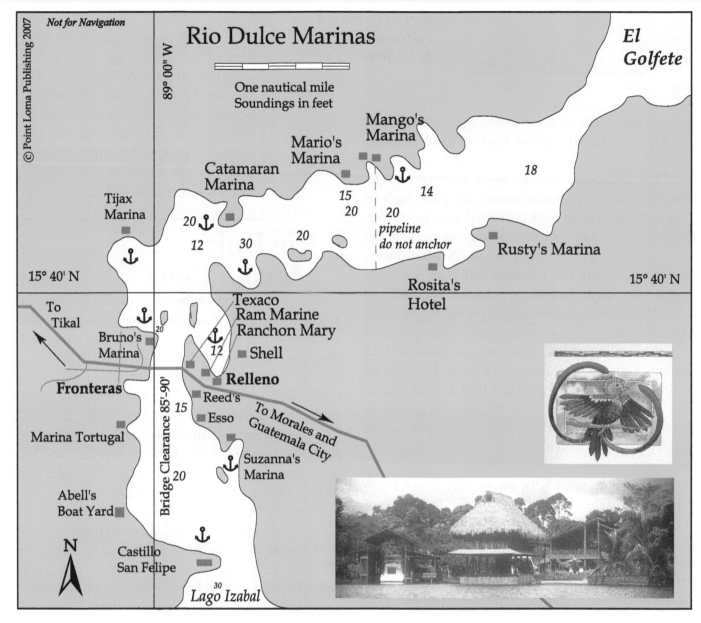

Not for Navigation

Rio Dulce Marinas

One nautical mile
Soundings in feet

El Golfete

Mango's Marina

Mario's Marina

Catamaran Marina

Tijax Marina

20

12   30   20

15

20   20

14

18

pipeline
do not anchor

Rusty's Marina

15° 40' N

15° 40' N

Rosita's Hotel

To Tikal

Texaco
Ram Marine
Ranchon Mary

Bruno's Marina

20

12

Shell

Relleno

Fronteras

Reed's

15

Esso

Marina Tortugal

To Morales and Guatemala City

Bridge Clearance 85'-90'

Suzanna's Marina

20

Abell's Boat Yard

N

Castillo San Felipe

30

Lago Izabal

west side of the river.

Puente Rio Dulce: The center span of the concrete bridge is 85' above the water, but wires and pipes hang down about 5', so consider it an 80' clearance at high water. The highway comes in from the east (Guatemala City, 5-hr drive) and goes west to Tikal and the Petén.

El Relleno: On the east side of the river, the village of El Relleno is "stuffed" around the bridge ramp. The Esso fuel dock is just before the bridge. Reed's Tienda and the Texaco fuel dock are past it.

Fronteras: On the west side of the river, Fronteras is a market town. Originally

Under the bridge on the Relleno side are 2 diesel docks and Reed's Tienda.

*Most of the marinas in Rio Dulce offer
services for yatistas living aboard.*

El Relleno was where the river dwellers gathered at the end of the only road into this region. After the bridge was built in 1980 and the road extended NW, Fronteras became a crossroads for buses and trucks carrying natives, cattle and basic supplies to and from the vast Petén. After Rio Dulce hotels and marinas were built, Fronteras got a bit touristy-hip.

Fronteras' main street is jammed with commercial traffic (no mufflers or smog control), open-air markets, eco-tourism offices and cheap hotels. Open-air cafes and an instant swap meet fills the side streets near the bridge. Pricey restaurants are tucked into jungle coves, helicopter pads stand next to vacation homes, internet cafes pop out of the backwaters and European backpackers and Mayan women wash their clothes in the river as yachties sail past – quite a mix.

Marinas: Some marinas have no road access, only boat, because the shore is marshy and subject to summer flooding. A new security patrol has been set up, keeping petty theft way down. Bravo!

Most marinas are full-service (up to 50-amp power, but outages are common) and they range from 10 to 85 slips, side ties or Med-moor slots. Some have nicer services (WiFi, cable TV, all-day restaurant, laundry, generator for backup power). Some are deeper, quieter, breezier, closer to eateries, cheaper. Most are managed by yatistas. Don't be shy about shopping around.

1.) **Mango Marina:** First small marina (5'5 to 6' depths) on west side of the river about 2.75 n.m. after Golfete. Docks on east side of a small peninsula get afternoon ventilation. Mango's is laid back. FMI, phone (502) 5213-6868 or email mangocharter@hotmail.com.

2.) **Mario's Marina:** Next little

peninsula south, same side, Mario's has 65 slips and slots at finger piers, many pleasant shore amenities, Club Cayuca bar & restaurant, gourmet store, very popular. FMI (502) 7930-5569 or visit www. mariosmarina.com

3.) **Catamaran Island Hotel & Marina:** About 1.25 n.m. past Mario's, the Catamaran Marina's 25 finger slips (6' to 8' depth) and docks (VHF 22) encompass 2 islets and a peninsula; hilltop restaurant, sail loft, hotel. Their rental bungalows have slips, great when you have guests. FMI (502) 7930-5494 and 95, or visit catamaran@intelgua.com.

4.) Monkey Bay Marina: between Mario's and Catamaran, Monkey Bay Marina has 20 slips, generator backup, community kitchen, workshop ashore, monitors VHF 68. FMI (502) 5368-9604 or Google them.

5.) **Ram Marine:** In sheltered Bahía Nana Juana NE of the bridge, Ram Marine has 25 slips to 70', minimum 6' alongside. It's also a boat yard with

*Most of the marinas are downstream
from the bridge (seen far right).*

Travelift, dry storage, some covered, small chandler, helicopter pad, snack bar, plans for another fuel dock. FMI (502) 7930-5408.

6.) Mar Marine: Also in Bahía Nana Juana but adjacent to the bridge, this marina has 15 slips to 70' LOA, but it's also a repair facility with close access to the highway through town. FMI (502) 7930-5089.

7.) Hacienda Tijax Marina: On the north side of Bahía Redonda, this marina & hotel has 40 Med-moor slots (6' depth) with rare road access to Fronteras. The 500-acre Hacienda Tijax behind the marina is a working rubber plantation with public tours. FMI (502) 7930-5505.

8.) Bruno's Marina: In Fronteras just west of the bridge, Bruno's has the easiest shore access for loading provisions, walk to town. Bruno's has 26 slips and side ties (7' depth) to 75' LOA, popular pool cantina, dink landing, Capt. Nemo's internet café. FMI call (502) 7930-5178 or email Bruno rio@guat.net.

9.) El Tortugal Marina: About 700 yards past the bridge, west side (right side going up river), Tortugal has about 20 well-ventilated Med-moor slots and side ties, restaurant, bungalows, no shore access to Fronteras. FMI call (502) 5306-6432.

10.) Nutria Marina: Just past Tortugal, same side of the river, Nutria Marina (named for the cute critter) has room for about 12 boats at its eco-lodge, monitors VHF 68. FMI (502) 5863-9635 or visit www.nutriamarina.com.

Bruno's Marina near the bridge in Frontera is handy for arrivals.

11.) La Jolla del Rio (formerly Suzanna's Laguna Marina)**:** On the Relleno side of the river past the bridge, tucked into a sheltered side basin is La Jolla del Rio with about 75 slips (6' depth) to 90' LOA. Restaurant, bungalows.

At press time, new owners Garon & Heidy Anderson are renovating this popular. FMI email La Jolla del Rio via rio@guat.net

Upstream from Tortugal, Marina Paraiso is a private club, no guest slips. We've not checked out Crow Bar Marina, Texan Bay Marina, Ranchon Mary's in Bahía Nana Juana, nor Lubi's or Xalaha and others. Check for Rio Dulce Updates on www.CentralAmericanBoating.com A few shops & private homes sometimes rent docks, but they're passed among friends, never advertised.

Local Services: Three diesel docks are at El Relleno: Shell (VHF 70) is inside Bahía Nana Juana; Esso is immediately before the bridge; Texaco (VHF 64) is just past the bridge.

Reed's Tienda (VHF 68) has marine hardware (West Marine order desk), outboard repairs, food staples and refrigerated groceries (ice cream) – and a convenient dock with 12' of water alongside, so you can shop by boat. FMI (502) 7930-5072.

Astillero Magdalena, also known as Abel's Boat Yard, has 3 marine ways for boats to 80 tons and 24' beam, all yard services. Owner Abel Ramirez and his crews are highly recommended by many cruisers. Astillero Magdalena is about half a mile past Tortugal, before the river narrows at the fort. FMI call Astillero Magdalena (502) 7930-5090 or 5060.

There's also The Shop boat repair & maintenance next to Bruno's Marina in Fronteras just before the bridge. FMI (502) 7930-5191.

RAM Marina at Relleno (7930-5408) before the bridge has a big Travelift, works on engines & outboards, plus a dry-storage yard, covered sheds, a few work docks and a major launch ramp. Several outboard repair shops are in the marina zone.

Tijax Hacienda Marina is popular also for sun-downers and dinner.

Capt. Nemo's computer repair and internet café is behind Bruno's Marina. They fixed our laptop quick & cheap. FMI (502) 7930-5174.

RioDulceChisme.com posts all the local yatista news, contact numbers, good forum, great folks.

Rio Dulce Boat Transport: Carlos the Welder (well-regarded in Rio Dulce) is also Carlos the Trucker (VHF 68). With his hydraulic lowboy trailer (46" x 15') and Mack truck, Carlos has reportedly safely moved more than 20 yachts from Rio Dulce to Puerto Quetzal on the Pacific or vice versa since 2004. This is a marvelous short cut if you simply gotta' get your boat to the other ocean faster than transiting the Panama Canal. FMI call Carlos at Rio Dulce Boat Transport (502) 5240-9104 or 5202-1702, at work and private home.

The Cruisers' VHF Net meets at 0730 on VHF

69. You'll be welcomed, get advice, directions. Each season, a new cruisers' guide lists all the latest minutia for comfortable daily life on the river. The NW Caribbean Net on SSB 6209 and 6212 at 1400 Z tracks yatista itineraries and shares WX info.

Restaurants, cafes and cantinas in abundance are either dinghy-up or within walking distance of a dinghy landing. Most cater to yatistas, backpackers and adventure eco tourists from all over the world.

Guatemala's wealthy citizens shuttle in and out of the marina zone by helicopter – private or chartered – because it's much faster and safer than driving the country's notoriously dangerous roads (twisty, 2-lane, steep) often clogged by big trucks, slow buses and

irrationally impatient drivers. Always expect oncomng traffic to be using your lane on blind corners.

Kidnapping for ransom has been a problem for wealthy Guatemalans, so many travel with a body guard. Attack for robbery is also reported against cruising boats in the Gorge and on Lago Izabal, so we urge boaters not to flaunt their comparative wealth and stay alert to all approaching vessels – even cayucas.

Rio Dulce has at least 2 places that haul & repair & store boats: RAM Marina, upper left and Abel's Boat Yard in Lago Isabel, lower left.
--- Above, truck your boat across the spine of Central America between Rio Dulce on the Caribbean and Puerto Quetzal on the Pacific? Talk with Carlos the Trucker who owns & runs Rio Dulce Boat Transport.

Lago Izabal

The marina zone of Rio Dulce again narrows before you move upstream into the vast Lago Izabal.

Castillo San Felipe: A lovely 1652 Spanish fort guards the narrow entrance to Lago Izabal – which once served as an anchorage for Spanish treasure ships. The fort defended valuable cargoes from constant pirate attack. The Spanish dug a channel to make this tip of land a tiny island, then gave the fort a drawbridge, many gun turrets and pediments. Spanish captains mounted their cannon on the fort's walls and stretched chains across the lake's entrance to prevent pirates from entering or getting away down river with stolen booty. Prettier than a fort, it was called a "castillo" – castle. After pirates were eradicated, the fort was used as a prison and municipal building.

Castillo San Felipe today is a well-maintained museum surrounded by a nice public park. Boaters can use the dinghy dock to visit the museum, and anchorage is possible on either side of the narrow entrance to Lago Izabal.

The navigable lake stretches 24 n.m. long and 10 n.m. wide, fed by dozens of streams and fringed by 3 broad estuaries. Mountain ranges around the lake run NE to SW, so they funnel the Trades – causing stiff sailing winds during winter cruising season. Average depths in Lago Izabal are only about 30'.

Denny's Beach is an anchorage on the lake's ESE shore where you can land a dink on Denny's private dock and enjoy the cantina and hammocks under palms. The village of Mariscos on the south shore a few miles west of Denny's Beach has a road to Trincheras on the highway.

The SW end of the lake is marshier, fed by many tributaries, and El Refugio bay opens to the south. Dozens of Mayan villages are found up these streams, but yatistas have been shy of visiting since an unfortunate boater and his family were attacked in this end of Lago Izabal in 2002.

On the lake's NW shore is El Estor, a small town with a road toward Flores. Finca Paraiso is on the north shore. The Crow Bar marina & hotel is on the north shore just past Castillo San Felipe.

Language School

Many of the 20 Spanish language immersion schools in Antigua are good. But the one we recommend and keep going back to is *Proyecto Linguistico Francisco Marroquin* (PLFM for short), a nonprofit school that – besides being the best at teaching Spanish – preserves the disappearing Mayan languages of the region. FMI visit www.languagelink.com/guatemala.html or call (309) 673-9220 or email info@plfm-antigua.org.

If you fly into Guatemala City (not a neat spot to visit), the school can have a van or taxi pick you up in front of the airport and bring you to Antigua. If you arrive in Antigua from either the Rio Dulce (Caribbean) or Puerto Quetzal (Pacific) side of Guatemala, just ask any taxi driver where the PLFM school office is located.

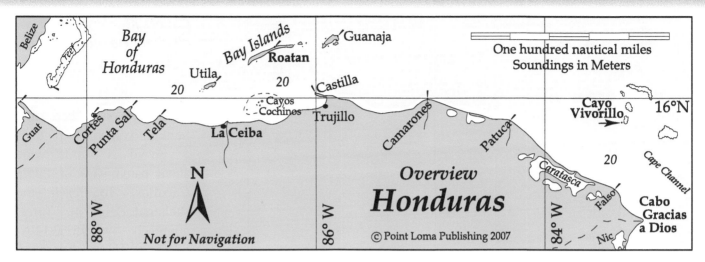

Honduras Itinerary: Honduras is new to this edition of *Cruising Ports*. In this chapter we will spend time point-hopping mainland Honduras' north coast, west to east (the more difficult direction), stopping mostly at La Ceiba where we'll find a marina with fuel and a boat yard.

Also in Le Ceiba is the main office of Adelante Foundation, a worthy organization supported in part by Point Loma Publishing.

In the Bay Islands, we'll primarily visit many of Roatan's yatista haunts, looking only briefly at the anchorages off Utila and Guanaja. Then continuing east, we'll stop at the remote Cayo Vivarillo anchorage before rounding Cabo Gracias a Dios toward Half Moon Cay, which is even more remote – entering the Western Caribbean.

The Honduran Lempira is the local currency – called "lemps" for short. However, US dollars are widely accepted for payment; in some places they're preferred.

Below is the list of charts useful for planning and cruising Honduras and the Bay Islands.

NIMA Chart 28140 Northern Reaches to Cabo Gracias a Dios.
NIMA Chart 28150 Barra de Caratasca to Tela.
NIMA Chart 28151 Approaches to Puerto Castilla.
NIMA Chart 28142 Puerto Castilla.
NIMA Chart 28154 Approaches to La Ceiba and Isla de Roatan.
NIMA Chart 28144 Port of La Ceiba.
NIMA Chart 28165 Puerto Castilla to Puerto Barrios.
NIMA Chart 28125 Isla de Guanaja.
NIMA Chart 28143 Isla de Utila and Bancos Salmedina.
NIMA Chart 28162 Tela to Pelican Cays.

Route Planning

Shoals form outside almost all the river and estuary mouths.

Coastal Route: From Livingston in Guatemala, you can round Punta Tres Puntos (10 n.m.) and lay a course into sheltered Puerto Cortés (38 n.m.) using the marked Punta Caballos channel.

Clearing the NW shore of Punta Caballos, you can lay a course to Punta Ulua (13.5 n.m.), being sure to clear it by at least half a mile to avoid reported 12' shoals. Then continue about 5 more miles into Puerto Escondido, which lies about 2.5 n.m. SW of the tip of Punta Sal.

Clearing Punta Sal (15°56'N, 87°35.77'W) you can lay a course SE into Bahia Tela (11 n.m.). From Punta El Triunfo at the north end of Tela Bay, give a .75 n.m. berth to the north end of Punta Izopo (about 4.25 n.m.) to avoid detached rocks. From off Punta Izopo, you can continue east to La Ceiba (48 n.m.).

From La Ceiba, it's about 47 n.m. NE to Trujillo Bay and Puerto Castilla. From the north side of Punta Castilla, it's about 56 n.m. east to low Punta Cameron, then another 45 n.m. SE to Punta Rio Patuca, being sure to clear it by a good 2.5 n.m. to avoid shoals.

Offshore Routes: From a mile north of Punta Izopo, you can lay a course of about 070°T for about 25 n.m. to a position about 3.5 n.m. south of Utila's south corner (thus leaving the dangerous Bancos Salmedinos about 3.5 n.m. to starboard and the uncharted cays off Utila's SW end about a mile to port). From that position, it's about 5.5 n.m. NE into Utila's East Harbour, which is on its SE side. From Utila's East

Canoes ply coastal waters all along Honduras.

Harbour, it's 20 n.m. NE to Roatan's West End point.

From La Ceiba on the mainland, it's about 37 n.m. NNE to French Harbour, and this route lays 9 n.m. west of the land part of the Cayos Cochinos.

From French Harbour, it's about 32 n.m. SE to Punta Honduras near Trujillo. From Pigeon Cays at the SE end of Roatan, it's about 10 n.m. east to Ochre Bluff at Guanaja's west tip. From Jack's Cay Pass off Guanaja to Cayo Vivorillo Grande, it's about 150 n.m. on a course of about 104°T.

From Rio Patuca you can lay a course almost due east to Cayo Vivorillo (55.75 n.m.) and then 54 n.m. SE to Half Moon Cay, which lies about 25 n.m. ENE of Cabo Gracias a Dios.

Puerto Cortés

This Port of Entry into Honduras is a busy cargo depot, but El Porvenir Navy Base has a haul-out yard that can handle 80' yachts. When in VHF range, yatistas need to hail the Port Captain (VHF 16), tell him why you're there, and he'll tell you where to go.

Avoid a 3-mile wide shoal patch west of Punta Caballos. To reach the sheltered Bahia de Cortés, approach 15°52.12'N, 87°58.09'W at the north end of the well-marked Caballos Channel (min. 30' depth) and follow it around the west end of Punta Caballos. If you anchor off the NE end of the bay don't block access to the freighter docks. The Port Captain's office is in the bay's NE corner.

El Porvenir Navy Base boat yard (507- 3389-9427) on the bay's E shore is just S of the lagoon mouth (15°49.672'N, 87°56.084'W), outside the first bridge. Call for yard booking, then hail on VHF 16 before approaching the Navy & boat yard too closely.

Departing Puerto Cortés eastward, stay a mile off the north shore of Punta Caballos to avoid a reported wreck and detached rock pinnacle. Stand half a mile off Punta Ulua to avoid reported shoals.

Puerto Escondido

NOTE: Two cruising yachts were attacked at anchor in Puerto Escondido (fatality) and Bahia Diamonte (armed robbery) on Punta Sal, both by local pangas. Stop here only in an emergency.

Located 5.5 n.m. ESE of Punta Ulua and 2.5 n.m. SW of Punta Sal, 3 small uninhabited bays line the NW face of Punta Sal, Escondido being the middle, our approach is 15°54.79'N, 87°38.05'W. Two detached rocks narrow the entrance. Diamonte about a mile to the NE is even smaller. Laguna Tinto is the larger estuary SW of Escondido, lined by mangroves. Escondido and Diamonte had been quiet places to await a weather window before pushing off for Utila and Roatan. But lawlessness makes them risky.

Garifuna communities thrive near Puerto Cortes, Tela, La Ceiba & Trujillo.

Puerto Escondido, Punta Sal and the west half of Bahía Tela lie within Kawas National Park, named for Jeanette Kawas, the environmentalist who was slain trying to protect this region from development.

Departing Puerto Escondido, avoid rocks jutting about half a mile farther NE than the Punta Sal nav light.

Bahía Tela

The eastern side of Bahía Tela (Punta Sal to Punta Izopo) is divided by Punta El Triunfo. The town of Tela lies south of Punta El Triunfo, and the train sidings of El Triunfo lies just north of that point.

As a banana port, Tela was abandoned in the 1970s and never recovered. The old United Fruit Company pier was rebuilt but collapsed in recent hurricanes. At about 15°47.24'N, 87°27.36'W, you can anchor (25' to 30' of water) about a quarter mile NE of the remnants of the old banana pier.

Ashore, this Garifuna village has mostly dirt streets and few services. However, on holidays the beaches SW of town are popular with tourists from San Pedro Sula who come down on the twice-weekly train.

Departing Bahia Tela eastward, give at least a half-mile berth to Punta Izopo due to detached rocks.

Bancos Salmedina: From a mile north off Punta Izopo, you can lay a course (095°T) directly to La Ceiba (meaning half a mile north of the point), which stays 2 miles south of Bancos Salmedina and 2 miles north of the shoals off Barra Rio Guerra.

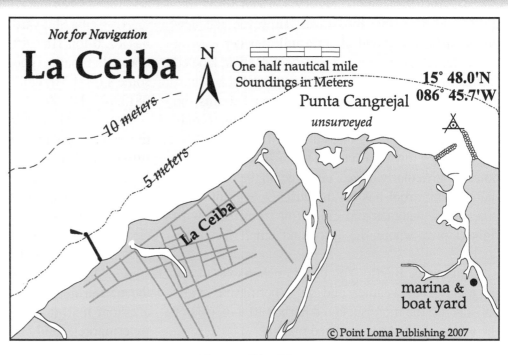

Not for Navigation
La Ceiba

One half nautical mile
Soundings in Meters

15° 48.0'N
086° 45.7'W
Punta Cangrejal
unsurveyed

La Ceiba

marina & boat yard

© Point Loma Publishing 2007

La Ceiba

La Ceiba is the largest town (pop. 80,000) that we cover on Honduras, and it's the easiest mainland Port of Entry for yatistas. It's also useful to yatistas, because nearby we find a real marina, fuel at the dock and a full-service boat yard – all located within a river mouth protected by large lighted breakwaters. La Ceiba town has a ferry and flights out to Roatan, and Adelante Foundation women (see below) bring their wares to town.

The mouth of Rio Congrejal has been rearranged several times by hurricanes and flash floods; today

Women around La Ceiba have learned to support themselves in small businesses - like this bakery - with education and micro-credit loans from Adente Foundation.

it's barely navigable by pangas. However, the new breakwaters are found about a mile farther east, at the mouth of what's now a shorter cutoff river, labeled Barra Boca Vieja on some charts. (NIMA Chart 28144 Port of La Ceiba.) Rio Congrejal drains the central highlands, and someday hurricane runoff may again change where it enters the Caribbean.

La Ceiba town was named by early mariners who noted a particularly large Ceiba tree on the beach, but that ancient arbol has bit the dust. Dole Fruit ships pineapples, bananas and grapefruit from the town's lighted pier, where the ferry and small freighters dock.

Anchor & Berth: You could anchor west of the town pier, but weather and draft permitting, most yatistas use the more sheltered harbor 10 n.m. east of the town - for its boat yard and marina.

Our approach about a quarter mile NW of La Ceiba harbor's lighted overlapping breakwaters is 15°48.103'N, 86°45.680'W. In strong north or NNE wind, breakers may inhibit entrance.

The harbor's outer lobe (8' depth) has the Roatan ferry dock, but keep bearing to port, and the main channel (6' to 8') starts in the far SE corner of the second basin. A dredge may be working.

Local Services: The boat yard and then the marina are down that channel less than half a mile on your right; follow the signs. Beyond the marina, the estuary channel ends in jungle.

La Ceiba Shipyard less than a mile into the harbor has a 120-ton Travelift (100' LOA, 25' beam), a ways, does all repairs (good reports), some dry storage, some slips. FMI, call La Ceiba Shipyard (504) 2408-9813, or VHF 69.

Lagoon Marina lies SE of the shipyard, down the estuary channel. Marina Laguna has about 25 full-service Med-moor slots, some sideties; showers, laundry, pool, cantina, shuttle van to town. Diesel, gas and propane can be delivered to the docks.

The marina office can usually arrange your port clearance with officials in town, so they come to the marina. FMI, Lagoon Marina (504) 2440-0614.

One bridge road crossing Rio Congrejal connects the marina area to La Ceiba. MegaPlaza in La Ceiba is a 2-story mall (usually air-conditioned) with movies, supermarket, food court, department stores. Around town you'll find several good grocery & hardware stores, English-speaking doctors & dentists, tour guides, etc. Eateries abound, from Ricardo's on the plaza to the Expat Bar & Grill.

Goloson International Airport is west of town. The D'Antoni hospital is about half a mile west of the bridge. Pico Bonito National Park is 10 miles SW of La Ceiba: toucans & motmot birds are thrilling, nice swimming hole, hiking trails, waterfalls. The peak reaches 8,284' above sea level.

Cultural Tourism: Adelante Foundation helps more than 4,800 of the poorest women in Honduras become self-supporting via micro loans and education. Point Loma Publishing supports its efforts with small donations from the price you paid for *Cruising Ports*. Adelante's micro-credit system is based on the Grameen Bank model (Nobel Prize winner).

Please call or email Mike Wiesner at the Adelante office in La Ceiba; he can often arrange a "cultural tourism day" for a group of yatistas to visit women's workshops & markets. Have lunch at their "pulperia," buy their homemade foods for your provisions, etc. Adelante Foundation (504) 443-1198 or visit www. AdelanteFoundation.org

This entrepreneurial seamstress now supports herself & family thanks to education and a micro-credit loan from Adelante Foundation in Honduras.

Departure: Eastbound, the 20-meter curve edges farther off shore, and the Sierra Nombre de Dios crowd closer to the coastline, sometimes rolling upland thunderstorms down onto the inshore waters.

Cayos Cochinos

From La Ceiba eastbound, you might make a side trip to the national park at Cayos Cochinos – Pigs Cays. The two tall cays (Little Pig, Big Pig) and 8 or 9 smaller reef-bound cays rise at the edge of the 20-meter curve about 10 n.m. north of Punta Catchabutan. A dozen detached reefs (submerged & awash) spread 6 n.m. SW from the cays, and numerous sand and broken shell banks litter the bottom south of the Cochinos.

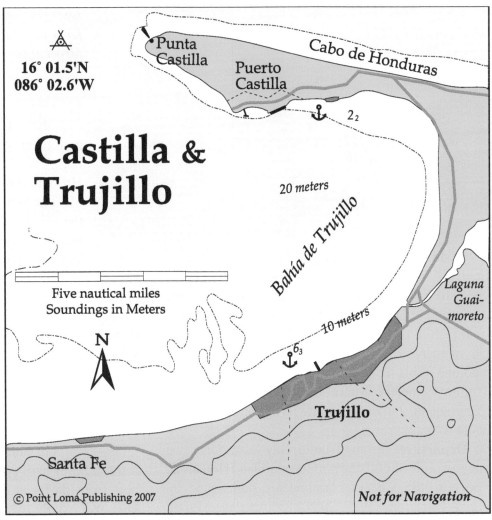

16° 01.5'N
086° 02.6'W

Castilla & Trujillo

Five nautical miles
Soundings in Meters

N

© Point Loma Publishing 2007

Not for Navigation

From La Ceiba, lay a course (17.5 n.m., about 061°M) for a point about .75 of a mile south of Cochino Pequeño, then turn north to come in behind the reef system SE of Cochino Grande. Screen for bugs.

Cochino Grande has a small dive resort and 3 public moorings, which you're supposed to use up first. If you hail Plantation Beach resort (VHF 12) and they're not too full, you might get to come in for dinner. Lion's Head (north end of Big Pig) and Pelican Point are reportedly the best scuba sights, but the snorkeling is good almost anywhere here. Or visit the Garifuna fishing villages of Chachuate and East End.

Puerto Castilla & Trujillo

Punta Castilla forming the north side of Bahía Trujillo (NIMA 28142) lies about 47 n.m. east of La Ceiba, about 26 n.m. ENE of Cayos Cochinos.

The small commercial Port of Entry (Puerto Castilla) has a commercial dock about 2.5 n.m. SE from low, wooded Punta Castilla. This is very isolated, but anchorage is permitted without clearing in here – unless you need to. The NE corner of the bay is shallow and lacks protection from prevailing winds. Between Punta Castilla and Trujillo town, the shoal mouth of Laguna Guiamoreto reaches the bay.

The pleasant town of Trujillo (pop. 30,000) along the SE side of the bay gains some shelter from 2 landmark peaks, Mount Caprio & Mount Calentura, that rise close east of town. Between Rio Cristales and Rio Negro, Trujillo has a municipal pier with about 7.5' of water at the seaward end (about 15°55.43'N, 85°57.06'W). Yatistas usually anchor (15' to 30') within a quarter mile downwind of the pier for beach access to town.

Trujillo has typical provisions, but isn't a mariner's hangout. The airport is just east of Rio Negro. Several small Garifuna villages are strung down the beach west of town. A cruise ship company may build a dock somewhere in this vicinity, which would change things a bit.

East Harbour on Utila has a ferry pier but not an all-weather anchorage.

History and Culture: Trujillo was occupied by English, French and Dutch colonists, and it has an interesting Spanish history as well. But Trujillo, once the capital of Honduras, is really more famous as the final resting place of William Walker, the infamous US mercenary. Trujillo might be a good place to read one of his many biographies. Then visit the Old Trujillo Cemetery where Walker was executed by firing squad (bullet holes preserved) and entombed in 1860.

Departure: From Trujillo Bay eastbound, we know of no more cruising ports on mainland Honduras. The next 185 n.m. of coastline are punctuated by Punta Cameron (19°59.20'N, 85°01.63'W), Punta Rio Patuca (15°49.0'N, 84°18.2'W), Barra Caratasca, Cabo Falso (15°12'N, 83°20'W) and Cabo Gracias a Dios. Inland from Barra Caratasca, the Puerto Limon Estuary has shoaled up. Vessels run this lee shore at least 5.5 n.m. off to avoid shoals.

The Bay Islands

The Bay Islands of Guanaja, Roatan, Utila and Cayos Cochinos spread about 70 n.m. SW to NE, lying 17 to 26 n.m. north of the Honduran mainland, except for the Cayos Cochinos, which lie about 10 n.m. north of Punta Catchabutan on the mainland.

Utila

Pronounced "oo-TIL-ah," this mostly low, 7-mile long island lies about 41 n.m. NE from Punta Sal, about 18 n.m. NW of La Ceiba. See NIMA chart 28143. The normal current pattern through the Bay Islands is west and north on rising tides, south and east on falling tides. However, a counter-clockwise eddy is observed north of Utila.

East Harbour, the only tiny harbor and anchorage, is on the SE side, gaining marginal shelter from landmark Pumpkin Hill and the harbor reef, but is open to the SE. The only nav light is on the reef forming the SE arm of the harbor. Utila's main duty is inexpensive dive charters for back packers and mainland tourists who arrive on the Municipal Pier via ferries from La Ceiba and cruise ship shore boats.

Try to approach Utila by coming in from the SSW, to a point about 3.5 n.m. south of Utila's SW corner, thus avoiding the large reef patch that trails 4 n.m. off the island's west and SW sides. From that offshore position, you can come straight into the harbor, heading generally 033°T toward the red and white radio antenna.

East Harbour holding is not good, eel grass over thin sand over hard coral. We have reports of dinghy theft from davits at night in Utila's East Harbour. Also, twice daily the fast ferry cuts straight through what little anchoring space is found, so try to avoid its direct path in to the ferry dock.

We're told that – with local knowledge (a pilot) – good anchorage is possible within the reef area west of the island, and our charts show a very narrow passage between Pigeon and Water cays, but we haven't tried it.

Utila town has small groceries, bike rentals, at least 5 internet cafes, lots of inexpensive eateries and scuba dive shops. Motorcycle jitneys taxi you around town. For exercise, hike up to the Iguana Research Station (north of the fire station, west end of town), open on cruise ship days. They preserve Utila's unique and endangered Swamper Iguana by breeding and releasing hatchlings into the mangroves.

In fair weather, tiny Shark Cove and slightly larger Black Rock Bay on the north side of Utila make a good hike or dinghy exploration, the latter bay being developed as a new town.

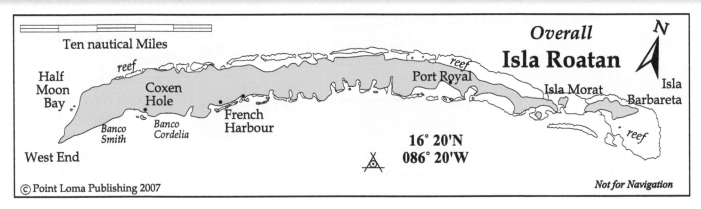

Ten nautical Miles

Half Moon Bay

reef

Coxen Hole

Banco Smith

Banco Cordelia

French Harbour

West End

Port Royal

reef

Isla Morat

Isla Barbareta

reef

Overall
Isla Roatan

N

16° 20'N
086° 20'W

© Point Loma Publishing 2007

Not for Navigation

Isla Roatan

Roatan Island lies about 30 n.m. NW of Punta Castilla, 180 n.m. west of Cayo Vivorillo, 290 n.m. south of Isla Mujeres and about 620 n.m. from the Panama Canal – depending on your route.

Roatan is the main island in the Bay Islands of Honduras, and it is the main cruising ground – and English is the main language. For yatistas, Roatan has dozens of sheltered bays and anchorages, a few marinas, fuel docks, funky fishing ports and fancy resorts.

Poorly charted, Roatan runs about 30 n.m. from NW to SE, yet only about 2 miles wide. Roatan's barrier reef fringes the entire north shore, most of the east end and some of the south side – so the openings are important. A high wooded ridge runs almost the island's full length. Most sheltered anchorages are along the island's south shores. Small canals or dinghy passages link some bays. Spring and early summer are the most delightful cruising seasons at Roatan. The Trade Winds can howl, especially in winter. In the summer, hurricanes pose a danger; this isn't a hurricane hole.

Roatan Southside Locations: From West End coasting NE, the useful indents, harbors and cuts are Coxen Hole, Dixon's Cove, Brick Bay, French Harbour (Sarah Cay cut), French Harbour (Big French Cay cut), Cocoview, Second Bight (trecherous), First Bight or Parrot Tree, Neverstain Bight with Half Moon dinghy cove, Caribe Bight, Jonesville (Bodden) Bight with Hole in the

Wall, Jonesville (east), Oak Ridge (fuel), Fiddler's Bight, Calabash Bight, then 1.75 n.m. over to the Fort Key cut (west side of Fort Key) to Lime Cay Bay and the larger Port Royal, then snug Old Port Royal Bay, Bailey's Bay, Helene Bay, Isla Barbeta and little Pigeon Cays.

We'll look at the Coxen Hole (the official Port of Entry), then French Harbour where yatistas more often clear in and hang out.

Coxen Hole

Coxen Hole (locally called Coxen's Hole) lies 4.25 n.m. NE of Roatan's West End tip. It's the seat of Bay Islands government and has the main airport, but it's not a comfortable harbor for yatistas since the big municipal pier was taken over for cruise ships and the ferries occupy the pier on the next point east.

In fact, Coxen Hole officials suggest that yatistas may opt to head first to French Harbour and get a marina slip there, then call for port officials to come by taxi (you pay the fare with your port fees) to perform your clearance dockside. Call "Coxen Hole

Roatan is blooming with new guest docks at nice residential developments.

Left: Looking west into Brick Bay and west French Harbour.
Below: Looking east into Old French Harbour & Big French Cay entrance.

Port Clearance" when you're within VHF range.

But if you want to clear here, approach from West End, coast in about a quarter mile off shore to avoid 2 reefs (Smith & Cordelia) that lie south and SE of the harbor and of Osgood Cay (Big Cay). Our approach position about half a mile WSW of big Osgood Cay is 16°18.40'N, 86°32.96'W.

Anchor (12' to 18' good holding mud) NW of Osgood Cay but not blocking cruise ship or ferry access. Swinging room may be restricted by the remnants of a shipwreck.

Port Clearance: The Port Captain (VHF 16) and Customs are at the head of the ferry pier, and Immigration is about 500 yards up the beach street going east. The captain alone goes to the Port Captain to notify them of the arrival. If you plan a short stay, clear papers from the last port and mention that Roatan is an intermediate stop only. This gives you a transient status, making it less expensive to clear.

If you wish to hire a ship's agent, we've used and recommend Mr. Beatman Ebanks, an energetic native English-speaker experienced with yachts, who has a good working relationship with Roatan officials. FMI email ebanksagency@yahoo.com in advance, and he'll give you his office and cell phone numbers.

Local Services: NW of the ferry pier (La Ceiba, Utila, Guanaja) is a multi-purpose dock. Warren's grocery is just east of there. An internet café is up the main street going north from Warren's. A bank for buying Lempira is just west of the ferry pier, and another one is on the way to Immigration but inland side of the street. The airport has flights to La Ceiba, San Pedro Sula and the capital Tegucigalpa.

French Harbour

French Harbour is the vortex of cruising life on Roatan. It has ample yacht anchorages and services – marinas, diesel gas, haul-out, repairs, groceries – and the laid-back tropical ambience.

Approaches: Coasting up island 4.5 to 6 n.m. NE from Coxen Hole, you'll see French Harbour traffic inside and outside the barrier reef.

Two entrances are marked on our French Harbour chart, along with paths to the anchorages and berthing facilities. Another chart shows the approaches to Brick Bay, Barefoot Cay Marina and the west end of French Harbour.

Use extreme caution when entering the reef, because we've found that the small

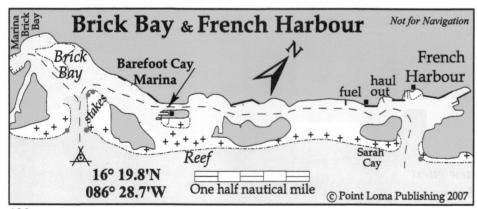

Brick Bay & French Harbour *Not for Navigation*

Marina Brick Bay

Brick Bay

Barefoot Cay Marina

French Harbour

haul out

fuel

Reef

Sarah Cay

16° 19.8'N
086° 28.7'W

One half nautical mile

© Point Loma Publishing 2007

stakes marking detached coral heads and shoals are sometimes knocked down.

Anchor & Berth: Anchoring is possible almost anywhere not blocking the docks and channels behind the reef. The area between Big French Key and Fantasy Island is frequently used as a well-protected all-weather anchorage by cruisers.

Barefoot Cay Marina & Dive Resort near the entrance to Brick Bay has 600' of full-service side tie dockage (yacht to 165') in their U-shaped basin, with 10' channel depth. This private island has a restaurant, pool, nice amenities, major dive center, friendly folks. Call "Barefoot Cay Marina" on VHF 18A and they'll either talk you in or send the skiff out to guide you in. Call ther new number (504) 2455-6235 or www. barefootcay.com.

Brick Bay Marina & Resort in a sheltered basin off the SW corner of Brick Bay has about 9' max in the basin, changed hands recently. FMI call Brick Bay Marina & Resort (504) 2455-1127.

Via the Big French Cay entrance, you can reach the basin of the old Roatan Yacht Club (formerly French Harbour YC) tucked inside Old French Harbour, best all-weather hidey hole (12' depth) on Roatan; avoid 4' shoal in W corner. It's not presently a marina, but you can ask them about dockage (504) 2455-5407.

Via the same Big French Cay entrance, Fantasy Island Resort (VHF 18) is a mile east (12' to 15' depth in channels) on tiny Ezekiel Cay. This dive resort has a 20-slip marina, 110' dock, pool, small fuel dock, great cantina, great new dockmaster, dink landing near the French Harbour East anchorage. FMI (504) 8798-5496 or www.fantasyislandresort.com

Continuing 2.25 n.m. upisland, Parrot Tree Plantation Marina has first 20 slips of 110 planned. FMI (504) 9706-9240.

Local Services: Jackson's Fuel Dock in the Sarah Cay end of French Harbour has diesel, gas, water, ice. A & D Dry Dock haul-out yard is widely used by cruising boats; ask for Seth Arch. French Harbour is a center for wooden boatbuilding & repair, has access to good woods, cheap labor. FMI (504) 455-5450. Also, G & G Hardware.

Provisions are mostly from Eldon's Grocery in French Harbour and Warren's in Coxen Hole. Stores are stocked when supply boats arrive, so in long periods of bad weather shelves can get a bit bare.

Radio Belize (830 Khz) gives news and weather

Marina & Guest Bungalows

* Sheltered concrete & wood marina - tender docks
* Accommodates up to 165 foot yachts, 10-foot draft
* 30- and 50-amp service, potable water
* Spacious bathrooms - large hot water showers
* WI-FI satellite internet - cable TV available
* Laundry service - ice - barbeque - mail service
* Pool: 50 feet long with whirlpool jets
* 260' dock with thatched palapa & hammocks
* Full security on-site 24 hours
* Dive shop on site - provisions nearby
* Between French Harbour and Brick Bay entrances
* Wide deep-water access from ocean
* VHF channel 18A monitored when in office
* Call for guidance through the Brick Bay entrance
* Ship's Agent available for customs processing

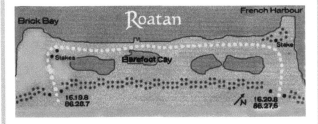

Barefoot Cay
Between French Harbour & Brick Bay
Roatan, Bay Islands, Honduras
www.barefootcay.com - info@barefootcay.com
VHF 18A (504) 2455-6235
From US: 1-866-246-3706 - 1-305-767-4576
E-FAX: 1-270-918-3621

forecasts in English for the Roatan area at 0100, 0300, 1300, 1500, 1700, 1830, 2100 and 2300 Zulu.

French Harbour has a good private medical center

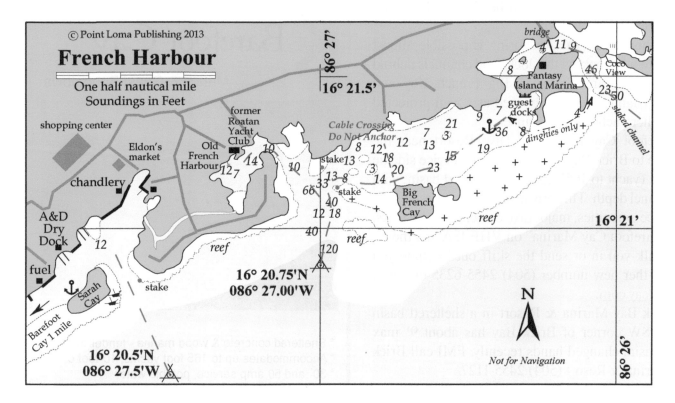

© Point Loma Publishing 2013

French Harbour

One half nautical mile
Soundings in Feet

shopping center

former
Roatan
Yacht
Club

Eldon's market

Old
French
Harbour

chandlery

A&D
Dry
Dock

fuel

Sarah
Cay

stake

Barefoot
Cay 1 mile

16° 20.5'N
086° 27.5'W

16° 20.75'N
086° 27.00'W

reef

reef

Cable Crossing
Do Not Anchor

stake

stake

Big
French
Cay

reef

bridge

Fantasy
Island Marina

Coco
View

guest
docks

dinghies only

staked channel

16° 27'

16° 21.5'

16° 21'

86° 26'

N

Not for Navigation

with English-speaking doctors and nurses. A public medical clinic is found in Coxen's Hole.

Oak Ridge has a fuel dock, an anchorage with excellent protection and a large fishing fleet.

Roatan History & Culture: Payan and Mayan villages on Roatan predated the arrival of Europeans. In 1502, Columbus named the country Honduras, meaning deep, because he thought deep waters were causing the rough seas he encountered. Actually it was rough because the water was shallow; perhaps the Admiral's depth sounder had blown a fuse.

About 50 years later, Spanish slaver ships seeking labor for mining and agriculture projects had almost depopulated Roatan and the other Bay Islands of their natives. In the 1600s, English, French and Dutch pirates took control of the Bay Islands and settled towns at what today are Coxen Hole and Port Royal. These pirates used Roatan as a base for their raids against the Spanish Main.

In 1797 after a huge slave uprising on St. Vincent, the British resettled 100s of Garifuna people on Roatan, primarily at Punta Gorda. Slaves were also brought here from Jamaica. In 1859, the Bay Islands politically became part of the nearby country of Honduras – but the island culture has remained unique.

The English-speaking descendants of these pirates and slaves still inhabit these islands. However they now spend their days sportfishing and running marinas. Pirate treasures have been dug up and smuggled off the island, so the authorities take a dim view of treasure seekers.

French Harbour fishing fleet ready to depart for the season.

Guanaja

Pronounced "wah-NAH-ha," this high island runs 10 n.m. SW to NE, and the whole NE end is wreathed in reefs. See NIMA chart 28125. Guanaja's prominent lighted western point Ochre Bluff is about 10 n.m. east of Pigeon Cays on Roatan's western end, and it's about 23 n.m. NNE of Punta Castilla or Cabo Honduras on the mainland.

From Guanaja, Cayo Vivorillo lies about 150 miles ESE, and this gives you a pretty straightforward approach to Vivorillo.

Isla Guanaja is almost divided by the Gully, a long canal (dinghy passible at high water) sheltering the air strip. Tacho Hill at the island's east end is an 850' peak, mostly recovered from denuding by Hurricane Mitch. But many of its historic Guanaja Pines were damaged.

Most of the population and services are found on tiny Bonacca Cay (original name of this island) or nearby at the south end of the Gully, or about 4.5 n.m. NE at Savannah Bight. But some of the lesser cays on the south side are also populated. Until recently, Guanaja Island had no cars, no roads, just boats and feet. Several anchorages are spread behind the sandbar and outer reefs.

Like at Utila, the easiest approach to Guanaja Settlement is from the SW. Ochre Bluff Light marks the SW tip, and you can coast NE behind the sandbar, avoiding a few isolated coral heads. Or enter to Bonacca Cay from the east, staying a quarter mile south of both Half Moon Cay and lighted Pond Cay, which has a sandbar off its south side.

Guanaja is going through a real estate boom; lots of new vacation homes. In future editions of *Cruising Ports*, we hope to have info about a marina just south of the airport.

Cabo Gracias a Dios

Hazard: Cabo Gracias a Dios, the major turning point in the Western Caribbean, has been reported to lie about 1.75 n.m. east of its charted position. Depths less than charted have been reported to lie 3.5 n.m. SE and from 3.5 to 10 n.m. east of the cape. Yachts should give this cape a berth of at least 10 n.m. and in

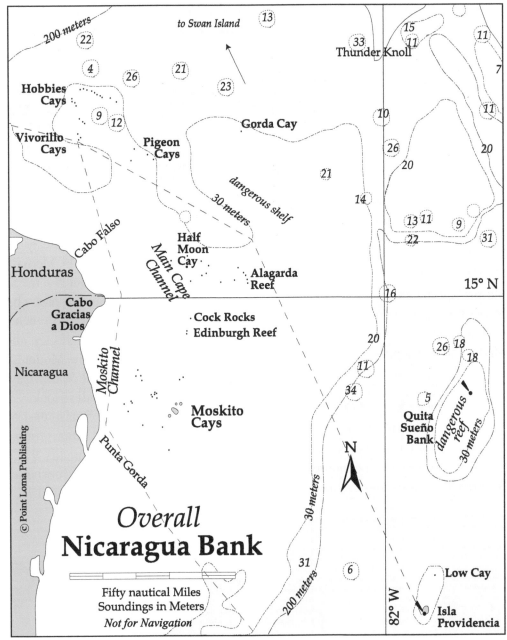

Overall
Nicaragua Bank

Fifty nautical Miles
Soundings in Meters
Not for Navigation

© Point Loma Publishing

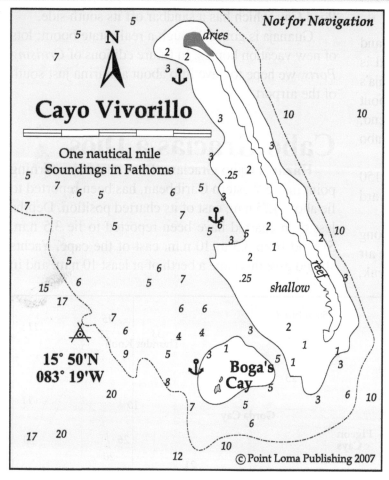

Cayo Vivorillo

One nautical mile
Soundings in Fathoms

Not for Navigation

15° 50'N
083° 19'W

Boga's Cay

dries

shallow

reef

© Point Loma Publishing 2007

Cayo Vivorillo Grande (15°50.0'N, 83°19.0'W), known locally as Boga's Cay, has the remnants of cement buildings (home of Old Man Boga) and a deep-water approach from SW. We've anchored many times west of this cay. A steep-to 2-mile long dry reef starts half a mile east of Cayo Vivorillo Grande and runs NNW for 2 n.m. lined with breakers. Anchorage is possible west of most of the reef. Numerous detached coral heads cover the 10-mile area NW from Boga's Cay.

This lovely outpost has been marred by vandals ashore, insistant beggars afloat and the murder of a cruising sailor several years ago. Honduran Navy patrols Vivorillo irregularly.

Media Luna Reefs: This group of tiny cays and mostly submerged reefs flank the east side of the unmarked Main Cape Channel; local knowledge is required to navigate these waters. Media Luna Cay is a barren rock (about 15°08.28'N, 82°41.77'W) at the SW corner of the group. It stands about 26 n.m. ENE of Cabo Gracias a Dios. A crescent reef juts half a mile north and NW from Cayo Media Luna.

Logwood Cay (Cayo Madero), another barren rock, is about 3 n.m. north of Cayo Media Luna. Logwood Cay is the SW corner of the vast Arrecifes de la Media Luna, which spreads 7 n.m. east and about 5 n.m. SE. Vessels in the Main Cape Channel may enter about 0.75 of a mile south of Logwood Cay to reach sheltered water about a mile SE of Logwood Cay, about 40' depth.

Also in the Media Lunas are Burn Cay, Savannah Reefs, the 2 South Cays, Port Royal Cay, Porpoise Cay and Hall's Rock.

About 5 n.m. east and SE of Savannah Reefs in the Media Luna group, another large reef, Arrecife Alagarda, spreads 9 n.m. north to south, 6 east to west. The NW corner of Alagarda Reef lies at about 15°08.5'N, 82°26.11'W.

thick weather should keep in depths of 60.

Main Cape Channel: The unmarked deep-water passage around Cabo Gracias a Dios is call the Main Cape Channel, lying about 24 n.m. off the actual cape. Vessels transiting around Cabo Gracias a Dios in the Main Cape Channel need to be aware of 2 groups of offshore cays and reefs that lie just outside the passage: the smaller Vivorillo group and the broader Media Luna group.

Cayo Vivorillo

The Vivorillo Bank lies from 33 to 53 n.m. NNE of Cabo Falso. This 675-mile square bank rises above the 20-meter curve and contains the Cayos Vivorillo, Becerro, Caratasca and Cajones (Hobbies) groups.

Boga's Cay at Cayo Vivorillo is visited by commercial fishing boats and yatistas.

Obstruction reported off Cabo Gracias a Dios; a 7' depth marked in 2008 with a stake at 14°55.57'N, 83°00.0'W.

Not for Navigation

This chapter briefly describes two of the many routes across the Nicaragua Bank, then jumps off shore to the Western Caribbean islands of Grand Cayman (British), Providencia and San Andrés (Colombian) and briefly the Corn Islands (Nicaragua).

Nicaragua Bank Routes

When rounding Cabo Gracias a Dios, it's normally safer to stay well off shore. The Nicaragua Bank reaches about 50 n.m. off the north coast of Nicaragua. Several offshore routes are possible through the Nicaragua Bank. See chartlet and below.

Moskito Channel Route, Vivorillo to San Andrés: We don't recommend planning to transit the Moskito Channel. However, the Mar Caribe's Trade Winds have been known to overpower smaller yachts and wear down their crews, and having a mechanical breakdown that renders one dead in the water in this region is extremely dangerous. So, for emergency purposes only, we include basic information about transiting the Moskito Channel.

From the Cayo Vivorillo Grande anchorage

(15°50'N, 83°19'W), clear the south end of those reefs and head about 53 n.m. SSE to a position (15°00.0'N, 83°02.5'W) about 5 n.m. east of Cabo Gracias Adios. Turn SSW into the Moskito Channel and continue for about 40 n.m. to a position (14°15.5'N, 83°09.00'W) about 4 n.m. east of Punta Gorda. The Moskito Cays to your east provide varying degrees of shelter from prevailing easterly wind and seas. From the Punta Gorda offshore waypoint, head SE (going back off shore) about 140 n.m. straight to the south end of Isla San Andrés. Total is about 233 n.m.

WARNING: The Moskito Channel is not well charted, and the edges have isolated coral heads. The safe passage is not marked, not maintained, not patrolled. Earthquake and hurricane activity have changed the bottom. Except in a faster-paced power boat, it's difficult to transit this 80 n.m. inshore passage entirely during daylight hours. Never travel this at night; besides logs, local fishermen string unlighted nets across the channel and sleep in flotillas of tiny unlighted cayucas, which are invisible to radar.

Cay Gorda Route, Vivorillo to Providencia:

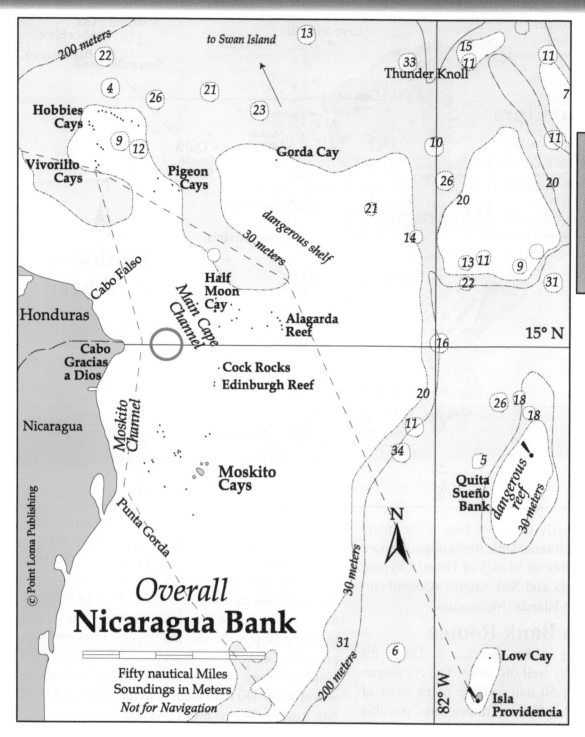

200 meters 22

to Swan Island 13

15
11

11

4 26 21 33
Thunder Knoll
23
7

Hobbies
Cays

9 12

Gorda Cay 10

11

Vivorillo
Cays

Pigeon
Cays

26
20

21 20

dangerous shelf

30 meters 14

Half
Moon
Cay

13 11 9

Cabo Falso

Main Cape Channel

Alagarda
Reef

22 31

Honduras

Cabo
Gracias
a Dios

15° N

16

Cock Rocks
Edinburgh Reef

Nicaragua

Moskito Channel

20

11

26 18

34 18

5

Quita
Sueño
Bank

dangerous reef

30 meters

Moskito
Cays

N

Overall
Nicaragua Bank

Punta Gorda

© Point Loma Publishing

31 6

Low Cay

30 meters

200 meters

82° W

Isla
Providencia

Fifty nautical Miles
Soundings in Meters
Not for Navigation

Obstruction
reported off
Cabo Gracias a
Dios; a 7' depth
marked in 2008
with a stake
at 14°55.57'N,
83°00.0'W.

From the Cayo Vivorillo anchorage (15°50'N, 83°19'W), we clear the south end of the Cayo and head SE for 75 n.m. to an offshore waypoint at 15°14.4'N, 82°16.6'W. This leg passes 2.5 n.m. south of the cay at the south end of the Cocorocuma Reefs. From the latter waypoint we turn SSE and lay a course 120 n.m. to the west side of Isla Providencia. Total distance is about 209 n.m. We easily continue from Isla Providencia to Isla San Andrés.

Grand Cayman Island

The Cayman Islands are composed of Grand Cayman, Little Cayman and Cayman Brac. All 3 are both British Crown Colonies where English is the official language. Almost in the center of the Western Caribbean, the Caymans are the emerging peaks of the submarine Cayman Ridge that extends from Cuba's Sierra Maestra range down to the Misteriosa Banks NE of Cabo Gracias a Dios in Honduras. The

Cayman Islands are formed of living coral reefs that crest the submerged mountain peaks. About 80 n.m. ESE of Grand Cayman, the Cayman Trench is 23,500' deep.

Grand Cayman Island is a long way from everywhere. It lies about 320 n.m. ESE of Isla Mujeres, 345 n.m. east of Punta Herrero in Mexico, about 230 n.m. NNE of Cayo Vivorillo and about 350 north of Isla Providencia. It's about 250 n.m. SE of Cabo San Antonio, Cuba, 180 NE of Swan Island and 185 WNW of Jamaica's west end. Little Cayman lies about 60 n.m. NE of Grand Cayman, and Cayman Brac lies only about 5 n.m NE of Little Cayman.

Grand Cayman is the largest of the Caymans, 20 n.m. E-W and 9.5 n.m. N-S. Except for George Town Harbour, the island is enclosed in coral reef with small cuts for local boats.

George Town

George Town Harbour on Grand Cayman's SW corner is the Port of Entry and deep-water harbor with a fuel dock. Although it's a long distance from everywhere else in the Caribbean, this is usually an easy stop for yatistas who want to clear in, take fuel and go.

But for a sheltered marina slip, vessels drawing less than 8' of water must go around the island's NW corner and enter the huge North Sound. Inside off separate channels we find the 3 older marinas and a dozen more in construction.

Approaches: Grand Cayman is a low island (max 50' at East End). When within 10 n.m. of the island, call "Port Security" on VHF 16 to announce your arrival. George Town is about 1.7 n.m. north of the island's SW tip. George Town Light (19°17.8'N, 81°23.0'W) is on the newly enlarged concrete pier forming the north side of the tiny harbor.

From the west, when 9 n.m. out from George Town, you cross Cayman Bank (about 19°20'N, 81°35'W), a popular scuba destination (90' depths). Cayman Islands Marine Park surrounds Grand Cayman, and Marine Conservation Regulations are

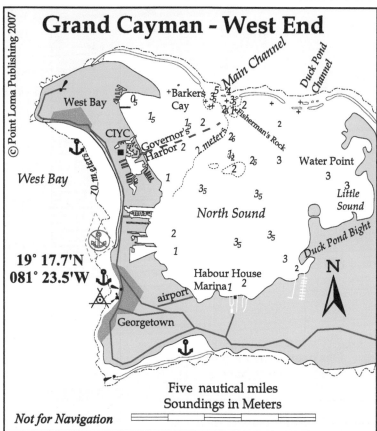

in effect. Use caution to avoid dive boats anchored or drifting along this spectacular wall. A tourist submarine submerges and rises in the vicinity.

From the south, stay a good mile off Southwest Point to avoid lighted Sand Cay (0.25 n.m. off shore) and unlighted Hastings Rock (13.2' depth) about 0.25 of a mile SW of Sand Cay. The current runs through here so strong that it's named Pull and Be Damned Point for good reasons.

Gorling Bluff Light (19°18.0'N, 81°06.3'W) stands on the SE end of Grand Cayman, and the breaking reef encircling the entire eastern end of the island is almost a mile off shore.

Anchorages: George Town's large concrete pier façade contains the Port Facilities and forms the

Rock in center of George Town harbor hinders the approach to shore.

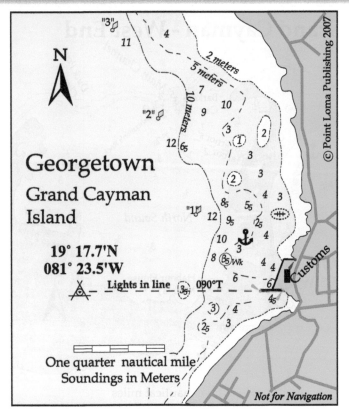

Georgetown
Grand Cayman
Island

19° 17.7'N
081° 23.5'W

Lights in line   090°T

One quarter nautical mile
Soundings in Meters

Not for Navigation

© Point Loma Publishing 2007

with hotels and eating or drinking establishments. In fact, Seven Mile Beach is actually about 4 n.m. long.

Caution: George Town and West Bay are not all-weather anchorages, because they offer protection only from the east. Yes, east is the prevailing wind, but any wind or swell from other quadrants is definitely felt in George Town Harbor and West Bay.

During a Nor'wester, which happens several times a winter, these anchorages become a lee shore. The season for Nor'westers is from November through April – the heart of cruising season – and these storms can strike with little or no warning, sometimes out of a blue sky. The presence of a swell out of the west may presage a storm. When anchored here, stay tuned to weather from NMG, and pay close attention to the portion for conditions in the Gulf of Mexico and the Northwest Caribbean. Remember that the colder the forecast for Miami, the more violent the storm here.

If you see a general exodus of local boats all heading to South Sound, by all means follow suit.

South Sound: The best anchoring shelter from a Nor'wester is off Spotts, one of the few places near South Sound that doesn't have a shielding reef.

South Sound is an open indent along the SW end of the island, west of Bodden Town. If you measure South Sound from Grand Pedro Point (the most southerly point on Grand Cayman) westward to Sand Cay and Southwest Point, then South Sound is about 6 n.m. wide. At the west end of South Sound, avoid lighted Sand Cay (a quarter mile off Southwest Point) and unlighted Hastings Rock (13.2' depth) about a quarter mile SW of Sand Cay. The more deeply indented western half of South Sound is foul with shield reef. By following a local guide boat, shallow draft cruisers may be able to get in behind the reef.

Spotts anchorage is about 4 n.m. east of Southwest Point and 1.25 n.m. west of Little Pedro Point, and it has a jetty near Prospect Reef Resort.

north seawall of a small sheltered cove called Grand Cayman Harbour. The small-boat anchorage is within a mile NW of the pier, in 18' to 36' of incredibly clear water. The bottom is coral sand and light mud. Dinghies have been allowed to land at the low dock used for cruise ship launches, which is right in the center of town. Just stream them off so the launches can land.

You may also anchor north of George Town in West Bay, along a beautiful white-sand stretch of shoreline called Seven Mile Beach, which is lined

Ships and yachts dock in George Town.

Yachts clear Customs at George Town's attractive waterfront.

Anchor as close as your draft will permit. The lee here comes from 120' high Great Pedro Point, which protrudes a bit farther south immediately east of Little Pedro Point. The main E-W road runs close along the shore, and the village of Savannah is half a mile east of Spotts.

Whenever the winds move more to the north or NW, cruise ships may move from George Town and re-anchor farther outside Spotts.

North Sound: North Sound is the shallow, shoal-ridden but sheltered 5-square mile lagoon covering 80% of the island's western half. A barrier reef shields the otherwise open northern expanse of North Sound.

The entrance gap (7' or less) into North Sound's Main Channel lies at 19°22.84'N, 81°19.61'W. Use your now acute visual coral-piloting skills. Inside several channels zig and zag around coral shoals.

The Port Captain can provide a chart for North Sound's channels. Main Channel and at least 4 side channels lead to boating centers. Ask the Port Authority when you clear in, and call the marinas on VHF to be sure of the present channel depths and directions. Meanwhile, there is plenty of swinging room to anchor in 8' to 15' depths, and it's also a snug place to ride out a Nor'wester. Mosquitoes are voracious here.

Boating locations on the west shore of North Sound are Head of Barkers Point, Morgan's Harbour Bay and Governor's Harbour (See marinas below.) and two golf courses. The swampy north and south perimeters inside Governor's Harbour have been dredged into residential channels with many private docks.

Along the south end are George Town Barcadero (back entrance to town), Owen Roberts International Airport, residential channel of Red Bay and Omega Gardens, then Duck Pond Bight. Along the east shore are Booby Cay, Little Sound, Water Cay and Rum Point.

Berthing: Bardcadero Marina (345) 949-3743 is the newest berthing in town, highly recommended.

located in the south end of North Sound near the airport. Check our UPDATES for more info.

Cayman Islands Yacht Club is located in the north end of Governor's Harbour, west side of North Sound. This full-service marina and yacht club has guest slips and side ties for yachts to 152' and maximum 7' draft. The marina has a Texaco fuel dock, restaurant and shore facilities; they monitor VHF-16.

To reach Cayman Islands Yacht Club from the entrance gap into Main Channel (19°22.84'N, 81°19.61'W), come due south for a quarter mile. At the bifurcation (19°21.49'N, 81°22.05'W), turn westward and follow the well-marked side channel (6' high PVC posts) into Governor's Creek, which cuts through the mangroves into Governor's Harbour. The channel contains 11' of water, but no more than 7' of draft is recommended. FMI on CYIC phone Dockmaster Benny (345) 945-4322.

The south end of Governor's Harbour contains numerous channels and side channels with private docks below resort homes. Some of these docks can be rented as guest slips, with or without the accompanying vacation home.

Harbour House Marina (See below.) in the south end of North Sound is a boat yard and chandlery, not a marina with guest docks.

Port Clearance: Once you get anchored call "Port Security" again. They will instruct you when to come alongside the pier's boarding platform for boarding and inspection.

We've tried to convince them to come out in our launch, but they won't. we don't like this pier, because it was designed for commercial ships and the surge is bad. It may seem calm for hours, but then a severe surge will burst in from nowhere. Unfortunately,

Looking south from the yacht docks in George Town.

everyone who enters the islands must dock at the pier; it's the rule. Make sure your vessel is well fendered.

In our experience, Grand Cayman is the easiest, least expensive and friendliest place in the Western Caribbean to clear official papers. The officials board your boat at the pier, and you fill out a few simple forms and present passports.

Be sure to declare any firearms. This is especially true in British or former-British possessions. Grand Cayman has very strong gun laws. If you declare your arms, no problem. They take them off and store them, and when you are leaving, you return to the same pier and they bring them back to your boat. If undeclared arms are found, everyone on board goes directly to jail and your boat is confiscated.

Spear guns (pole spears or Hawaiian slings) are prohibited from use in the Cayman Island waters, and live plants or cuttings and fruits and veggies cannot be brought ashore. If you have questions about prohibited items, call Grand Cayman Customs (345) 949-2473.

Once the officials have cleared you in, you are free to leave the pier.

To clear out, you walk a few steps to the Port Authority building. Your first office is Customs, where you fill in a clearance form and pay a small fee. However, they do charge a $50 overtime fee after 1600 weekdays, after 1200 Saturday and anytime Sunday. Then you walk upstairs to Immigration, where they put an exit stamp in your passports and clearance form. That's it.

Local Services: To make fuel arrangements, call Beefer's Fuel Pier on VHF 16. Beefer's own private pier lies on the south side of the harbor bight, only 100 yards south of the municipal pier where you cleared in. This tiny, exquisitely beautiful bay is called Hog Sty Bay. This fuel pier too suffers from surge but isn't as jagged. Beefer's Pier has its own tanks and pumps, and good drinking water is available. As on most Caribbean islands, both fuel and water are expensive. Cayman uses Imperial Gallons (1.0 Imp G = 1.2 US gallons) and the potable water is metered.

Fuel is also available at two places inside North Sound. Cayman Islands Yacht Club (See marinas.) inside Governor's Harbour has a Texaco dock and requires 7' draft or less. Call them on VHF-16.

Harbour House Marina has a diesel dock and haul-outs for boats up to 75 tons and 22' beam, and the water depth to reach this large boat yard and chandlery is 6' at MLW. Harbour House Marina is located in Red Bay Estates along the south end of North Sound. They use a Travelift with soft straps to haul. Services are complete hull and prop repair, welding, wooden-hull shipwrights, fiberglass repair, sail repair, marine electronics repair and install, diesel engine mechanics, plus towing and salvage.

Their chandlery has British Admiralty charts, radios, navigation electronics, filters, fittings, fenders, anchors, batteries (US amperage), chain and more.

Harbour Drive is the main drag behind the harbor.

Crystal clear water along West Bay makes good snorkeling from the swim step.

This thoroughfare runs up and down the entire west side of the island. But north of town it's called North Church Street, and south of town it's South Church Street. Near the harbor you'll find banks, restaurants, banks, grocery stores, banks, laundry services, banks, T-shirt shops and a few more banks.

For a fresh produce, visit George Town's open-air markets early each morning. A good Fosters Food Fair supermarket is at Governor's Harbour in the Strand Shopping Centre.

The flowering gardens of Queen Elizabeth II Botanic Park are a wondrous treat for the eyes of mariners bleary after so much blue. This 65-acre park contains trails, visitor center, café and the Cayman Blue Iguana captive breeding and reintroduction facility; open daily 0900 to 1830.

Cayman Maritime & Treasure Museum houses many pirate and shipwreck artifacts. During the French Revolution, the British captured a French frigate and renamed her *H.M.S. Convert.* In 1794, Convert was escorting a fleet of 58 merchantmen when she was accidentally rammed and pushed onto the East End reef – followed by nine other ships. Check out the Ten Sails exhibit. The Cayman Maritime & Treasure Museum is on West Bay Road. FMI call (345) 947-5033.

Cayman Islands National Museum is in the Old Courts Building; phone (345) 949-8368. The Links at Safe Haven is an 18-hole championship golf course near Cayman Island Yacht Club. Britannia golf course is a mile south. Pedro Castle on Great Pedro Point is the oldest surviving building on Grand Cayman, built in 1780.

When more than one cruise ship is visiting Grand Cayman, their passengers swarm the Turtle Farm, museums and T-shirt shops. Over the past few years, an annual average of 900 port calls were made at George Town by cruise ships. That's about 2.5 cruise ships per day.

Side Trip: It's fun to send home a Post Card from Hell. About 5 n.m. north of George Town is the community of Hell – complete with a devilish billboard near the post office, great for hilarious snapshots.

Local Events: Each June, George Town hosts an international sportfishing tournament that brings lots of big boats to the island. Despite Grand Cayman's laid-back beach-resort ambiance, it is primarily an offshore banking center – depicted beautifully in John Grisham's best selling novel *"The Firm."* Grand Cayman enjoys the highest standard of living of any island in the Caribbean. Prosperity is evident, and prices are higher. Cayman's fairly steady exchange rate is unlike everywhere else in Central America. For example, US$1.20 equals only $1.00 KYD or Cayman dollar. We were surprised to be charged US$10 for a simple hamburger. Since your cruising kitty won't stretch as far here as elsewhere along this route, don't plan to provision in Grand Cayman. You may decide to eat more meals on board than you normally would. On the other hand, you might be enticed to stay longer by renting a private dock with attached beach cottage up near Rum Point.

History & Culture: Columbus, the original tourist, stumbled onto these three islands in 1503 on his fourth voyage of discovery, and he named them Las

Scuba diving is the main attraction for fly-in tourists. Grand Cayman has many "resort course" scuba programs. Photo by Larry Benvenuti.

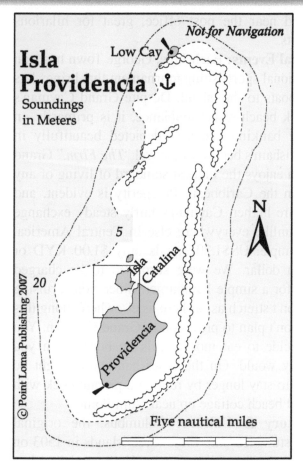

Tortugas for the many sea turtles. When Britain annexed Jamaica in 1655, these islands came along as dependents and were named for the "cayman," a small crocodile that was already disappearing from the region.

Pirates ruled the Cayman Islands, staging attacks on Spanish merchantmen and treasure ships. Henry Morgan prepared here for his famous siege on Panama, and the novel "*Treasure Island*" is based on Blackbeard's shooting of Israel Hinds. The many caves around the Caymans are all said to have held pirate booty.

Great Britain populated Grand Cayman with colonists and freed slaves. It was administered as a dependent of Jamaica until 1962, when Jamaica voted for independence. To this day, the Cayman Islands remain a British Crown Colony.

Local holidays: the Queen's Birthday (second Monday in April), Discovery Day (May 18), Constitution Day (July 6) and Remembrance Day (November 6).

This neck of the Western Caribbean is a good place to read *The Far Tortuga* by Peter Matthiessen. It's a brief slice of life as impoverished Cayman turtle

divers face the last days of fishing by sailing schooner. "Sign of the times, Mon!"

Isla Providencia

The island of Providencia (Heaven) lies only 55 n.m. NNE of her bigger sister, Isla San Andrés. Cabo Gracias a Dios is about 175 n.m. NW of here. The Panama Canal lies about 280 n.m. SSE.

Although Providencia and San Andrés are closer to Honduras and Nicaragua, both islands and their off-lying cays belong to distant Colombia in South America. Spanish is the official language, but English is also fairly common.

You may first think of these beautiful islands as twins, but we agree with the locals who insist that Providencia is the more laid-back baby sister. Mountainous little Providencia measures only 4 n.m N-S and 2.5 n.m. E-W. San Andrés is broader but lower. However, official clearance can be made at either island's main port.

Providencia's islanders are genuinely friendly to visitors. Their first greeting of any cruising yacht is usually, "Welcome to our island!" Business owners may offer to show you around town – or you can get a taxi to glimpse the whole island in less than an hour. With its population of only 4,800, this island is a tropical paradise unspoiled by tourism – a very rare thing in the Caribbean.

Santa Catalina Harbor

Providencia is connected by a low wooden foot bridge off its NW corner to smaller but hilly Isla Santa Catalina (about .75 of a mile square), and generally they're thought of together as Providencia.

Providencia's only wharf and anchorage is Santa Catalina Harbor. The harbor lies south and SE of Isla Santa Catalina and west of Providencia's main town, Isabel. The small harbor is well protected from prevailing NE Trade Winds. Although the anchorage is open to the west, only very rarely do local winds blow from that direction.

You will enter the harbor by coming around Isla Santa Catalina's west and south sides. The 600' long concrete wharf (9' of water alongside) is busy with small fishing and cargo boats. The passenger ferry from San Andrés arrives two or three times a week,

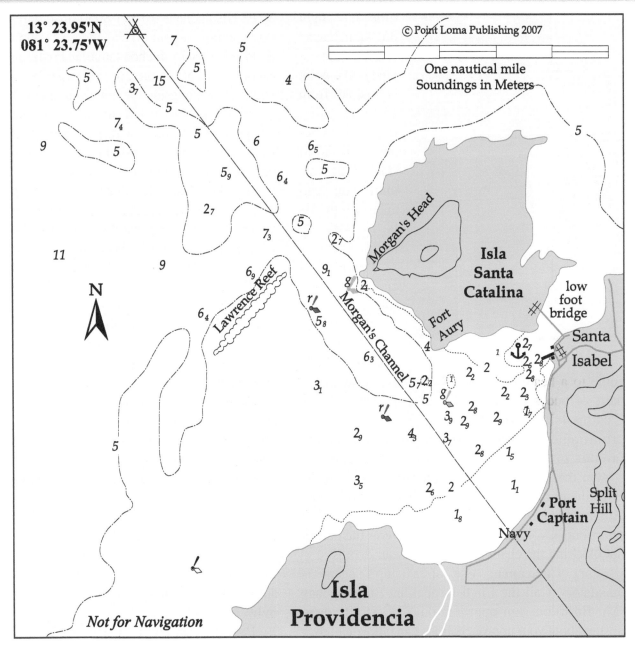

13° 23.95'N
081° 23.75'W

© Point Loma Publishing 2007

One nautical mile
Soundings in Meters

N

Morgan's Head

Isla
Santa
Catalina

low
foot
bridge

Santa
Isabel

Fort
Aury

Lawrence Reef

Morgan's Channel

Split
Hill

Port
Captain

Navy

Isla
Providencia

Not for Navigation

and from Isabel, a paved road circles most of the island.

Approaches: The south end of the 30-n.m. N-S Quito Sueño Banks (about 14°29.2'N, 81°08.2'W) lies about 50 n.m. north of Providencia. Quito Sueño means Quit Dreaming – translated as "set your depth sounder alarm."

Seranna Banks are about 100 n.m. NE of Providencia. About 90 n.m. east of Providencia is Roncador Bank. A *"roncador"* is someone who snores – signifying that these shallow coral banks gurgle and spout.

All three of these broad offshore banks are owned by Colombia and patrolled by naval gunships. However, rumors of drug smuggling persist, so we suggest yatistas use caution or avoid these banks.

Providencia's 1,200' central peak makes a good radar target. Providencia's entire north, east and south sides are shielded in breaking coral reefs, and its west side is mostly foul with shoals and isolated corals. The only approach to the harbor and anchorage is a narrow natural channel coming in from the NW side.

If your approaching from the north, you'll see 15-mile Cayo Palma Light (13°24.0'N, 81°22.1'W) on a coral cluster about 7 n.m. inside the north reef, which extends 8 n.m. north of the island. Cayo Palma (close off Isla Santa Catalina) is about 1.4 n.m. due east of the Providencia sea buoy. (See below.)

If you're arriving from the south or SW, an 18-

mile nav light on Manchancel Hill on the island's SW point is visible from 157° to 318°. But the safer approach is to stay well off until you can approach the island's NW corner.

Providencia sea buoy rides at GPS 13°23.95'N, 18°23.75'W.

From there, come to a heading of 143°M and pass between the pairs of buoys that take you close aboard of Santa Catalina Island and Morgan's Head, the rocky prominence that looks like a profile of the infamous pirate who raided from this island.

On the bow, you'll see a prominent cleft in the ridgeline of the main island; the charts call this Split Hill, but the locals call it Morgan's Ass. After the last set of buoys you may anchor anywhere in the harbor not blocking the channel, but watch your depths.

Port Clearance: Use of a ship's agent is mandatory. Call the English-speaking Bush Agency (Mr. Bush) on your approach on VHF 16. If you're unsure about your approach, Bush can talk you in over VHF. His phone is (6) 334-8050 Bush will inform the Port Captain of your arrival and give you instructions as to whether to anchor (smaller boats) and dinghy ashore north of the pier, or (for larger boats) to bring your vessel alongside the town's municipal pier.

If you're instructed to come to the pier (9' alongside), it requires a turn to port. Because of a shoal, you need to keep slightly right of a straight line between the pier and the last set of buoys.

The Port Captain monitors VHF 16 and 24, and he has a repeater on the island's highest peak with a range of 60 n.m., enabling him to communicate with Isla San Andrés. Port clearance is easy and inexpensive, and the officials are very friendly.

Local Services: You can fuel at Providencia, but you can't be in a hurry. All supplies come into the island by barge or boat from Isla San Andrés, 55 n.m. to the south, so you might have to wait a couple of days. They will bring it down to the pier by tank truck or you can jerry jug smaller quantities.

At the head of the pier is a bank, but it doesn't exchange US dollars, and traveler's checks are not accepted anywhere on the island. The bank's cash machine accepts Visa/MC for cash advances. We have exchanged US dollars for Colombian pesos with various merchants.

The island's few grocery stores have limited supplies, but by visiting all the stores you can get by just fine. Fresh fruits and veggies arrive by boat from Costa Rica once a week. A handful of restaurants dot the harbor – none of them great but the price is right.

Providencia's paved airstrip is only 1,500 meters in length, but it has daily flights in small planes to and from Isla San Andrés, where you can connect to Miami once a week.

Rented motor scooters are a quick and easy way to tour the whole island of Providencia in a couple hours.

Take a walk for about a mile and visit the ruins of the old fort that protected the harbor. Cross the low wooden footbridge

Bush is the yacht agent on Isla Providencia, here waiting at the dinghy dock with VHF to talk you in.

Johnny Cay on north approach to Isla San Andrés is inside the reef.

to Santa Catalina Island and head SW along the waterfront to the end of the path. Then climb the hill through the jungle. Old canon still overlook the entrance channel.

Free Town is the village SW of Isabel, cut through by Bowdon Gully. The half-mile wide bay off Free Town is sheltered but less than 6' deep. If a marina ever were to be built at Providencia, this probably would be the spot.

Continuing around the island counter clockwise you'll encounter the low-lying village of Agua Dulce, where galleons once anchored to row in for fresh water from the mountain streams. Bottom House is the good sized settlement on the SE end, then the small communities of Smooth Water Bay, Rocky Point and Smith Bay. These four clusters of homes also have about a dozen Mom-and-Pop hotels for scuba divers who fly in to explore the western reef. Pangas launch from small boat houses on the beach. Boxon is the village just east of Isabel, facing Cayo Congrejo and a series of close-in reef segments.

Diving: The 15-n.m. of coral reef that circle Providencia provide snorkeling and scuba diving that are absolutely superb – lots of colorful reef fish and exotic fauna not found elsewhere. Providencia's reefs have recently been declared an Underwater Nature Preserve, so look and take photos, but don't hunt. Only locals may take the delicious native conk (*strombus gigas*), lobsters (*panulirus argus*), and only during certain seasons.

Local Pirates: "*Piratas en Santa Catalina*" is a short historical novel about Providencia's pirate history and racial mixtures, by local author Jaime Vasquez M. Providencia has been populated by various Caribe tribes, English pirates, Spanish colonists and freed African slaves. Several gift shops in Isabel have this interesting little book, and the Spanish version is good practice.

Isla San Andrés

The larger island sister, San Andrés (pronounced "*AHN-drayz*") also lies directly on the Western Caribbean route, making it another logical stop for rest, fuel and refuge – but you probably won't need to stop at both. A ship's agent is required for a stop here, but pilotage into the harbor is optional for recreational boats.

San Andrés is as beautiful an island as will be found anywhere in the world. Its low palm-covered plateau and transparent blue-green waters are surrounded by coral reefs and isolated cays fringed with tall coconut palms swaying in the Trade Winds.

Like Providencia, San Andrés is owned by Colombia and has friendly locals, but here tourism is much more developed. San Andrés is to mainland

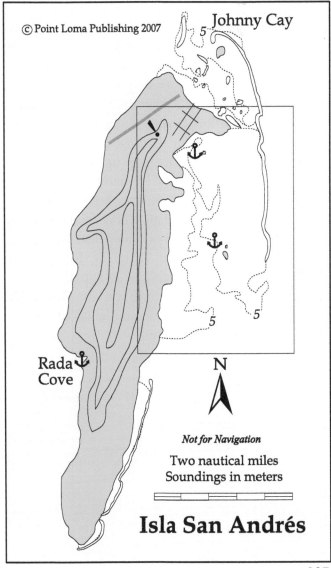

© Point Loma Publishing 2007

Johnny Cay

Rada Cove

N

Not for Navigation

Two nautical miles
Soundings in meters

Isla San Andrés

Fuel dock at Nene's Marina is also charter dock, not very secure.

Colombia what Hawaii is to the US – a favorite vacation getaway.

For yatistas, San Andrés has a larger harbor than Providencia and direct international flights. But if you need emergency parts and can make it to Panama, that's usually your better option.

Bahía de San Andrés

The harbor of San Andrés is on the island's NE side, but it's sheltered behind a dangerous reef and reached by a well marked channel. Formerly the harbor wharfs were used primarily by small cargo ships and commercial fishing boats. One small marina has diesel, and 2 other even smaller marinas are handy for shallow-draft boats or dinghy landing. Wharves and passenger loading docks are being renovated in the harbor to keep up with the cruise ships now anchoring outside the harbor.

Approaches: Isla San Andrés lies 55 n.m. SSW of Isla Providencia, 215 n.m. NNW of the Panama Canal and 110 n.m. ENE of Bluefields, Nicaragua. The radar-target peaks of Cayos de Este Sureste (12°24.0'N, 81°27.0'W) are about 20 n.m. ESE of San Andrés, and a racon B (dah, di, di, dit) also marks this approach. Cayos Albuquerque lie about 25 n.m. south and SSW of San Andrés.

Although the harbor is on the NE corner of the island, a direct approach from the north is impossible due to the large reef that encircles the harbor. Several wrecks high and dry on San Andrés Reef are a good reminder, as well as a good visual landmark. No matter which direction you're traveling, an approach from the south or SE end of San Andrés is safer.

Our GPS approach waypoint about a quarter mile SE of the San Andrés sea buoy is 12°23.2'N, 81°41.2'W. If you've opted to hire a pilot, he or they will board you here and guide you through 2.5 n.m. of coral shoals into the harbor and anchorage. But the buoys have been upgraded and are pretty clear.

Ship's Agent: Because this is part of Colombia, you must hire a ship's agent to handle your port clearance here. Since the death of friend Livingston, we use and recommend Rene of the Serrana Agency. You should begin calling the agency on VHF 16 when you enter range.

Call "Rene at Serrana Agency" in English on VHF 16. He will initiate and then perform your port clearance, arrange fuel and whatever you need. Since he carries a hand-held VHF when away from his office, you may have to be close and on the east side of the island in order to reach him. But Nene's Marina will hear your call and find Rene for you. FMI, phone Rene at the Serrana Agency (578) 512-04628.

Port Clearance: You must have a Zarpe from your last port. Capitania hours are M-F, 8-12, 2-5. This is not the cheapest place to visit in the Caribbean. But San Andres and Providencia are stratigically located for this route.

Colombian Coast Guard patrol boats fuel up at Nene's Marina.

yatista. For details, phone (578) 512-3234 .

If Thomas Livingston is not available, the other is Serrana Agency, also on VHF 16. FMI, phone Rene (578) 512-04628.

Anchorage: Visiting yachts must first come into the upper harbor while port clearance is performed. Vessels deeper than 6' draft will anchor east of the commercial piers. Shallower boats can anchor in 12' to 15' of water in the north end of the harbor, but beware of a couple shoals that uncover at low tide, some with shipwrecks marking them – some without. From the main anchorage you can not reach Johnny Cay off the northern part of the island except by dinghy or by going outside the reef and around.

After you're cleared in, you can ask permission from the Port Captain to move to any of the other anchorages.

One popular spot within the harbor reef is just NW of Cayo Cordoba (12°33.2'N, 81°41.4'W), also called Haynes Cay, which is about a half mile north of the sea buoy. Anchor in 15' of turquoise water over gray-white coral sand. An aquarium and water park on this spot brings tourists and jet boats by day.

Rada Cove is on the SW side of Isla San Andrés. This small but sheltered anchorage has a landing dock and a few hotels, and a Colombian Army sentry routinely searches visitors. Apparently smugglers would also like to use this cove.

Berth: If your boat draws 6' or less, you can Med-moor at Nene's Marina (pronounced "NAY-nayz") on the north shore of the harbor anchorage. Nene's has standard shore power hookups.

CAUTION: Avoid problems by not leaving a vessel unattended in San Andrés, and allow no one aboard but officials and known friends. The open but illegal use of cocaine and marijuana is widespread, and smuggling intrigues abound.

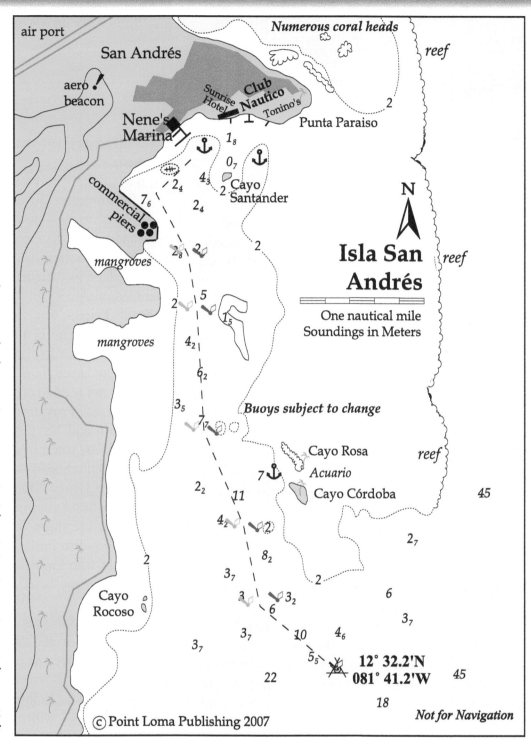

Rada Cove on SW side of Isla San Andrés.

Club Nautico lies NE of Nene's, or just east of tall Sunrise Hotel (most expensive hotel on the island). Club Nautico berths mostly water-ski and jet boats, but yatistas often make arrangements to use their dinghy dock for shore access. Their shore facilities are much nicer and more secure than Nene's.

Tonito's Marina just east of Club Nautico has been for local sportfishing charter boats, but they may have an occasional berth for shallow-draft yachts.

Local Services: The owners of larger yachts may have their agent make arrangements for fuel alongside one of the concrete piers SW of the anchorage. They are high rough concrete, sometimes busy with commercial traffic. The prevailing wind pins you strongly down against the pier, so use fender boards and fenders to avoid damage.

Otherwise, for most cruising boats Nene's Marina has a long fuel hose that reaches anywhere in the marina. If you're not moored in this marina, make arrangements to fuel before bringing your boat over to these crowded docks.

Some boat supplies, repairs and parts are available in Barrio Obrero west of the commercial docks. San Andres has at least 2 propane shops, lots of internet cafes and tackle shops. Scooters are an easy way to see the island, a trip of less than 2 hours. Taxis are readily available.

The divided malecon road that runs past Nene's Marina continues north into the business part of San Andrés, dominated by the Chamber of Commerce, Government Palace, restaurants, hotels, casinos, jewelry and dress stores, dive shops and banks. San Andres is no longer duty free, but it's a shopaholics' delight.

The island has flights to Colombia, Panama and other Central American capitals.

Side Trips: For longer-range cruising, try Cayos Albuquerque to the south. To the north lies Isla Providencia (described above), which is less developed and even more beautiful than San Andrés. Boaters do not need to check in at San Andrés before stopping to visit Providencia; Providencia has its own Port Captain and Navy base. With good navigation gear and skills, you might also check out the cays of Roncador, Quito Sueño Bank and Serrana Bank.

History: Henry Morgan used this island, like Providencia, as a base from which to raid the passing Spanish treasure ships. San Andrés was first settled in 1629 by English Puritans and later by planters and woodcutters who brought slaves from Jamaica. The descendants of the latter are the majority of present inhabitants.

Isla San Andrés was awarded to Spain in 1786, but in 1821 after the Spanish-American Wars of Independence it became part of Colombia – 440 n.m. away.

Until the 1980s, Colombia's mainland government had little to do with these two islands. Their residents remained English-speaking and Protestant. However in recent years island schools no longer teach English.

Little Corn Islanders arrive by ferry panga from Big Corn Island.
Photo by Willey Seven.

Corn Islands, Nicaragua

Little Corn Island, Big Corn Island and Blowing Rock are known as the Corn Islands, spreading NNE to SSW over about 18 n.m. In about the middle of the chain, Big Corn Island lies about 78 n.m. ESE from the south tip of Isla San Andrés and about 28 n.m SE from Punta Set Net, Nicaragua, and about 130 n.m. north of Puerto Limón, Costa Rica.

Big Corn Island (pop. 8,000) has anchorage with shelter from moderate NE Trades, a small diesel dock, a patrol base of the Nicaraguan Armada, several diving and fishing resorts and flights from Managua.

Approach: When in VHF range of Big Corn Island, hail "Pasenic Corn Island" on VHF 16, and port officials will give directions or escort you into Southwest Bay anchorage. From the SE, avoid Blowing Rock located 6.3 n.m. SE of the south end of Big Corn Island.

Anchorage: Anchorage is possible in Southwest Bay (12°09.31'N, 83°04.54'W) in 26' to 30' of water located, surprise, off the SW corner of Big Corn Island. Also, anchorage is reported at Brig Bay, the smaller indent on the west side of Big Corn, in 30' to 36' of water. In periods of calm, anchorage is reported off the SE side of Big Corn.

At Little Corn, the only anchorage is in Pelican Bay on the SW side of Little Corn.

Port Clearance: This is not a port of entry into Nicaragua. However, port officials at Big Corn welcome yachts in transit to stop for rest, shelter, fuel and to visit the island. They will meet you at the main pier.

Local Services: The main pier, CAF Dock (12' at the end), at the head of Southwest Bay on Big Corn provides diesel and ice for the shrimping fleet, also off loads fishing boats for

Map: Corn Islands, Nicaragua. Five Nautical Miles. Soundings in Meters. © Point Loma Publishing 2007. Little Corn Is., Big Corn Island, Scylla Rock, 10 meters, 20 meters, reef, 12° 10.0'N 083° 00.0'W. Not for Navigation.

the nearby cannery. Near that dock is a smaller pier (dinghy landing) for fishing and diving excursion boats.

Taxi rides are $1. Ashore are 2 groceries, many small resorts & restaurants, hospital, airport, etc. Casa Canada Resort overlooking Southwest Bay is owned by Canadians and welcomes yatistas to their restaurant and hotel. Ferry service to mainland Nicaragua is irregular.

Departure: Identify and avoid Blowing Rock, 6.8 n.m. SSE of the south end of Big Corn Island. It rises only about 4' above sea level at MLW, and a blow hole in its center occasionally spouts like a whale, but in big seas Blowing Rock is difficult to see. A 30' bank surrounds the north side of Blowing Rock.

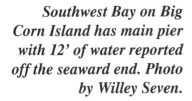

Southwest Bay on Big Corn Island has main pier with 12' of water reported off the seaward end. Photo by Willey Seven.

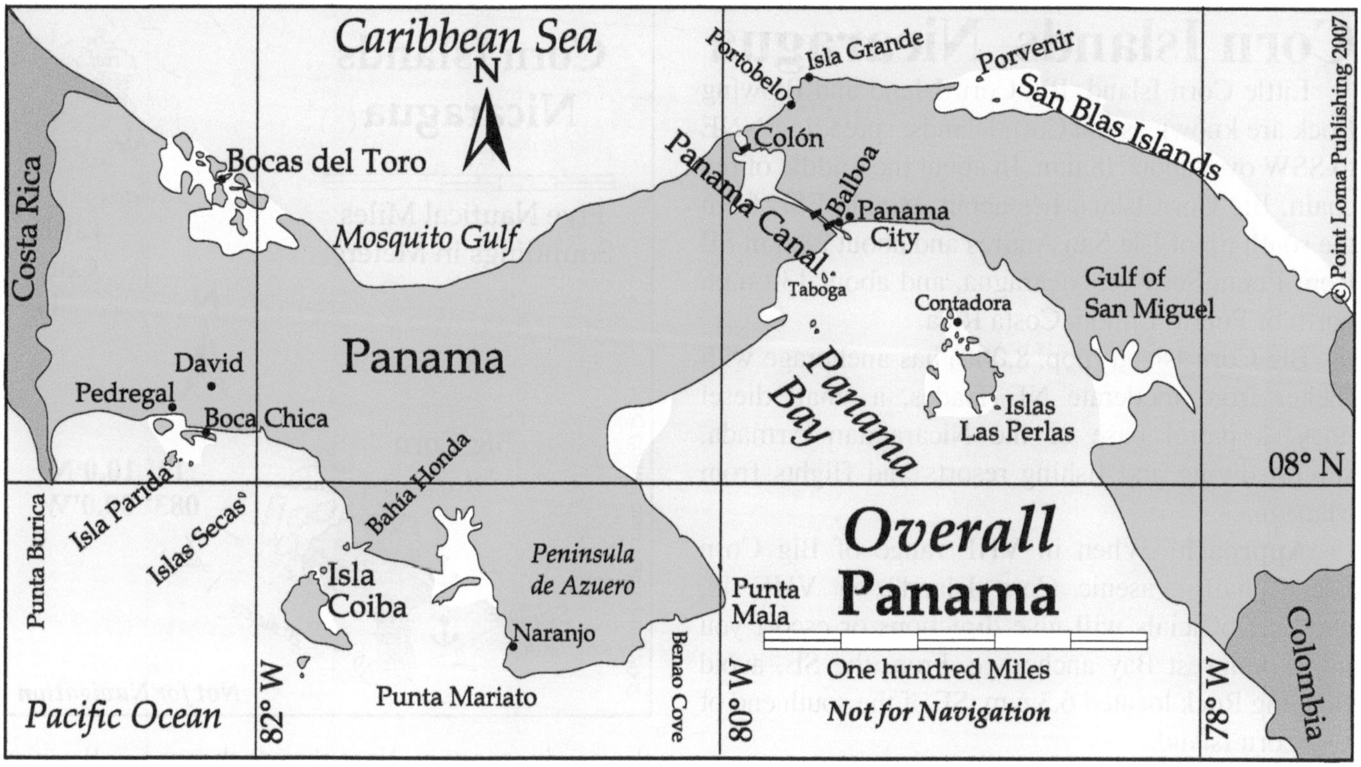
Caribbean Sea
N
Bocas del Toro
Mosquito Gulf
Costa Rica
Panama
David
Pedregal
Boca Chica
Isla Parida
Islas Secas
Bahía Honda
Isla Coiba
Peninsula de Azuero
Naranjo
Punta Mariato
Punta Burica
Pacific Ocean
82° W
Benao Cove
80° W
Portobelo
Isla Grande
Porvenir
San Blas Islands
Colón
Panama Canal
Balboa
Panama City
Taboga
Contadora
Gulf of San Miguel
Panama Bay
Islas Las Perlas
08° N
Overall Panama
Punta Mala
One hundred Miles
Not for Navigation
78° W
Colombia
© Point Loma Publishing 2007

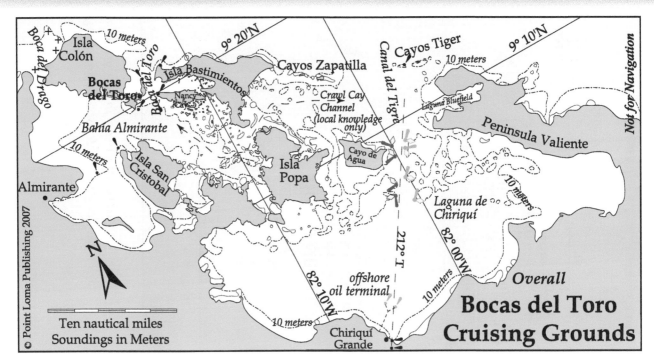

© Point Loma Publishing 2007

Ten nautical miles
Soundings in Meters

**Overall
Bocas del Toro
Cruising Grounds**

We think of this as the Southwestern Caribbean, but to Panamanians it's called the Atlantic side – a holdover from the glorious canal-building days. However, we respect local customs and preferences. On this side of Panama, we'll look first at the primary cruising grounds east to west: Bocas del Toro, Portobelo, Islas Lintón and Grande and the San Blas Islands. Then we'll hop back to Colón and Bahía Limón at the entrnace to the Panama Canal.

Bocas del Toro

The entire Republic of Panama is shaped like an S lying on its side. Along Panama's NW shores is the sparsely populated province of Bocas del Toro (Mouths of the Bull) and the 3 large bays: Bahía Bocas del Toro, Bahía Almirante (Admiral) and Chiriquí Lagoon. Taken together, this is considered the Bocas del Toro cruising grounds.

The heart of this cruising ground is the town of Bocas del Toro (pop. 3,500), called Bocas Town. It's the capital of Bocas del Toro Province. For yatistas, the Bocas Town offers 2 marinas, a fuel dock, sheltered anchorage and good provisions. Nearby you'll find scads of jungle-clad islands, pristine anchorages and dinghy coves, deep channels, national parks, wildlife preserves, Chiriquí villages and resort developments.

November and June are the best cruising months, when rainy season has ended or not quite begun, yet the Trade Winds aren't in highest gear. However, the

6-month period from December through May is also very pleasant - if well ventilated.

Bocas is south of the Atlantic hurricane belt, but summer brings frequent rainstorms with intense squalls, lightning and thunder. They roll in from the ocean, pile up against the Cordillera de Talamanca behind Bocas and deluge the coast.

SE of the Bocas region, the coast curves south then north, forming the huge sheltered Gulf of Mosquitoes – named for good reason. Mosquitoes carrying yellow fever killed thousands of workers during initial efforts to dig the Panama Canal. Yellow fever is no longer a problem in Panama, but mosquitoes still are.

Approach: The Bocas del Toro region lies about 190 n.m. SSW of Isla San Andres and 140 due west of the Panama Canal. Bocas Town covers the SE appendage of 6-mile long Isla Colón, which is 400' high and protrudes about 5 n.m. from the low coast north of it – a good landmark. Isla Colón lies 60 n.m. SE of Puerto Limón, Costa Rica, and 20 n.m. SE of the unmarked Costa Rica-Panama border.

To reach Bocas Town and the marina area, use the Canal de Bocas del Toro, which lies between Isla Colón and Isla Bastimentos. (Don't confuse this with the Boca del Drago on the west side of Isla Colón, which is favored by ships heading to Puerto Almirante.)

Our GPS approach position 09°22.0'N, 82°12.8'W is about .75 of a mile WNW of Bastimentos Island's NW tip, called Cabo Toro. The western face of Isla

213

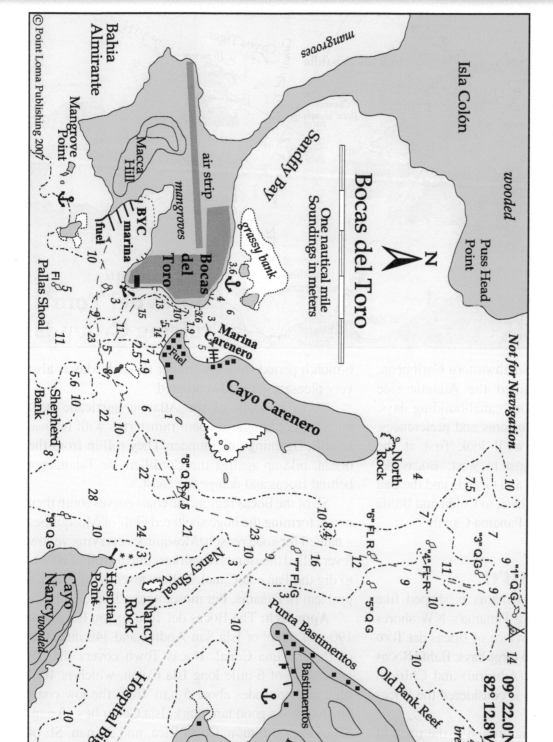

Red buoy #6 east of North Rock at north end of Cayo Carenero.

Yellow buoy: Boca del Toro is to port (antenna), Carenero Cay is to starboard.

© Point Loma Publishing 2007

Isla Colón

Puss Head Point

wooded

Bahia Almirante

Mangrove Point

Macca Hill

BYC marina

fuel

air strip

mangroves

Sandy Bay

grassy bank

Bocas del Toro

Bocas del Toro

One nautical mile
Soundings in meters

N

Not for Navigation

Fl 5
Pallas Shoal

10

3

15 13 7

9 11

5 8

5.6 10
Shepherd 8
Bank

23

2.5 1.9

Marina Carenero
Fuel

5

Cayo Carenero

22

6

North Rock

"6" FL R

"8" Q R 7.5

"7" Fl G

Nancy Shoal

Nancy Rock

Hospital Point

Cayo Nancy
wooded

Hospital Bight

10

wooded

Isla Bastimentos

Punta Bastimentos

Bastimentos

Old Bank Reef

"5" Q G

"3" Q G

"4" Fl R

"1" Q G

14

09° 22.0'N
82° 12.8'W

breakers

Cabo
Toro

Red Frog Beach Marina on Isla Bastimentos opened in 2010. Call (507) 6910-8700, or VHF 68 for approach instructions & slip reservations.

Bocas Yacht Club & Marina has a fuel dock south of the slips.

Colón is about 1.75 miles to the west of this position. Carenero Cay (2 n.m. long) lies between the two larger islands, and a shoal juts 350 yards off its east side. The Canal de Bocas del Toro (10' to 15' deep) runs along the east side of Carenero Cay just east of its shoal.

Earthquakes in 1991 changed the bottom, so the channel buoys shown on NIMA Chart 28052 (Canal de Bocas del Toro) aren't accurate. We use the following GPS waypoints courtesy of Marina Carenero and Capt. Tom Knueppel, and we've verified them ourselves:

R-2	09°22.074'N by 82°12.771'W
G-3	09°21.762'N by 82°13.057'W
R-4	09°21.517'N by 82°13.211'W
R-6	09°21.259'N by 82°13.268'W
G-7	09°20.924'N by 82°13.310'W
R-8	09°20.451'N by 82°13.488'W

Berthing: (1.) Bocas Yacht Club & Marina (also called Bocas Marina) has a fuel dock and 100 full-service floating slips for boats to 100' LOA and 10' draft (15' of water at MLW). This modern facility is located at Bocas Town, in the quarter-mile wide cove just past the big ferry pier on the south tip of Bocas Town.

To reach Bocas Yacht Club & Marina, pass the red buoy located about 350 yards off the south tip of Carenero Cay, keeping the buoy to starboard. See chartlet. Continue about 600 yards WSW to the yellow and black buoy (09°20.2'N by 82°14.8'W) off the south end of Bocas Town, then another 600 yards

Marina Carenero on Careening Cay is popular with long-term cruisers.

NW into the marina. Bocas Marina monitors VHF 12, 69 and 16, so call for directions when in range.

Slip fees include town water, and the 30- and 50-amp shore power is metered. Ashore are showers, laundry, a restaurant, a gazebo hangout on the point and some apartments behind the docks. The marina can handle your domestic port clearance, baby-sit your boat while you're out of town, provision it from a gourmet shop in town and line up minor repairs in the slip. FMI on Bocas Yacht Club & Marina, visit www.BocasMarina.com or phone (507) 757-9800.

(2.) Marina Carenero is in the cove on the SW side of Carenero Cay, but to reach it, you go around that island's south end. See chartlet. After passing the red buoy located about 350 yards off the south tip of Carenero Cay, aim toward the big ferry pier at the south tip of Bocas Town. You'll then coast up the channel off the east side of Bocas Town (15' of water) until you have the landmark microwave tower on your port beam. From there, head ENE toward Carenero Cay, aiming for the 2-story house above Marina Carenero. The center of their cove is 16.5' deep, and the slips have about 13' of water. Marina Carenero monitors VHF 68, so call when you're within range.

Marina Carenero has 26 full-service slips to 60' LOA. The lighted finger piers have 120/240-volt (60 Hz), 120-amp shore power and water. Ashore the marina has showers, laundry, an Internet hookup and can perform monthly maintenance for absentees.

Mary Robertson manage this marina. As former cruisers, she and Mack built this marina as their children grew up on Carenero Cay. The Robertsons are selling their other marina on the Pacific coast of Panama, at Boca Chica, as we go to press.

Marina Carenero is the designated Seven Seas Cruising Station for Bocas del Toro, so they'll forward free information whether you're planning to stay here or not. Translated as Careening Cay, the island was named by Spanish explorers who regularly careened their ships on the eastern shoal. FMI on Marina Carenero, visit www.CareeningCay.com or email MarinaCarenero@hotmail.com or (506) 757-9242.

(3.) Red Frog Beach Marina on the S side of Isla Bastimentos is open, has 100 slips, restaurant; (507) 6910-8700 or www.RedFrogResort.com/marina

Small private docks and boat houses line Bocas Town, the south end of Carenero Cay and the inner cove of Bastimentos village – useful for dinghy landing (ask permission) and sometimes as long-term

*Waterfront along Bocas Town
on south end of Isla Colón.*

berths without shore services.

Anchorages: The 3 most useful anchorages near the marinas are (1.) just south of Marina Carenero inside the same bight on the SW side of Cayo Carenero, (2.) off the NE side of Bocas Town but south of the two grassy-bank islets, (3.) close SE of Bocas Yacht Club & Marina docks. Both town anchorages have periods of wakes and noise, and the southern one has some mosquitoes when the wind drops.

Along the SW side of Isla Colón anchorage is found in Big Bight, in the slot east of Conch Point, in Ground Creek and Knapp's Hole. Probably 100 anchorages are found in remote coves scattered around Bahía Almirante and Laguna Chiriquí. But you'll also find lots of shoals and coral heads, so explore with caution.

Port Clearance: Bocas is a Port of Entry, so you can clear into Panama here. The Capitania overlooks the ferry pier on the south tip of Bocas Town. Hail the Port Captain on VHF 16 as soon as you're in range, and he'll direct you to the present clearance dock. Many yatistas arrive here with a Zarpe from Roatán or San Andrés.

Local Services: Bocas Yacht Club & Marina's fuel dock (6' to 8' depth) is at the south point of the marina, approached from the south end of Bocas Town. FMI, see marinas above. Other fuel docks are on the SE side of Bocas Town and the south tip of Cayo Carenero.

Bocas Town is a pleasant, funky center of services that resonates with reggae and CNN on cable. We found several grocery stores with good provisioning (check out Super Gourmet Grocery & Deli), 2 hardware stores with some marine stuff, dive shops that fill tanks and provide guides. We found lots of eateries; one traditional menu item is rice and beans soaked in coconut milk.

Bocas has a water taxi and car ferry to Almirante on the mainland, where you catch a bus down to David and on to Panama City. Bocas airport has flights from Panama City (one hour) and David (20 minutes) with Aeroperlas (email iflyap@aeroperlas.com) and Mapiex (aero@sinfo.net). Many boaters opt to bus up to Costa Rica and back to renew their visas.

NOTE: If you decide to summer over here from July through October, bring rain awnings and mosquito netting for every portal, lots of mosquito spray, mildew inhibitor and some method of dehumidifying your boat's interior.

History & Culture: Bocas Town is almost entirely of wooden structures. The primary architectural style

*Port Captain's office in Bocas del Toro is
an easy place to clear into Panama.*

Fresh tropical produce arrives at Bocas Town markets by canoe from remote village docks around Bahías Almirante and Chirique.

Afro-Caribe families who settled here from Islas San Andrés and Providencia mostly fished and grew a few kitchen gardens. Agriculture has been based on vast banana plantations and a few coconut groves, but the new economy is based on tourism.

Departure: When it's time to head toward Colón, most yatistas pick a good weather window and make passage.

From the sea buoy outside the Bocas del Toro channel, Isla Escudo de Veraguas lies 45 n.m. ESE. The island is about 180' high, jungle clad, about 2.25 n.m. long. A nav light marks the cays trailing off its east tip, but the north shore is reef bound.

Anchorage with shelter from moderate Trades is possible off Isla Escudo de Veraguas' SW corner (09°05.68'N, 81°34.57'W) and in non-reefy holes along its south side.

is called Caribbean Colónial – a quaint Victorian style modified for tropical comforts, often brightly painted.

Diving tourism is the primary industry, based on tours out to Bastimentos Island National Park, Zapatilla Cays, Crawl Cay, Red Frog Beach and the waters and mangroves that surround the islands. Banana plantations dominate farming and commercial shipping.

Long before Columbus visited here in 1502, this beautiful and fertile region was inhabited by Guaymi, Terraba, Moskito and Changuina tribes, but it was the scene of constant tribal wars that repelled Franciscan missionaries.

During the 1600s and 1700s, the islands of Bocas del Toro and Laguna Chiriquí were havens for British and French Huguenot pirates. The few British and

Portobelo

Portobelo lies 17 n.m. NE of the Atlantic entrance to the Panama Canal. Portobelo is a handy anchorage for boaters awaiting canal transit – and a stepping stone to Isla Lintón and the San Blas Islands. Portobelo is one of our favorite places in Panama, but it has no services to speak of.

Portobelo (beautiful port) is a perfect natural harbor, about a mile long sans the mud flats, providing excellent shelter from the strongest easterly Trade Winds but a bit vulnerable to westerly conditions of rainy season. The large anchorage is surrounded by steep hills and magnificent examples of 17th and 18th century military architecture, built by the Spanish

Chartlet covers next 3 pages.

Map

Portobelo to Isla Grande

Not for Navigation

Los Farallones

09° 37.35'N
79° 35.50'W

Isla Lintón

Isla Grande

Los Mogotes

Panamarina

Puerto Garrote

Salmedina Reef

Playa Blanca

Portobelo

Ensenada Indio

Buenaventura

N

79° 40'W

09° 35'W

Five nautical miles
Soundings in Meters

© Point Loma Publishing 2007

Portobelo town spreads around historic Treasure House and one of 4 forts around the bay.

crown to protect its trade and shipments of gold ripped off from the natives.

Port Clearance: Portobelo was recently made a Port of Entry, so new Migracion and Aduana offices should open soon.

Approach: When coming from the Panama Canal, we avoid shipping traffic by not going into the Bahía Las Minas area – an oil refinery port. But about 2 n.m. NE of the entrance to Bahía Las Minas, a pleasant fair-weather anchorage (09°25.45'N, 79°84.22'W) is found off the south side of Isla Naranjo Abajo. Avoid the reefs surrounding the N, W and SW sides of this island and its twin, Isla Naranjo Arriba. Only 2 n.m. SW of the entrance to Portobelo is Bahía Buenaventura, with a rich history and small anchorage.

Breakers surround Salmedina Reef, which lies .75 of a mile west of steep-sided Punta Mantilla (09°34'N, 79°41'W), the northern arm of Portobelo Bay. We find deep water halfway between Salmedina and Isla Drake. The south point of Portobelo's entrance is low Punta Coco, and this mile-wide entrance quickly narrows to about half a mile.

Anchorages: Thirty cruising boats may anchor in here. The quietest spot is along the north wall of the bay, in the indent half a mile east of steep Iron Castle Point. You can drop the hook in about 30' of water over soft mud and sand. From here you can hike up the middle ravine to a small dam and pool.

If you don't mind sight-seers and wakes from pangas and excursion boats, you can anchor along the south side of the bay below the village and forts in about 30' of water. This gives quicker shore access to town.

Or, anchor toward the E end of the bay, off the mud shoal containing Careening Cove and Rio Cascajal. To stay off the shelf, anchor in 30' to 46' of water. Lots of

dinghy docks, but small tips insure security.

Local Services: Good cell phone coverage. The brightly painted bus round-trips to Colón twice daily, 2 hrs each way. It also runs to an El Rey Mercado in Sabanilla, which may be handier for just groceries. Portobelo has convenience stores and laundry.

For eats, Captain Jack's Canopy Bar overlooks the harbor, has WiFi and VHF, often hosts the morning cruisers' net; backpackers' hostel. Portobelo has a popular hot-dog stand and an organic juice bar-art gallery combo, a tiny artist community, but less in rainly season. Fantasy sculptures line walkways. The Colon road continues to Juan Gallego and Puerto Garrote near Isla Lintón, ends at Isla Grande.

History & Culture: Columbus anchored here in 1502 but didn't name it. When the Spanish were searching for an eastern terminus of the land route across the Isthmus of Panama, they eventually discovered Portobelo. For decades, this bay was the Pacific embarkation point for mountains of stolen

Guard towers and canon overlook the anchorage at Portobelo.

Inca gold and "taxes" en route to the coffers of Spain.

Sir Frances Drake loved to sack the Customs House here, and lurking at Buenaventura and Playa Blanca he ambushed many gold ships. El Draco died of dysentery in 1596, reportedly buried at sea in a lead coffin a short distance off the harbor entrance, probably near what's called Isla Drake. Another famous pirate, Henry Morgan, once captured Portobelo. Forts 300 yrs old, gun turrets are fun to explore.

For more than 200 years, Portobelo was lost to the civilized world; during construction of the Panama Canal, stone blocks from Portobelo's Iron Castle were barged out and dumped in the ocean to form the foundation of Colón harbor's center breakwater. Portobelo's 900 residents (West Indian, native Panamanian and a few Kuna) live a simple existence amid the ruins of 300-yr old forts.

Panamarina: Between Portobelo & Isla Linton but still inside the national park, this nifty low-key marina (09°36.90'N, 79°36.70'W) has 37 eco moorings, shore facilities. See Approaches next column.

Isla Lintón

Isla Lintón (aka Juan Joaquin Island or Isla Grande Resort) is an uninhabited island, well-protected anchorage and popular yatista hangout located 8.5 n.m. NE from Portobelo or about 25 n.m. NE of Colón breakwater

Panamarina lies between Portobelo and Isla Linton.

Long before the Panama Canal Yacht Club in Colón was destroyed by the ports company, some far sighted club members built an annex here to serve as an alternative. Good thing. Since then, Shelter Bay Marina across Limón Bay has become a more practical place for yatistas to prepare for transit or to enter the Caribbean. But this remains a popular cruising gunk hole away from the busy canal area.

Approaches: From Portobelo, it's about 5.5 n.m. up to Punta Cacique via the north side of Dos Hermanas Islands (aka Tres Marias), then 1.5 n.m. ESE to the west side of Isla Lintón. Our GPS position a quarter mile north of Punta Cacique is 09°37.35'N, 79°35.5'W. Avoid the reef jutting about a third of a mile NE from the bulk of Punta Cacique.

(En route to Lintón, wedged into the east end of the narrow slot .75 of a mile SSE from Punta Cacique, Panamarina moorings advertise as long-term boat storage. This is a very sheltered spot, but breakers line the circuitous path past Cacique village, so hail Panamarina on VHF 69 for their tender's guidance. Or call Panamarina (507) 6680-2003.)

The lighted Los Farrallones rocks (09°39'N, 79°38'W) and their adjacent Sucio Shoal lie 1.75 n.m. NW of Punta Cacique, and the smaller submerged La Lavandero lies about half a mile north of the entrance to the Lintón anchorage. You'll come just east of Roca Pelado, which is usually the breaking east end of the Mamey Cays. Our GPS position in the entrance to the Lintón anchorage is 09°37.09'N, 79°35.55'W.

In flat weather, approach is possible

Approach to Isla Lintón anchorage from NW side of the island (right side of photo).

Isla Grande (lower left) shelters this anchorage a few miles east of Isla Lintón.

from the east side of Isla Lintón, then weave between 3 reefs at the island's south end to reach the sheltered anchorages.

Anchorage: We anchor SW of the island or in the 200-yard-wide slot between Isla Lintón's SW side and the mainland, anywhere in 20' to 40' over sand. The dink dock is on the island, and the owners usually allow yatistas to use it. We've seen 20 cruising boats swinging here at a time.

Local Services: Along the mainland to the south are the villages of Juan Joaquin Gallego and Puerto Garrote, where you can get basic provisions and water, sample the cantinas and catch a bus that runs 3/day to Colón. PCYC's annex is in the SE end of the little bay about half a mile south of the anchorages.

Isla Grande

At 2 n.m. NE of Isla Lintón you come to Isla Grande, which has a nav light on its NE corner. Isla Grande and tiny Islas Tambor and Tamborita off the NE side of Isla Lintón form the northernmost point in Panama. Enjoying the full brunt of the Trades, Isla Grande's east side is famous for surfing competitions.

Home to more than a dozen small hotels and cantinas, the island gets packed with vacationers arriving by bus on weekends. A water taxi runs from the end of the road at La Guayra to the island. Jet boats run at full throttle have reportedly become a nuisance for yatistas anchored here at night or dinghying ashore.

Approach: Our GPS approach waypoint just west of the cove on the SW side of Isla Grande (09°37.61'N, 79°34.43'W) is in the channel between Isla Lintón and Isla Grande. By dinghy, you can get here via the south side of Isla Lintón in 2.5 n.m.

Anchorage: Isla Grande is not as well sheltered as Isla Lintón during any season. Isla Grande's best anchorages are in a cove on its SW side and along its south side in the 400-yard wide channel between the island and mainland. Anchor lights help jet boaters see you at night. However, during rainy season, Isla Grande's anchorages have almost no shelter from westerly conditions.

Departure: Continuing toward the San Blas Islands, avoid Mafu Rocks off Punta Manzanillo, but there's deep water along the north side of Los Mogotes. Passing Isla Mogote Afuera (09°38.24'N, 79°31.30'W) astern, you're in Bahía San Cristóbal. Mark this tiny island as a useful reference.

Escribanos is a tiny but sheltered port between Isla Grande and Porvenir.

En route to San Blas Islands

Nombre de Dios: In the SE corner of Bahía San Cristóbal, a good Trade Wind anchorage is found in historic Bahía Nombre de Dios about 4 n.m. SE of Isla Mogote Afuera; our GPS approach half a mile north of Nombre de Dios is 09°35.85'N, 79°28.59'W.

Green Turtle Bay Marina opened in 2010 inside a sheltered basin less than 3 n.m. E of Nombre de Dios. Green Turtle's basin with 75 slips is entered from the W. Check our UPDATES for more info soon.

Miramar: Fair-weather anchorage is reported at Miramar village, in the mangrove indent along the SW side of non-distinct Punta Cuango. Punta Cuango lies 11.75 n.m. ESE of Isla Mogote Afuera and about 10 n.m. WNW of Bahía Escribanos. (See aerial photo of Escribanos on previous page.) Our GPS position about half a mile north of Punta Cuango is 09°35.18'N, 79°19.17'W. Yatistas anchor SW of this point and may dinghy up the narrow channel to a fuel dock.

From Punta Cuango, it's about 12 n.m. east to the south side of lighted Bajos Escribanos and another 12 n.m. east to the entrance to the San Blas Channel entrance to this cruising ground.

San Blas Islands
(*Kuna Yala*)

This 80-mile swath of picture-perfect islands is what cruising dreams are made of – more than 300 small islands and coco-palm cays, blazing white sand, turquoise waters so clear you can see every link in your chain, 100s of coral reefs for snorkeling – plus exotic natives eager to sell you their handicrafts or fresh catch. You can feast every night on lobster, crab, conch and fish without straining your budget. If you have a watermaker and solar or wind power, you might never find an excuse to wake up from this dream.

But it's not all romantic. Mother Nature and Kuna law rule these waters. Locally, the San Blas islands are called *Kuna Yala*, one of the 3 self-governing *comarcas* or territory of the 50,000 Kuna people, a matriarchal society. They primarily speak *Delugaya*. The women wear long skirts, red & yellow head scarves, gold earrings and nose rings, beads wrapping their legs and blouses built around twin *molas*. (See below.) Very superstitious and formal, the Kuna retain their ancient beliefs and gods.

Kuna law delegates up to 3 *sahilas* or chiefs to govern each of the 40 inhabited islands. Under Kuna law, every island, anchorage, tree, fish, shell and coconut has a rightful Kuna owner, so don't step ashore or take anything from the water without asking permission and paying for it. Not long ago, Kuna law prohibited foreigners from anchoring overnight in the islands except El Porvenir, and any yatista who broke local customs or overstayed his welcome was run out by the *sualipetmar* or Kuna police. Yatistas are still required to ask permission from an island's *congreso* of chiefs to be ashore after dark.

The NE Trades and heavy seas would sweep the San Blas Islands if they weren't kept at bay by the

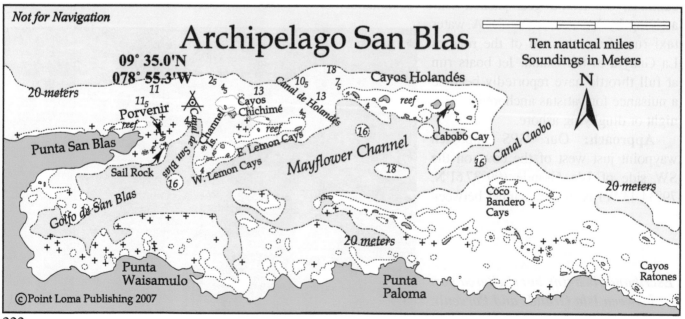

Not for Navigation

Archipelago San Blas

09° 35.0'N
078° 55.3'W

Ten nautical miles
Soundings in Meters

N

20 meters

Porvenir
Punta San Blas
Sail Rock
Golfo de San Blas

Cayos Chichimé
Canal de San Blas
W. Lemon Cays
E. Lemon Cays

Canal de Holandés
Cayos Holandés
reef

Mayflower Channel

Cabobó Cay
Canal Caobo

Coco Bandero Cays

20 meters

Punta Waisamulo
Punta Paloma

Cayos Ratones

©Point Loma Publishing 2007

Looking north, Porvenir is upper right, Wichubhuala is center, Nalunega is on left and barrier reef spans top of photo.

intermittent outer reefs and steep edges of this vast coral shelf. The bottom is usually easy to read with high sun at your back or overhead, so learn your way around before cloudy days or milky-water conditions.

Limited scope: This vast cruising ground spans 213 islands, 30 coral cays and 100s of detached reefs. In truth, we can't begin to do it justice within a guidebook that covers 9 countries and 3,750 miles of coastline. For more detail of the San Blas Islands, I highly recommend Eric Bauhaus' *The Panama Guide*, available at Isla Morada chart store in Balboa.

But to get you launched on your own explorations of the Kuna Yala, we're going to mention El Porvenir and a few initial anchorages and channels in the more popular 20-mile western section.

El Porvenir

Located 37 n.m. east of Isla Grande, 200 n.m. ESE of Cartegena, Colombia, and about 1.25 n.m. east of Punta San Blas, the tiny capital island of El Porvenir (09°33.37'N, 78°56.93'W) lies at the west end of the San Blas Islands (Kuna Yala). Isla El Porvenir (the Future) has a few palm trees and lies about a mile south of the large breaking reef running E-W off Punta San Blas.

El Porvenir is the Port of Entry for the Comarca of Kuna Yala, and you are required to clear in here before visiting any of the islands.

Approach: First-timers should use the deep-water San Blas Channel,

which is 2 n.m. wide at its narrowest (between Sail Rock on the El Porvenir side and Cayo Gallo in the Lemon Cays). To approach the north entrance of the San Blas Channel, stay 3.0 n.m ENE of Punta San Blas and come to a position 2.25 n.m. ESE of Cayos Chichimé. Or come to our GPS position 09°35.0'N, 78°55.3'W.

From there, head SSW for about 2.0 n.m. along the west side of the San Blas Channel, heading toward Sail Rock. You'll run alongside the eastern edge of the reef jutting east from Isla El Porvenir. About half a mile before you would reach Sail Rock (avoid shoals NE of it), take the narrow side channel (23' least depth) that branches SW; this Porvenir Channel curves around the south side of Isla El Porvenir and forms the arrival anchorage.

With local knowledge, a longer and more circuitous path through the reefs NW of El Porvenir is possible.

Anchor: Just off the Porvenir Channel, staying in 20' to 50' of water about 200 yards off Isla El

SW corner of El Porvenir has anchorage, docks and port clearance facilities, also access to the airport.

Porvenir, you can anchor almost anywhere south or SW of the island. Land your dinghy at the main dock on the SW shore. Cruise ships sometimes anchor in the San Blas Channel, shuttling passengers to Isla El Porvenir to buy molas.

Port Clearance: The Port Captain, Immigration and Customs clearance are all accomplished in the airport terminal building just to the right of the dinghy landing. Because El Porvenir is a Port of Entry, you can get cleared into Panama, visas and 3-month cruising permit, but the fee has been higher to clear on weekends, and the Kuna Yala comarca adds a small fee.

Local Services: El Porvenir is tiny, but has a fuel dock, a mini market, a small hotel run by the Kuna islanders, a water taxi service and an airport with one daily flight to Albrook at Panama City. El Porvenir is the best place to meet guests flying in to join you, but if the El Porvenir Hotel here is closed, a larger Hotel Anai is on Nalunega Island less than a mile SW by water taxi, and it has an anchorage off the SW side.

During all February, the Kuna celebrate their 1925 revolution that won them autonomy; special artwork, dances, foods and fermented drinks are part of the ceremonies held on various islands, some open to visitors, some not.

West Lemon Cays
About 2.5 n.m. ESE across the San Blas Channel, the West Lemon Cays are a triangular cluster of more

Molas of the Kuna

Kuna women create and sell their unique "*molas*" – 3-, 4- or 5-layer fabric panels embellished with reverse appliqué and embroidery. The ingenious designs depict scenes from the Kuna's daily life in the Kuna Yala – fishing, marine animals, flowers, jungle birds, religion and children. Molas are made in identical pairs, intended to become the front and back bodice panels of a Kuna blouse, to which a yoke and puffy sleeves of different fabrics will be added later.

The Kuna are a matriarchal society – women are the traders and hold most financial power. Anthropologists believe Kuna women have been tattooing intricate designs on their faces, arms and legs since at least the 1300s. During the 1800s Christian missionaries hoping to clothe and domesticate the rebellious women taught them the European fabric arts of embroidery, appliqué and reverse appliqué that were then so popular in the civilized world. The Kuna women turned their new talents into making mola blouses that carried their traditional designs. However, they still wear gold rings through their noses, wrap their legs in strings of beads and sometimes tattoo their faces.

If you're collecting molas to sell back home, the older molas are more valuable in art galleries. You can distinguish them by their 100% cotton fabrics and threads, possibly a bit worn, and the complete use of hand stitching. The top layer is usually a frame of slightly coarse black or dark red cloth. If mounting behind glass, leave the slightly frayed edges showing.

Newer molas with machine stitching, brighter colors and synthetic fabrics are fun, too. Immediately after the invasion of Panama, I saw molas depicting helicopters zooming low, soldiers marching with guns and troopers parachuting from the sky. The Kuna women said they saw it on satellite TV-CNN, so it's part of their lives. To please the tourists, the market-savvy Kuna women now make pot-holder mitts, eye-glass cases, patch-type emblems and a wide range of useful fabric items. They add mola details to ready-made T-shirts and sport shirts.

Molas can be purchased from Kuna women throughout the canal region at slightly higher prices, because it costs them to travel from home and stay in the cities with relatives. But the best mola deals are struck in the Kuna Yala or San Blas Islands.

Looking SE, Tia Dup (top of photo) lies SE of this snug anchorage in the West Lemon Cays. Mayflower Channel is upper right.

than a dozen islands. The west leg of the triangle runs 2 miles along the east side of the San Blas Channel.

Channel Island (Kagan Dup) lies about in the middle of that leg, and a channel runs ESE along its south side. Anchorage is possible (20' over sand) off the SW side of Channel Island.

Or continue about 800 yards ESE into a narrow channel that quickly turns SSE between 2 reefs jutting from the next 2 islands (Miria Dup to the SW, Nagu Archi Dup to the NE). The anchorage area is nestled between these 2 islands and a third one, Tia Dup, SE of the anchorage.

To exit this anchorage via a continuation of this channel to the south, you'll need to cross a 7' bar. That takes you into the Mayflower Channel, the wide, deep-water passage running generally E-W between the offshore islands and the coastal ones. Otherwise, turn around and retrace your path back to the south side of Channel Island – Kagan Dup. In calm weather, another channel opens north from along the east side of Kagan Dup, but it's quite exposed in north wind.

Cayos Chichimé

At the NE entrance to the San Blas Channel (See El Porvenir above.), you'll find the popular Chichimé Cays. The northern barrier reef shielding both the Chichimé and the East Lemon Cays spreads about 4.5 n.m. WNW to ESE between the San Blas Channel to the west and the Holandes Channel to the east.

But the Cayos Chichimé section alone consists of a 1-mile wide barrier reef (often breaking), the 2 primary islands (Achu Tupu Pipi and

Nalunega village has hotels, small groceries, water taxi.

Achu Tupu Dummat), a sheltered central anchorage and lots of detached reef patches. In heavy Trades, seas thunder onto the barrier reef, yet the anchorage stays smooth.

Cayos Chichimé lie 2.5 n.m. NE from Channel Island in the West Lemon Cays or about 4 n.m. ENE of El Porvenir. Enter the anchorage from the WSW off the San Blas Channel, keeping close south of a detached shoal .25 of a mile west of Achu Tupu Pipi (the smaller NW island) and then keeping on your port side the detached sand-palm islet and connecting submerged reef jutting west off Achu Tupu Dummat (the larger SE island).

Between the 2 Chichimé Cays and the large Icacos Island at the east end of the East Lemon Cays are 13 other cays and numerous reefs (protected by the same barrier reef) spreading south to the Eden Channel. With local knowledge, several other anchorages are found here.

Holandes Cays

Farthest east of the outer cays groups, the 12

Traditional Kuna Yala mode of transportation.

Holandes islands are enmeshed in their northern barrier reef system that stretches 7.5 n.m. E-W, between the Holandes Channel to the west and the Caobos Channel to the SE. Being farther off shore, these islands have deep water close around them, narrowing the margin for anchorage.

In prevailing NE Trades, a small protected shelf is found south of the 2 westernmost islands (Holandes Cay and Walsala Dup), which are connected by reef. Enter from Holandes Channel and anchor off the reef connecting these 2 islands.

Another anchorage is found at 1.75 n.m. farther ESE. Run along the deep south edge of this reef system and anchor in the 200-yard wide bight north of Miria Dia Dup and south of the larger Miria Dup.

At the east end of the Holandes Cays, 3 islands strung N-W form the edge of the barrier reef. In moderate weather, a navigable passage (9.5' of water) running west is found between the large middle island and the smallest northernmost. Less than a quarter mile in you'll find a tranquil anchorage dubbed the Swimming Pool. A more sheltered access route to this anchorage is possible from the SW along the SE side of Caobos Cay (largest in the Holandes group) with local knowledge.

That's the last of the western section San Blas Islands that we'll look at for initial anchorages. The deep-water Caobos Channel comes in SE of the Holandes Cays, between them and the Coco Banderos Cays. The Caobos Channel connects with the Mayflower Channel, leading you west into Bahía San Blas. Off its south side lie all the cays close to the mainland.

The middle section of the San Blas Islands (Coco Banderos Cays to the Cayos Ratones) lacks the offshore barrier reefs and runs close along the mainland, now curving more southerly.

The eastern areas (Cayos Ratones to Punta Brava) are mostly uninhabited and reported to be troubled by drug smuggling and turf wars – so we avoid that area. As we go to press, Colombia and Panama are working on new regulations to safeguard and restrict yatistas traveling in that region.

Colón & Bahía Limón

The town of Colón covers the peninsula east of Bahía Limón inside the breakwaters enclosed harbor at the Atlantic entrance to the Panama Canal. Colón was named for Christopher Columbus (Cristóbal Colón), and the community just south of Colón is Cristóbal, but they run together. Bahía Manzanillo on Colón's NE side is accessed by the newer eastern breakwater, but that opening and bay are not for yachts. Duty-free shops fill the Free Zone on Colón's SE corner.

Blighted by high unemployment, Colón streets are very dangerous, infamous for violent crime, especially daylight muggings. It's absolutely stupid to walk around Colón streets with a purse, backpack, wallet, gear bag, watch, necklace, earrings or other jewelry – even for big men in daylight hours. Hire a taxi to provision; never leave the PCYC grounds alone. The sad expression remains in use: "If you've been at Colón for a week, you've been mugged once. If you've been here two weeks, you've been mugged twice."

Shelter Bay Marina (opened in 2006) in the NW corner of Limón Bay has about 90 full-service slips for boats to 200' and is pleasant and very secure. See

If you didn't buy all the molas you wanted in the San Blas Islands, don't worry, the Kuna women bring them to Colón and Balboa.

Marinas below. The historic Panama Canal Yacht Club on Colón's western waterfront was demolished under protest. Largo Remo may open a marina or moorings in Bahia de las Minas in 2012; check UPDATES.

On Colón's western waterfront on Limón Bay, the huge Muelle Cristóbal 2000 (Piers 6, 7 & 8) was renovated for souvenir sales to cruise-ship passengers, and charter buses start tours inland and across to Balboa.

Club Nautico sportfishing dock and a small T-dock on the NE corner of Colon on Bahia Manzanillo have welcomed yachts, but dock space is very limited, no moorings are set and the anchorage gets wakes.

Anchorage F or "the Flats" is where yatistas who don't have a reservation at Shelter Bay Marina (or unwilling to chance Manzanillo Bay) must anchor right before or after transit of the canal. Unfortunately, dinghies are restricted in the Flats, due to lack of security, so call for a water taxi. Hopefully, Panama may develop some safer alternatives for yatistas.

Approach: Vessel movement in the approaches to Colón and in the harbor are tightly regulated, like a busy international airport. When in VHF-range of Colón hail "Cristóbal Control" (pronounced "kris-TOE-bahl") with your boat name on VHF 12. When they respond, tell them your LOA and type of vessel, and tell them your ETA at the "Western Breakwater" (opening is 09°23.8'N, 079°55.1'W), not the Manzanillo opening 1.25 n.m. farther east. And tell them if you have (a.) a ship's agent and (b.) a slip reservation at Shelter Bay Marina or not.

When Cristóbal Control responds, they may tell you to call again when you're so many miles out, or direct you to anchor outside the breakwater among the ships, or to enter the breakwater after such and such ship exits. AIS is helpful here.

Blinding rain or thick haze often limit your visibility and your radar picture in these waters. The land east of Colon and the harbor is higher than west of it. But don't accidentally approach the eastern breakwater opening into Margarita and Manzanillo bays. A racon marks the Western Breakwater entrance, but it can be blanketed by anchored ships until you're closer.

Several shipping lanes converge as you approach the Western Breakwater, so traffic is dense. Two tall, square skeleton-type light towers mark the entrance (red to starboard, green to port), but don't cut in too close, because the towers stand 100 yards inside the harbor.

Shelter Bay Marina in the NW corner of Limon Bay is a great stop, also the only true marina in town.

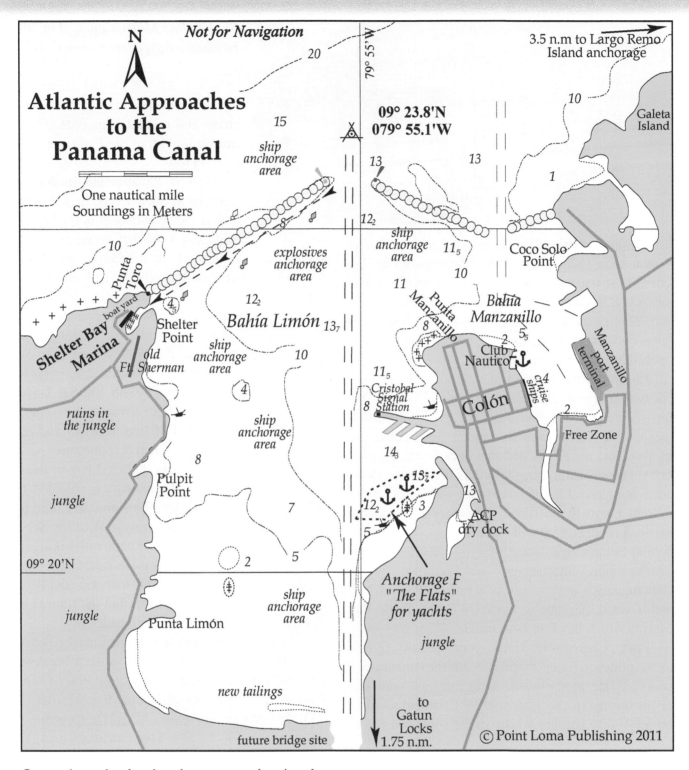

N

Not for Navigation

20

79° 55'W

3.5 n.m to Largo Remo
Island anchorage

Atlantic Approaches
to the
Panama Canal

One nautical mile
Soundings in Meters

**09° 23.8'N
079° 55.1'W**

15

10

Galeta
Island

*ship
anchorage
area*

13

13

1

Coco Solo
Point

10

12₂

*ship
anchorage
area*

11₅

10

13

Punta
Manzanillo

*Bahía
Manzanillo*

Manzanillo
Port
terminal

10

*Punta
Toro*

boat yard

8

*explosives
anchorage
area*

11

8

Club
Nautico

5₅

4
cruise
ships

2

Shelter Bay
Marina

4
5

Shelter
Point

12₂

Bahía Limón 13₇

11₅

Cristobal
Signal
Station

8

Colón

2

old
Ft. Sherman

*ship
anchorage
area*

10

*ruins in
the jungle*

4

Free Zone

*ship
anchorage
area*

14₃

jungle

8

Pulpit
Point

7

13₇

13

12₂

3

ACP
dry dock

09° 20'N

2

5

5

*Anchorage F
"The Flats"
for yachts*

jungle

jungle

Punta Limón

*ship
anchorage
area*

new tailings

to
Gatun
Locks
1.75 n.m.

future bridge site

© Point Loma Publishing 2011

Once through the breakwater, you're in the Main Ship Channel that runs N-S through Bahía Limón. Don't cross the outbound traffic lane without permission from Cristobal Control Signal.

Anchorage: With or without a slip waiting for you, you may be told to proceed to Anchorage F for yachts (also called "hand lines") and small commercial fishing boats. This anchorage is also known as "the Flats."

Proceed south in the Main Ship Channel until abreast of the control tower atop Muelle Cristóbal to port. The Flats anchorage is off your port bow, marked by yellow buoys and yellow lights, bounded on the west by the busy Main Ship Channel leading to Gatun Locks, on the south by mud shoals (low tide) and marsh, on the east by Pier 16. During winter, the Trade Winds often blow 20 knots or more in this anchorage, and the soft mud bottom is poor holding.

Shelter Bay Marina opened in 2005 in Limón Bay, across from Colón.

Chagres Alternative: Instead of entering Bahia Limon, some yachts anchor below the ruins of Fort San Lorenzo at the mouth of Rio Chagres (09°19.243'N, 89°08.068'W), about 7 n.m. SW from the breakwater gap. This is sheltered from E Trades, but beware of huge outflow that occurs whenever Gatun Dam is opened, usually announced on VHF 16.

Largo Remo (Long Oar) Island has a small enclosed cove on its SE side (09°23.458'N, 79°50.351'W) for free anchoring. Ex-cruisers are hoping to install inexpensive yacht moorings and a dink dock, but locals (avoid the abandoned ship dock on the cove's S side) block the isthmus road from Samba Bonita. Don't enter commercial Bahia Las Minas, which lies farther E from Largo Remo Island. Whenever this mooring marina gets opened, it will link at Cativa, 4 road miles behind Colon's Free Zone.

For more alternatives, see Portobelo, where Captain Jack's now serves as a yatista HQ and YC; and if you'd like nice services, try Green Turtle Bay Marina which lies E of Isla Grande.

Port Clearance: Hoist your yellow Q-flag (quarantine) on your port spreader and the Panamanian courtesy flag to starboard. After reaching your slip or anchoring in the Flats, notify Cristóbal Control on VHF that you are where you're supposed to be,

then wait for the Colón port officials to arrive and inspect your boat. *The blue star on the luff of the Panamanian flag goes on top.*

Next is Panamanian Immigration. If you're at Shelter Bay, they'll come to you. If you're anchored in the Flats, you wait there until they come clear you in, then either stay in the Flats for free or ask Cristóbal Control for permission to proceed to a marina slip if you have one.

Marinas: Shelter Bay Marina (opened in 2006) has about 90 full-service concrete floating slips to 200' LOA, 20' depth, diesel & gas service, WiFi, restaurant & bar, laundry, showers, 24/7 security, a chandler shop, haul-out yard with 100-ton Travelift, etc. The marina office can arrange for your port clearance, provide a list of line handlers and repair services and assist your transit preparations.

Located inside a small sheltered bay in the NW corner of Limón Bay, this marina is shielded from wind, seas and ship wakes. This property used to be Fort Sherman (US Army Jungle Warfare School), surrounded by a huge national park with hiking trails and beaches. Water taxi service takes you over to Colón whenever needed. The marina's shuttle uses the road around from Cristóbal, but the future Gatun Bridge will shorten the drive considerably.

Shelter Bay Marina has its own marked channel along the south side of Colón's western breakwater, so turn to starboard as soon as you enter from the Caribbean. FMI, contact Shelter Bay Marina (507) 433-3581 or visit www.ShelterBayMarina.com.

The Panama Canal Yacht Club was bulldozed by the Panama Ports Company.

Local Services: As we go to press, diesel is available

Club house and office at Shelter Bay Marina has restaurant, repair yard, shops, water taxi dock.

Fuel barge in Shelter Bay Marina fills this sportfisher and a bonefish skiff.

at Shelter Bay Marina by tying up to the fuel barge, docked along the basin's wooded outer peninsula. Try to fuel well before your transit, so too many aren't jammed up together.

The required 125' transit lines can be rented from your ship's agent or from Shelter Bay Marina. They keep a list of recommended agents and experienced line handlers, locals and yatistas who have already transited. Find out the going rate, which has been $50/day plus all meals, a sheltered place to sleep onboard if you must overnight in the canal, plus return bus fare.

Provisioning is good at Cuatros Altos shopping center, and Sheler Bay's van makes several daily round trips for shopping, errands, etc. Or, if you run errands in Colón, ask the SBM office to call a recommended (safe) taxista who will pick you up, know his way to what you need, wait while you make purchases and bring you back; they deserve a tip for being bodyguard and local guide.

First-timers are surprised to see armed guards at Colón businesses – especially the grocery store and banks. If you arrive at a bank with no guard outside or inside, leave and come back later. Colón's regular taxi drivers may not speak English, so be sure they wait for you with the meter running. You don't want to be left without a guard or safe ride home.

En Colon, basic provisions come from the El Rey market and Super 99 Grocery, such as unrefrigerated eggs, fresh meats that can be ground or cut to your order, frozen meats & fish, sometimes limp produce, canned goods, sodas and bottled water by the case, cleaning supplies and a sundries department.

Automotive-type repairs are available in Colón, found by asking the marina office to recommend a trusted taxista to scout them out for you. Some taxistas will run errands, knowing that Colón is a dangerous place for any visitors. (Beware; not all taxistas are trust-worthy. And just because a taxista speaks English doesn't make him a ship's agent.)

Otherwise, we suggest traveling to Panama City for most marine spares and repairs. It's an hour taxi or bus ride. Train service between Colón and Balboa is still limited to cargo, but the new regime hopes to resume passenger service soon.

Third Lane Update: To expand the canal's super-tanker capacity, a wider lane with locks is being be added along the east side of the existing Gatun Locks. It will run from the old Mindi Dock ESE along the former Fort Davis, entering Gatun Lake about 1700 yards east of Gatun Locks or just west of the old Dock 45 facilities. At Balboa, the new lane cuts west of the existing locks. Yachts won't use the new lanes, but be prepared for construction delays and sudden changes during transit. We will post Updates on www.CentralAmericanBoating.com.

Newest outer docks (left) at SBM, with a sailboat entering the marina basin.

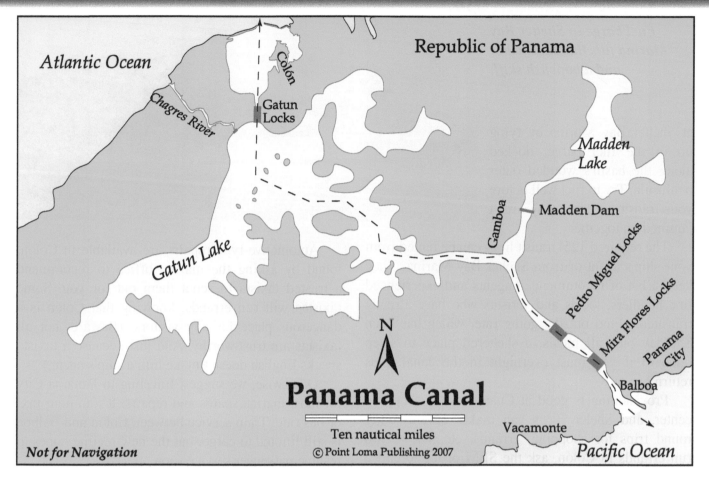

Our Transit of the Panama Canal

Vessel name	Vessel type
Crew names	
Linehandlers' names	
Transit date & start time	Actual start time
Pilot/transit advisor's name	
Events of transit	
Notes	

As we go to press in early 2011 (limited edition 6.5), changes are being proposed to the requirements, fees and procedures for yachts to transit the Panama Canal, and some may have been implemented by the time you arrive here. Panama Canal changes usually are implemented in Juary, May and October of any year. For the latest official word, visit www.pancanal.com and click Maritime Operations, then Customer Forms. From the list, click Procedures for Securing a Handline Transit of the Panama Canal. That PDF will contain the latest requirements, fees and procedures. Get a new one just before arriving here.

Major changes affecting yatistas are quickly reported over the cruising nets and nautical magazines. Check our websites for updates: www.CentralAmericanBoating.com.

We start this chapter with a word about Ship's Agents, the ACP and hand lines. Then we'll look at the official Requirements for Transit (equipment & personnel) and Methods of Transit (center chamber, side wall, tug). Paperwork & Fees are next. Finally we'll walk through a typical Transit of the Panama Canal step by step, so you'll know basically what to expect while up-locking and down-locking – and entering a different ocean.

Ship's Agents

You don't need a ship's agent, but if you're in a hurry to get to the other side, hire a bonded ship's agent who is licensed to operate in the Panama Canal, because he or she will get you into the locks much faster and way less ruffled, and they'll return your unused Buffer Fee - unlike some gypsy agents.

While delivering yachts from one US coast to the other, my husband and I have transited the canal more than 50 times in a variety of vessels, sometimes hiring an agent - and sometimes doing it ourselves. We always get through faster when we hire an agent. For boats over 65' LOA, an agent can usually get you through in 24 to 48 hours. From arriving at Colón to departing Balboa, our fastest time so far is 9 hours.

Since Panama took control of the canal in 2000, yachts requesting transit have been assigned a much lower priority, and the incentives to hire an agent have increased – because the Panama Canal is gearing up for larger ships and a greater volume of them.

When you hire an agent, he or she will stay in contact via SSB, cell phone or email while you approach Colón or Balboa, then they meet with you in person upon your arrival. Make a list of exactly

Top Right: Ship's Agent Pete Stevens (on cell phone) and ACP Admeasurer handle our papers.
Right: Ship's Agent Tina McBride (far right, red T-shirt) transits the canal with clients.

Panama Canal Agents

1.) **Alex Reese (megayachts)**
Associated Steamship
Cel (507) 6614-0485

2.) **Roy Bravo**
Emmanuel Agencies
(507) 441-5652
Cel (507) 6678-6820
emanuelagencies@emanuelagenciessa.com

Other licensed Canal agents we know of:
Enrique Plummer
Agencia Naviera Plummer
Cel (507) 6674-2086, Fax (507) 314-0895
Email eplummer@hotmail.com

Ms. Tina McBride (not under 40')
Panama Canal Transits
Cel (507) 6637-2999, Fax (507) 314-0977
Email PanamaTransit@gmail.com
www.PanamaCanalTransits.com

David Manrique, Match Ship Management
Cel (507) 6615-8157, Tel (507) 314-0850
Fax (507) 314-0841, www.matchship.com

Stanley Scott, Naviera Stanley S.A.
Cell (507) 6680-7971
Email: Sscot@cwpanama.net

what services you need and strike a deal.

A bonded ship's agent will pick up all the required official forms for your Colón and Balboa port clearances and your ACP transit, bring them to your boat for your signature, then go make all the copies needed, drop them off and get them recorded at the various offices where they belong before closing time. He or she will cut through the miles of red tape and quickly get you set up with your two most important appointments: Admeasurement and Transit Date, according to your preferences.

Beyond those basic services, he or she can provide you with canal lines, a cell phone, qualified line handlers, temporary fenders, total provisions, diesel, laundry service, guest pickup at the airport, a trusted English-speaking taxi driver to run errands, etc.

Hiring a bonded ship's agent licensed to operate in the Panama Canal eliminates the $850 Buffer Fee. He or she can fix 101 potential problems before they become problems for you. Their fees vary widely ($175 to $900) depending on your needs, but because we're always in a hurry to get through the canal, we've always found our agents' fees a worthy investment. As crime increases in Colón and parts of Balboa, we're not fond of hanging out there longer than necessary.

Bonded Agents: Pete Stevens and Tina McBride are the only 2 bonded Panama Canal ship's agents who we have hired many times and can highly recommend. Their contact information is on this page.

Fake Agents: Some taxi drivers in Colón and Balboa call themselves "agents," and they may be able to drive you to the various offices and find some old car tires for you to buy. But they are not bonded, not licensed by the ACP and have no legal responsibility to you or anyone if, for example, you have a delay or glitch caused by following their advice, if you have an accident during transit or - if your $850 buffer fee disappears in a puff of electronic smoke.

Do It Yourself: If hiring a ship's agent isn't in your budget, skip ahead to the Paperwork & Fees section of this chapter.

Panama Canal Authority (ACP)

The ACP (*Autoridad del Canal de Panamá*) is the Panamanian government organization that directs and controls all aspects of the Panama Canal (admeasurement, fees, transit scheduling, pilots & transit advisors, lockage, tugs, work boats, dredges, etc.) and the surrounding canal region (no longer called "the canal zone").

However, the canal region is treated like a separate port from either Colón or Balboa, because you must perform an additional port clearance in and out of the canal region. Once you enter the canal region (approaches to Colón or Balboa and the canal itself), you're within controlled space and can't move anywhere without requesting and being granted permission.

The ACP supplies a full-fledged Pilot to yachts 65' LOA and over, while smaller yachts get a Transit

Panama Canal lines leading to top of lock walls as chamber fills rapidly from below.

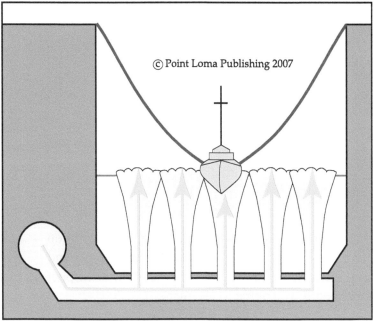

Advisor. Pilots have more experience in general, but unfortunately much of their time has been on big ships; some Pilots are uncomfortable with delicate yachts. Transit Advisors usually have worked their way up from being the mate or captain on one of the many canal work boats or tugs. For $2,250 extra, you can request (well in advance) to be assigned a Pilot instead of a Transit Advisor.

To the ACP, yachts are officially called "hand lines" because we don't require locomotives in the locks (except yachts 125' or more). Yatistas who have never transited before are informally referred to as Y-jobs, which isn't necessarily derogatory. If you've never been through before, be sure your Pilot or Transit Advisor knows that fact, so he or she will explain things more clearly and point out the more interesting sights in the canal.

Yachts documented or registered as *commercial* have different procedures and require a ship's agent.

Requirements for Transit

Here's our checklist of equipment and personnel required for transit. An ACP Admeasurer will inspect your boat and discuss your gear, line handlers and what's required for transit. The Port Captain has final authority about any questionable equipment or personnel you may have.

1. Steady & reliable propulsion: Your onboard engine must be capable of pushing your boat all day at the 5-knot minimum. (This may be increased to 8 knots.) Your propulsion must be capable of moving your boat forward and reverse. If you can't maintain the required minimum speed, tell the Admeasurer. It might be possible to hire a fellow yatista with a power boat to tow you through at 5 knots.

If you are scheduled to transit through in 1 day but for any reason can't maintain a required speed when asked to during the transit, you might break your transit into an unscheduled 2 days, in which case you'll forfeit the $440 transit delay fee. Or you might be required to hire an ACP tug, which is far more expensive.

2. Panama Canal lines: You must have four 125' lines of a diameter and strength sufficient for your vessel's size and weight, and one end of each line needs a 3' diameter eye to quickly fit over huge bollards. These lines come under tremendous strain, so we recommend good quality 7/8" line when possible. Each of your four 125' canal lines must be all of one piece, that is, no joint of two lines to make 125'. A 3' wide bowline on the outboard end is an awkward but acceptable alternative to a 3' eye splice. One 250' line on the bow is not acceptable. Polypro-line or frayed

Bollards atop lock walls are 12 inches wide, recessed amid concrete, so large eyes are required.

TIP: Your deck cleats must be roomy enough to easily handle the diameter of these lines in a figure 8 that won't slip off while constantly being paid out or hauled in – even while wet. Test them ahead of time, to make sure your lines and cleats are compatible. If a canal line under strain suddenly slips off a cleat, it could cause serious injury and damage. Sailboats may run the 2 aft lines forward to 2 cockpit winches.

lines are not acceptable. Panama Canal lines are often rented from ship's agents or the marinas on either end of the canal, but these lines see heavy use; inspect them before you agree to use them.

3. Chocks & bitts: Before you can transit, the ACP's office of the Port Captain will require you to sign a legal waiver releasing the ACP from liability for any damages that may result from your inadequate chocks and bitts.

Because of the extreme forces exerted on your cleats and the extreme upward angle of the lines during transit, the ACP requires four sturdy "closed chocks." A large cleat sturdily mounted along the gunwale that has an eye through its center will usually work. But if a cleat is mounted inboard and its fairlead at the gunwale is open on top (allowing the line to be lifted upward), the ACP may require you to weld a steel bar across the top to close it.

Cleats that are flimsy or not through-bolted to a backing plate below decks may have to be replaced, or you may have to install sturdy backing plates that are through-bolted below decks. The working area around each of these four cleats must be cleared of obstructions, so the 125' lines can be worked freely.

4. Fenders: The ACP requires you to have "adequate fendering," but if your boat is slammed against the jagged concrete walls and one of your fenders bursts, then obviously it wasn't adequate.

Yes, do buy special fenders just for your transit, 2 or 3 fenders to a side - depending on the size and weight of the boat. Buy the largest, toughest fenders you can find, because they are your best insurance against damage. For large yachts, we recommend using four of the spherical or slightly tear-drop balls that measure about 3' across. Storage is always a problem on smaller boats, so keep them deflated and stowed until reaching Panama, inflate them and test for leaks before transit, then after transit perhaps sell them to others who arrived unprepared. Tubular dock fenders are useful only between rafted boats, not for protection from the chamber walls.

Tires make a poor substitute for fenders, but you can rent them cheaply in Balboa. Garbage bags meant to keep tires from marring the gel coat seldom last through the transit.

5. Onboard line handlers: Besides the helmsman, each yacht needs a well-rehearsed team of four very strong people to serve as its onboard line handlers, one to constantly work each of the four 125' Panama Canal lines throughout the transit. Everyone handling lines should know what's about to happen, constantly pay attention to directions given by the Pilot or Transit Advisor, because their job is to keep the boat from smashing into the concrete walls.

This is not a job for lightweights. Line handling

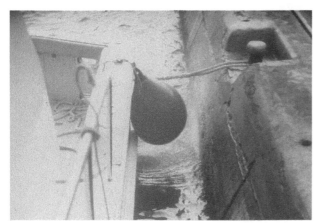

These fenders are 2.5' in diameter, heavy-duty and lashed 4 to a side on 60' motoryacht.

requires stamina, a strong back, tall stature for leverage and callused hands (wear sturdy gloves). Turbulence and current can be tremendous, requiring strength and stamina to keep the lines under tight control while hauling them in or paying them out. If one line slips, the hull can be thrown against the concrete walls or steel gates.

While you are up- or down-locking center chamber (See below.), line handlers cannot set down their lines to take pictures, to eat, rest or get out of the sun or rain. Line handlers must take the job seriously. On larger boats, having an extra body to tail each line handler may be a good idea, but smaller boats get way too crowded for extras.

If you don't have enough of your own crew, fellow yatistas with different transit days enjoy helping each other out by serving as line handlers. Your first choice should be someone who has worked as a line handler at least once before, preferably three or four times, because each transit involves a different set of circumstances. Everybody wants to learn, but there are fewer teachers.

Professional line handlers are a good option. The offices of Shelter Bay Marina, the PCYC and the Balboa Yacht Club fuel dock have a list of local line handlers who work full time for yachts in transit. But get a strong recommendation and then interview them before hiring. The going rate has been $50/day if completed in one day, $65/day if overnighting in the canal, plus $15 bus fare back from the end of the transit. Also, the ACP requires you to supply your line handlers (and your Pilot or Transit Advisor) with up to 3 meals/day and plenty of drinking water or soft drinks, access to a sanitary bathroom, shelter from sun and rain and a place for your line handlers to sleep if you are required to overnight in Gatun Lake. For an extra tip, your line handlers might carry your rented lines back to where you began.

You must be prepared to transit "center chamber" using your four line handlers, even if you end up being nested or rafted

Line handler gets starboard bow set up for transiting center chamber.

to other boats or are lucky enough to find a passing tug – in which cases you'll have an abundance of line handlers.

6. Helmsman: The helmsperson will steer and maneuver the boat through the locks and channels of the Panama Canal, so the helmsman cannot also be a line handler. This means you'll have at least five people in your crew.

You must maneuver in and out of the lock chambers, each 110' wide and 1,000' long. You enter behind or in front of a ship, and you must hold the boat steady in position while the lines are being made up. You may maneuver out of the locks rafted with other yachts alongside.

Although an ACP Pilot or Transit Advisor comes on board and directs your course and speed, he or she is not required to steer your boat. However, some might enjoy steering for a few minutes across Gatun Lake.

TIP: Don't leave the helmsman stuck on the flybridge without a gopher during transit.

7.) Anchor & Head: You must have an anchor and ground tackle ready to go, in case of emergencies. You must also have a sanitary place for going as well, with privacy. A bucket in the cockpit will not get it. Be prepared with an empty holding tank.

Methods of Transit

One of the papers you'll sign asks, "Which one of these three methods of transit do you prefer?" You don't always get what you request, because the final decisions are made by the ACP Lock Master the

night before - or sometimes within minutes of your approach to each set of locks. However, you must be prepared and equipped to transit center chamber – the most demanding method.

1.) Center Chamber: This requires holding position in the center of the 110' wide chamber despite turbulence, prop wash and current simply by the skipper coordinating engine(s) and the actions of the four line handlers (two on bow, two on stern) each with a 125' line going up to the lock bollards. Transiting center chamber solo is usually the safest method, but it demands more maneuvering expertise from the helmsman (who is also directing the line handlers), and it's much more physically demanding on line handlers. On a larger boat, try to have one person relaying orders from the skipper to the line handlers.

An offshoot of Center Chamber is called "nested," meaning rafted alongside other yachts or a small ship scheduled to transit the same chamber. You form a raft in the center of the chamber width. The largest yacht should be placed in the middle of the nest and must use its engine(s) to maneuver the whole raft. The line handlers might work from that boat or from whichever smaller boats are nested outboard on both sides of the nest. So, coordination is required to keep

from drifting out off center. (It's often a zoo.)

The Transit Advisors direct the nesting process, placement of fenders and breast lines. Take care that standing rigging (shrouds, spreaders, outriggers) doesn't get tangled when the boats roll during turbulence. Except at Gatun, you may be nested in one chamber but not the next.

2.) Side Wall: Two lines attempt to hold you steady alongside the jagged concrete wall on one side of the chamber. Unfortunately, it's almost impossible to stay put during the turbulence of filling the chamber during up-locking, especially in the first chamber where fresh and salt water are mixing. The boat is likely to get slammed into or scraped against the side wall, damaging the topsides and rigging.

So, when you sign your papers, you should reject Side Wall as a preferred method for up-locking. However, for the less turbulent

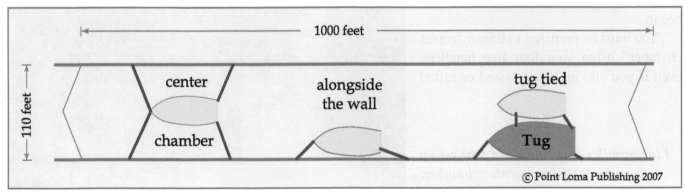

center
chamber

alongside
the wall

tug tied

Tug

1000 feet

110 feet

Fishing boat transits sidewall. Yachts should not up-lock sidewall, but it may be OK for down-locking.

down-locking process, side wall is usually harmless if you're well fendered and winds are calm. Still, beware in the final chamber when fresh and salt water mix turbulently as the gates are opened.

3.) Tug Tied: Requesting an ACP tug boat in advance is very expensive; ask your agent. But if one happens to be transiting your same chamber and isn't engaged, the lock master might assign you to tie up alongside it for free. Transiting alongside a tug is convenient for the helmsperson and crew, and it's safe for the boat IF you have excellent fendering.

TIP: Let the tug get secured side wall before you come alongside. Use your bow, stern and spring lines, plus all your fenders or even fender boards against the tug's nasty black fenders. When down-locking, get your stern quickly secured first to counteract the "down hill" current. Don't let the tug get underway with your boat still tied alongside.

Transit Paperwork & Fees

Cruising Permit: Before applying for transit, you should have obtained a Panamanian Cruising Permit from the office of *"Consular y Naves."* Take along a copy of the vessel's document and the serial numbers of your engines. The fee for this permit is about $30. Panama uses US dollar bills for its own currency, which is called the Balboa.

Visit the Panamanian Immigration offices to get a visa stamped (about $10 each) in the passports for all your crew members. If you have access to a Panamanian Consulate in the US, you can take care of this stamp for free before you leave on your voyage.

Admeasurement: When your boat is ready to transit, you start the official ball rolling by calling the Admeasurer's Office to make an appointment to be admeasured and inspected.

Colón Admeasurer (507) 443-2293.

Balboa Admeasurer (507) 272-4571.

They may schedule your appointment for tomorrow or a week from tomorrow. If the boat has transited the Panama Canal previously (even different owner) and no structural changes have been made, the Admeasurer may have it on file and you might avoid being measured again. (Someday yachts may not be admeasured. Check www.pancanal.com for updates.) But the Admeasurer still needs to inspect the boat and all its transit gear.

An Admeasurer comes aboard with tapes and measures the LOA (including bow sprit, davits, swim step) to determine your Transit Fixed Fee. If a davit extends your boat to more than 50', you might want to take it off until your transit is done. He or she also inspects the boat and all transit equipment, has a little talk explaining to everyone how it all works, answers questions and determines by which methods your boat can transit.

From the Admeasurer, you get the Admeasurer Clearance (one copy sent to the Port Captain) and Handline Inspection Form, which you'll need for the Port Captain, bank and Transit Scheduler.

Fees, Fees & More Fees: Once you've been admeasured, take all your papers and visit the Port Captain's office, where you'll request to transit, fill out

Basic fees as published by ACP in Sept 2013			
Vessel LOA	Transit Fee	Buffer	Delay
less than 50'	*$800.*	*850.*	*440*
50' to 79'	*$1,300.*	*850*	*440*
80' to 99'	*$2,000.*	*850*	*440*
100' or more	*$3,200.*	*850*	*440*
However, additional fees now apply			

Yachts 65' or more are required to have AIS, or rent a device like this from the ACP for about $161 to use during your transit.

more papers and ask to pay all the fees.

The basic Transit Fee is based on your boat's LOA. Add $54 Inspection Fee if you have no agent; see the box above. Yachts or "hand lines" pay the $891 Buffer Fee and $471 Transit Delay Fee in advance, returned by the ACP to you or your agent in 3-4 weeks if you don't damage the locks, cause a delay or need to be towed. Locomotives are required to transit yachts 125' or more; consult your agent.

Additionally, if your boat is 65' or more and you don't have an AIS (Automatic Identity System), you pay $161 to rent a portable device, which must be employed on your boat during transit. On the horizon may be a $320 launch fee for everybody.

Cash is accepted at the Port Captain's office, and you get a receipt. Or, safer than carrying cash, you can pay by Visa credit card at two Citibank locations:

In Colón, the Citibank (507-441-6303 and 441-6144) is next to the Cristobal Piers entrance. Fees may be paid 8:30 a.m. to 1 p.m. Mon – Fri; closed weekends and holidays. Keep the receipt.

In Balboa, the Citibank (507-228-0165 or 314-1596) is in Niko's Plaza. Fees may be paid 8:30 a.m. to 2 p.m. Mon – Fri; closed weekends and holidays. Keep the receipt safe, make copies.

Transit Schedule

Take the receipt for paying your fees back to the Port Captain with all your papers. When the Port Captain clears you to proceed, after 6 p.m. that same day (but within 30 days of being Admeasured) you must contact the Marine Traffic Scheduler (507) 272-4202 to request your preferred transit date. The MTC will give you a transit date and a tentative pilot time.

As we go to press, the MTC is trying to schedule hand lines to start transiting very early in the morning (0430) and get out the other side in one day. If they take 2 days, no fee. If you request to take 2 days, you may or may not be assessed the $471 Delay Fee.

The afternoon or evening before your tentative pilot time, you must phone the MTC to confirm (a.) the exact time the pilot will board and (b.) that you are ready. If you don't call the MTC to confirm, you may lose your transit date.

About Scheduling: You don't always get the transit date you request, and even after you get a transit date, the MTC can change it. Enough hand lines need to be awaiting transit to make it worth the canal's time. Waits of three weeks are now rare. But once you're scheduled, you, your boat and your line handlers must remain ready to transit.

If many hand lines are waiting to transit, the scheduler may try to contact you (via VHF or your ship's agent) to see if you're ready and able to transit earlier than previously scheduled.

Pilots and Trip Advisors occasionally arrive later than scheduled. But once he or she arrives, if you aren't ready or you fail to complete your transit as scheduled, you will probably forfeit all or part of your Transit Delay Fee.

Once you start transiting, if something delays your transit that is NOT under your control, then you may be rescheduled to overnight on a buoy in Gatun Lake and finish the following day – without

ACP Pilot boat delivers our pilot onboard in the Flats to begin our transit.

ACP Pilot (right) directs all boat movement, while skipper drives the boat and directs our onboard line handlers.

forfeiting your Transit Delay Fee. Overnighting in Gatun, the Pilot leaves but everyone else must stay aboard. Line handlers must be fed, berthed and paid for two full days.

Panama Canal Transit

After you've gathered all your transit gear and people, after all your paperwork is in order and fees paid, you'll be assigned either an ACP Pilot or an ACP Transit Advisor. If your boat is under 65' you'll get Transit Advisor who acts as your Pilot while you are in transit. If your boat is 65' or more, you'll get a Pilot. The difference is described above, but for the sake of clarity, we'll say you have a Pilot.

Your Pilot gives helm orders and directions and coordinates all transit activities by radio, but he or she does not actually drive your boat. A typical transit normally runs through breakfast, lunch and dinner, so you must feed your Transit Advisor and line handlers. (Now there're at least six people on board.) By the time you pop out the other side, you'll be exhausted and elated.

Typical Transit

Let's examine a typical transit from north to south (Colón to Balboa) aboard a 70' twin screw motoryacht. Our assigned ACP Pilot comes aboard at 0700 at the Shelter Bay Marina, and we offer him coffee and breakfast muffins. He checks that we have already untwisted and flaked out our four 125' Panama Canal lines, have the 3' eyes properly fed through the closed chocks and going outboard, that we have plenty of elbow room to work each line, nothing snaggable nearby. After the Pilot gets the word on his hand-held VHF, we move out into the Main Ship Channel through Limon

Sportfisher maneuvers at center of the nest or raft with 2 sailboats alongside as they up-lock.

Bay, down the jungle-lined approach to the first set of three chambers called Gatun Locks.

Gatun is the easiest set of locks to transit, because all three chambers are connected within a mile, each raising us about 28' until we're at the canal's highest elevation (85'). As we approach Gatun, the Lock Master tells our Pilot that we're going to transit this one "center chamber." Ahead of us is our first lock partner, a crusty Liberian freighter moving slowly into the first chamber, which begins at sea level filled with sea water. After the freighter is secured, we begin to enter behind him slowly until the Pilot says to stop. We're very close to his stern.

The ACP line handlers on the port wall toss down a monkey fist with light messenger line. We scramble to grab the monkey fist before it goes overboard, then we lightly secure the eyes of both our portside 125' canal lines (bow & stern) to their messenger line. The ACP line handlers hoist up our lines while walking them forward and secure the eyes over two widely spaced bollards in the chamber. Same happens on starboard.

(In spite of horror stories, the ACP line handlers don't deliberately smash solar panels, windows and spot lights, but it does happen by accident. Pad your panels. You could be knocked senseless by a monkey fist if you don't pay attention.)

Now, by adjusting our canal lines on the deck cleats, we must quickly get our hull centered exactly in the middle of the 110' width, and we must keep our bow and stern parallel to the side walls. Meanwhile, the lock gates will be closing behind us, so we must quickly get centered, secured and ready before the bell rings. At that instant, our ascent begins.

Up-locking

Up-locking is more turbulent than down-locking. Violent, erratic currents boil beneath us, when 52 million gallons of fresh water gushes up from big holes in the chamber floor, filling it in 15 minutes. That current pushes up on the rudder and hull surfaces, which is NOT like steering up or down a river. Because it's the first chamber, we get added turbulence from all that fresh water forcing its way upward, displacing all the salt water and trying to mix.

What's everyone doing? As helmsman, John keeps the boat centered, but he can't move very far forward or back due to the constraint of the lines. Maneuverable twin screw boats have a better time of it. John also directs the line handlers, so they keep us from getting crooked.

Each line handler must constantly keep hauling

in his or her rapidly slacking line, never cleating off the line with a locked figure 8. As a team, they must coordinate to keep the boat exactly on station: the bow and stern lined up with the centerline of the chamber, not drifting or twisting. If one line handler hauls in too fast or too slow, the boat will get cross-wise or get tossed violently against one wall or the gates. ACP Pilots seldom warn you if we're getting crooked; it's up to the skipper and line handlers. Turbulence lessens when the chamber is three-quarters full.

After we reach the maximum height, the gates open and our giant lock partner is hauled into the next chamber by electric locomotives, still called mules. To help get moving, that Liberian freighter's helmsman gives a few turns of his screw.

LOOK OUT! The prop wash sets us back on our lines forcefully. (Many accidents occur at this point.) John helps ease the strain by going slow ahead with our lines still secured. But we can't let go of any lines until well after the visible prop wash has passed.

Option: The Lock Master may have assigned us to "nest" or raft up in the middle of four smaller sailboats. With the Pilot's and Transit Advisors' help, we're careful to position all five of the hulls so their rigging (spreaders, shrouds, outriggers) won't touch or tangle when turbulence jerks and bounces the raft around. We fender well between hulls, but we hang at least two of the biggest and sturdiest fenders outboard – in case we get slammed against the walls or gates.

Our twin-screw power boat acts as the only propulsion for the whole raft. The four outside corners of the raft are where the 125' lines are worked from, so the best cleats should be positioned there. Only four of the 20 line handlers are required to work, but since the job is now complicated by their being farther apart, one of the extra crew relays the skipper's orders to limit confusion and keep the raft from twisting. Extra bodies can tail the big lines and keep the lazy ends flaked out.

Two lines are black so not visible as we lock through one of the chambers.

Prop wash from the ship ahead can suprise you, so be prepared at the lines and throttle.

Two rafts might transit in the same chamber, and they may also share the chamber with a dreaded Liberian freighter.

If we had been a nest of three boats, we might have carefully motored the raft into the next chamber. But five boats is too gangly a mess, so get all the bodies back where they belong, untie and move off separately.

After Gatun's first chamber has filled and opened into the second chamber, our 125' lines are cast off the lock walls, and we quickly haul them in with the ACP's messenger lines still attached. The other ends of the messenger lines are held by the ACP line handlers. As we power slowly forward into the middle of the second chamber behind the freighter, the ACP line handlers walk the heaving lines forward with us. When we're in position directed by the Lock Master and our Pilot, the ACP line handlers haul our heavier lines back up and re-secure them to bollards in this second chamber.

We repeat this entire procedure in Gatun's second and third chambers until the line handlers cast us off and we enter Gatun Lake, the man-made, freshwater lake 85' above sea level.

Gatun Lake spreads 163 square miles, and it's one of the most picturesque parts of the Panama Canal. Here's where line handlers can get their camera, eat, take pit stops, spell the helmsman, etc. If we had time to kill, our Pilot might let us take the Banana Channel or Monkey Cut, which run east of the Peña Blanca Reach near Gatun, but we can't because we have a schedule to keep.

At 10 knots, we zig and zag 23.5 miles along various stretches and curves, all within the well marked Panama Canal channel as it passes through island-dotted Gatun Lake, until we arrive at Gamboa Anchorage across from the Chagres River entrance.

Option: If we were under 65', the ACP might have scheduled us to stop here overnight and finish our transit tomorrow. If so, we are directed to a large mooring buoy, and the Transit Advisor is taken off by one of the ACP work boats (Sorry, ACP boats can transport only ACP employees.). We spend the rest of the day and the night on the buoy with our line handlers, watching ships pass close by.

Canal rules specify that boat owners must feed their line handlers and provide them a toilet and dry place to sleep. Small boats may want to bunk their extra crew on deck, but it often rains at night here. By VHF radio, all arrangements are made for a different Transit Advisor to arrive the following morning to complete the transit.

Because this boat is over 65', we aren't scheduled to stop and spend the night on a buoy at Gamboa. We continue the same day into the Gaillard Cut, the narrowest part of the canal, where we motor across the Continental Divide, past Gold Hill and Contractors Hill and zoom beneath the majestic Centenario Bridge.

Because of a geological weakness on the Pacific side, two sets of locks had to be built: Pedro Miguel

Upwelling turbulence is considerable, not navigable like river current.

For down-locking we're close enough to the gate to see into the lower chamber.

Locks with one chamber and Mira Flores Locks with two chambers. Between them lies man-made Mira Flores Lake.

At Pedro Miguel, because we are now down-locking we go ahead of our lock partner, which this time is a Monrovian freighter. Lucky us, we get to tie alongside an ACP tug boat that is already secured to the lock walls.

Securing alongside a tug is tricky maneuvering, because the strong current is now behind us. We get our stern line over first, then our bow and crossed spring lines. We give the tug hands our eyes, so we retain control of our destiny as much as possible. Dock lines are seldom sturdy enough for this, so use the 125' canal lines from our starboard stern and bow. We fender well on the tug side, but reserve at least one big fender for the open side, just in case an accident puts you hard against the far wall.

Somewhat thrilling, we are looking over the top of the chamber gate – it's 31' straight down – into the next chamber, which is empty.

Down-locking

Descending is much easier for 2 reasons. We don't have the prop wash from the large ships, because they usually down-lock behind yachts. And the turbulence of the violent up-welling isn't present. Someone in the control booth just pulls the plug and down we go, like a toy boat in a really big bathtub.

On the other side of the tug, its hands are paying out its canal lines, which lead almost straight up to the top of the chamber walls by the time we've completed this descent.

(If an ACP tug had not been available, and if we'd been down-locking side wall, our 125' lines would have been leading straight up. If our chocks had not been completely closed over the top, we could not

244

have kept them from popping out.)

At the end of this down-locking, we take back our lines from the tug hands and move away, being prepared for some wash turbulence from the inward opening of the gates. Never let a tug get underway with you still alongside. This is not a service; much damage occurred to yachts when this practice was still widely used.

We enter Mira Flores Lake and traverse the short distance to the last set of locks, called Mira Flores. We learn that we will transit center chamber in both chambers. We receive the ACP line handlers' monkey fists, send up our lines and get secured in center chamber. While going down 54' at Mira Flores, our four line handlers slacken the lines slowly and evenly. The last pair of these chamber doors opens into the Pacific Ocean. As in Gatun's first chamber, John is prepared for the mixing of fresh and salt water, but this time it occurs after the gate has opened.

Just before we go beneath the Bridge of the Americas, an ACP Pilot boat comes alongside (we maintain 5 knots) and picks up our Pilot.

See the section on Balboa & Panama City at the end of Chapter 3.

We pass the Balboa Yacht Club moorings and fuel pier and continue down the fairway, because we have obtained permission to go around to the east side of Flamenco Island to Fuerte Amador Resort & Marina, aka Flamenco Yacht Club. En route, we pay off our line handlers and help them pack up their belongings. At the marina, we get plugged into our slip, say good-bye to our line handlers and fall into an exhausted stupor.

How long did it take? We have done the entire transit in 7 hours, but usually it takes about 14 hours – all depending on the boat's cruise speed, on other ships' schedules and on the extemporaneous decisions of our ACP Pilot or Transit Advisor and the various Lock Masters.

Marinas & Yacht Clubs

Bahía Ballena Yacht Club, Tambor, Costa Rica, (506) 683-0095 Bahíabyc@racsa.co.cr

Bahia del Sol Hotel & Marina, El Salvador (503) 2327-0300.

Balboa Yacht Club, Balboa, Ancon, Republic of Panama, (507) 228-5794 bycmarina@cwpanama.net.

Banana Bay Marina, Golfito, Costa Rica, (506) 2775-0838 www.BananaBayMarina.com

Barefoot Cay Marina, Roatan, Honduras, (504) 2455-6235 www.barefootcay.com

Barillas Marina Club, Bahía Jiquilisco, El Salvador, (503) 2675-1131, fax 1134, or 2263-3650, 3620. info@barillasmarina.com

Belize Yacht Club, San Pedro, Ambergris Cay, Belize, (510) 226-4338 www.BelizeYachtClub.com

Bocas Yacht Club & Marina, Bocas del Toro, Republic of Panama, (507) 757-9800 www.BocasMarina,com

Bruno's Marina, Frontera, Rio Dulce, Guatemala, (502) 7930-5121 or 5174 rio@guat.net

Catamaran Inn & Marina, Frontera, Rio Dulce, Guatemala (502) 7930-5494 and 95 catamaran@intelgua.com.

Cayman Islands Yacht Club, West Bay, Grand Cayman Island, Benny, (809) 947-4322.

Club de Yates de Veracruz, Mexico, (229) 932-0917.

Club de Yates de Yukalpetén, Yucatan, Eduardo Ponce, (969) 935-2969.

Costa Rica Yacht Club, Puntarenas, Costa Rica, www.costaricayachtclub.com (506) 661-0784.

Cozumel Club Nautico, (919) 872-1113 or 1118.

Cucumber Beach Marina, Belize City, (501) 222-4153 marina@oldbelize.com

Denny's Beach Marina, Rio Dulce, Guatemala (502) 4636-6156.

El Tortugal Marina, Fronteras, Guatemala (502) 5306-6432.

El Relleno Marina, Rio Dulce (502) 7930-9739.

Enrique's Marina, Isla Mujeres, Quintana Roo, Mexico, (998) 877-0211.

Fantasy Island Island Resort & Marina, Roatan, Honduras (504) 2445-7612, or 7510 www.fantasyislandresort.com.

Fish Hook Marina, Golfito, CR (305) 248-2810, or (506)775-1624

Fort George Radisson Marina, Belize City, (501) 223-3333 www.radissonbelize.com.

Fuerte Amador Marina & Resort, Balboa, Panama, (507) 314-1980 or 0665 www.fuerteamador.com

Hacienda Tijax, Fronteras, Rio Dulce, Guatemala (502) 7930-5505.

Harbour House Marina, George Town, Grand Cayman, (345) 947-1307

Hemingway International Yacht Club, Cuba, (537) 204-6653, fax (537) 204-1689 yachtclub@cnih.mh.cyt.cu

Isla Xalaja, Rio Dulce (502) 5991-9645.

Lagoon Marina, La Ceiba, Honduras (504) 440-0614.

La Marina, Livingston, Rio Dulce, Guatemala (502) 974-0303

La Jolla del Rio Marina, Rio Dulce, Guat (502) 7902-7539 rio@guat.net

Los Sueños Resort & Marina, Costa Rica, (506) 2630-4200, or 637-8886 US toll free (866) 865-9759. www.lsrm.com

Cruising Ports: the Central American Route

Mango Marina, Fronteras, Rio Dulce, Guatemala (502) 5213-6868 mangocharter@hotmail.com
Maria La Gorda, Cuba (53) 827-1306, fax (53) 827-8131

Marina Carenero, Bocas del Toro, Panama, (506) 757-9242 MarinaCarenero@hotmail.com www.CareeningCay.com

Marina Cayo Guillermo, Cuba (53-33) 30-1738 or 30-1637, fax (53-33) 30-1737, psol@cayo.cco.tur.cu

Marina Cayo Largo del Sur, Cuba (53) 548-213 or 548-133, fax (53) 548-212 gcom@psol.cls.tur.cu

Marina Chapelín, Cuba (53) 566-7550 or 566-7566, fax (53) 566-7093.

Marina El Cid Cancun, Puerto Morelos, Quintana Roo, Mexico, (998) 871-0184 dockmaster at elcidcaribe@prodigy.net.mx

Marina El Colony, Cuba (53) 619-8181 and 8182, fax (53) 619-8420 carpeta.colony@gerona.inf.cu

Marina Hemingway, Havana, Cuba: (537) 209-7270 or 7928 or 7201, fax (537) 204-5280 Sergio Ameneiro at rpublicas@prto.mh.cyt.cu or Ing. Isuara Oraz Perez at comercial@prto.mh.cyt.cu

Marina Miramar, Panama City, Panama, (507) 206-8888 panama@interconti.com

Marina Papagayo, Playa del Coco, CR (506) 2690-3 602.

Marina Pez Vela, Puerto Quetzal, Guatemala (502) 2379-5778.

Marina Pez Vela, Quepos, Costa Rica, (866) 739-8352, or (506) 777-4141 www.MarinaPezVela.com

Marina Puerto Aventuras, Quintana Roo, Mexico, (984) 873-5110 marina@puertoaventuras.com.mx

Marina Puerto Azul, Puntarenas, CR (506) 2282-9204.

Marina Puertosol Cienfuegos, Cuba (53-43) 245-1241, fax (53-43) 245-1275 mpsolcfg@ip.etecsa.cu
Marina Puertosol Trinidad, Cuba (53) 419-6205, marinastdad@ip.etecsa.cu

Marina Puesta del Sol, Nicaragua, (505) 883-0781 or 880-0013 or (cellular, extra digit) 880-00190 mpuestadelsol@yahoo.com

Marina Tortugal, Rio Dulce, Guat (502) 7742-8847 or 5306-6432.

Marina Santiago de Cuba (53) 226-91446, or fax 226-86108.

Marina Varadero, Cuba (53) 566-7755 or 566-7756, or fax (53) 566-7756.
Marina Vita, Cuba (53) 243-0132, or fax 243-0126.

Mario's Marina, Fronteras, Rio Dulce, Guatemala (502) 7930-5569 or visit www.mariosmarina.com

Mar Marine, Rio Dulce, Guatemala, (502) 7930-5090.

Milagro Marina, Isla Mujeres, Quintana Roo, Mexico (988) 877-1708 or (805) 698-8165.

Monkey Bay Marina, Rio Dulce, Guatemala, (502) 5368-9604 harbormaster@monkeybaymarina.com

Nene's Marina, Isla San Andrés, Colombia, (578) 512-6139.

Nutria Marina, Fronteras, Guatemala (502) 5863-9635 or visit www.nutriamarina.com

Panama Club de Yates y Pesca, Panama City, Panama, (507) 2227-0145.

Paradise Marina, Isla Mujeres, Qintana Roo, Mexico (998) 877-0252 marinaparaiso@yahoo.com.mx.

Parrot Tree Plantation, Roatan, (504) 9700-9240.

Puerto Isla Mujeres, Quintana Roo, (998) 287-3340 marina@puertoislamujeres.com

Red Frog Beach Marina, Bocas del Toro area, Panama (281) 576-8792   www.RedFrogBeach.com

Shelter Bay Marina, Colón, Panama, (507) 433-3581 www.ShelterBayMarina.com

Taboga Island Moorings, Balboa, Panama (507) 6442-5712, VHF 74.

Texan Bay Marina, El Golfete, Rio Dulce, Guatemala (502) 5758-8748   www.TexanBayMarina.com

Tijax Hacienda Marina, Rio Dulce, Guatemala (502) 7930-5505.

Fuel Docks

Banana Bay Marina, Golfito, Costa Rica, (506) 2775-0838 www.BananaBayMarina.com.

Barefoot Cay Marina, Roatan, Honduras (504) 2455-6235 www.barefootcay.com

Barillas Marina Club, Bahía Jiquilisco, El Salvador, (503) 2263-3650 x 3620. info@barillasmarina.com

Bocas Yacht Club & Marina, Bocas del Toro, Panama, (507) 757-9800 www.BocasMarina.com

Cucumber Beach Marina, Belize City, (501) 222-4153 marina@oldbelize.com

Fantasy Island Resort & Marina, Roatan, Honduras, (504) 2445-7612 lr 7510 www.fantasyislandresort.com

Fuerte Amador Marina, (Flamenco YC) Panama City, R.P. (507) 314-1980 or 314-0665 www.fuerteamador.com

Los Sueños Resort & Marina, Costa Rica, (506) 2630-4200, or 637-8886 US toll free (866) 865-9759. www.lsrm.com/marina

Marina Carenero, Bocas del Toro, Panama, (506) 757-9242 www.CareeningCay.com

Marina El Cid Caribe, Cancun area, Quintana Roo, Mexico, (998) 871-0184.

Marina Hemingway, Havana, Cuba: (537) 209-7270 or 7928 or 7201, fax (537) 204-5280.

Marina Miramar, Panama City, R.P. (507) 2206-8888 panama@interconti.com.

Marina Papagayo, Playa del Coco, Costa Rica (506) 2696-2262, US toll free 888.863.0301

Marina Pez Vela, Puerto Quetzal, Guatemala (502) 2379-5778.

Marina Pez Vela, Quepos, Costa Rica, (866) 739-8352, or (506) 777-4141 www.MarinaPezVela.com

Marina Puerto Aventuras, Quintana Roo, (984) 873-5110 marina@puertoaventuras.com.mx

Marina Puesta del Sol, Nicaragua (505) 883-0781 or 880-0013 or (cellular, extra digit) 880-00190 mpuestadelsol@yahoo.com

Nene's Marina, Isla San Andrés, Colombia, (578) 512-6139.

Puerto Isla Mujeres, Quintana Roo, Mexico, (998) 287-3340 marina@puertoislamujeres.com

Ram Marine, Rio Dulce, Guatemala (502) 7930-5408

Shelter Bay Marina, Colón, Panama, (507) 433-3581 www.ShelterBayMarina.com

Haul Out Yards

Abel's Boat Yard (Astillero Rodriquez) Lago Izabel, Rio Dulce, Guatemala (502) 7930-5059

A & D Dry Dock, French Harbour, Honduras, (504) 455-5450.

Fuerte Amador Marina & Resort, Panama City, Panama, (507) 314-0665 www.fuerteamador.com

Island Marine, Bahía Jaltepeque, El Salvador, (503) 7724-8221 or 7947-2132

La Ceiba Shipyard, La Ceiba, Honduras (504) 440-0614.

Mar Marine, Rio Ducle, Guat (502) 7930-5089.

Ram Marine, Fronteras, Rio Dulce, Guatemala (502) 7930-5408.

Shelter Bay Marina, Colón, Panama, (507) 433-3581 www.ShelterBayMarina.com

Island Marine, Bahia del Sol, El Salvador (503) 7724-8221.

Varadero Puerto Barillas, Bahía Jiquilisco, El Salvador (503) 278-3298, fax 278-3292.

Ship's Agents

Panama Canal: Stevens, Pete: Delfino Maritime Agency, Panama, (507) 6735-7356, or 261-3554

Cel (507) 6613-1134 6613-1599 Fax (507) 261-3943 delfinomaritime@hotmail.com

Panama Canal: McBride, Tina: Panama Canal Transits, Panama, Cel (507) 6637-2999 Fax (507) 232-8843 (request tone) tinamcbride@hotmail.com www.PanamaCanalTransits.com

Panama Canal: Manrique, David: Match Ship Management, Panama, Cel (507) 6615-8157 (507) 314-0850 Fax (507) 314-0841 www.matchship.com

Panama Canal: Plummer, Enrique: Agencia Naviera Plummer, Panama, Cel (507) 6674-2086 Fax (507) 314-0895 eplummer@hotmail.com

Providencia: Bush Agency: Isla Providencia, Colombia, (6) 334-805

Puerto Quetzal: Ovalle, Manuel de Jesus or "Miguel Oscar" (502) 7881-3679. Or Eduardo Perez (502) 2407-9026.

Puntarenas: Andrade, Ernesto: Puntarenas, Costa Rica, (506) 661-0948 eandrade@racsa.co.cr

Rio Dulce: Langdon, M.E. ("Emy"): Fronteras, Rio Dulce, Guatemala (502) 5612-1415

Rio Dulce: Raul the Customs Agent: Fronteras, Guatemala, (502) 7947-0083.

Roatan: Ebanks, Beatman: Roatan, Honduras (504) 2445-1271, and 2445-0469 ebanksagency@yahoo.com

San Andrés: Rene at Serrana Agency (578) 5120-4628.

Useful Contacts

Aeroperlas, Panama, iflyap@aeroperlas.com)

Balboa Admeasurer, Panama Canal, (507) 272-4571.

Belize Tourism, www.travelbelize.org

Cabañas Parida, Isla Parida, Panama (507) 774-8166

Carlos the Yacht Trucker, Rio Dulce, Guatemala rio@guate.net.gt   See photo this page.

Citibank, Balboa, Panama, (507-228-0165)

Citibank, Colón, Panama, (507-441-6303 and 441-6144)

Colón Admeasurer, Panama Canal, (507) 443-2293.

Cruising World Magazine www.CruisingWorld.com Dancing Roots, Crocodile! herbal insect repellent. www.dancingroots.com (603) 357-5050.

Grand Cayman Customs, (345) 949-2473

Hotel Bahía del Sol, Bahía Jaltepeque, El Salvador info@Bahíadelsolelsalvador.com

International Health Certificate (Pets), www.aphis.usda.gov

Islamorada (chart store), 808 Balboa Ave, Balboa, Panama, (507)-228-4348 info@islamorada.com

Livingston, Guatemala, Port Captain's office, (502)-7947-0029

Mapiex, charter planes, Panama, aero@sinfo.net

Medical Kit, www.medicalofficer.net

Mexican Fishing Licenses, SEMARNAT Office, 2550 Fifth Ave., Suite 101, San Diego, CA 92103-6622 (619) 233-6956.

Panama Canal information & forms, www.pancanal.com

Passport application (US), http://travel.state.gov/passport/passport_1738.html

Pilot Service, Barillas Marina, Bahia Jiquilisco, El Salvador, (503) 632-1802 info@barillasmarina.com

Proyecto Linguistico Francisco Marroquin (PLFM), Spanish & Mayan Language School, Antigua, Guatemala (309) 692-2961 www.langlink.com/guatemala **or** info@plfm-antigua.org

San Pedro, Belize. Customs & Immigration officers, (501) 422-3869.

Turneffe Island Lodge, Belize, (713) 313-4670

US State Dept. travel advisories, http://travel.state.gov/travel/travel_1744.html

US Treasury Department's Office of Foreign Asset Control (OFAC) http://www.treas.gov/offices/eotffc/ofac/

Seabreeze Books and Charts, worldwide, San Diego, (888)-449-7011 www.seabreeze.com

The Log Newspaper, Southern California & Mexico Boating News, www.thelog.com

Weather Routing International, (318) 798-4939, www.wriwx.com

Cruising Ports: *the Central American Route*

28004
28006

27005
26001
56
462
Caymans

411

Your home-away-from-home on the Central American Route!

Moorings: 80 heavy-duty moorings for yachts to +194' within sheltered marina channel.
Free pilot service from outside Bahia Jiquilisco to Barillas Marina Club.
Port Clearance: all offices are on marina premises, open 7/24.
Fuel dock: diesel, gasoline, Texaco products.
Boat yard: marine ways & Travelift for vessels to 500 tons.
Dinghy landing, work dock, 24-hr security patrols.
Beautiful gated community within El Salvador National Park.
Clubhouse, restaurant, patio bar, sat TV, convenience store.
Air-conditioned internet cafe, outdoor laptop hookups.
Pools, patios, bungalows, helicopter pad & private air strip.
Courteous English-speaking owner, management & staff.

"Barillas is a great place to summer over south of the hurricane belt. It's our home-away-from-home on the Central American route."

Capt. John E. Rains & Capt. Patricia Miller Rains

Central American Route - Chart List

Pacific Central America
Planning Charts
W145 Gulf of St. Lawrence to Strait of Juan de Fuca
21026 Puerto Madero to Cabo Velas (Pacific Coast)
21500 Punta Remedios to Cabo Matapalo
28006 Caribbean Sea-Southwest Part (Velas to Panama)

Coastal Charts
21510 Puerto Madero to Acajutla
21520 Acajutla to Corinto
21540 Corinto to Punta Guiones
21550 Cabo Velas to Cabo Blanco
21560 Punta Guiones to Punta Burica
Plan: Approaches to Quepos
21580 Cabo Metapalo to Morro de Puercos
Inset: Golfo Dulce
21601 Morro de Puercos to Panama
Plan: Aguadulce Anchorage
21605 Panama to Bahia Pina
Plan: Bahia Pina

Extensive Cruising
21483 Puerto San Jose and Puerto Quetzal
21489 Approaches to Puerto San Jose and Puerto Quetzal
21521 Golfo de Fonseca
21526 Bahia de San Lorenzo
Inset: Puerto de Henecan
21529 Bahia de La Union and Approaches
Plan: La Union
21525 Corinto and Approaches
Plan: Corinto Harbor
21543 Plans on the West Coast of Costa Rica
A. Bahia Brasilito and Bahia Potrero
B. Bahia Santa Elena
C. Bahia Murcielagos
D. Bahia Carrillo
21547 San Juan del Sur and Approaches
Plan: Bahia San Juan del Sur
21544 C.R. 006, Gulf of Nicoya
21546 C.R. 008, Puntarenas and Puerto Caldera
21562 Golfo Dulce
21563 Golfito
21581 Plans within Bahia de Charco Azul

A. Puerto Armuelles
B. Approaches to Pedregal
21582 Golfo de Montijo
Continuation of Rio San Pedro
21583 Isla de Coiba (South Coast of Panama)
21584 Approaches to Puerto Armuelles and Pedregal
21603 Approaches to Balboa

Caribbean Central America
Planning Charts
28004 Caribbean Sea-Northwest Part
28006 Caribbean Sea-Southwest Part

Coastal Charts
27120 Yucatan Channel
28190 Ambergris Cay to Isla Cozumel
28167 Ambergris Cay to Pelican Cays
28162 Tela to Pelican Cays
28150 Barra de Caratasca to Tela
Panels: A. Cabo Farallones to Tela
B. Barra de Caratasca to Cabo Farallones
28140 Northern Reaches to Cabo Gracias a Dios
28130 Cabo Gracias a Dios to Puerto Isabel
28120 Puerto Isabel to Laguna de Perlas
28110 Laguna de Perlas to Rio Colorado
26070 Rio Colorado to Cristobal
Plan: Isla Escudo de Veraguas
26060 Puerto Cristobal to Cabo Tiburon
26066 Approaches to Cristobal
Plans: A. Portobelo
B. Puerto de La Bahia de las Minas 15,000
26068 Puerto Cristobal

Extensive Cruising
28202 Isla Mujeres, Cancun and Approaches
28201 Puerto Morelos (Mexico)
28197 San Miguel de Cozumel
Plan: Banco Playa
28168 Belize City Harbor
28164 Approaches to Puerto Barrios and Puerto Santo Tomas de Castilla
28165 Puerto Santo Tomas de Castilla and Puerto Barrios
28170 Approaches to Puerto Cortes (Gulf of Honduras)
28171 Approaches to Puerto de Tela (Gulf of

Honduras)
28161 Tela Harbor
28143 Isla de Utila
Plan: Bancos Salmedina
28144 Port of La Ceiba (Honduras)
28154 Approaches to La Ceiba (Roatan)
28125 Isla de Guanaja
28151 Approaches to Puerto Castilla
28142 Puerto Castilla
28049 Approaches to Puerto Limon and Bahia de Moin
28051 Puerto Limon and Bahia de Moin
28041 Approaches to Bocas del Toro and Laguna de Chiriqui
28042 Entrance to Laguna de Chiriqui and Chiriqui Grande
Plan: Chiriqui Grande
28052 Canal de Bocas del Toro
28053 Northwestern Passage into Bahia Almirante (Boca del Drago)
28054 Bahia Almirante (Southwestern Part)
26065 Cayos Chichime to Punta Rincon and Approach to Golfo de San Blas
26063 Punta San Blas to Bahia Concepcion
28082 Bluefields (Nicaragua)
Plan: El Bluff and Booth Docks
28103 Cayos Vivorillo, Becerro and Caratasca
Plans: A. Cayos Becerro
B. Cayos Vivorillo
28104 Puerto Cabezas and Approaches
Plan: Puerto Cabezas

Publications Recommended

Mexico Boating Guide, Rains
Cruising Guide to Belize and Mexico's Caribbean Coast, Rauscher
The Panama Cruising Guide, Bauhaus
The Panama Guide, Zydler
Reed's Nautical Almanac Caribbean
Sailing Directions for the West Coast of Mexico & Central America
Sailing Directions for Caribbean Sea Vol I & II
Tide Tables Pacific & Atlantic
Light List Pacific & Atlantic
Pilot Charts: Caribbean Sea, Pacific, Gulf of Mexico

28140 Northern Reaches to Cabo Gracias a Dios
26081 Isla de San Andres and Adjacent Cays
Plans: A. Rada el Cove
B. Cayos de Albuquerque
C. Cayos del Este Sudeste
26083 Isla de Providencia
27241 Cayman Islands (West Indies)
Plans: A. Little Cayman and Cayman Brac
B. Grand Cayman
27243 George Town Harbor and West End Point
Plans: A. George Town Harbor (Grand Cayman)
B. West End Point (Little Cayman)

Gulf of Mexico
Planning Charts
411 Gulf of Mexico
28300 Bahia de Campeche

Coastal Charts
28330 Guajardo to Barra de Chavarria
28320 Tampico to Punta Zempoala
28310 Punta del Morro to Barra de Tupilco
28260 Barra Tupilco to Isla Piedra
28221 Plans in Campeche Bank
A. Cayos Arcas
B. Arrecife Alacran
C. Cayo Arenas
D. Arrecifes Triangulos
E. Alacran Anchorage
28210 Progreso to Isla Contoy

Extensive Cruising
28302 Veracruz and Approaches (Mexico-East Coast)
Plan: Port of Veracruz
28321 Approaches to Tuxpan
Plan: Rio Tuxpan
28323 Approaches to Tampico and Altamira
28325 Ports of Tampico and Altamira
Plans: A. Tampico
B. Altamira
28265 Campeche
28281 Coatzacoalcos
28282 Approaches to Coatzacoalcos
28261 Approaches to Frontera
28263 Laguna de Terminos and Approaches
28264 Laguna de Terminos-Western Entrance
28223 Progreso-Yukalpeten

Lats & Longs

The following positons along the Central American Route are for general planning purposes only, primarily in geographic order inbound to the Panama Canal. These positions not for navigation. Do not program these positions into your autopilot as a route, because their sequence could drive you ashore or onto offshore hazards. Some positions are offshore approach waypoints, and others are hazards and navigation lights on land. These positions were accumulated over several years using a variety of GPS devices, not all calibrated the same.

Guatemala
Puerto Quetzal (13°54.90'N,90°47.03'W)

El Salvador
Puerto Acajutla (13°34.4'N, 89°50.5'W)
Estero Jaltepeque (13°16.6'N, 88°53.6'W)
Bahía Jiquilisco (13°07.01'N, 88°25.2'W)
Punta Ampala (13°09.5'N by 87°53'W)

Nicaragua
Punta Consiguiña (12°54.5'N, 87°41.83'W)
Speck Reefs (12°41.27'N, 87°25.47'W)
Marina Puesta del Sol (12°36.6'N, 87°22.4'W)
Corinto (12°28.67'N, 87°11.23'W)
San Juan del Sur (11°15.1'N, 85°53.1'W)

Costa Rica
Bahía Santa Elena (10°57.0'N, 85°48.3'W)
King Kong Rock (10°36.52'N, 85°42.28'W)
Playa del Coco (10°33.8'N, 85°42.1'W)
Isla Catalina (10°29.2'N, 85°53.0'W)
Cabo Velas (10°22'N, 85°53'W)
Punta Guiones (09°54'N, 85°41'W)
Bahía Carillo is (09°51.00'N, 85°29.46'W)
Cabo Blanca (09°33.18'N, 85°06.90'W)
Ballena Bay (9°42.5'N, 84°58.4'W)
Islas Tortugas (09°46.14'N, 84°53.55'W)
Isla Muertos (09°53.13'N, 84°55.60'W)
Puntarenas Pier (09°58.10'N, 84°49.81'W)
Bahía Herradura (09°38.7'N, 84°41'W)
Quepos (09° 25.50'N, 084° 11.70'W)
Punta Uvita (09°08.55'N, 83°45.85'W)
Drake Bay (08°42.61'N, 83°39.67'W
Punta Llorona (08°35.44'N, 83°44.10'W)
Puerto Jiménez (08°32.81'N, 83°17.06'W)
Golfito (08°36.5'N, 83°11.5'W)

Panama Pacific
Punta Burica offshore (08°00'N, 82°53'W)
Montuosa offshore (07°27.3'N, 82°17.3'W)

Isla Jicarita offshore (07°11.5'N, 81°48.0'W)
Punta Mala offshore (07°27.5'N, 79°59.0'W)
Isla Bona (08°33.8'N, 79°39.2'W)
Isla Taboguilla (08°48.0'N, 79°29.5'W)
Panama Canal sea buoy (8°51.5'N, 79°29.0'W)
Ladrones (07°52.0'N, 82°26.0'W)
Isla Parida SW light (08°06.0'N, 82°22.0'W)
Boca Chica approach (08°09.5'N, 82°14.3'W)
Marina Boca Chica (08°12.5'N, 82°11.5'W)
Islas Secas Light (about 07°57'N, 82°01'W)
Isla Canal de Afuera (7°41.8'N, 81°38.4'W
Bahía Honda anchor (7°45.9'N, 81°31.7'W)
Machete Bay (07°37.8'N, 81°43.6'W)
Naranjo Cove (7°16.49'N, 80°55.6'W)
Benao Cove (7°25.5'N, 80°11.3'W)
Pacheca Light (08°40'N, 79°03'W)
Playa Galeon (08°38.06'N, 79°02.09'W)
Isla San Jose Light (08°12.8'N, 79°07.8'W)
Bodega Bay (08°15.70'N, 79°08.07'W)
Punta Cocos (08°13'N, 78°54'W)
Rio Cacique (08°17.75'N, 78°54.19'W)
Isla Galera (08°11.7'N, 78°46.6'W)
Flamenco Island (08°54.5'N, 79°31.2'W)

Gulf of Mexico & North Yucatan
Rio Grande (25°58'N, 97°09'W)
El Mezquital (25°14.3'N, 97°25.3'W)
Boca La Pesca (23°46.2'N, 97°43.9'W)
Punta Jerez (22°52.8'N, 97°45.44'W)
Altamira (22°29.2'N, 97°50.8'W)
Tampico Light (22°15.9'N, 97°46.3'W)
Cabo Rojo Light (21°33'N, 97° 20'W)
Isla Lobos Light (21°28.2'N, 97°13.7'W
Barra Corazones (21°15.52'N, 97°24.82'W)
Barra Galindo (21°05.88'N, 97°21.61'W)
Punta Cazones (20°43.5'N, 97°12.0'W)
Barra Tecolutla (20°28.63'N, 97°59.58'W)
Rio Nautla (20°14.53'N, 96°46.84'W)
Isla Bernal Chica (19°40.27'N, 96°22.95'W)
Chachalaca Light (19°24.8'N, 96°19.3'W)

Cruising Ports: the Central American Route

Galleguilla Reef (19°14.39'N, 96°07.37'W)
Sacraficios Reef (19°10.17'N, 96°05.57'W)
Coatzacoalcos (18°10.17'N, 94°24.86'W)
Dos Bocas (18°27.25'N, 93°12.33'W)
Punta Buey (18°38.8'N, 92°43.2'W)
Carmen sea buoy (18°42.5'N, 91°54.0'W)
Punta Zacatal (18°36.7'N, 91°51.4'W)
Punta Atalaya Light (18°38.7'N, 91°51.7'W)
Bucaneros YC (18°38.33'N, 91°47.58'W)
Rio Chompotón (19°21.6'N, 90°45.4'W)
Sebaplaya (19°39.0'N, 90°42.5'W)
San Bartolo Light (19°49'N, 90°35'W)
Darsena de Pesqueros (19°49'N, 90°36.6'W)
Cayos Arcas (20°13'N, 91°58'W)
Obispo Shoals (20°29'N, 92°12'W)
Cayos Triangulas (20°54'N, 92°14'W)
Isla Arena Light (20°36'N, 90°28'W)
Real de Las Salinas (20°45'N by 90°26'W)
Celestún breakwaters (20°50.9'N, 90°24.5'W)
Las Palmas Light (21°03.7'N, 90°15.2'W)
Sisal Reef (21°21'N, 90°09'W)
Alacran Reef (22°20.14'N, 89°42.64'W)
Puerto Sisal (21°13.63'N, 90°04.84'W)
Progreso Pier (21°20'N by 89°40.8'W)
Yukalpetén approach (21°17.8'N, 89°42.7'W)
Puerto Telchac (21°20.7'N, 89°18.7'W)
Bajo Pawaschick (21°31.5'N, 88°46.2'W)
D'zilam de Bravo (21°23.92'N, 88°52.9'W)
Punta Yalkubul (21°31.2'N, 88°36.7'W)
Rio Lagartos approach (21°37'N, 88°11'W)
Isla Holbox (21°30.19'N, 87°23.77'W)
Cabo Catoche (21°46.52'N, 87°06.29'W)

Cuba
El Morro light (23°09.0'N, 82°21.4'W)
Marina Hemingway sea buoy
(23°05.44'N, 82°30.55'W)

Yucatan Channel (Mexico)
Isla Contoy Light (21°30'N, 86°49'W)
Isla Mujeres north approach (21°16.3'N, 86°45.1'W)
Becket Rock (21°10'N, 86°44'W)
Bajo Pepito buoy (21°12.5'N, 86°45.3'W)
Puerto Juarez (21°11.02'N, 86°48.26'W)
Cancun's lagoon entrance (21°08.73'N, 86°47.22'W)
Puerto Morelos Light (20°51.7'N, 86°53.0'W)
Puerto Morelos sea buoy (20°48.3'N, 86°52.9'W)
Punta Hut (20°43.5'N, 86°58.0'W)

Punta Celerain (20°16.17'N, 86°59.39'W)
Puerto Abrigo, approach (21°31.68'N, 86°56.47'W)
Zubel Reef (approach 20°37.9'N, 87°03.5'W)
Aventuras approach (20°29.757'N 87°,13.479'W
Punta Allen Lighthouse (19°46.9'N, 87°28.0'W))
Cayos Culebra (19°41.7'N, 87°28.0'W)
Punta Pajaros Light (19°35.8'N, 87°24.8'W)
Punta Tupac (about 19°28.4'N, 87°26'W)
Punta Herrero (19°18.7'N, 87°26.8'W)
Zaragosa approach (18°13.05'N, 87°49.48'W)
Chetumal pier (18°29.41'N, 88°17.96'W)
Banco Chinchorro Light (18°45.8'N, 87°18.9'W)
Cayo Lobos Light (18°23.5'N, 87°23.2'W)

Belize
San Pedro Cut approach (17°54.0'N, 87°57.2'W)
Goff's Cay Sandbore (17°20.3'N, 88°02.2'W
English Cay (17°19.6'N, 88°03.0'W
North East Split Light (17°22.8'N, 88°05.5'W)
Port Island (17°28.38'N, 88°12.03'W)
Turneffe reef north (17°37.5'N, 87°45.3'W)
Rendezvous Point (17°32.68'N, 87°49.80'W)
Blue Creek (17°12.39'N, 87°55.83'W)
Bokel Cay Light (17°09.8'N, 87°54.4'W)

Guatemala, Atlantic
Rio Dulce sea buoy (15°50.25'N, 88°43.70'W)
Livingston fuel dock (15°49.148'N, 88°45.043'W)
La Marina (15°48.673'N, 88°45.504'W)
Cayo Grande anchorage (15°47.18'N, 88°49.71'W)

Honduras, Atlantic
Punta Sal (15°56'N, 87°35.77'W)
Bahia de Cortés approach (15°52.12'N, 87°58.09'W)
Pto Escondido approach (15°54.79'N, 87°38.05'W)
Tela anchorage (15°47.24'N, 87°27.36'W)
La Ceiba Lagoon Marina (15°48.0'N, 86°45.7'W)
Trujillo pier (15°55.43'N, 85°57.06'W)
Punta Cameron (19°59.20'N, 85°01.63'W)
Punta Rio Patuca (15°49.0'N, 84°18.2'W)
Cabo Falso (15°12'N, 83°20'W)
Coxen Hole (16°18.40'N, 86°32.96'W)
Barefoot Cay approach (16°19.8'N, 086°28.7'W)
French Harbor approach (16° 20.5'N, 086° 29.0'W)
Cayo Vivorillo (15°50.0'N, 83°19.0'W)

Western Caribbean
Gracias a Dios offshore (15°00.0'N, 83°02.5'W)

George Town, Cayman Light (19°17.8'N, 81°23.0'W)
North Sound, Cayman (19°22.84'N, 81°19.61'W)
Quito Sueño Banks south (14°29.2'N, 81°08.2'W)
Providencia Isla sea buoy (13°23.95'N, 18°23.75'W)
San Andrés, Isla approach (12°23.2'N, 81°41.2'W)
Cayos de Este Sureste (12°24.0'N, 81°27.0'W)
Corn Island, SW Bay (12°09.31'N, 83°04.54'W)

Panama, Atlantic
Bocas del Toro approach (09°22.0'N, 82°12.8'W)
Isla Escudo de Veraguas (09°05.68'N, 81°34.57'W)
Cristobal breakwater (09°23.8'N, 079°55.1'W)
Punta Mantilla (09°34'N, 79°41'W)
Los Farrallones rocks (09°39'N, 79°38'W)
Isla Lintón approach (09°37.09'N, 79°35.55'W)
Isla Grande approach (09°37.61'N, 79°34.43'W)
Isla Mogote Afuera (09°38.24'N, 79°31.30'W)
Nombre de Dios approach (09°35.85'N, 79°28.59'W)
San Blas Channel approach (09°35.0'N, 78°55.3'W)
El Porvenir (09°33.37'N, 78°56.93'W)

Spanish Lexicon
Quick Reference for General Boating Terms, Mechanical, WX and Navigation

General Boating Terms
Anchor (to): fondear
Anchor: ancla
Anchorage: anclaje
Arrive (to): llegar
Beam: manga
Boom: botavara
Bow: proa
Cabin: cabina
Captain: capitán
Cook: cocinero(a)
Copies: copias
Customs: Aduana
Deck: cubierta
Deckhand: marinero(a)
Draft: calado
First Mate: Segundo a Bordo
Halyard: driza
Helm: timón
Helmsman: timonel
Hull: casca
Immigration: Migración
Jib: foque
Jibe (to): virar
Launch (to): botar
Launch, skiff: lancha
Leave port (to): embarcarse
Line: linea
Mast: mastíl, palo
Oar: remo
Oarlock: chumacero
Papers: papeles, despachos
Pleasure craft: yate de placer
Port Captain: Capitán del Puerto
Port Captain's office: Capitanía
Port hole: tromera
Port: babor, puerto
Power yacht: crucero
Propellor: helice
Sailboat: velero
Sailor: marinero(a)
Screwdriver: tornillador
Sea sick: maréo

Cruising Ports: the Central American Route

Starter: arranque
Tool: herramiento
Winch: molinete, winche
Wrench: llave

Mechanical Terms

Battery: batería, pila
Bearing: cojinete
Bolt: tornillo
Breakdown: parada
Cable: cable
Diesel: diesel
Engine: maquina
Exhaust: escape
Fuel: combustible
Gasket: empaquedura
Gasoline: gasolina
Grease: grasa
Head: cabeza
Hose: manguera
Injector: inyector
Mechanic: mecanico
Nut: tuerca
Oil: aceite, lubricante
Piston: piston
Pump: bomba
Row: (to): remar
Rudder: timón
Screw: tornillo
Sea level: nivel de mar
Seamanship: marineria
Sheet: escota
Ship: barco, buque
Speed: velocidad
Starboard: estribor
Stern: popa
Tank: tanque
Tiller: caña del timón
Tow (to): remolcar
Tugboat: remolcador
Wharf: muelle, embarcadero

Marine Meteorology

Barometer: barometro
Breakers: rompientes
Breeze: brisa
Calm: calma
Clear up (to): aclarar
Clouds: nubes
Degrees: grados
Ebb tide: marea menguantes
Fog: niebla, neblina
Forecast: predición
Front: frente
Gale: viento duro
Gentle breeze: brisa debil
GMT: hora media de Greenwich
Gust: rafaga, racha
Haze: calima
High pressure: alta presión
Horizon: horizonte
Hurricane: huracán
Light air: ventorina
Mist: neblina
Moderate: brisa moderada
Norther: nortada
Rain: lluvia
Shower: chubasco
Squall: turbonada
Surf: oleadez
Surge: resaca
Thunder: trueño
Tide: marea
Trade winds: vientos alisos

Navigation Terms

Altitude: altitud
Barometer: barometro
Bearing: orientación
Breakwater: rompeola
Buoy: boya
Chart: carta
Chronometer: cronometro
Compass: brujula
Course: rumbo
Depth: profundidad
Deviation: desviación
Dividers: compas
East: este, oriente

Fathom: braza
Knot: nudo
Lighthouse: faro
Magnetic: magnetico
Meridian: meridiano
Observation: observación
Parallel: paralelo
Position: posición
Radar: radar
Reckoning: estima
Reef: arrecife
Sextant: sextante
South: sur
Star: estrella
Track: trayectoria
West: oeste, poniente
Waves: olas

Add Your Own New Terms

Transmission Time	Contents of Transmission	Valid Time	Map Area
0000/1200	Test Pattern		
0005/1205	US/Tropical Surface Analysis (W. Half)	18/06	1
0020/1220	Tropical Surface Analysis (E Half)	18/06	2
0035/1235	24 Hr. Wind/Wave Forecast	00/12	3
0045/1245	48 Hr. Wind/Wave Forecast	00/12	3
0055/1255	72 Hr. Wind/Wave Forecast	00/12	3
0105/1305	24 Hr. Surface Forecast	00/12	3
0115/1315	48 Hr. Surface Forecast	00/12	3
0125/1325	72 Hr. Surface Forecast	00/12	3
0135/1335	Cyclone Danger Area* or High Wind/Waves	21/09	6
0150/----	72 Hr. Wave Period/SwellDirection	0000	3
----/1350	(Rebroadcast of 0150)	0000	3
0200/1400	Goes IR Tropical Satellite Image	00/12	4
0215/1415	00 HR Sea State Analysis	00/12	3
----/1425	Product Notice Bulletin		
0225/1445	High Seas Forecast (In English)	22/10	5
0600/1800	Test Pattern		
0605/1805	US/Tropical Surface Analysis (West Half)	00/12	1
0620/1820	Tropical Surface Anlysis (E Half)	00/12	2
0635/1835	24 Hr. Wind/Wave Forecast	06/18	3
0645/1845	(Rebroadcast of 0045/1245)	00/12	3
0655/1855	(Rebroadcast of 0055/1255)	00/12	3
0705/1905	(Rebroadcast of 0105/1305)	00/12	3
0715/1915	(Rebroadcast of 0115/1315)	00/12	3
0725/1925	(Rebroadcast of 0125/1325)	00/12	3
0735/1935	Cyclone Danger Area* or High Wind/Waves	03/15	6
0750/1950	48 Hr. Wave Period/Swell Direction	00/12	3
0800/2000	Goes IR Tropical Satellite Image	07/18	4
0825/2025	Request for Comments/Broadcast Schedule		
0845/2045	High Seas Forecast (In English)	04/16	5

Carrier Frequency is 1.9 kHz below the assigned Frequency.

Frequency kHz	Times
4317.9	continuous
8503.9	continuous
12789.9	continuous
17146.4	1200Z - 2045Z

	Map Areas
1	5S-50N, 55W-125W
2	5S-50N, 0W-70W
3	0N-31N, 35W-100W
4	12S-44N, 28W-112W
5	7N-31N, 35W-98W
6	05-N-60N, 0W-100W

NMG New Orleans - Radio Fax & Voice Broadcast Schedule

Ham & Single Side Band Nets

Name	MHZ	UTC	WX	Coverage
Waterways Net*	7.268	0730 EST	x	East US to Yucatan Channel
Cent Am Breakfast Club*	7.083	1300		Central America
NW Caribbean Cruisers' Net	8.188	1400		Mexico to San Andrés
Southbound II Net	12.359	2000	x	Atlantic/Caribbean
Halo Net	21.390	2100		US/Carib/South America
Pacific Maritime Mobile Net	21.402	2200		entire area
Maritime Mobile Net	14.313	24 hrs		world wide emergency
			*	7 Mhz is lsb, all others usb

US Coast Guard WX & Emergency

MHZ	UTC	Coverage	WX
4.125	2300-1100	NMG entire area	x
6.215	24 hrs	NMG entire area	x
8.290	24 hrs	NMG entire area	x
12.290	1100-2300	NMG entire area	x

Sample of 72-hr NMG chart

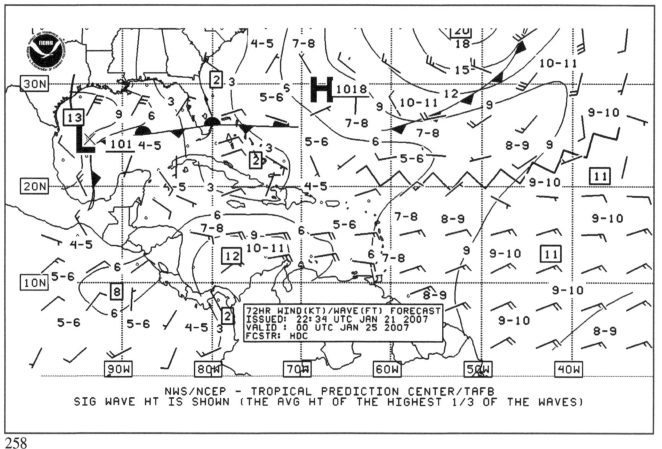

Cruising Ports: the Central American Route

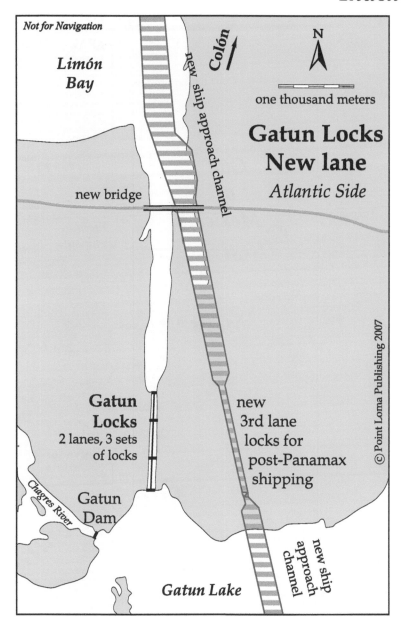

Not for Navigation

Limón Bay

new bridge

Colón

N

one thousand meters

Gatun Locks New lane
Atlantic Side

new ship approach channel

© Point Loma Publishing 2007

Gatun Locks
2 lanes, 3 sets
of locks

Gatun Dam

Chagres River

new
3rd lane
locks for
post-Panamax
shipping

new ship
approach
channel

Gatun Lake

Cruising Ports: *the Central American Route*